A WORLD PARLIAMENT

'Jo Leinen and Andreas Bummel have provided us with a seminal contribution to the discussion on a world parliament and world governance. Grounded in the past, their comprehensive and bold work points to a future where the forces of human solidarity can prevail.'

—**Andrew Strauss**, Dean and Professor of Law at the University of Dayton School of Law

'Congratulations to both authors on this great book! It is an impressive overview of the international challenges of our time, their historical roots, and approaches for a better future of the world. A world parliament is an important catalyst for this.'

—**Franz Josef Radermacher**, Professor at the University of Ulm

'A bold, articulate, competent and courageous view on the evolution of world politics and, more importantly, what is needed to achieve humane governance.'

—**Daniele Archibugi**, Italian National Research Council, Rome, and Birkbeck College, University of London

'In this clear, precise and comprehensive book, Andreas Bummel and Jo Leinen discuss the history, rationale and possible implementation of a democratic constitution of the world. Everybody who cares about the big issues that confront humanity – war, climate, povery, injustice, rule of law – will be presented with a promising and well-conceived approach to finding solutions.'

—**Thomas Pogge**, Professor of Philosophy and International Affairs at Yale University

'This is a truly visionary book that should be read by all concerned by the lack of direction of global politics. Maybe a global democratic transformation will be called utopian but it is a very realisable utopia it paints. Based on solid research, well presented and very readable.'

—**Ronaldo Munck**, Professor at Dublin City University and author of 'Globalisation and Contestation: the new great counter-movement'

'A comprehensive, informative, well-researched and insightful study of a subject of momentous importance to the future of humanity.'

—**Garry Jacobs**, CEO of the World Academy of Art & Science

'This book is utopian in the best sense. At a time when politics is increasingly reduced to short-term reactions to previously neglected problems that have now become threatening, this book presents long-term thinking on the only adequate form of political organization for our planet in light of the various global threats.'

—**Vittorio Hösle**, Professor at the University of Notre Dame, Indiana

'Climate, oceans, world trade – all this requires global rules. We need a parliament at the world level – at the United Nations – that allows the people to exercise oversight. The present book is an excellent work on this subject, in particular with regard to its history and the logical approach.'

—**Ernst Ulrich von Weizsäcker**, Co-President, Club of Rome

'This recommendable book succeeds in reconciling the opposites: it is, at the same time, analytic and holistic, rooted in history and futuristic, realistic and visionary.'

—**Susanna Cafaro**, Professor of EU Law, Università del Salento

ABOUT THE AUTHORS

JO LEINEN has been a member of the European Parliament since 1999. He was chair of the parliament's environmental committee and of its committee on constitutional affairs. From 2011 to 2017 he was president of the European Movement, an international umbrella organization that is advocating for a democratic and enlarged European Union. From 1997 to 2005 he was presiding the Union of European Federalists that is dedicated to the promotion of European political unity. From 1985 to 1994 he was minister of the environment in the German state of Saarland. He graduated in law and was born in Bisten, Germany, in 1948.

ANDREAS BUMMEL is co-founder and director of Democracy Without Borders and of the international Campaign for a United Nations Parliamentary Assembly that was launched in 2007. He has dedicated his career to the promotion of global democracy and world federalism. Since 1998 he has been a Council member of the World Federalist Movement, an international NGO that promotes the rule of law, world peace, federalism and democracy. He was trained in business administration, studied law and worked at a management consultancy firm. He was born in Cape Town, South Africa, in 1976.

A WORLD PARLIAMENT

Governance and Democracy in the 21st Century

JO LEINEN
ANDREAS BUMMEL

Translated from German
by Ray Cunningham

© Democracy Without Borders, Berlin, 2018

This book is published with the support of the
Foundation For European Progressive Studies (FEPS)
and the European Parliament. The view of the authors does not
necessarily represent the ones of FEPS or of the European Parliament.
www.feps-europe.eu

In addition, we wish to thank
The Workable World Trust and Stiftung Apfelbaum
for their kind support.

The original edition was first published in German in 2017 under the title
Das demokratische Weltparlament: Eine kosmopolitische Vision
by Verlag J.H.W. Dietz Nachf. GmbH

Translated from German by Ray Cunningham
www.raycunningham.eu

Cover design by Hermann Brandner, Cologne

Please contact the publisher if you are interested in acquiring
foreign language or other rights to this publication.

ISBN 978-3-942282-13-0

Visit our website at
www.democracywithoutborders.org

Contents

Detailed Contents

PART II

Introduction

For the first time in history, all the people in the world are linked together in a shared civilization which reaches around the entire Earth. Technological advances in the fields of communications, transport, the media and information are driving forward planetary integration. Cross-linking through the internet is omnipresent and all-pervasive and has become indispensable for business and society. Our modern life is only possible because of the globalization of trade, the flow of capital, services and production chains. However, the worldwide consumer society and its use of resources are not sustainable. Important natural resources will eventually run out. Many renewable resources may collapse because of overdepletion. The increase in the amount of CO_2 released into the atmosphere due to the use of fossil fuels continues unabated and the consequences of the expected increase in global temperature are unpredictable. Our planet's climate system could tip into a life-threatening state unless urgent action is taken. The provision of essential public goods such as food security or the stability of the financial and economic system also depends heavily on the functioning of global structures and processes.

The direct and complex interconnections mean that the actions of every individual, no matter how apparently insignificant, impact on everyone else. Humanity, taken in aggregate, now shares a common fate. We have the means to destroy our highly developed human civilization. For instance, there are still thousands of nuclear missiles ready to be launched within minutes. At the same time, world society is sufficiently productive to enable all people to live a decent life in which basic needs, education and health care are provided. And yet this has not yet happened. Just as slavery and colonialism were overcome, so too must extreme poverty, economic exploitation and the institution of war, together with the military-industrial complex, be consigned to the history books. Extreme social inequality is also a crucial concern. The benefits of globalisation and growing productivity must be fairly distributed within individual societies and around the world. Achieving all this requires more than having the right policies; rather, it is an issue of having the *right political structures* that allow for their implementation. There are no political institutions for effective global governance. All attempts to date have been in vain. World civilization cannot be created in this way. The world order is in a crisis, one which carries a risk of catastrophic collapse.

The United Nations and its many specialised agencies, the international financial institutions, the World Trade Organisation and various intergovernmental networks already fulfil many functions of a world government. However, this apparatus is ineffective, opaque and undemocratic. The inertia of the economic and political elites who benefit from the status quo is provoking the rise of nationalist, anti-modern and counter-enlightenment forces which considerably increase the risk of global decline.

Effective institutions of world law enabling world governance are needed in order to overcome this unstable state of affairs. The question is whether the process of globalization will finally be extended and completed in the world of politics as well. The decisive building blocks for the creation of a sustainable and just global market economy are the principles of democracy, federalism and subsidiarity. There is no doubt that democracy must be improved and strengthened. However, this will only succeed with a holistic approach that pays particular attention to the global level. Following the emergence of democracy in the ancient Greek city states and its expansion to the modern territorial states in the 18th century, the next step is now imminent.

This book is the outcome of our longstanding concern with the topic of a world parliament and is based on intensive research work over many years. It is not a neutral consideration of the issue but rather a passionate plea. We are convinced of the necessity of a democratic world parliament. To write a neutral book was not our intention, nor would it even have been possible for us. As one practical step, eleven years ago we were co-founders of the international campaign for a parliamentary assembly at the United Nations, or UNPA for short, which is now endorsed by thousands of politicians, former UN officials, distinguished scholars, cultural innovators, representatives of civil society organizations, and many committed citizens from over 150 countries.

We know that a world parliament and a world legal order cannot be realized from one day to the next. But we argue that it is high time to set this process in train by establishing a UNPA. We have not allowed ourselves to be guided by what is possible in terms of Realpolitik but by what is needed. Not much would have been accomplished in the history of humanity without visionary forward thinking. The era of Utopias is not over, quite the contrary. Now, at the beginning of global modernity, there is an urgent need for serious thought, without prior constraints or reservations, about the condition and the ends of planetary civilization. Our aim quite simply is to move the question of a world parliament and a world legal order into the spotlight and to spark a serious debate on it.

The world parliament project is the key to the realization of a world order which is democratic, sustainable and based on solidarity. It is a vehicle for a new global enlightenment. The creation of a world parliament is among the most important political preconditions for the long-term survival of world civilization in the Anthropocene. Though the global risks and challenges of our time are severe, even existential, we do not want to succumb to alarmism. Even if all the world's problems did not exist, the argument for a world parliament would remain valid. It follows from the recognition that all people are equal and that they are globally interlinked in one world civilization. The way decisions are reached in a community is of crucial importance as it shows how members of the community relate to each other and what influence they have over their destiny. A world parliament is not a panacea, but it is the instrument that enables all members of the world community – and that means *all people* – to be involved in decisions of global significance.

In a certain sense, this book is a work of archaeology. On the one hand, the idea of a world parliament is not new. The first part of the book explores its historical-philosophical foundations since antiquity and traces, for the first time, the history of the idea and the attempts to bring it about from the French Revolution to the present day. We sketch important historical contributions and outline the project's impressive theoretical and practical foundations. The narrative touches on the history of parliamentarism and democracy and general plans for peace. It is important for supporters of the idea to know that they stand in a tradition that goes back hundreds of years.

On the other hand, the call for a world parliament is today more relevant than ever before. To underline this, in the second part of the book we set the issue of a world parliament in the context of some of the most important global challenges and long-term developments of our time. Our starting point is the recognition of planetary boundaries, dealing with climate change, global public goods and the problem of growth. We address the crisis of the financial system as well as the race for deregulation and the need to stop tax evasion globally. Transsovereign problems are evident everywhere. World civilisation is fragile and, due to the rapid technological developments in the fields of bio- and nanotechnology, robotics and artificial intelligence, fundamental questions are arising for which humanity is not institutionally prepared. The same applies to nuclear disarmament, collective security, the protection of human rights and the fight against crime. As we will point out, the construction of global democracy is also crucial for combating hunger, poverty and inequality, and for global water policy. These issues are not dealt with in an isolated way, however. Instead, there is an overarching narrative that describes the structural dysfunctions and failings of today's international order. At the same time, the alternative of a democratic world order and its underlying principles is presented in growing detail. The second part describes the contours of a process of global state formation that is already taking place. We contend that currently this process primarily serves a transnational elite and that the world's citizens need to assert control through the establishment of a world parliament. Against the backdrop of the global power structures of the transnational elite, we argue for the implementation of a new global class compromise. In all this, the traditional understanding of national sovereignty must be put to the test. In the last chapter of the second part, we discuss the socio-political evolution of humanity in the context of long-term trends in cognitive, moral, and psychological development and trace the formation of a planetary consciousness.

We want to offer pointers and create connections which have received insufficient attention to date. As often as possible we do this by citing in the original those sources and authors that are especially noteworthy and relevant. Our aim is not to set out academic or political debates in detail; given the vast number of topics addressed, that would not be possible anyway. The book demonstrates the breadth of the support for a world parliament and analyses the flaws of the contemporary debate on a world order. Sometimes we go into the policies we believe a world parliament ought to implement, such as nuclear and conventional disarmament, a global basic income or global regulation of commodity markets. Throughout the book we also look at other proposals that we think should be part of democratic world governance under the control of a global parliament. Among other things, we explore the introduction of a uniform taxation of multinational corporations, the creation of a global reserve currency and global taxation, the establishment of a global anti-trust authority, a strengthening of the International Criminal Court and a broadening of its mandate to include money laundering and economic crimes of global relevance, the establishment of a global criminal police force, the creation of a permanent UN peacekeeping force, the establishment of strategic worldwide food reserves, and a world constitutional court. Finally, the third part offers a possible path towards the implementation of a world parliament and the transition to a democratic world legal order. In addition to those already mentioned in the first part, it includes details of important design features for a world parliament as a constituent part of a world legislature.

We would like to thank the Foundation for European Progressive Studies, The Workable World Trust, Stiftung Apfelbaum and Democracy Without Borders for their support in publishing the book. We would also like to take this opportunity to pay tribute to the important role played by Democracy Without Borders (formerly the Committee for a Democratic UN), the World Federalist Movement-Institute for Global Policy, the Society for Threatened Peoples and, more recently, The Workable World Trust in the Campaign for a UN Parliamentary Assembly. In the course of the UNPA campaign there have been countless encounters, discussions and events all over the world in the past eleven years and in the time preceding the campaign, all of which have shaped our thoughts and this book in one way or another. We thank everyone who has contributed to this exchange and the campaign. We hope that you will understand that mentioning all by name is an impossible task that would excessively over-extend this introduction.

It is our desire that this book will not only initiate a serious debate, but also significantly strengthen the efforts for a world parliament. You are cordially invited to join our project. Give this book to friends, colleagues and acquaintances. Visit the campaign's website and sign the international appeal for a United Nations Parliamentary Assembly. Become a supporter of Democracy Without Borders, which is leading the work for a world parliament and global democracy. Become part of a new cosmopolitan movement!

www.unpacampaign.org
www.democracywithoutborders.org

TRANSLATOR'S NOTE

Unless an English-language source edition is given for a quotation originally in a foreign language, all translations are by the authors and/or the translator. Some terms for political and legal concepts from the Germanophone world are notoriously difficult to translate into English, e.g. *Rechtsstaat* and its derivatives (such as *Rechtsstaatlichkeit*), or *Völkerstaat* (even, arguably, *Volk*). *Rechtsstaatlichkeit* is close to the term 'the rule of law' in Anglo-American legal discourse, but in addition to the legal it includes a moral dimension of justice or fairness, so it means something like 'the rule of law and justice'. I have tried to signpost any important distinctive nuances in the text, but sometimes have simply kept the German original where repeating such signposting would become a distraction.

PART I

The idea of a world parliament: its history and pioneers

The idea of a world parliament raises the question of the role played in the world order by each individual person. It is based on the conviction that all people, regardless of their many differences, are members of a single family of human beings encompassing the whole world. By virtue of their humanity alone they are, without exception, citizens of the world, with equal status and equal rights. As such, they share responsibility for the planetary community and its habitat, the Earth. The world parliament is the political institution in which all people will be directly represented by delegates whom they elect. The task of this institution is to stand guard over the wellbeing of all people and their common interest. It is a product and a symbol of the self-determination and sovereignty of humanity as a whole, and the foundation for a legitimate world state system.

The concept of global popular representation brings together historical and philosophical developments that can be traced back over many centuries. From at least the Enlightenment up to the present day, an important developing dynamic has been humanity's quest for emancipation, democracy, self-determination and peace. Given the number of autocratic regimes still in place today, the idea of a world parliament, because it is conceived as an institution whose members are elected by universal, equal and free votes, also represents a plea for continuing and progressive political emancipation and democratization. In this sense, the idea of a world parliament has its roots not only in the values of the Enlightenment, which had the goal, in the words of Immanuel Kant, of freeing mankind from its 'self-imposed state of dependency', but it continues to further the cosmopolitan dimension of the Enlightenment programme. The establishment of a world parliament is thus the central goal of a new global enlightenment, because it would make every human being an autonomous subject of a world legal order. The project thus overturns the centuries-old international law paradigm of the sovereign nation state and ushers in the end of the era of international law opened by the Peace of Westphalia of 1648. At that time, after almost a third of the population of central Europe had died in the Thirty

Years' War and entire regions had been depopulated, agreement was reached on the sovereign equality of rulers and the co-existence of differing confessions. 'The right of free communication between sovereigns as independent, equal rulers, recognising no higher authority, was termed the 'law of nations' following the Roman ius gentium, although everyone knew that there was no question of the nations, in the sense of their peoples, having rights', as Otto Kimminich aptly remarks.[1] For this reason, Kant had thought that it would be better to speak of the 'law of states' rather than the 'law of nations'.[2]

If sovereignty was initially a personal attribute of feudal lords and monarchical rulers, in the course of the American and French revolutions in the 18th century it metamorphosed into the sovereignty of the people in domestic affairs and that of the modern state in foreign affairs. In this way the republican state seamlessly took over the legacy of the monarchies. The further continuation of the Enlightenment project in the global age must adopt as its objectives the overcoming of the enclosure of human beings in the nation states, the embedding of governance and democracy in clear global public structures, where necessary, and the successful achievement of the leap from international law (i.e. law between nation states) to a cosmopolitan world law. The aim of international law – which is inherently paradoxical, because at its core it recognizes no higher authority for decision or enforcement, built as it is on sovereign entities - must ultimately be that of its own abolition, as Vittorio Hösle has aptly put it.[3] World law, in contrast to international law, will genuinely possess the characteristics of law: universally binding determination through legislation, the obligatory adjudication of disputes before a court, and the necessary means for enforcement. Our focus is on the first of these aspects, and within that on the legislative institution.

The aim of establishing a world parliament is closely connected with our contemporary problems and challenges. In order to understand this, it is essential to have a clear picture of the philosophical roots and historical dimension of the project. In this section, we provide a historical overview from its beginnings up to the present day.

---

1   Kimminich, Otto. 1997. Einführung in das Völkerrecht. 6th ed. Tübingen, Basel: UTB, p. 64.
2   Kant, Immanuel. 1797. The Metaphysics of Morals. § 53.
3   Hösle, Vittorio. 1997. Politik and Moral. München: C.H. Beck, p. 933.

1.

From the Stoics to Kant: cosmopolitanism, natural law, and the idea of a contract

Cosmopolitanism in ancient Greece

One of the founding principles on which the idea of a world parliament is based is that the entire Earth must be comprehended as the home of all human beings. The history of cosmopolitanism is usually traced back to the Greek philosopher Diogenes of Sinope (ca. 400 to 323 BCE), who, when asked about his home city, is supposed to have answered that he was a 'kosmopolitês' – a citizen of the world. An important, if ambiguous, role was played by his contemporary Alexander the Great (356 to 323 BCE), who brought Persia, Asia Minor and Egypt under his rule, and extended it as far as the Indian subcontinent. Peter Coulmas writes in an account of the history of cosmopolitanism that Alexander was the first to express the view that all people should be regarded as brothers and kin. He pursued the vision of an 'empire of the human race' encompassing many different peoples and countries.[1] He is supposed to have advanced the idea that 'the habitable Earth' was 'the common fatherland of all'. As the historian of antiquity Alexander Demandt recounts, Alexander, according to Plutarch, saw himself as the 'arbitrator and steward of humanity' whose task it was 'to merge all people together into a single body and to mix the peoples in a giant mixing bowl of friendship' and 'to unite them into a single family'. His philosophy was based on the idea that all people, Greeks as well as barbarians, were equal.[2] Although he may not have wanted to be regarded by Persians and other peoples as an alien ruler, the reality was different. Their incorporation into his empire was achieved by force.

In Stoic philosophy, the idea of a natural community of humankind and of the unity of all life was firmly established by around 300 BCE. This viewpoint was contrary to the prevailing particularism and parochialism of the ancient Greek world, which after the collapse of the Alexandrian empire was fragmented into rival city-states. The idea that 'this whole universe should [be]

1   Coulmas, Peter. 1990. Weltbürger. Geschichte einer Menschheitssehnsucht. Reinbek: Rowohlt, p. 90.
2   Demandt, Alexander. Alexander der Große. München: C.H. Beck, 2012. pp. 373, 378, 373.

thought to be one city in common between gods and human beings', as Cicero (106 to 43 BCE) put it[3], had no explicit political intent, and was not meant to imply the idea of a world state. Nevertheless, as Coulmas observes, 'the secular and unique historic achievement of the Stoics was to project the community of citizens as realized in the Polis onto the community of humanity and thus to universalize it'.[4]

In one of Cicero's dialogues, the view is advanced that human solidarity and shared responsibility extend to the whole of humanity. A human being, it is argued, 'simply by reason of the fact that he is human, should not be considered a stranger by any other human being'. Every single person is connected to the human community. It is a natural duty 'to place the common interests of all people above our own'.[5] As the classical scholar Klaus Bartels remarks, the dialogue culminates in the concept of treason against humanity and in the astoundingly modern hypothesis that people have a duty not only towards the human community but also towards future generations. 'Whoever sacrifices the common interests or welfare of all for his own interests or welfare' deserves just as much censure as 'someone who betrays their fatherland'. And later on it is argued that steps must also be taken to ensure the welfare of 'those generations that will live in times to come'.[6]

The idea of a democratic world community was then formulated by Philo of Alexandria (ca. 15 BCE to 40 CE), one of the best-known representatives of Hellenic Jewry. There are two species of cities, he wrote in a treatise, and one of them is better than the other, namely the one 'which enjoys a democratic government, a constitution which honors equality, the rulers of which are law and justice'.[7] The ultimate purpose of the rise and fall of people and nations, he philosophized in another text, was 'in order that the whole world may become, as it were, one city, and enjoy the most excellent of constitutions, a democracy'.[8]

Cosmopolitan roots in India and China

Cosmopolitan thought is also found, and from very early on, beyond the cultural borders of ancient Greece. For example, in the collection of Old Tamil

3 Cicero. De Legibus. I. 23., citation from Coulmas, ibid., p. 118.
4 Ibid., pp. 114ff.
5 Citation from Bartels, Klaus. 2011. Jahrtausendworte in die Gegenwart gesprochen. Darmstadt/Mainz: Philipp von Zabern, p. 74.
6 Citation from ibid., pp. 74f.
7 On the Confusion of Tongues, Section XXIII (108), in: Philo Judaeus. 1993. The Works of Philo. Transl. by C.D. Yonge. New updated edition. Hendrickson Publishers. p. 243.
8 On the Unchangeableness of God, XXXVI (175), ibid., p. 172.

poetry 'Puṟanāṉūṟu', which is part of Sangam literature from the period between 100 BCE and the fifth century, it is said in a poem by Kaṇiyaṉ Pūṅkuṉṟaṉ that 'every country is my country, every man is my kinsman'.[9] The Hindu Upanishads, which are in part much older, and other ancient Indian Sanskrit texts contain the philosophical concept 'Vasudhaiva Kutumbakam', which in Sanskrit means 'the whole world is one family'.[10] In the 'Book of Rites', one of the five classics of the Confucian canon, which are derived from the teachings of the Chinese philosopher Confucius (551 to 470 BCE), can be found the idea of the 'Great Unity', according to which the world should be shared equally and harmoniously by all. Still older is the concept of 'Tianxia', which means roughly 'everything under heaven'. This rose to importance in the Zhou dynasty, around 1046 to 256 BCE and includes the idea that the Chinese Emperor unites and rules the world as the Son of Heaven. In the Zhou dynasty, according to the Chinese philosopher Zhao Tingyang, the starting point of all political thinking was the world as a whole. It was regarded as the 'uppermost political entity', to which all other political entities should be subordinate. According to the theory of 'Tianxia', a political system can only claim to be in a state of peace 'when the notion of externality no longer exists; in other words, when nothing and nobody is excluded', as Tingyang explains. The philosopher points out that the Tao Te Ching, for example in Chapter 54, has a global perspective.[11]

Vitoria's 'republic of the whole world'

The first detailed formulation of the idea of the whole of humanity as a state-like community appeared at the start of the European colonization of Central and South America. The Dominican theologian Francisco de Vitoria (1483 to 1546), who from 1526 onwards gave lectures at the University of Salamanca, and who was a contemporary of Christopher Columbus and Hernán Cortés, developed the concept of a 'res publica totus orbis', a community spanning the entire globe. There had of course been other sketches for a world state, notably that for a tiered universal monarchy developed by Dante Alighieri (1265 to 1321). However, the latter was conceived around the establishment of an impe-

---

9   There are many translations of these lines, with slight variations.
10 See e.g. the fable 'The Brahman and his weasel' in the Hitopadesha; cf. Śarman, Lakshmīnarayaṇa. 1830. The Hitopadesha: A collection of fables and tales in Sanskrit by Vishnusarmá. Calcutta: Shástra Prakásha Press, pp. 508-509 (Ch. 4, Fable 13).
11 Tingyang, Zhao. 2009. 'A Political World Philosophy in terms of All-under-heaven (Tian-xia)'. Diogenes (56) 221: 5–18. pp. 8ff.

rialist Christian empire. 'In contrast to the universal monarchy,' writes the Vitoria scholar Johannes Thumfart, 'Vitoria appears as the champion of a concrete, democratically legitimated and pluralistically structured global polity.'[12]

For us, accustomed as we are to the division of the world into states, Vitoria's conceptual approach is not very easy to grasp. As Josef Soder explains, the community imagined by Vitoria is 'neither a state like other states, nor a super-state, but simply the summation of the whole of humanity, whether divided into states or not'.[13] In Vitoria's conception, the global state community of the 'totus orbis' is aboriginal. It precedes the formation of separate individual polities and is therefore also not annulled by their emergence. Indeed, the 'totus orbis' can issue laws that are binding on all people and all states. Remarkably, this requires only the assent of a majority. Vitoria, to be sure, does not explain exactly how such decisions on the part of 'the whole globe' are to be reached in practice. At any rate, the goal or purpose of what he believes to be this naturally occurring community is the wellbeing of all people.

The aboriginal community of all human beings in Vitoria's conception is the starting point for state organization, and every individual is by nature a subject of international law entitled under certain conditions to certain rights. Vitoria assumes in all of this that all people are essentially equal, regardless of their religion or other characteristics. He formulated this view at the beginning of the era of globalization, just as Europeans were coming across peoples who had until then been entirely unknown to them. It was in stark contrast to the unchecked inhumanity of the Spanish Conquista, which Hans Magnus Enzensberger described in 1981 as 'genocide perpetrated against 20 million people'.[14] According to Vitoria's doctrine of international law, non-Christian communities such as those found in the 'New World' also had a right to self-governance and property. Their subjugation was therefore wrong, and at the very least required justification.[15] Rolf Grawert comments: 'at a time when Spaniards are murdering Aztecs and overthrowing their rule, and when Francis I of France forms an alliance against Charles V with Suleiman the Magnificent and Moors

12 Thumfart, Johannes. 2011. Francisco de Vitorias Philsophie: globalpolitisch, nicht kosmopolitisch. In: Die Normativität des Rechts bei Francisco de Vitoria, ed. by Kirstin Bunge, Anselm Spindler and Andreas Wagner, 229-254. Stuttgart-Bad Cannstatt: frommann-holzboog Verlag, p. 249.
13 Soder, Josef. 1955. Die Idee der Völkergemeinschaft. Francisco de Vitoria and die philosophischen Grundlagen des Völkerrechts. Frankfurt am Main: Alfred Metzner Verlag, pp. 53ff.
14 Las Casas, Bartolomé de. 1981 [1552]. Bericht von der Verwüstung der Westindischen Länder. Ed. by Hans Magnus Enzensberger. Insel Verlag, p. 124.
15 Although Vitoria deprected the atrocities of the Conquista, he did offer one argument for the justification of the Spanish campaign. He argued that the Spaniards had a right to intervene in the Indian communities in order to provide protection against the practice of human sacrifice.

as well as Jews are being persecuted, this appeal to a universal human nature is of extreme political significance, and has remained so up to the present day'.[16]

Conceptions of peace under the 'sovereign power of the state'

Vitoria's reflections on a cosmopolitan human community, which in his view afforded every individual the right of freedom of movement, remained an exception until the 18th century Enlightenment. Already in Dante's time, 'the actual development of history had begun to move away from the idea of a supranational political unity. At the start of the 14th century it was no longer possible to imagine that the Emperor or the Pope could once again become a universal power. The cohesion of the Christian world was being increasingly broken down by the claims of the territorial rulers to independence', writes Maja Brauer in her history of world federalism.[17] In the course of the transition from the Middle Ages to the modern era, the princes and the other sovereign rulers, in a development that spanned generations, fought ever harder to bring geographical territories that were as homogeneous as possible under their sole control. The French political theorist Jean Bodin (ca. 1529 to 1596) formulated the concept of sovereignty as the most important political objective of the new power of the state. According to Bodin, the sovereign ruler is the owner of all armed force within his territory, is independent of others, especially of the Emperor and the Pope, and recognizes only God alone above him. 'The principal characteristic of sovereign majesty and absolute power,' wrote Bodin in 1583, lies in the power 'to impose laws on all subjects without their consent.'[18] This, together with the development at the same time of administrative institutions, led to the gradual formation of discrete, 'sovereign' territorial states.

'For centuries, the model of a great community of peoples was replaced by the model of the association of sovereign monarchs who agreed rules for the peaceful resolution of disputes and common responses to violent acts committed by individual members', as Brauer summarizes the period following Dante.[19] In the face of the continuing Ottoman expansion into Europe since the 15th century and of the sieges of Vienna in the years 1529 and 1683, the idea of a pooling of Christian forces against the 'Turkish threat' was an important aspect of the peace plans of this period, one that often gave them an imperialist

---

16   Grawert, Rolf. 2000. 'Francisco de Vitoria. Naturrecht - Herrschaftsordnung – Völkerrecht'. Der Staat 39: 110-125, p. 117.
17   Brauer, Maja. 1994. Weltföderation - Modell globaler Gesellschaftsordnung. Frankfurt am Main et al.: Peter Lang, p. 26.
18   Bodin, Jean. 1976 [1583]. Über den Staat. Stuttgart: Reclam, p. 31f., see also p. 42.
19   Brauer, ibid., p. 27.

orientation. One example of this is the plan for 'a perpetual and general peace among all the peoples of Europe' put forward from 1711 onwards, piecemeal and in several versions, by the French diplomat the Abbé Castel de Saint-Pierre (1658 to 1743). His proposed Christian-European alliance of states, which would have a court of arbitration and a common army, did not include the Ottoman Empire as a full member. On the contrary: in a third volume about the project in 1716 he described the 'expulsion of the Turks' as an 'urgent necessity'.[20]

The numerous proposals for international peace alliances usually envisaged congresses and assemblies meeting on a regular basis. They had little to do with a world parliament in the sense of cosmopolitan and democratic popular representation by independent delegates. What was envisaged as a rule was assemblies made up of delegates of the aristocratic rulers bound by their instructions; such was the case with Saint-Pierre, and also with the peace concept of Émeric Crucé (1590 to 1648), which distinguishes itself by virtue of its ecumenical approach, notably including the Islamic world. It was often assumed, for example by Saint-Pierre and Crucé, that these rulers' congresses should be able to come to binding decisions for safeguarding peace between states, right up to determining common sanctions against peace-breakers. It had nothing at all to do with representation for the 'subjects' of their rule in international law. If there is a reference within these peace plans to a parliament, then it is generally in the pre-modern sense of a simple council of representatives of interested parties, and in this case of the sovereign rulers in particular. The term parliament derives from the Old French 'parlement', which literally means parley or interlocution.

The idea of the social contract in Hobbes and Locke

The founder of Pennsylvania, William Penn (1644 to 1718), argued in 1693 in an essay on a peace model for Europe that the sovereignty of the rulers would not be constrained by a guarantee of collective assistance, but on the contrary would be strengthened by increased security against reciprocal attacks. Penn regarded the concept of the 'sovereign equality' of rulers as naïve. In the assembly of representatives of the sovereigns which he proposed, he envisaged that votes would be weighted according to economic strength in order to mirror in the assembly the 'inequality between the rulers and between the states' and to make participation more attractive to the greater powers. In 1710, John Bellers (1654 to 1725), a friend of Penn's and like him a Quaker, also put forward a peace model envisaging weighted votes. However, he uses population as his weighting basis. Bellers is one of the first to address the rights of the subjects in

20 Borner, Wilhelm. 1913. *Das Weltstaatsprojekt des Abbé de Saint-Pierre*. Diss. Berlin, Leipzig, pp. 31ff.

the context of the consideration of a federation of states: 'by consent of the General Council [of the alliance of states] ...there should be established an order
and regulation, between sovereigns and subjects, to hinder on one side, the oppression and tyranny of princes; and on the other side, the tumults and rebellion of subjects'. [21] One had to accept a tyrannical prince, wrote Crucé almost a
hundred years earlier, in the same way 'one accepts a year with a poor harvest,
in the hope of better times to come.'[22]

With 'De Cive' in 1642 and 'Leviathan' in 1651, Thomas Hobbes heralded
the end, in political philosophy, of the legitimation of political rule by divine
right. In its place came the theoretical concept of contractual self-commitment
by the individual, the idea of the social contract. Hobbes constructed a hypothetical state of nature in which, because of what he believed to be the competitive attitude inherent in man's lupine nature, and because of mutual distrust,
selfishness and fear in the absence of a general power capable of imposing justice and law, an anarchic 'war of all against all' prevails. In order to escape this
general condition of insecurity, a state, with an absolute ruler and a monopoly
on force, is established by means of a reciprocal contract between each and
every individual. This contract comes into general force as soon as a majority
gives assent. It is a unique and irreversible hypothetical act, from which Hobbes
derives the unlimited power of an absolute sovereign, who should be as invin-
cible as the Leviathan, the sea monster of the Old Testament.

In the year 1649, the English Civil War between the parliamentary forces
around Oliver Cromwell and the Royalists around Charles I ended with the ex-
ecution of the King and the abolition of the English monarchy (which was restored in 1660). The so-called Levellers, who represented a new interpretation
of democracy, formed a strong grass-roots political movement within the revolutionary camp. 'The Levellers were convinced that political rule derived from
the rational will of originally free and equal men by way of a contract of each
with all,' writes the political scientist Richard Saage.[23] They had recognized that
relations between rulers and subjects were designed and maintained by human
beings and not 'natural', as Aristotle had argued. Hobbes used the same insight
to justify a rigorous absolutism. But the theory of the social contract which underpinned this also made possible a radical reappraisal of the question of legitimate state rule and its relation to the individual. 'The history of the modern

21 Bellers, John. 1710. Some Reasons for an European State. London, p. 19. Nb this citation: ed. of 1723, in:
    Alan P.F. Sell, et al. (eds.). 'Protestant Nonconformist Texts Volume 2: The Eighteenth Century'.
22 Crucé, Émeric. 1953 [1623]. Der neue Kineas. In: Ewiger Friede. Friedensrufe und Friedenspläne seit der
    Renaissance, ed. by Kurt von Raumer, transl. by Walther Neft, 289-320. Freiburg: Verl. Karl Alber, p. 314.
23 Saage, Richard. 2005. Demokratietheorien. Wiesbaden: VS Verlag für Sozialwissenschaften, p. 82.

state is the history of the taming of the Leviathan – by human rights and rational law, by the rule of law in the state, by *Rechtsstaatlichkeit* and constitutionalism, by the separation of powers and democracy,' writes Wolfgang Kersting, professor of philosophy at Kiel.[24]

The model of the state proposed by John Locke (1632 to 1704) represented one milestone in this process. In his 'Two Treatises of Government', published anonymously in 1689, this English philosopher took up the idea of the social contract and used it as a starting point for the deconstruction of the concept of absolute monarchy. He argued that in the hypothetical state of nature human beings were completely free, equal and independent. His underlying view of human nature, in contrast to Hobbes, is positive. The purpose of the community created by the social contract was the maintenance of order and the protection of the natural rights of the individual, especially the right to life, liberty and property. The state's powers were limited to serving 'the public good of the society'. 'It is a power, that ... can never have a right to destroy, enslave, or designedly to impoverish the subjects' writes Locke.[25] This is followed by ruminations on how the social contract might be designed to control political power. An elected legislature is envisaged as sovereign, 'made up of representatives chosen for that time by the people'[26]; its laws, passed by majority, are universally binding, including on the lawmakers and on the state itself. Here Locke formulated a system of popular rule via elected representatives and the principle of the rule of law. In arguing for separating law enforcement, or the exercise of the monopoly on force, from the legislative function, in order to prevent abuses of power, Locke is also emphasizing for the first time the need for the separation of powers. Should the legislature betray the people's trust and act against the state interest, then sovereignty is forfeited and returns to the people, who can renew the social contract and replace the legislature.

The idea of the social contract in Hobbes and Locke was particularistic rather than universal and applied to specific communities rather than to the foundation of a world state. But Hobbes showed how the individual sovereigns, too, could be understood to be in an anarchic state of nature, without law and order. 'Concerning the Offices of one Soveraign to another, which are comprehended in that Law, which is commonly called the Law of Nations, I need not say any thing in this place; because the Law of Nations, and the Law of Nature, is the

---

24 Kersting, Wolfgang. 2002. Thomas Hobbes zur Einführung. 2nd ed. Hamburg: Junius, pp. 12f.
25 Locke, John. 1689. Two Treatises of Government, § 135, p. 103.
26 Ibid., § 154, p. 118.

same thing', wrote Hobbes.[27] Thus the original 'war of all against all', a hypothetical relationship between individuals in the state of nature, becomes a reality between sovereigns in the international sphere. In this view, to ensure the preservation of their capacity to act, indeed of their existence, under these conditions, states must make the greatest possible efforts for their own security and must prevent the development of excessive power imbalances. The consequence is a perpetual increase in alliance-building and in expenditure on armed forces, which in turn simply increase insecurity yet further. This gives rise to what the German-American scholar of international law John H. Herz described as the 'security dilemma'.

A similar understanding of international relations underlay most conceptions of peace under international law and remains influential today. 'Let us admit then' as Saint-Pierre wrote in his plea for a federal Europe at the beginning of the 18th century, 'that the Powers of Europe stand to each other strictly in a state of war, and that all the separate treaties between them are in the nature of a temporary truce rather than a real peace.'[28] A lasting general peace through a balance of powers was 'a mere figment of the imagination' wrote Kant in 1793.

The social contract and Wolff's 'Völkerstaat'

In a subsequent logical step, the idea of the social contract then offers an escape route out of the international 'state of nature' by way of a sovereign common polity encompassing all states. In his noteworthy study of cosmopolitan models for a global state, the Zürich philosophy professor Francis Cheneval identifies Christian Wolff (1679 to 1754) as the first person to use the theory of the social contract as the foundational rationale for a world state (a 'Völkerstaat', or 'peoples' state'), and therefore as the person who heralded 'a shift to the supra-national in the philosophy of international law'.[29] Following Cheneval's analysis, the philosophical concept put forward by Wolff in 1749 and 1750 must indeed be seen as a significant milestone in the evolution of cosmopolitan models of world order. In Wolff's abstract conception of the social contract, which is extended to include all levels of human social interaction, he outlines (according to Cheneval) a universal community of cooperation between people, a 'civitas

---

27 Hobbes, Thomas. 1651. Leviathan. Ch. XXX.
28 Rousseau, Jean Jacques. 1953. Auszug aus dem Plan des Ewigen Friedens des Herrn Abbé de Saint-Pierre. In: Ewiger Friede. Friedensrufe and Friedenspläne seit der Renaissance, ed. by Kurt von Raumer, transl. by Gertrud von Raumer, 343-368. Freiburg, München: Verlag Karl Alber, p. 348.
29 Cheneval, Francis. 2002. Philosophie in weltbürgerlicher Bedeutung. Über die Entstehung und die philosophischen Grundlagen des supranationalen und kosmopolitischen Denkens der Moderne. Basel: Schwabe & Co, pp. 132ff.

maxima', which has as its goal and purpose the wellbeing of all people, and which ultimately leads to a democratically constituted 'Völkerstaat'. Wolff not only transforms the theory of the social contract, and thereby supersedes the theory of divine right, but – as probably the first person since Vitoria – in his model of international law he resurrects the idea of a community of the human race, comprising all individuals. This 'societas magna' of all people, and the human rights embedded within it, are the foundation of all further social development, according to Wolff.[30]

As Cheneval explains, Wolff's argument for a 'Völkerstaat' follows the logic of social contract theory and attempts to derive from this a general validity for a universal legal system. Wolff shows that the justification for government in social contract theory cannot logically be restricted to the nation state level only to disappear beyond that in a reversion to the 'state of nature' at the international level. 'A contractualism limited to the national level is therefore incoherent, because at the level of international law it turns against its own principles' writes Cheneval.[31] The theory logically requires that states bind themselves together in a superordinate 'Völkerstaat', or superstate. 'Wolff argued for a federal superstate, one which comes into being through an originating contract between the individual state and the group and the group with the individual state, one in which an assembly of state representatives, a senate of the peoples, passes binding laws on the principle of majority rule, laws on which limits are set by the acknowledgement of a community of mankind based on principles of natural law and of certain basic laws', Cheneval summarizes.[32] Yet this would not give rise to a global Leviathan, precisely because Wolff underpins this with a tiered and functionally differentiated conception of sovereignty under which the resulting superstate has only those powers that are assigned to it by the states and necessary for the fulfilment of its responsibilities. For Wolff it is clear that this 'Völkerstaat' does not yet exist. The conception is rather an ideal of a rational, social world order to be aspired to over the course of history.

Kant's cosmopolitan project

Cosmopolitan thinking reached a highpoint in the philosophical work of Immanuel Kant (1724 to 1804). In the essay 'Idea for a Universal History from a Cosmopolitan Point of View', published in 1784, Kant outlined, following social contract theory, how world history was leading to 'the civic union of the

30 Ibid., p. 172.
31 Ibid., p. 202.
32 Ibid., p. 135.

human race' under a 'lawful constitution'.[33] In his famous essay 'Perpetual Peace' of 1795, Kant wrote that from a universalist perspective the state of nature could only be overcome if three elements of a civic constitution are combined: namely, citizenship rights within a nation, international law between states, and cosmopolitan rights, where 'individuals and states ... may be regarded as citizens of one world-state (jus cosmopoliticum)'.[34] Similarly, Kant's conception of a world republic by no means abolishes the states, but rather makes them into constituent parts, into 'citizens', of a superordinate world constitutional order.

However, Kant recognized several different impediments which meant that the ideal 'Völkerstaat', with its three specified elements for the overcoming of the state of war, could not be established immediately, but only step by step, by 'a continuous approximation' through 'gradual reform'.[35] For one thing, he believed that 'with the too great extension of such a Union of States over vast regions any government of it ... must at last become impossible'.[36] For another, he cites the potential risk of despotism,[37] given that most states were still autocratic themselves. But what was decisive was his judgement that the states, that is the rulers of his day, would not be prepared to abandon the international 'state of nature' for the establishment of a shared republican 'Völkerstaat'. As a first practical step, therefore, and as the only one possible, only a federation of states came into question for him. 'For states, in their relation to one another, there can be, according to reason, no other way of advancing from that lawless condition which unceasing war implies, than by giving up their savage lawless freedom, just as individual men have done, and yielding to the coercion of public laws. Thus, they can form a State of nations (*civitas gentium*), one, too, which will be ever increasing and would finally embrace all the peoples of the earth. States, however, in accordance with their understanding of the law of nations, by no means desire this, and therefore reject *in hypothesi* what is correct *in thesi*. Hence, instead of the positive idea of a world-republic, if all is not to be lost, only the negative substitute for it, a federation averting war, maintaining its ground and ever extending over the world may stop the current of this tendency

---

33   Kant, Immanuel. 1963 [1784]. Idea for a Universal History from a Cosmopolitan Point of View, in: On History, ed. by Lewis White Beck, The Bobbs-Merrill Co., 7th and 9th theses.
34   Id. 1903 [1795]. Perpetual Peace, transl. by M. Campbell Smith. London: George Allen & Unwin, p. 119.
35   Ibid, 3rd definitive article; and id., The Metaphysics of Morals, § 61 and conclusion.
36   Ibid., § 61.
37   Id. 1798 [1793]. On the Popular Judgment: That may be Right in Theory, but does not Hold Good in the Praxis, in: Essays and Treatises, Vol. I., transl. by John Richardson, London: Richardson, p. 188.

to war and shrinking from the control of law. But even then there will be a constant danger that this propensity may break out.'[38] The federation of states proposed here has no sovereignty in the way that a civil constitution does and is therefore incomplete. The limitation of cosmopolitan rights to a right to visit foreign countries should be understood, in line with Kant's philosophy of history, as a concession to the reality that the rulers would not be willing to allow more. He compares the unwillingness of the states to subject themselves to legal and self-drafted binding powers to the 'attachment of savages to their lawless liberty', which should be regarded 'with profound contempt as barbarism and uncivilisation and the brutal degradation of humanity'.[39]

The federation of states outlined by Kant as a minimal solution is in line with traditional international peace conceptions and is not innovative. However, a new way forward is suggested by the notion of a cosmopolitan programme envisaging a development from this federation of states to a world republic, one in which not only the states but also the people would be subjects of a community of humanity. The dogma of absolute sovereignty within international law was thus broken in two ways simultaneously. On the one hand, by the partition of sovereignty between individual states and the world republic; and on the other hand, by the participation of the individual alongside the states in the sovereignty of humanity. Kant said nothing about the specific institutional shape to be taken by the 'state of nations' as the incorporation of perpetual peace, the greatest political good. But as Kant 'made the idea of representation the defining characteristic of the republic, the representation of the citizens of a state by its government or by directly elected delegates at the supra-national level was not a problem for him,' reasons Cheneval.[40] Thus it is in Kant's philosophy that the idea of a world parliament is implied for the first time.

---

38 Id., Perpetual Peace, loc. cit., 2nd definitive article.
39 Ibid.
40 Cheneval, loc. cit., p. 620.

2.
The 18th century: enlightenment, revolutions, and parliamentarism

The American federal state and representative democracy

In the course of the Enlightenment, from the middle of the 18th century onwards, an 'unprecedented enthusiasm for cosmopolitanism' spread across Europe and North America, as Coulmas writes.[1] Diogenes' claim that he was a citizen of the world became a programmatic statement of the era, repeated by Thomas Paine, David Hume, Voltaire and Gotthold Ephraim Lessing among others. Of course, the monarchs pursued their dynastic and geopolitical interests just as ever before, by means of war if necessary, but the spirit was blowing in a new direction.[2] 'The barriers that separated states and nations in their antagonistic pursuit of self-interest have been breached. All thinking minds are linked together now by a cosmopolitan bond,' Friedrich Schiller (1759 to 1805) enthused in his inaugural lecture in Jena in May 1789.[3] For a short period, intellectual and bourgeois forces saw themselves as united in the spirit of enlightenment and cosmopolitanism. From this crucible there emerged for the first time the explicit idea, indeed the concrete political demand, for a world parliament. The cosmopolitan ideal combined together with the theories of representation and of democracy, which had just burst through into practice in such spectacular and historic fashion in North America, and joined forces with the French Revolution.

In the American Declaration of Independence of 1776, the equality and liberty of all people was for the first time proclaimed and made the foundation of a new state order. Following the British victory in the war with France for domination in North America, from 1763 onwards the tension between London and the colonists mounted. 'No taxation without representation' became the slogan for their unsuccessful demand for representation in the English parliament. They argued that when a government infringed unalienable human rights, as

---

1   Coulmas, Peter. 1990. Weltbürger. Geschichte einer Menschheitssehnsucht. Reinbek: Rowohlt, p. 333.
2   Ibid., pp. 333ff.
3   Schiller, Friedrich. 1789. 'Was heißt und zu welchem Ende studiert man Universalgeschichte?'

King George III of England (1738 to 1820) had done, a right of resistance was thereby created. In the war of independence which followed, the colonists threw off English rule and ushered in a new era, a 'novus ordo seclorum'. In this they had one great advantage: they could make a clean start. 'We have every opportunity and every encouragement before us, to form the noblest purest constitution on the face of the earth. We have it in our power to begin the world over again,' declared Thomas Paine.[4] With the Articles of Confederation of 1777, the thirteen former colonies at first established a loose confederation which did not impinge on the sovereignty of the individual states, not even with respect to foreign or trade policy. Common resolutions were hardly implemented at all, and were therefore ineffective. It proved impossible, for example, to create a common economic area. In the pursuit of their individual interests, the states divided and came into conflict. Eventually the Federalists prevailed. The United States of America was established as a genuinely federal state with the Constitution of 17 September 1787. Legislative power in this new, geographically extensive federal state, whose citizens mainly originated from all over Europe, was in the hands of a Congress consisting of two chambers: the House of Representatives, directly elected (initially by male census suffrage) to represent the people, and the Senate, made up of representatives of the individual federal states elected by their parliaments (and from 1913 also directly).

The early proto-democracies in the Greek city states (up to about 300 BCE) and in the Roman Republic (up to the beginning of the principate in 27 BCE) were based on assemblies of the (male) electorate, and were limited to comparatively small city states. Referring to these early models, Jean Jacques Rousseau (1712 to 1778) was still saying in 'The Social Contract' of 1762 that only an assembly of the whole people could constitute a sovereign legislature expressing the common will. As popular sovereignty could neither be subdivided nor delegated to representatives, a republican system could only ever be realized in small states. The political scientist Robert Dahl (1915 to 2014) described the gradual shift in the interpretation of democracy, away from its historical roots in the city states to the more extensive areas of rule of a nation, a country or a nation state, as 'the second democratic transformation' of history.[5] The example of the USA showed that democracy, understood as representative democracy, could be organized not only in a large territory but also in the innovative political form of a federal state. Benjamin Franklin, for example, expressed the idea

4   Paine, Thomas. 1995 [1776]. Common Sense. In: Rights of Man, Common Sense and Other Political Writings. Oxford University Press.
5   Dahl, Robert. 1989. Democracy and its critics. New Haven: Yale University Press, pp. 213ff.

in 1787 already that the new American federal constitution might function as a model for a 'federal union' in Europe.[6]

The historical roots of parliamentarism

The United States of America heralded a new epoch in the history of representative democracy. The founding fathers of the USA regarded their system as unique, on account of its embedding of popular sovereignty in a written constitution, of its republicanism and federalism. 'Yet it is also clear,' according to the historian Colin Bonwick, 'that the state constitutions as well as the United States Constitution (which were all drafted during the revolutionary era and must be taken together) owe much to the experiences of other countries – and especially to the British constitutionalism from which Americans were escaping.'[7] The development of parliamentarism, which reached its zenith up to that point in the US Constitution, can be traced back over many centuries to the societies of the Middle Ages and the early modern period, with their hierarchical estates of the realm. Representatives of the nobility, the clergy, and later also of the higher classes from the cities were able to achieve some rights to political participation or consultation vis-à-vis their rulers. Membership of the assemblies of the estates which then developed was exclusive, and usually based on personal privilege, public office, property or guild or trade membership, often itself in turn based on birth. The members of the assemblies of the estates represented only their own interests, and not those of the subjects in general at all. The rulers were often dependent on their cooperation and assent, especially for raising taxes. The development of the representation of the estates and of parliamentarism followed complex paths, with interruptions and with peculiarities specific to every region. However, the first assembly of the estates to be established on a long-term basis and with some powers over the king, and which moreover included representatives not only of the nobility and the clergy but of the cities, was convened in 1188 by Alfonso IX (1171 to 1230), King of León in the Iberian peninsula.[8]

The development of parliamentarism in England was a special case. For England, according to the political scientist Klaus von Beyme, 'was the only

---

6   Letter of Benjamin Franklin to Rodolphe-Ferdinand Grand, 22 Oct. 1787, in: Benjamin Franklin Papers, ed. by The American Philosophical Society and Yale University, digital ed. by The Packard Humanities Institute.
7   Bonwick, Colin. 1999. The United States Constitution and its Roots in British Political Thought and Tradition. In: Foundations of democracy in the European Union. From the genesis of parliamentary democracy to the European Parliament, ed. by John Pinder, pp. 41-58. Basingstoke: MacMillan Press. p. 41.
8   Zanden, Jan Luiten van, Eltjo Buringh, and Maarten Bosker. 2012. 'The rise and decline of European parliaments, 1188–1789'. The Economic History Review, 65 (3), pp. 835–861.

country in the world to develop parliamentary government with no significant break in continuity in the constitutional development from a system based on the estates of the realm from the late Middle Ages onwards'.[9] Following his conquest of England in the year 1066, William I (1027 to 1087) introduced regular consultations with the clergy and the landed nobility in order to ensure their assent on important questions and thus to make them into supporting props for his rule. After the 'Magna Carta' was successfully pushed through in 1215, the English King was for the first time obliged to obtain the assent of an assembly of the landed nobility in order to introduce new taxes. From 1295 onwards, representatives from the towns and boroughs also took part in the English parliament. And from 1341, the 'commons' assembled separately from the nobility and the clergy. The English parliament thus developed into a two-chamber system. In the 15th century a general census suffrage was introduced for the lower chamber, the 'House of Commons'. By 1619, twelve years after the founding of Jamestown as the first permanent settlement of English colonists in the 'New World', the first assembly of elected political representatives of the colonists in North America was formed in the province of Virginia, and valuable experience of democracy began to be gained.

The long evolution of 'sovereign' territorial states produced a 'tendency among the monarchs and princes, who had occupied the pinnacle of the medieval feudal pyramid, to claim the new sovereignty for themselves alone, and to exclude the estates, which had developed in the medieval state into co-holders of public political power,' according to the historian Heinz Schilling.[10] The conflicts over power and privilege between monarchs and representatives of the estates during the three centuries from 1500 onwards were a central aspect of all great socio-political confrontations of the epoch.[11] Often, kings would simply refuse from the outset to convene the assembly of the estates, as for example Charles I did in the decade prior to the outbreak of the English Civil War in the year 1642. Eventually, in the Revolution of 1688/89, the English parliament made itself the bearer of the sovereignty of the state by means of the 'Bill of Rights'. Even if the monarch continued to determine the overarching political questions, and in particular to decide on war and peace, from now on he had to win a majority in the newly independent parliament for the government budget.

9   Beyme, Klaus von. 1999. Die parlamentarische Demokratie. 3rd ed. Opladen/Wiesbaden: Westdeutscher Verlag, p. 21.
10   Schilling, Heinz. 1994. Aufbruch and Krise: Deutschland 1517-1648. Vol. 5. Siedler Deutsche Geschichte. Berlin: Siedler Verlag, p. 20.
11   Cf. Zanden, loc. cit.

Cosmopolitanism in the French Revolution

Developments in England, and the ideas of John Locke, did not fail to have an impact in France, the centre of the Ancien régime. In the course of the 18th century they slowly but surely undermined the authority of the monarchy. When Louis XVI found himself forced to convene the Estates General of France in 1789, for the first time since 1614, in order to legitimate and implement tax reforms, it was a signal that electrified people far beyond the borders of France. Following the elections to the Estates General, in the so-called Tennis Court Oath of 20 June 1789 the Third Estate, representing around 98 per cent of the population, declared itself to be a National Assembly for the creation of a constitution. The storming of the Bastille on 14 July is regarded as the symbolic moment of birth of the Revolution. The Declaration of the Rights of Man and of the Citizen was issued on 26 August, beginning with the declaration of the equality and liberty of all and of the sovereignty of the people, and identifying the principles on which the new order would be based.

In the turmoil of the Revolution, one of the issues at stake was whether the establishment of a republican system beyond France for those other peoples of Europe still under monarchical rule should be among the aims. Republicanism 'at that time of upheaval and at the historical birth of modern European democracy was not yet particularist but rather European and cosmopolitan', Cheneval emphasizes. The concept of the 'nation' was not necessarily synonymous with the nation-state during the first few years of revolution.[12] The external situation was decisive at this point. In May 1790 the National Assembly declared its renunciation of wars of conquest, but revolutionary fever, sparked by the proclamation of the right of peoples to self-determination, was spreading, and increasingly unsettling the European monarchies. Louis XVI discussed with them the possibility of armed intervention 'in order to put a stop to the agitators'.[13] In April 1792 military conflicts began between France and an alliance led by Austria and Prussia which continued until 1797, in the course of which France would occupy the Southern Netherlands and the Dutch Republic.

It was an expression of the cosmopolitan revolutionary spirit of the time when, on 26 August 1792, the National Assembly awarded French citizenship to seventeen foreigners who had rendered outstanding service to the Revolution, including Jeremy Bentham, Alexander Hamilton, James Madison, Thomas Paine, Johann Heinrich Pestalozzi, Friedrich Schiller and George Washington.

---

12 Cheneval, Francis. 2004. 'Der kosmopolitische Republikanismus - erläutert am Beispiel Anacharsis Cloots'. Zeitschrift für philosophische Forschung 58 (3): 373-396, pp. 376, 378.
13 Tulard, Jean. 1989. Frankreich im Zeitalter der Revolutionen 1789-1851. Geschichte Frankreichs. Vol. 4. Stuttgart: DVA, pp. 90ff.

Among those honoured was Johann Baptist Baron de Cloots, also known as Anacharsis Cloots (1755 to 1794), born in Kleve in Prussia but with Dutch family roots. Like Paine, Cloots lived in Paris, and had been an active member of the Jacobin Club since 1789. In September 1792, again like Paine, he was elected to the National Assembly, and was called on from time to time to help draft the Constitution. It is remarkable that Cloots, the first person to explicitly formulate the idea of a world parliament, was not a philosopher but a revolutionary.

Cloots' 'republic of humanity'

For Cloots, the Revolution had a universal character and mission. He was emphatically of the view that a world republic should be established, starting with France. In his work 'Bases constitutionelles de la République du genre humain' of 1793, Cloots argued for a radically individualistic interpretation of sovereignty. From human rights he derived the 'mutually supportive and indivisible sovereignty of the human race'[14] Nations that were in any kind of reciprocal contact, or even simply knew about each other, could not both be sovereign simultaneously. In Cloots' view, autonomous self-determination is then no longer possible, and the foundations for conflict are given. In contrast, 'the Republic of Mankind' would 'never be in dispute with anyone, for there is no communication between the planets', argued Cloots.[15] Thus he rejected at the same time the idea developed by his colleague Paine in the book 'Rights of Man' from 1791/92 that universal peace and prosperity could be achieved when all countries had established representative democracy as their form of government (thereby founding the 'democratic peace theory' still debated today). Sovereignty requires that all people are unified in a universal community based on human rights. And this is achievable, given that all share the same goals of liberty, equality, security, justice and the protection of property and peace and from oppression.[16] According to Cloots, the constituent subjects of the world republic can only be individual persons, on account of the indivisibility of sovereignty. At the centre of the world republic stands a directly elected parliament as legislature. *Départements* are envisaged as subsidiary administrative units, at the same time serving as the electoral constituencies for the parliamentary delegates. In accordance with his design, Cloots proposed that France, with its new

14 Cloots, Anacharsis. 1793. Bases constitutionnelles de la république du genre humain. Paris: L'Imprimerie Nationale, p. 3.
15 Ibid., p. 14.
16 Ibid., pp. 35f.

constitution, should be a universal republic to which all nations liberated from monarchy should accede as *départements*.

The end of cosmopolitanism

To Cloots' great joy, the parliament brought into being by the first experiment in democracy in German history, the 'Rheinisch-German National Convention' elected under French occupation in Rhine-Hesse and the Palatinate in February 1793, voted for the 'Republic of Mainz' which it had proclaimed to accede to France. However, only one month later the territory of the Republic west of the Rhine was retaken by troops of the Prussian-Austrian alliance. When the offensive pushed forward into French territory and the French National Convention felt compelled to introduce general conscription, the Levée en masse, the revolutionary mood turned. Prompted by Maximilien Robespierre, Cloots and other foreigners were arrested as saboteurs of the Revolution, tried and found guilty, and executed by guillotine on 24 March 1794. During the 1970s, the renowned German performance artist Joseph Beuys (1921 to 1986) would sometimes use the name 'Josephanacharsis Clootsbeuys' in memory of Cloots, his ideas and his fate.[17] Thomas Paine escaped the guillotine by sheer good fortune.

Republicanism joined forces with xenophobia and French nationalism.[18] In July 1793, Schiller was already lamenting the failure of the Enlightenment in forceful terms. 'The attempt by the French people to claim their sacred human rights and to win their political freedom ... has cast not only that people, but with them a substantial part of Europe and a whole century back into barbarism and slavery ... So it was not free people who were being oppressed by the state, no, it was only wild animals, which it held in benevolent chains.'[19]

17 Guido de Werd. 1988. Vorwort. In: Anarchasis Cloots - Der Redner des Menschengeschlechts, ed. by Städtisches Museum Haus Koekkoek. Kleve: Boss-Verlag, p. 7.
18 Cf. Cheneval, 2004, loc. cit., pp. 377ff.
19 Letter from Friedrich Schiller to Herzog Friedrich Christian von Augustenburg, 13 July 1793, in: Schillers Werke. Bd. 26, ed. by Edith Nahler and Horst Nahler. Weimar: Verlag Hermann Böhlaus Nachf., 1992, pp. 257-268, p. 262.

3.
From Vienna to The Hague:
the dynamics of integration and
the inter-parliamentary movement

In the nascent nation states of Europe, the transition from monarchical regimes to parliamentary forms of government was a long drawn-out process that oscillated between revolution and restoration. In France, for example, the Constitution of 1799 practically abolished general elections again and prepared the ground for the military dictatorship of Napoleon Bonaparte. Following Napoleon's military defeat in the 'Battle of the Nations' at Leipzig in 1813, the Congress of Vienna of 1814/15 established a new balance of power in Europe and set itself the goal of restoring monarchical authority. Nevertheless, parliamentary bodies were now regularly considered in the context of the intellectual debate over peace plans for Europe and the world.

Sartorius' 'peoples' republic'

For example, in an article published in 1837, the political scientist Johann Baptist Sartorius (1774 to 1844), born in Lorraine, put forward a plan for a representative popular republic of the human race in which legislative power was vested in a senate to be elected by global popular vote - indirectly, via electoral colleges, 'in order to make the election quick and easy to oversee and run'.[1] Every six years, one third of the Senate (the seats of the longest-serving members) would be elected anew. This would ensure continuity. The right of initiative would lie with a regent, also elected by popular vote. There is no provision for the representation of individual states in this world state, which is to be founded by a voluntary treaty between the states. Like Cloots, Sartorius too argues that there can only be one sovereignty and that this must lie with the collective, that is, with the world state. Within their own 'spheres of authority', however, the nations would have 'free rein'. Limits would be set on the power of this peoples' state by 'positive constitutional norms'.

---

1   Sartorius, Johann Baptist. 1837. Organon des vollkommenen Friedens. Zürich: S. Höhr, p. 272.

Pecqueur's concept of worldwide integration

One of the most important contributions to the thinking about a world parliament in the first half of the 19th century came from the French social and economic theorist Constantin Pecqueur (1801 to 1887). In his work 'De la Paix' in 1842 he presented detailed reflections on how a democratic federal world state could be established. The division of humanity into nations, he argued, was a 'relic of barbarism', and meant – entirely in line with the tradition of social contract theory – that the states were in a state of nature which entailed regular outbreaks of armed conflict. In Pecqueur's work, the peace question is strongly linked to what was called the social question. This must also be understood in context, at a time when industrialization and urbanization, together with the incipient population explosion, were bringing increasing immiseration of the hired labour force. According to Pecqueur, global prosperity was directly related to the duration and continuity of peace. Ever closer economic exchange between nations served not only to promote more peaceful relations but also to increase prosperity. Pecqueur develops a programme for a step by step integration which is to begin with trade and customs unions. He took as his model the German Customs Union established in 1834, which in turn grew out of a merger of the Prussia-Hesse Customs Union, the Central German Trade Union and the South German Customs Union. 'These partial mergers,' wrote Pecqueur, 'can be understood as preparations for a comprehensive union, first European, then cosmopolitan.'[2] By means of a gradual dismantling of trade barriers, complete global free trade is to be achieved incrementally; the path to that point requires avoiding national trade imbalances while occasionally allowing protectionist measures as an exception. With his support for the idea of free trade, Pecqueur set himself against the dogma of mercantilism, which had been the prevailing practice and theory since the 16th century, and according to which governments should use public policy to try to promote exports and obstruct imports. Friedrich List, who also spoke out in favour of global free trade, described the mercantilist system in 1819 as an 'unfortunate delusion' which fed 'a perpetual war for wealth'. 'I am convinced,' wrote List, 'that humanity will only be able to achieve the highest peak of physical wellbeing, as well as of intellectual perfection, when over the entire surface of the Earth civilized peoples are able to extract from Nature her treasures and to exchange the surplus of their products in mutual free trade.'[3]

---

2   Pecqueur, Constantin. 1842. De la Paix. De son Principe et de sa Réalisation. Paris: Capelle, p. 212.
3   Friedrich List. 1929. Schriften, Reden, Briefe. Ed. by Erwin von Beckerath et al., Vol. 1, Berlin, p. 571.

But economic convergence was not sufficient for Pecqueur. It was also intended to set in train the political integration of the states. Economic integration would 'inevitably' be followed by 'political convergence'.[4] This perspective, one we would like to term the dynamics of integration, and one which Pecqueur was the first to use as the foundation for a project to establish a federal world state, was not the arcane opinion of an outsider. The project for a German customs union, for example, which had been under discussion at various political levels since 1820, also derived from an 'unambiguously grand political perspective' from a Prussian point of view, as Thomas Nipperdey writes.[5] Thus, the Prussian finance minister Friedrich von Motz wrote in a memorandum of 1829 to King Frederick William III that 'if it is accepted in political science that import, export and transit duties are simply the consequence of the political divisions between states (and this is true), then by the same token it must also be accepted that the unification of those states into a customs and trade union will lead at the same time to unification into one common political system. And the more natural is the combination into *one* commercial customs and trade system ... so the closer and stronger will be the combination of those states into *one* political system'.[6]

Pecqueur's world federation and world parliament

In contrast to the Prussian finance minister, who was dreaming of a unification of the German states, including Austria, under the leadership of Prussia, Pecqueur had in mind a 'complete union' of the entire globe. All nations and peoples, beginning with Europe, should be gradually joined together into a world state with world institutions, without however having to forfeit their own statehood. The federal constitution of the USA served as his model. Sovereignty was to be tiered between the individual states and the common federal state envisaged. Pecqueur emphasized that, in addition to customs and trade issues, defence, foreign policy and policing were to be the province of the federal state. This would involve the establishment of a federal diplomatic service, while the foreign ministries of the individual states would be abolished. Once the federal state had become universal, the entire service could be disbanded. The same applied to national armies. Within the federal state, a common 'cosmopolitan police' would ensure security and law enforcement. Supra-national authority

---

4 Pecqueur, loc. cit., p. 320. See also pp. 189ff.
5 Nipperdey, Thomas. 1998. Deutsche Geschichte 1800-1866: Bürgerwelt und starker Staat. München: C.H. Beck, p. 359.
6 Eisenhart, Wilfried von and Ant Ritthaler (ed.) 1934. Vorgeschichte und Begründung des Deutschen Zollvereins 1815-1834. Vol. 2. Berlin: Verlag R. Hobbing, p. 534.

would be based on the principle of justice, which for Pecqueur meant equality, fraternity and liberty. Disputes would be resolved in court on the basis of world law. The organs of the world federal state would have to be established by direct elections. If the best form of government for the individual nations was representative (that is, democratic), then this applied to their union, too. Pecqueur regards as the ideal legislative organ a congress directly elected by popular vote. 'The members of this European or cosmopolitan Congress can be elected neither by the legislative nor by the executive branches of the states they are to represent,' Pecqueur writes in order to underline the necessity for direct elections. If this is not possible to begin with, then at the very least the appointed members have to be 'absolutely independent'. [7] It would be absurd to believe that the congress would be able to operate as a higher authority if its members were dependent on the individual states.

Pecqueur saw the monarchical regimes as being the greatest problem and obstacle for the project of integration. In the year 1842, when Pecqueur published his work, there was – in today's terms – only one democracy in the entire world: the USA. But dynastic rule in the individual states was incompatible with the establishment of a supranational authority. As long as it was not possible for a federal state congress to be freely elected by popular vote, then the fear must be that its decisions would do the people more harm than good. For the congress, as an assembly of aristocrats, would continually make decisions in the interests of the governments and against the interests of the governed. In which case the project of achieving universal peace through the agency of a universal congress would find itself jeopardized by 'a renewal of the alliance of the kings against the people'. [8] In any event, monarchical regimes would be very concerned about their sovereignty and not at all inclined to subordinate themselves to a supranational authority.

Pecqueur saw the ideal solution as starting the project in the form of a merger between a small group of states with democratic forms of government. All states, however, regardless of their form of government, should be invited to join. However, it must be a condition of membership that, at a minimum, the representatives of the individual states in the federation should be elected by 'more or less' general suffrage. This would doubtless apply initially more often to small countries, as these had an interest in strengthening their protection against the great powers. The growing union would then gradually become of more interest for the larger countries. As the autocratic regimes would not want to find themselves isolated, Pecqueur thought they would eventually agree to

7   Pecqueur, loc. cit., p. 290.
8   Ibid., p. 333.

the clause concerning representation in the common congress in order to be allowed to join. 'This Congress would be a school of liberty and of cosmopolitan representation, an advanced course in politics for the enlightened masses of all countries,' wrote Pecqueur.[9] The initial aim would be a step-by-step unification of Europe, in the form of a confederation of states on the model of the first US constitution. As civilization progressed, so competences and functions could be developed further to the point where cooperation would eventually lead to a federal state whose congressional delegates were all directly elected.

Each country would send an equal number of deputies. Proportionality according to population size would contradict the principle of the equality of the states and could provoke mistrust on the part of countries with smaller numbers of seats. However, if the great powers would not agree to equal numbers for all, it might still be acceptable. For the great powers favoured the pursuit of their own conflicting interests over the idea of uniting against the small countries. Consequently, small numbers of seats could be of great significance in determining majorities in particular circumstances. The interests of smaller countries would therefore have to be considered if they were to be won over.

Tennyson's 'Parliament of Man'

The poem 'Locksley Hall', written in 1837 by the English poet Alfred Tennyson (1809 to 1892), was published in the same year as Pecqueur's book. It is about a soldier who comes upon a place familiar from his childhood and is moved to mixed emotions. In the course of a utopian dream of the future, he sees 'the vision of the world, and all the wonder that would be'. Among the peoples and nations, war prevails, until a world parliament and world federation, with universal law, bring peace:

> Till the war-drum throbbed no longer, and the battle-flags were furl'd
> In the Parliament of man, the Federation of the world.
> There the common sense of most shall hold a fretful realm in awe,
> And the kindly earth shall slumber, lapt in universal law.[10]

The poem had considerable influence, especially in the Anglo-American world, and the lines quoted above are still often quoted today. The British historian and political scientist Paul Kennedy (born 1945), for example, inspired by this poem, titled his 2006 book on the United Nations 'The Parliament of

9   Ibid., p. 381.
10   Tennyson, Alfred. 1842. 'Locksley Hall', in: Poems. Boston: W. D. Ticknor, lines 127-130.

Man'. Kennedy writes that US President Truman (1884 to 1972) often fished out and read aloud a copy of these lines.[11]

The long struggle to extend the right to vote

The period in which Pecqueur and Tennyson published these two works was turbulent. In many states, forms of popular representation were slowly but surely evolving. The disintegration of the hierarchical medieval order which accompanied the growth of industrialization, and the so-called 'social question', placed monarchical ruling structures in Europe under relentless pressure to change. A key issue was the inclusion of the power-hungry bourgeoisie in political decision-making. The American Revolutionary slogan 'no taxation without representation' now came to be seen as relevant and significant in this context too. As a rule, what emerged initially was a plutocratic parliament based on male census suffrage. The balance of power vis-à-vis the crown varied, and was another source of conflict. For most reformers and revolutionaries, the goal was universal male suffrage, though the demand to extend the right to vote to women as well was heard as early as 1791 during the French Revolution. The revolutionary activist Olympe de Gouges (1748 to 1793) protested against the fact that the National Assembly's Declaration of the Rights of Man and of the Citizen in practice applied only to men, and she drew up a 'Declaration of the Rights of Woman and of the *Citoyenne*'. In 1793 she too was executed. It was only from the end of the 19th century onwards that the right to vote among the world's states was gradually freed from conditions such as property ownership and the payment of taxes and also extended to women.

In the USA, too, where the right to vote was a matter for the federal states, there were restrictions in some states until around 1860 on the basis of tax payments or property. The first examples of the permanent introduction of universal male suffrage occurred in Europe, for example in the revolution of 1848 in France and in Switzerland. Otto von Bismarck (1815 to 1898) introduced it in the North German Confederation in 1867, and in 1871 it was adopted in the new German Empire. At the time, Bismarck probably calculated that the poorer rural population would be more inclined than the urban bourgeoisie to vote for the monarchist camp, which is why the abolition of restrictions on suffrage would favour that party. The research programme 'Polity' has analysed all countries with more than 500,000 inhabitants from 1800 to today and classified them by year and form of government. According to this programme, of the 56 states

---

11 Kennedy, Paul. 2006. The Parliament of Man. The Past, Present, and Future of the United Nations. New York: Random House, pp. xi f.

analysed for the year 1871, six were democratic: Belgium, Greece, Columbia, New Zealand, Switzerland and the USA. 34 were classified as incoherent mixed forms between democracy and autocracy, or 'anocratic', and 16 as autocratic.[12]

The birth of the inter-parliamentary movement

With the advance of parliamentarism and of universal voting rights, the concept of a world parliament, too, began to develop. 'Naturally, over the course of time,' according to Claudia Kissling, 'the thinking about international parliamentarism adopted the democratic principle being enacted at the nation state level and transposed this to the international level.'[13] For example, in the public law teaching of Georg Jellinek (1851 to 1911), the concept of parliamentary representation is already integrated quite naturally into the institutional framework of a federation of states. Jellinek wrote in 1882 that, for a federation of states, it was not out of the question 'that for the purposes of agreeing common standards the representatives of the governments might be joined by representatives of the people, such as parliamentarians from the contracting states'.[14] He differentiated thereby between a federation of states and a federal state. The nature of the latter namely required 'a parliament elected by direct popular vote, whose members conceive of themselves not as agents of the individual states but as direct agents of the collective state'.[15] One of the intellectual pathbreakers of the Argentinian constitution of 1853, the lawyer and later diplomat Juan Bautista Alberdi (1810 to 1884), stressed in 1870 in his book 'El Crimen de La Guerra' that the human being as an individual is ultimately the basic unit of every human community. A world community would therefore be based not only on states but also on the people themselves. On the road to a political world union, the sovereignty of the individual states would have to gradually give way in favour of the sovereignty of the human race, he argued.[16]

From the 1830s onwards, the idea slowly took root and grew that the delegates to the various popular representative bodies should work directly together in order to promote international understanding and the establishment of a permanent peace. The paramount issue of foreign policy, namely that of war and peace, should not – this was the idea of interparliamentarism – remain solely in the hands of the cabinets and heads of government. The erstwhile

---

12 Polity IV Annual Time-Series 1800-2010 (www.systemicpeace.org/inscrdata.html).
13 Kissling, Claudia. 14 February 2005. 'Repräsentativ-parlamentarische Entwürfe globaler Demokratiegestaltung im Laufe der Zeit'. forum historiae, no. 5.
14 Jellinek, Georg. 1882. Die Lehre von den Staatenverbindungen. Wien: Alfred Hölder, p. 186.
15 Ibid., p. 283.
16 Alberdi, Juan B. 1900. El Crimen de la Guerra. Buenos Aires: Talleres Gráficos Argentinos, ch. 10.

Spanish parliamentarian Don Arturo de Marcoartu stressed in an essay of 1876 the necessity of finally codifying the relationship between the states, and their rights, by means of general treaties. In the future he envisaged an international congress being held for this purpose at which not only representatives of the executive branch of government would take part; a full and proper reflection of the representative system required that other political forces at the state level also needed to be represented. Marcoartu proposed a 'Constituent Assembly' to establish a 'Magna Charta [of] the constituent rights of nations in peace, in war, and in cases of dispute'.[17] This assembly, which he saw as the inception of an international parliament, should include representatives of the executive, legislative and judicial branches from the individual states, all equal in status: in each case, one delegate appointed by the government, two members or former members elected by the parliament (one each from the majority and minority groups), and one magistrate nominated by the highest court and the universities. In order to implement and enforce the laws passed by this assembly, an international tribunal of arbitration would be needed – an old idea, whose roots Marcoartu traces back as far as the assembly of the Greek city states convened by the Athenian King Amphictyon around 1497 BCE. If no existing government were to demonstrate its willingness to convene such an assembly in the foreseeable future, then the delegates of the national popular representative bodies should prepare the ground with their own parliamentary conferences. 'To encourage parliamentarians to cooperate on promoting international understanding as representatives of the people rather than of their governments was a logical consequence of the movement for the emancipation of the bourgeoisie, which over the course of the 19th century had advanced into the margins of political power' writes Ralph Uhlig in his history of the early interparliamentary peace movement. [18]

The establishment of the IPU

Under the slogan 'Peace through arbitration', the 'Inter-Parliamentary Union' was founded in 1889 in Paris, initially with the name 'inter-parliamentary conference on arbitration'. It was the first international union of national parliamentary delegates. Very soon it was working on models for a standing international tribunal of arbitration. An early highpoint was the annual conference in

---

17 Marcoartu, Don Arturo de. 1876. Internationalism and Prize Essays on International Law. In: the same, A.P. Sprague and Paul Lacombe. Internationalism. London, New York: Stevens and Sons, E. Stanford, Baker Voorhis and Co, 6-55, pp. 17f.
18 Uhlig, Ralph. 1988. Die Interparlamentarische Union 1889-1914. Wiesbaden: Franz Steiner Verlag, p. 3.

Budapest in 1896, when 250 parliamentarians took part and approved proposals for submission to the European governments by the administrative office of the organization. The aim was to press the governments to hold a diplomatic conference for the establishment of a tribunal. The members of the IPU supported these efforts in their national parliaments. The idea was to create parliamentary majorities for peace policies, and especially for the principle of international arbitration, in the individual popular representative assemblies, and thereby to exert influence on the governments. Russian diplomats, too, took part in the conference in Budapest. 'It appears that the Russian observers in Budapest were impressed by the arguments of the friends of peace' writes Uhlig.[19] In order to avoid the expense of having to modernize the Russian artillery, the idea arose in Moscow to conclude an agreement with the Austro-Hungarian Empire on mutual limits on such weapons. Tsar Nicholas II eventually proposed a general peace conference, which then did indeed take place in The Hague in 1899, with representatives from 30 states.

The Hague Peace Conferences as a catalyst

At the first Hague Peace Conference, it was agreed that a court of arbitration should be established for the voluntary resolution of international disputes, and the Hague Convention with respect to the Laws and Customs of War on Land was issued. This document stipulates, among other things, that in the event of war, civilians and civilian establishments are to be spared to the greatest extent possible; and in an annex it forbids the use of chemical weapons. The court of arbitration is not a standing court for the judgement of cases, but an administrative bureaucracy which is available when needed to enable temporary tribunals or investigative commissions to be set up quickly and easily. Overall, the Hague Peace Conference and its outcome were judged a success by the inter-parliamentary movement. As a next step, it hoped to develop the court of arbitration into a full court. The IPU and the wider peace movement also saw the need for further action in the area of arms control, where no progress had been made, and in the development of standards of international law. From 1903 onwards, the calls grew louder for a second Hague Conference, and in general for regular meetings of a world congress, in order to achieve these goals. These calls were linked once more, in the USA especially, to the idea of a world parliament.

19 Ibid., p. 245.

Internationalism in the USA

As Warren F. Kuehl relates in his history of internationalism in the USA, the year 1903 marked 'the beginning of the modern movement for an international organisation'. [20] For example, the two chambers of the Massachusetts legislature, prompted by a citizens' petition initiated by the journalist Raymond L. Bridgman (1849 to 1925), sent a resolution to the US Congress requesting the US President to launch an initiative for 'the governments of the world' to establish 'a regular international congress'. This idea received a great deal of attention in the press, and was supported by the iron and steel magnate Andrew Carnegie (1835 to 1919) among others. Bridgman expanded on the proposal in his book 'World Organization' from 1905. He undertook a critical analysis of the concept of sovereignty and concluded that it made sense only at the global level, and not for nation states. The time had come to acknowledge this, and to organize humanity into one common polity. This would need to have legislative, executive and judicial branches. Business necessities, and not political theories, demanded speedy action. 'Already the necessity is upon us for world legislation, because business transactions now extend all over the world and no national legislature will be adequate to protect the people from world monopolies,' Bridgman adduced by way of example. [21] The USA, whose own constitution was the model for the proposed world organization, should take the lead in establishing it. This idea was not unique to Bridgman. The New York lawyer Hayne Davis (1868 to 1942) also saw the constitution of the USA as the model for the global level. Beginning in 1903, and independently of Bridgman, he promulgated in numerous articles the idea of an international organization which in fact was already under construction. The Hague tribunal, he argued, had already endowed humanity with 'the united nations' (which made Davis in all probability the first person to use this term). [22] Following the creation of the Hague tribunal, an executive and a legislature were now needed. With regard to the last, he added that all laws passed by the world congress should become binding on all parties when they had been ratified by four-fifths of all countries, representing four-fifths of the world's population.[23]

---

20 Kuehl, Warren F. 1969. Seeking World Order. The United States and International Organization to 1920. Nashville: Vanderbilt University Press, pp. 62ff.
21 Bridgman, Raymond L. 1905. World Organization. Boston: Ginn & Company, pp. 46f.
22 Davis, Hayne. 12 February 1903. 'The Perpetuation of the Union of Nations'. The Independent (Boston), vol. 55, pp. 384-386.
23 Davis, Hayne. 7 July 1904. 'A World's Congress'. The Independent (Boston), vol. 57, pp. 11-19.

Davis eventually joined forces with Congressman Richard Bartholdt (1855 to 1932) from Missouri in order to work on this internationalist project. Bartholdt, who was originally from Germany and had emigrated to the USA in 1872, established an IPU group within the US Congress in 1904 and in that same year, with the support of the Congress, organized the first annual meeting of the IPU outside Europe, in St Louis. There, at his instigation, a resolution was passed calling on US President Theodore Roosevelt (1858 to 1919) to convene a second Hague conference. The request was delivered to Roosevelt in person at a reception at the White House. One month later, Secretary of State John Hay took the matter up on behalf of the President. However, it was not until September 1905, after the conclusion of the Russo-Japanese War in which Roosevelt had acted as a mediator between the parties, that the time seemed propitious. The USA left it to the Tsar to officially launch the initiative to convene the second Hague Peace Conference.

An initiative at the IPU

Meanwhile, Bartholdt was working hard to try and make the establishment of a world parliament a central aim of the IPU. '[I]n order to perfect the peace machinery there lacked only, first, an international parliament or a World Congress, and second, a general arbitration treaty to guide the court as well as the ruling powers', as Bartholdt recalled. [24] The US American delegation to the IPU submitted a proposal to this effect at the annual conference in Brussels in 1905. The proposal included the suggestion that the IPU should lobby for the establishment of a standing 'international congress', consisting of a senate and a chamber of deputies. In fact, the proposal was for each nation to be given two seats in the senate, while seats in the chamber of deputies would be allocated in proportion to the respective share of world trade, though this was not spelt out in more detail. Every member would receive one vote. Any decision passed by a majority vote in both chambers would be legally binding unless an as yet unspecified number of national parliaments were to reject it. The competence of the congress was restricted to international matters, and decisions would have to respect the 'territorial and political integrity' of every nation represented there. The proposal also invoked equal treatment with respect to trade issues as a matter of principle. Finally, the states represented in the congress should have

---

24 Bartholdt, Richard. 1930. *From Steerage to Congress. Reminiscences and Reflections*. Philadelphia: Dorrance & Company Inc, p. 261.

a duty to place their armies at its disposal for the enforcement of the decisions made by the Hague court.[25]

The proposal was not put to a vote, but passed on to a study commission. There, the American proposal met with 'some surprising counter-arguments' from the more conservative Europeans, as Uhlig reports.[26] It was objected that the prospects for success were small in view of the prevailing international tensions, and that the efforts of the IPU should be focused on the issue of ensuring that the Hague conference became a recurring event. An 'academic discussion over the purely hypothetical organisational structure of a world parliament' would add nothing to this. But the Italian delegate Beniamino Pandolfi brought the discussion to a point. He made a blunt plea that no parliamentarians should take part in the proposed congress. This 'untypical viewpoint' for an IPU parliamentarian, as Uhlig writes, was based on his judgement of the 'essential and foundational interests of interparliamentarism', for Pandolfi believed that the American plan put the existence of the IPU itself in jeopardy. 'The incorporation of a parliamentary element into the Congress, elected by the local parliaments, would leave the Interparliamentary Union no other option but dissolution. So we are voting not only on a dangerous and anarchic institution but at the same time on our own suicide,' in the words of Pandolfi's own submission.[27] By the end of the next IPU Conference in London in 1906, nothing was left of the original proposal from the US American group. The call for an international parliament was not included in the IPU's programme for the second Hague Peace Conference. The Conference took place in October 1907 but saw no notable progress made. The introduction of obligatory arbitration failed, in large part because of its rejection by the delegation from the German Empire.

Once the project of a world parliament had effectively been stalled within the IPU, enthusiasm among the early activists in the USA slowly began to ebb away over the next few years. In France, the socialist deputy Francois Fournier (1866 to 1941) instigated an attempt in parliament in July 1913 to prompt the French government into a diplomatic initiative for a world parliament. The government resisted, and Fournier's proposal was roundly defeated in the National Assembly.

25 Lange, Christian (ed.). 1911. Un Congrès International, Conférence de Bruxelles, 1905. In: Union interparlementaire. Résolutions des Conférences et Décisions principales du Conseil, 93-94. 2nd ed. Brussels: Misch & Thron.
26 Uhlig, loc. cit., pp. 413f.
27 Citation from ibid., p. 413.

Arguments emerging out of the German peace movement

In Germany, powerful supporting voices emerged in the shape of the historian and later Nobel Peace Prize winner Ludwig Quidde (1858 to 1941) and the international law specialist Walther Schücking (1875 to 1935), both leading members of the German Peace Society founded by Bertha von Suttner (1843 to 1914) in 1892. Suttner herself promulgated the 'vision of a united congress of all states, working for a new international federation and international co-operation' on the model of the USA.[28] Schücking argued, in a book published in 1908, for a world federation of states with a world parliament, and criticized 'Germany's reactionary position' at the Hague, much to the annoyance of the Kaiser's government. Referring to already extant shared administrative bodies under international law such as the Universal Postal Union, founded in 1874, Schücking wrote that it would be a 'pointless waste of time, energy and money' if 'as happens today, the same group of states sets up a new union of states for each new international purpose because no general international organisation yet exists'.[29] Such ad hoc unions should be superseded by the general federation of states. In a study of the Hague Conferences, which concluded that they had 'if not *expressis verbis*, then implicitly and *ipso facto*, created a world federation of states',[30] Schücking explained in more detail that the world parliament, alongside the congress of states, should initially have only an advisory role and should be made up of delegates from the individual member states of the federation. He illustrated the advantages offered by the involvement of such a world parliament in international negotiations and in the setting of international laws by means of two examples of possible constellations arising 'in the struggle between national and international law' (Jellinek). In the first, it is postulated that the world parliament might help overcome government resistance in the course of negotiations if a majority within the world parliament – and within that a majority within the respective national parliamentary delegation – were to take a position different from that of the government. At the second Hague Conference, for example, it would have been possible to get the obligatory recourse to arbitration adopted, at least with respect to some matters. 'For if this had revealed that the implacable resistance of the German government did not even have the backing of their own parliament, then it would probably have given

---

28 Citation from Walker, Barbara (ed.). 1993. Uniting the Peoples and Nations. Readings in World Federalism. Washington D.C. and New York: World Federalist Movement & World Federalist Association, p. 97 ('A Message to American Women' in: The Women Voter, Vol. V., October 1914).
29 Schücking, Walther. 1908. Die Organisation der Welt. Tübingen: J.C.B. Mohr, pp. 610f.
30 Id. 1912. Der Staatenverband der Haager Konferenzen. Ed. by Walther Schücking. Vol. 1. München, Leipzig: Duncker & Humblot, p. 6.

way', according to Schücking.[31] In the second example, it was possible to imagine a case where there was resistance in a national parliament to agreement to an international norm negotiated by the national government. In such a case, the world parliament could help avoid a dispute between the executive and the legislature over the ratification of treaties, because its existence would mean that a delegation from the national parliament took part from the very beginning in the 'legislative tasks of the world federation of states'. Such participation would make it easier to persuade a possibly sceptical national parliament of the argument for ratification, especially in states such as the USA where the powers are rigorously separated.

The idea of a world parliament was taken up repeatedly over the following years. For example, the lawyer and former German Reichstag deputy Ernst Harmening (1854 to 1913) highlighted in a lecture given in the year 1910 that 'national economic and governmental interests' were now international, and 'could not be adequately safeguarded without the help of other nations'. The concept of sovereignty needed to be revised. It was 'no longer a guarantee for the unlimited self-determination of a polity', and even less so for the welfare of the population. Instead, people were adopting 'a new belief in the solidarity of the interests of the entire civilized world, and ultimately of humanity'. The need for 'self-government by the peoples' in the framework of a 'federal community of nations' would in his view be met by a world parliament. The IPU represented the beginning of this process, he argued, citing its influence on the Hague Conferences.[32]

In the Christmas edition of the 'Berliner Tageblatt' of 1912, the renowned social critic, author and dramatist Frank Wedekind (1864 to 1918) complained that the 'edifice of missions, legations and embassies' of international diplomacy was 'a completely medieval apparatus' that operated 'without taking any account of either the rotary press or wireless telegraphy'. The best Christmas present he could imagine would be the establishment of a world parliament. 'The world parliament would of its nature be a permanently open peace conference, with all the instruments of power of the entire world at its disposal, unlike the peace congresses to date, which were a convocation of dilettantes and notorious business opportunists', wrote Wedekind in a deliberate provocation of the

---

31 Ibid., p. 302.
32 Harmening, Ernst. 1910. Das Weltparlament. Vortrag gehalten in der Staatswissenschaftlichen Gesellschaft zu Jena. Jena: Bernhard Vopelius, pp. 6f., 11, 31, 25.

diplomatic establishment.[33] He had come to this idea in tandem with the anarchist and anti-militarist writer Erich Mühsam (1878 to 1934), who also reported on their collaboration shortly afterwards in his 'Magazine for Humanity'. Mühsam wrote that despite their differing views on the state they had quickly agreed that 'currently the most serious danger for the people of the world lies in the lack of control over those persons to whom are entrusted humanity's most effective instruments of power'. What was frightening was above all the 'shadowy secrecy' in which 'these people' habitually consorted. Overnight, an argument could break out between the foreign ministries of the great powers, and a war could begin. 'The world parliament for which we call', wrote Mühsam, 'has as its purpose the constant public supervision of international diplomacy.' All the factors affecting relations between nations were by their nature public affairs, and would indeed be public affairs were it not for the pathological secretiveness of the intermediaries. 'When we know that peace is no longer threatened by any diplomat or by any international quarrel, then we will have fulfilled our task', he wrote.[34] There were many other lesser-known proponents of a world state and an elected world parliament at the time.[35]

33 Wedekind, Frank. 25 Dec. 1912. 'Weihnachtsgedanken'. Berliner Tageblatt, no. 656, 1. Beiblatt, p.1/2. Also printed in: the same. 1920. 'Weihnachtsgedanken (1912)'. Schweizerland Vol. 2 (2nd half-year): 849–854.
34 Mühsam, Erich. 1913. 'Das Weltparlament'. Kain. Zeitschrift für Menschlichkeit (2) 10: 145–163., pp. 150f., 163.
35 E.g. Eduard Loewenthal or Kurt Wolzendorff, see Riehle, Bert. 2009. Eine neue Ordnung der Welt: föderative Friedenstheorien im deutschsprachigen Raum zwischen 1892 und 1932. V&R unipress, pp. 81ff., 112ff.

4.
World War and the League of Nations

The programme of the 'Round Table' group

Beginning in 1909, an international network was formed of people concerned for the future of the British Empire, which was felt to be losing its grip on its predominant position in world affairs. The group, called the 'Round Table', can be traced back to the influence of Cecil Rhodes (1853 to 1902), the South African politician and co-founder of the diamond company De Beers. All his life, this British imperialist dreamed passionately, albeit without concerning himself with detail, of an Anglo-American federation that would ensure that 'the peace of the world would be secured for all eternity'.[1] After Rhodes' death, his fortune was left to the Rhodes Trust, which not only established one of the most prestigious scholarship programmes in the world but was created with the additional purpose of pursuing this goal.[2] With the support of the Rhodes Trust, the 'Round Table' developed a plan for the transformation of the British Empire into a federal state, a 'Commonwealth of Nations'. This would entail the end of the dominance of the Empire by the United Kingdom. Like its former colonial possessions, it would become just a member state of the new federation. At the centre of this federation there would be 'a central sovereign imperial authority directly elected by the people of the Empire. to conduct foreign policy and control the armed services, raising taxation through its own officers'.[3] This programme accorded with the proposals made by Lionel Curtis (1872 to 1955), one of the leading members of the group, who was committed to the cause of international integration and who had played a role in the setting up of the Union of South Africa in 1910. The Empire Parliamentary Association of 1911 was the world's second international network of parliamentarians (after the IPU). The

---

1   Rotberg, Robert I, and Miles F Shore. 1988. The founder: Cecil Rhodes and the pursuit of power. Oxford University Press, p. 666, see also pp. 102, 281, 316.
2   On the plans for a secret society see Bummel, Andreas. 8 October 2003. 'Kritische Anmerkungen zur Urlegende moderner Verschwörungstheorien'. Telepolis.
3   Lavin, Deborah. 1995. From Empire to Commonwealth. A Biography of Lionel Curtis. Oxford: Clarendon Press, p. 108.

purpose of this association was to improve contacts and information flows between the parliamentarians of the Dominions (the self-governing colonial territories of the United Kingdom) and the British Parliament. After the end of the First World War, consideration was given to the idea of transforming the association into a genuine common parliament in the context of an institutional reformation of the Empire.[4]

The theory of sociocultural evolution and a world federation

The outbreak of the First World War in 1914 destroyed all hopes for a third Hague conference. On account of its hitherto unimaginable, monstrous scale, the War was experienced, not only by pacifists and internationalists, as an apocalyptic rift. The 'great edifice of nineteenth-century civilization', wrote Eric Hobsbawm, 'crumpled in the flames of world war, as its pillars collapsed'.[5] The members of the 'Round Table' were alarmed. Some of them now began to think beyond the original plan. The historian Carroll Quigley, who studied the group, describes their fear 'that all culture and civilization would go down to destruction because of our inability to construct some kind of political unit larger than the national state, just as Greek culture and civilization in the fourth century B.C. went down to destruction because of the Greeks' inability to construct some kind of political unit larger than the city-state'.[6] The original hope for a 'Commonwealth of Nations' and a British-American Union was seen from then on as a part of the project of a universal federation of nations.

The idea of establishing a worldwide organization for peace began to receive mass support. All over the world, peace associations and societies sprang up and campaigned for a league of nations. The 'League of Nations Union', established in England by the writer H.G. Wells (1866 to 1946) among others, grew into the largest group in the British peace movement and in 1931 could count over 400,000 members.[7] Wells, Curtis and others joined together in order to argue, based on their reading of world history and against the backdrop of total war, the essential necessity of a world federation if civilization was to have any future. World history showed human affairs to be a story of 'the oscillating ac-

---

4   Hall, H. Duncan. 1920. The British Commonwealth of Nations. A Study of its Past and Future Developments. London: Methuen & Co., pp. 306ff.

5   Hobsbawm, Eric. 1995. Age of Extremes. London: Abacus, p. 22.

6   Quigley, Carroll. 1981. The Anglo-American Establishment. New York: Books In Focus, p. 137.

7   Baratta, Joseph Preston. 2004. The Politics of World Federation. United Nations, UN Reform, Atomic Control. Vol. 1. Westport, Connecticut; London: Praeger Publishers, p. 74.

tion of separatist and unifying forces', and the time had now come for the unification of the whole world.[8] At the root of their argument lay the theory of
sociocultural evolution, which by 1912 - on account of an influential essay by
the anthropologist Franz Boas (1858 to 1942) - had become closely associated
with the peace issue, and which now became a fixed basic element of the ideology of world federalism. 'The history of mankind,' wrote Boas, 'shows us the
grand spectacle of the grouping of man in units of ever increasing size that live
together in peace, and that are ready to go to war only with other groups outside
of their own limits.'[9] Notwithstanding all temporary revolutions and the provisional collapse of larger units, the progress towards unification had been so regular and so marked that the only possible conclusion was that this tendency
would continue to govern history in the future. Units of the size of modern nation states would have been inconceivable earlier, just as now the idea of the
unification of the whole world seemed to exceed the power of imagination. But
the assumption that this development would now halt at the nation state could
not be justified. In his observations, Boas agreed with other early theorists of
sociocultural evolution such as Herbert Spencer (1820 to 1903) and Lewis
Henry Morgan (1818 to 1881), although he disagreed with and strongly criticized them on other aspects, especially as regards their belief in a teleological
development of human civilization. His approach was developed and extended
by social scientists such as Norbert Elias (1897 to 1990) and Gerhard Lenski
(1924 to 2015) within a 'neo-evolutionary' framework which rejects any element of determinism.

A world parliament on the Versailles agenda

After 17 million deaths, the greatest massacre in the history of the world to that
point was brought to an end with a ceasefire in November 1918. In February
1919, the Paris Peace Conference, under the leadership of Great Britain, France,
Italy and the USA, approved the establishment of a League of Nations, as proposed one year earlier by US President Woodrow Wilson (1856 to 1924) in the
last of the 'Fourteen Points' of his peace plan. During the negotiations over the
operating rules for the planned League of Nations, the idea of including a parliamentary body was proposed from various quarters. An important member
of the 'Round Table' group was appointed as one of the British negotiators in
the person of Lord Robert Cecil (1864 to 1958), later President of the League

---

8   Wells, H. G., et al. 1919. 'The idea of a League of Nations'. The Atlantic Monthly 123: 106-115, 265-275, p. 106.
9   Boas, Franz. 1912. 'An Anthropologist's View of War'. The Advocate of Peace 74 (4) (April): 93-95, p. 94;
     First published in: International Conciliation, no. 52 (March 1912).

and a Nobel Peace Prize winner. In his proposals for the setting up of the League of Nations he raised the idea of a 'periodical congress of delegates of the Parliaments of the states belonging to the League, as a development out of the existing inter-Parliamentary Union'. This interparliamentary congress could discuss the reports from the inter-state conference and other international bodies and thus 'cover the ground that is at present occupied by the periodical Hague Conference'. [10] However, the only committed supporter of this idea was the second leading member of the British delegation, the South African politician Jan Christiaan Smuts (1870 to 1950) (who, incidentally, had for a short period been Rhodes's legal adviser at De Beers in 1895). On 12 February 1919, at his insistence, the British delegation submitted a proposal to the drafting committee to add to the organizational infrastructure of the League 'a Representative Assembly elected by the legislative bodies of all States members of the League'.[11] This assembly of parliamentarians would provide advice for the work of the assembly of government representatives and the Executive Council envisaged in the current draft. Further details of its operations could be left to the Executive Council. At the ninth session of the drafting committee on the following day, Smuts amended the proposal in a much less ambitious direction. Now the draft Covenant should include only the stipulation that 'at least once in every four years, an extraordinary meeting of the Body of Delegates shall be held, which shall include representatives of national parliaments and other bodies representative of public opinion'. In the discussion that followed, Cecil was given the first word. Surprisingly, he rejected the proposal, on the grounds that the time was not yet ripe. Smuts' initiative was not supported by any of the other 18 participants in the session. It was objected that such a provision was unnecessary, as states were already free to appoint parliamentarians as their delegates. In the opinion of the French negotiator Léon Bourgeois, delegates chosen by a government represented the majority views of the citizens anyway, and, as Wilson said, would without doubt 'be true representatives of the people at large'. The leader of the Belgian delegation, Paul Hymans, expressed fundamental reservations. If a beginning was made of giving representation to 'social groups', it would end up with an international parliament holding yearly meetings. Such a body might lay before the League all sorts of questions, and its scope of action would be too widely extended. Ultimately, elections would take place, and 'the international parliament would no longer bear any relation to the present conception of the Body of Delegates'.[12] With that, the proposal was off the table.

10　Miller, David Hunter. 1928. The Drafting of the Covenant, vol. 2. New York: G.P. Putnam's Sons, p. 62.
11　Ibid., vol. 1, pp. 218, 273.
12　This and previous citations from ibid, vol. 2, pp. 299-301.

The intention to constitute the League as an exclusive space for governments did not meet with the approval of the peace movement. In March 1919 over 60 organizations from 22 countries gathered in Bern for the international conference of 'League of Nations Societies', among them H.G. Wells' English group, to consult on the constitution drafted in Paris, which had now been published. The first of 26 amendments they proposed was for the establishment of a world parliament as the principal body of the League. 'An international parliament elected by the peoples should replace the assembly of delegates proposed in the Paris text. This parliament should have full prerogatives and legislative powers, each country electing one member for each million inhabitants.'[13] Magnus Hirschfeld (1868 to 1935), the German doctor and sexologist who is regarded as a global pioneer for gay rights and the emancipation of sexual minorities, was another who spoke out for a world parliament. In a speech in front of the Berlin Reichstag he declared on 10 November 1918 that the slogan of the future should no longer be 'workers' but '*people* of the world unite'. 'We want people's tribunals and a world parliament', Hirschfeld proclaimed to a crowd of several thousands.[14]

The 'German Plan' for the constitution of the League

The German Empire, as one of the parties responsible for war and one of the losers, was not able to take a direct part in the Paris negotiations, nor to bring about any changes to the work carried out by the Allies on the treaty. But following the November Revolution of 1918 and the forced abdication of William II (1859 to 1941), who fled into exile in Holland, Germany was on the path to a republic, with a new government in charge. The elections of January 1919, which took place for the first time on the basis of a universal, equal, secret and direct franchise (for women, too), resulted in the appointment of Philipp Scheidemann (1865 to 1939) as Prime Minister. In order to give their own ideas for a league of nations concrete form, Scheidemann's cabinet issued a 'German plan' on 23 April 1919 for the constitution of the league, drawn up in the foreign ministry with Schücking's participation. One of the key features of the plan, alongside other organs such as a congress of states (i.e. an assembly of representatives of the member states) and a permanent international court, was a 'first world parliament', made up of representatives of the individual parliaments of the member states. The Scheidemann cabinet was therefore the first

---

13 'Berne Conferees Suggest Amendments'. New York Times, 19 March 1919.
14 Hirschfeld, Magnus. 'Ansprache vom 10. Nov. 1918'. Vierteljahresberichte des Wissenschaftlich-humanitären Komitees während der Kriegszeit hg. statt des Jahrbuch für sexuelle Zwischenstufen (18) 4: 165–166, p. 166.

government ever to support and call for the establishment of a world parliament, and to the best of our knowledge remains the only one to have done so to date. In this plan, the assent of the world parliament would be required for 'a) changes to the constitution of the federation; b) the creation of universal international legal standards; c) the creation of new administrative organs for the federation; d) the determination of its budget'.[15] The individual parliaments should be entitled to one representative per one million inhabitants, up to a maximum of ten. These were regarded as provisional regulations for a first world parliament, which would then – with the assent of the congress of the states – determine its own future composition itself. Other regulations were also discussed within the foreign ministry, such as direct elections and sliding scales for the allocation of seats. However, according to Gottfried Knoll in a study of 1931, the aim was to keep the regulations pragmatic, simple and clear, so that ordinary people would be able to understand them, and in order to avoid creating unnecessary obstacles to this first step. In Knoll's view, the German proposal for a world parliament was intended perfectly seriously. The government saw the world parliament as a potential 'counterweight against the megalomania of the Allied governments', and hoped that it might exert a moderating influence and bring 'a breath of the spirit of cosmopolitanism' into the League of Nations.[16] If the League were constructed only on the basis of states, there was a danger that 'the old politics' would infiltrate it by way of its various corporate organs. There was also the consideration that a world parliament might generate positive feedback for the democratic parliamentary system of the new German Republic. In this vein, Foreign Minister Ulrich Graf Brockdorff-Rantzau (1869 to 1928) said that German democracy could not be secure 'unless and until the necessary measure of democracy exists in the League of Nations'.[17]

Disappointment over the League of Nations

The German position was irrelevant to what was going on in Paris. The agreed constitution was signed by the negotiating parties as part of the Versailles Treaty on 28 June 1919. Although the League of Nations project had been driven principally by US President Wilson, in March 1920 the US Senate refused to ratify it. The reason for this was not only, as is usually claimed, Amer-

---

15 Knoll, Gottfried. 1931. Der Deutsche Regierungsentwurf zu einer Völkerbundssatzung vom April 1919. Leipziger rechtswissenschaftliche Studien 61. Leipzig: Verlag von Theodor Weicher, p. 87.
16 Ibid., pp. 22, 25.
17 Citation from ibid., p. 21 (Daily News, 25 February 1919).

ican isolationism. On the contrary: Kuehl's study, for example, reports a striking level of popular support for the idea of a league of nations in the US. But the
specific form this idea was given in the Versailles Treaty did not stir any enthusiasm. 'The court has almost disappeared international law, I think, is hardly
mentioned; and the thing has turned into a plain political alliance', the Senate
majority leader Henry Cabot Lodge complained in a letter.[18] Above all, the Senate felt itself ignored by Wilson, who had only belatedly and grudgingly consulted that body.

It was not only in the USA that the majority of internationalists and pacifists,
for various reasons, were disappointed by the League of Nations. Hadn't the
democratic countries prevailed over the autocratic regimes? The Romanov,
Habsburg and Hohenzollern dynasties, like the Ottomans, had vanished from
the political screen. In 'The Outline of History', in the last section of which he
argues for a democratic world state, H.G. Wells expressed his outrage over the
absence of democracy in the League of Nations. '[T]his League of Nations', he
wrote, '[…] was not a league of peoples at all; it was a league of "states, dominions, or colonies". … There was no bar to a limited franchise and no provision
for any direct control by the people of any state. …An autocracy would no
doubt have been admissible as a "fully self-governing" democracy with a franchise limited to one person. The League of the Covenant of 1919 was, in fact, a
league of "representatives" of foreign offices.'[19] Gerhart Hauptmann (1862 to
1946), winner of the Nobel prize for literature in 1912, regarded America as the
'great shining model for Europe', and for the world. The League of Nations was
not even worth mentioning. 'We all long for a world parliament. We need a real
league of peoples,' was how Hauptmann described the feelings of many intellectuals in the midst of German hyperinflation and the heightened conflict over
reparations.[20] The debate over a world parliament at first continued unabated
following the foundation of the League of Nations. Quidde called for a revision
of the Covenant of the League to introduce a world parliament, among other
things. However, the structure of the parliament must not be based 1:1 on population, 'for that would condemn the whole of Europe to impotence in the face
of the gigantic empires of East Asia'.[21] He rejected the measures put forward in
the German government plan as being too undifferentiated. There would have

18 Kuehl, Warren F. 1969. Seeking World Order. The United States and International Organization to 1920.
    Nashville: Vanderbilt University Press, p. 335.
19 Wells, Herbert George. 1920. The Outline of History. Being a Plain History of Life and Mankind. Vol. 2. New
    York: The MacMillan Company, p. 558.
20 Citation from Tschörtner, Heinz Dieter (ed.). 1994. Gespräche and Interviews mit Gerhart Hauptmann. Ber-
    lin: Erich Schmidt Verlag, p. 79 (New York Times, 10 September 1923).
21 Quidde, Ludwig. 1922. Völkerbund and Demokratie. 2nd ed. Berlin: Verlag Neuer Staat, p. 16.

to be a sliding scale between small and large states in order to take full account of both population size on the one hand and the principle of equivalence of the states on the other. The Austrian-born sociologist Rudolf Broda (1880 to 1932), who had made a detailed study of this issue, drew attention in 1920 to an important argument for a world parliament. Delegates to a peoples' parliament would regard themselves 'to a much greater degree as representatives of humanity in general or as members of an international party crossing national borders' than as representatives of their country.[22] The parliamentary history of the German Empire, he argued, had demonstrated that the Reichstag deputies had regarded themselves as representatives of the people as a whole, and that this had suppressed potential conflict between the constituent states. In a world parliament, it would no longer be countries that stood in opposition to one another but ideas. The danger of inter-state conflict would be reduced by the parliament. It was clear that the prospects for structural reform of the League of Nations were poor. But sooner or later, in the view of Quidde among others, this idea would prevail, because people would grasp 'that the security of their vital interests would only be made possible by the construction of something over and above the nations, something which would prevent these nations from raping one another in their brutal egotism; by establishing the sovereignty of humanity over and above the individual states, the sovereignty of the League of Nations'.[23]

---

22 Broda, Rudolf. 1920. 'Das kommende Weltparlament'. Der Völkerbund: 347-358, p. 348.
23 Quidde, loc. cit., p. 27.

5.
The Second World War and
the atomic bomb: world federalism
in the early years of the UN

Federalism under pressure from fascism

The time between the beginning of the First and the end of the Second World Wars is regarded by historians such as Hobsbawm or Arnold J. Mayer as one continuous world conflict lasting thirty-one years. The sociologist and political scientist Sigmund Neumann spoke in 1946 already of a 'second Thirty Years' War'.[1] Democracy and the parliamentary system came under pressure in many places. Fascist regimes sprang up. In the years between 1911 and 1929, according to the Polity programme, there were consistently more democracies than autocracies in the world of states (the rest were hybrid forms). But from 1930 the proportions were reversed. The Inter-Parliamentary Union, despite its dogged work on international issues such as disarmament or the strengthening of international law, sank slowly into political irrelevance. By the end of the Second World War at the latest, the IPU was 'out of the race', as Kissling writes.[2] The 'Round Table' group's aim of transforming the British Empire into a federation of states foundered on the will to independence in the dominions. Their sovereignty was finally sealed by the Statute of Westminster of 1931. The British Commonwealth became a loose association of independent states. However, the federal idea now reappeared in a new form as a response to the rise of National Socialism and fascism. In the 1939 book 'Union Now', Clarence Streit (1896 to 1986), originally from the German Palatinate but an emigrant to the USA in 1911, bemoaned the lack of cooperation between the democratic countries, who in the international political sphere behaved like autocracies, and proposed a political union of democracies as a counterweight to the fascist dictatorships. This would begin with the USA, Great Britain, Canada, Australia,

---

1   Neumann, Sigmund. 1946. The Future in Perspective. New York: G.P. Putnam's Sons, pp. 6ff.
2   Kissling, Claudia. 2006. Die Interparlamentarische Union im Wandel. Frankfurt: Peter Lang, p. 145.

New Zealand, South Africa, Ireland, France, Belgium, the Netherlands, Switzerland, Denmark, Norway, Sweden and Finland, and with the gradual accession of new members would ultimately grow to a universal world organization. As Geneva foreign correspondent of the *New York Times*, Streit, who was in contact with Curtis and greatly admired him, had observed at close quarters the agony of the League of Nations. 'The Union's existing and potential power from the outset would be so gigantic, its bulk so vast, its vital centres so scattered, that Germany, Italy and Japan even together could no more dream of attacking it than Mexico dreams of invading the American Union now,' wrote Streit, who had been a Rhodes Scholar at Oxford.[3] At the centre of his plan for a Union was a congress directly elected by popular vote in the member states, consisting of a house of representatives and a senate. The federal union, based on guaranteed human rights and Union citizenship, would among other things have sole responsibility for foreign and defence policy as well as currency and trade issues, and would guarantee a democratic form of government in the member states.

The growth of world federalism

Streit's book became a bestseller, translated into many languages, which gave new impetus to the idea of a supra-national federal union. In many free countries, new groups were established to press for the idea of supranational integration. In 1939, the organization 'Federal Union' was founded in the USA, with Streit as its chair; it advocated as a first step a union between the western democracies, and it is still active today under the name 'Streit Council for a Union of Democracies'. Alongside Brauer, the historian Joseph Preston Baratta has been especially active in researching the history of world federalism and the multifaceted world federal movement, in a two-volume study published in 2004 (it is only possible to touch on the history of world federalism in the margins of the present work). The 'campaign for a world government', established in 1937 by the feminists and peace campaigners Rosika Schwimmer (1877 to 1948) and Lola Maverick Lloyd (1875 to 1944), is regarded as one of the earliest world federalist organizations. They published a pamphlet calling for a worldwide constitutional convention and sketching out their ideas for a directly elected world parliament as the basis for a future democratic world federation.[4] The issue of a world parliament was now inseparably commingled with the dis-

---

3   Streit, Clarence K. 1939. Union Now. A Proposal for a Federal Union of the Democracies of the North Atlantic. London: Jonathan Cape, p. 25.
4   Schwimmer, Rosika, and Lola Maverick Lloyd. 1942. Choas, War, or a New World Order. 4th ed.

course of the federalists. World federalism without a democratic world parliament is logically not possible, even if this institutional aspect was often not fore-grounded or explicitly articulated. The issue of federalism had long played an important role in some resistance movements. In Italy there had been a tradition of federalist thinking since the First World War. In the 'Ventotene Manifesto' of 1941, which was to prove very influential, the Italian anti-fascists Altiero Spinelli (1907 to 1986) and Ernesto Rossi (1897 to 1967) set out the goal and ideal of a federal European state. They denounced the 'ideology of national independence' as the root of the formation of totalitarian states and the out-break of wars. The principle of non-intervention as adopted by the League of Nations had proved absurd, leaving each nation 'free to choose the despotic government it thought best'. And they were already looking beyond Europe. '[O]nce the horizon of the Old Continent is passed beyond,' runs the text of the Manifesto, written during their imprisonment, 'and all the peoples who make up humanity embrace in a grand vision of their common participation, it will have to be recognized that the European Federation is the single conceivable guarantee that relationships with American and Asiatic peoples can exist on the basis of peace cooperation; this while awaiting a more distant future, when the political unity of the entire globe becomes a possibility.'[5]

The idea of a world federation was to be found in other regions of the world as well, for example among the opponents of British rule in India. 'While [we] must primarily be concerned with the independence and defence of India in this hour of danger, the Committee is of opinion that the future peace, security and ordered progress of the world demand a world federation of free nations, and on no other basis can the problems of the modern world be solved', read the text of the famous 'Quit India' resolution adopted by the All-India Congress Committee in 1942, supported by the future Indian Prime Minister Jawaharlal Nehru (1889 to 1964) and by Mohandas Gandhi (1869 to 1948) among others.[6] As the historian Manu Bhagavan writes, the idea of 'One World' that Nehru and other politicians advocated 'had become a common euphemism for a global parliament'. 'A global parliament is exactly what Nehru had in mind,' he points out.[7] The Indian politician (and defence minister 1957 to 1962) and UN Ambassador Krishna Menon (1896 to 1974) described a world government and a world parliament in a speech to a committee of the UN General Assembly in

5   Spinelli, Altiero, and Ernesto Rossi. 1941. 'The Manifesto of Ventotene'.
6   All-India Congress Committee. 1942. 'Quit India Resolution'.
7   Bhagavan, Manu. 2013. India and the Quest for One World: The Peacemakers. Houndmills, Basingstoke, Hampshire: Palgrave Macmillan, p. 66.

1954 as 'very desirable'.[8] According to Bhagavan, this reflected the official position of Nehru and of the Indian government.

The Guardian of the Bahai Faith, Shoghi Effendi (1897 to 1957) from near Haifa, a great-grandson of the Founder of the Faith Bahá'u'lláh (1817 to 1892), also spoke in 1938 about the necessity of a world state with a world parliament whose members would be elected by the people of all countries.

At this time, the debate about world federalism was dominated by three questions. Should the aim be to create a world federation step by step, via a union initially involving only a limited number of states, or in one great universal step encompassing all of them? Should it be restricted to certain narrowly defined core policy areas, i.e. minimalist in scope, or should it be given much more wide-ranging powers? After the founding of the UN, the additional question arose of whether the aim should be to establish a world federation as a new organization or as the outcome of a reform of the UN. A substantial stream of thought within the federalist movement supported the idea of an international convention tasked with drafting a constitution for a world federation, which would then be submitted to the individual countries for ratification. One early outcome of these efforts was the 'Declaration of the Federation of the World' passed by the House of Representatives and Senate of North Carolina in 1941 which supported this goal and which in the ensuing period up until 1950 was adopted in nineteen other US federal states.

Planning the post-war order

However, the establishment of a world parliament and of a federal world order was not given serious consideration by the Allies either during the war or afterwards. In December 1941, US President Franklin D. Roosevelt (1882 to 1945) had a team set up within the US foreign ministry, the State Department, to work on political plans for after the war. Although there was some initial discussion in the planning team of a federal structure for a future world organization, it was adjudged to be politically impossible and therefore abandoned. 'The various governments and peoples are not believed to be ready for an international federal government even if it were theoretically desirable', ran the minutes of a planning meeting.[9] A solution was required that would be acceptable to all governments, and particularly to the Soviet Union.

8　Official Records of the General Assembly, Ninth Session, First Committee, 26 October 1954, p. 215-25. Citation from Reddy, E.S., and A.K. Damodaran (ed.). 1994. Krishna Menon on Disarmament. Speeches at the United Nations. New Delhi: Sanchar Publishing House, p. 12.

9　Citation from Baratta, Joseph Preston. 2004. The Politics of World Federation. United Nations, UN Reform, Atomic Control. Vol. 1. Westport, Connecticut; London: Praeger Publishers, p. 97.

At the end of 1942, the Soviet Union went on the offensive in the Battle of Stalingrad, and the Battle of El Alamein ushered in the end of the German-Italian presence in North Africa. The Allies declared their war aim to be the unconditional surrender of the Axis powers. Looking ahead to the post-war order, the founder of the Ford Motor Company, Henry Ford (1863 to 1947), called for the creation of a world parliament directly elected by worldwide vote 'to put the world on a peace basis'.[10] The Governor of Minnesota, Harold Edward Stassen (1907 to 2001), also took up the theme. He urged in January 1943 that the Allies begin planning for a world organization. The most important body of the organization, according to Stassen, should be a parliament consisting of only one chamber, which would elect the chairperson of the executive, which in turn would take the form of a world council. The representatives of each country in the parliament should be appointed on the same basis used for the respective national legislature. In the face of such calls, the team in the US foreign ministry considered the possibility of a world legislature empowered to create binding law as the basis of a new world organization. 'Unless a broadly federal scheme of international organization is adopted, which is unlikely, it would be difficult to secure support for this proposal, particularly in the United States. This proposal would create a serious constitutional problem in the majority of states', opined the State Department.[11]

Fundamental criticism of the UN, and the shock of the atom bomb

At the conference of the United Nations in San Francisco from 25 April to 26 June 1945, representatives from fifty states finally came together to discuss and adopt the charter of the coming world organization. Beginning in August 1944, the piecemeal liberation of the German concentration camps brought the industrialized mass murder of millions in the Holocaust to the attention of the global public in all its horror. On 8 May, Nazi Germany surrendered. In the Pacific the war continued. On 6 and 9 August 1945, the USA dropped atomic bombs on Hiroshima and Nagasaki on the orders of President Truman. About 200,000 people were killed instantaneously. Estimates set the total number of deaths in the Second World War at up to 70 million.

The most important cornerstones of the Charter of the UN, which came into force on 24 October 1945, are the principles of national sovereignty and of non-intervention in internal affairs. The organization took the form of an associa-

10 'World Parliament is Predicted by Ford'. New York Times, 2 January 1943.
11 Citation from Baratta, vol. 1, loc. cit., p. 99.

tion of sovereign states. According to the provisions of Chapter VII of the Charter, however, the Security Council can decide on universally binding coercive measures 'to maintain or restore international peace and security'. The five victorious powers of the World War secured for themselves permanent seats, with a right of veto, on this body, the most important one. In the event of the use of armed force by the UN, a Military Staff Committee should take over the command of the forces provided by the members. However, this provision has never been implemented. In the General Assembly, which cannot pass any universally binding resolutions, all states are equally represented with one vote.

Internationalists criticized the structural principles behind the new world organization, and evoked the failure of the American confederation and of the League of Nations. The logical conclusions had not been drawn from the lessons of the past. 'The League of Nations, which had failed in [its] task,' wrote Curtis for example, 'was reconstructed as the United Nations Organization. Both were based on the same principle as the Articles of Confederation, that is to say on a compact between sovereign States, which in terms maintained their sovereignty.'[12] This view was shared in the United States by a broad cross-section of the population. The polling institute Roper, for example, conducted a survey which included the following question: 'If every other country in the world would elect representatives to a world congress and let all problems between countries be decided by this congress, with a strict provision that all countries have to abide by the decisions whether they like them or not, would you be willing to have the United States go along on this?' Of those questioned, 62.8 per cent answered 'yes' and only 19.8 per cent 'no'. [13]

Prominent support for a federal world order

The dropping of the atom bomb came as a great shock, and led to an even more urgent prioritization of the problem of 'international anarchy'. Leading atomic scientists such as Robert Oppenheimer or Philip Morrison, who had themselves worked on the Manhattan project for the development of the bomb, condemned its use, and issued urgent warnings against a nuclear arms race and nuclear war, which would mean the destruction of human civilization. In a volume of essays entitled 'One World or None', Leó Szilárd wrote in 1946 that the problem could only be contained by a world government. Twenty prominent figures, including the Nobel Prize winners Albert Einstein (1879 to 1955) and Thomas Mann (1875 to 1955), the philosopher and author Mortimer J. Adler

---

12 Curtis, Lionel. 1949. World Revolution in the Cause of Peace. New York: Macmillan, p. 33.
13 Cf. Guma, Greg. 11 Sep. 2013. 'Waking Up from World Order Amnesia'. Global Research (www.globalresearch.ca).

(1902 to 2001), the former US Supreme Court Judge Owen J. Roberts (1875 to 1955) and US Senator William Fulbright (1905 to 1995), published a joint statement on 10 October 1945 making the same point. 'The first atomic bomb destroyed more than the city of Hiroshima,' they wrote. 'It also exploded our inherited, outdated political ideas.' Since the San Francisco Charter upheld the absolute sovereignty of rival nation states, it was similar in spirit to the Articles of Confederation of the thirteen original American republics. 'How long will the United Nations Charter endure? With luck, a generation? A century?', they asked. But it was not enough to rely on luck. 'We must aim at a Federal Constitution of the world, a working world-wide legal order, if we hope to prevent an atomic war.'[14]

Reves' critique of democracy, the nation state and sovereignty

With this statement, the prominent signatories were at the same time also expressing support for the recently published book 'The Anatomy of Peace' by the Hungarian-born American journalist Emery Reves (1904 to 1981), in which he made a powerful attack on the concept of the sovereignty of nation states and a plea for world democracy. The book sold in tens of thousands of copies in several translations, and can be seen as a modern update on cosmopolitanism. Just as in the transition from the Ptolemaic to the Copernican worldview, it argued, a revolution in thinking was required. Currently, the only point of reference and starting-point for all political analysis was one's own 'sovereign' nation state. But the nation state system was like the era of feudalism, as there was still no recognition of any higher legal authority. In the highly integrated world of the industrial age, this perspective was 'bankrupt'. The principle of national self-determination propounded by President Wilson was already an anachronism by then, and had laid the groundwork for the Second World War. Peace was not a question of a static international mechanism which would maintain the status quo and suppress aggression between states; rather, it had to be understood as a dynamic social system with the capacity to react to the changes and developments in human society and to steer them. This could only be achieved through a universal legal order - something that was not even conceivable on the basis of the Ptolemaic ideology of nation states. 'The modern Bastille', wrote Reves, 'is the nation-state, no matter whether the jailers are conservative, liberal or socialist. That symbol of our enslavement must be destroyed if we ever want to be

---

14 Citation from Nathan, Otto, and Heinz Norden (ed.). 1960. Einstein on Peace. New York: Simon and Schuster, pp. 340f.

free again.'[15] By this, Reves meant not the abolition of the nation states but a radical reorientation of our understanding of democracy, one that would no longer have the nation state as its point of reference. 'We cannot have democracy in a world of interdependent, sovereign nation-states, because democracy means the sovereignty of the people. The nation-state structure strangulates and exterminates the sovereignty of the people, that sovereignty which, instead of being vested in institutions of the community, is vested in ... separate sets of sovereign nation-state institutions.'[16] He concluded, as had Cloots and others before him, that popular sovereignty and democracy could now only be achieved within the framework of a universal and worldwide legal order.

Albert Einstein and Albert Camus as advocates

One of the internationally best-known advocates of a world federation and world parliament after the war was Albert Einstein. From 1933 onwards, he lived in exile, and in 1939 he warned US President Roosevelt of a possible German atom bomb programme. He had long since adopted the peace question as a cause. Along with many other prominent figures, such as John Boyd Orr (1880 to 1971), the Scottish Nobel Prize winner and founding Director of the UN Food and Agriculture Organization, and Brock Chisholm (1896 to 1971) from Canada, the first Director-General of the World Health Organization, he was a supporter of the international umbrella organization of world federalists known today as the World Federalist Movement, WFM, founded in August 1947 in Montreux in Switzerland. Einstein intervened time and again in the public debate. In October 1947, for example, he published a widely-admired open letter to the UN General Assembly. In this, he lamented the fact that the member states had failed to transfer any of their competences upwards to the supra-national level of the United Nations, and he made three suggestions for the future development of the organization. Firstly, the UN General Assembly needed to be strengthened, and the Security Council made subordinate to the Assembly. Secondly, the method of representation had to be substantially changed. 'The present method of selection by government appointment,' Einstein wrote, 'does not leave any real freedom to the appointee. Furthermore, selection by governments cannot give the peoples of the world the feeling of being fairly and proportionately represented. The moral authority of the United Nations would be considerably enhanced if the delegates were elected directly by the people. Were

---

15   Reves, Emery. 1946. The Anatomy of Peace. 10th ed. New York, London: Harper and Brothers, p. 270.
16   Ibid., p. 162

they responsible to an electorate, they would have much more freedom to follow their consciences.'[17] Thirdly, the General Assembly should remain in permanent session, and should take the initiative in the construction of a 'supranational order'. If necessary, the other countries should proceed without Russia,
as long as it was made clear that the door remained open and that the 'partial
world Government' would never be misused as an alliance against others.

The philosopher Albert Camus (1913 to 1960), who had joined the Résis-
tance during the war and who received the Nobel Prize for literature in 1957,
also spoke out for a world parliament. In November 1946 he wrote that democracy was 'a form of society in which the law is above those who govern, the law
being the expression of the will of all, represented by a legislative body'. International law, however, according to Camus, 'is made and unmade by governments, that is, by the executive. We are therefore in a regime of international
dictatorship. The only way out is to place international law above governments,
which means that that law must be made, that there must be a parliament for
making it, and that parliament must be constituted by means of worldwide elections in which all nations will take part.' Until such a parliament existed, the
only option was resistance against the 'international dictatorship'.[18] Camus later
became a member of the international council of the WFM, and alongside Abbé
Groués-Pierre (who was also active in the WFM), André Breton, Georges Alt-
man, Robert Sarrazac-Soulage and other French intellectuals was in the solidarity committee supporting the former US Air Force bomber pilot Garry Davis
(1921 to 2013). In 1948, Davis had generated considerable publicity by handing
in his US passport at the US Embassy in Paris as a protest against nationalism
and declaring himself 'the first citizen of the world'. He then camped illegally
on the 'world territory' set aside for the UN General Assembly, which was holding its third meeting there, thereby creating an international furore and launch-
ing a mass movement for world citizenship.

The position of the Catholic Church

During the fourth world congress of the WFM in Rome in 1951, Pope Pius XII
agreed to receive a delegation from the movement in the Vatican. In an address
to the delegation, the Pope declared that the aim of a federal political world
organization with 'effective authority' was in accordance with the 'traditional

---

17 Einstein, Albert. 'Open Letter to the General Assembly of the United Nations, October 1947'. In: Einstein on
Peace, Otto Nathan and Heinz Norden (ed.), 440–443. New York: Simon and Schuster, 1960, p. 442.
18 Camus, Albert. 2007. Camus at 'Combat': Writing 1944-1947. Ed. by Jacqueline Levi-Valensi. Transl. by Arthur Goldhammer. Princeton University Press, p. 268.

teachings of the Church'. 'Nothing is more in concurrence with its proclamation on just and unjust war, particularly under today's circumstances', he said. Whoever was engaged in trying to realize a 'comprehensive political organisation', for example in the form of a world parliament, should be thinking about it precisely from a federalist standpoint.[19] Following Pius XII, the call for an 'effective political organization of the world' has become a fixed component of papal teaching. In 1963, for example, it was expressed by John XXIII, in 1967 by Paul VI, in 2009 by Benedict XVI, and in 2015 by Pope Francis in the encyclical 'Laudato Si''. 'The creation of a parliamentary world legislature that supervises a global executive branch and that allows for the participation of the world's citizens in global political affairs', wrote Maja Brauer and Andreas Bummel in a study of 2016, is set out in Catholic doctrine and is 'fully in conformity with papal teaching.'[20]

The British initiative of November 1945

One important government politician of the post-war period who spoke out explicitly in support of a world parliament was the Labour politician and British foreign minister Ernest Bevin (1881 to 1951). Curtis, one of the co-founders of the Royal Institute of International Affairs in 1920 and a prominent figure in London foreign policy circles, had met with Bevin (whom he had known for a long time already) in October 1945 and put to him the idea of an international assembly.[21] In a parliamentary speech one month later, Bevin said that a new study was needed 'for the purpose of creating a world assembly elected directly from the people of the world, as a whole, to whom the Governments who form the United Nations are responsible and who, in fact, make the world law which they, the people, will then accept and be morally bound and willing to carry out.' He would be willing to sit down with anyone, regardless of their party or nation, in order to work on the constitution of such a world assembly. International law presupposed conflict between nations; it would be replaced by world law, with a world judiciary to interpret it, with a world police to enforce it, created by a sovereign world authority elected by the people themselves.[22] These

---

19 Reprinted in Brauer, Maja. 1994. Weltföderation - Modell globaler Gesellschaftsordnung. Frankfurt: Peter Lang, pp. 332f.
20 Brauer, Maja, and Andreas Bummel. 2016. 'The Federalist Principle in the Catholic Social Doctrine and the Question of a World Parliament'. Committee for a Democratic UN, p. 8.
21 Lavin, Deborah. 1995. From Empire to Commonwealth. A Biography of Lionel Curtis. Oxford: Clarendon Press, p. 301f.
22 Hansard Debate, House of Commons. Series 5, Vol. 416, 23 November 1945, 759-846, pp. 786f.

arguments were not without impact. The Canadian foreign ministry, for example, considered supporting Bevin's initiative if it were to be officially proposed by the British government. In his speech to the first UN General Assembly, the Canadian foreign minister Louis St. Laurent (1882 to 1973) spoke of the transformation of the UN into a world government. In an internal memo for the Canadian delegation to the third session of the Economic and Social Council of the UN, the Canadian foreign ministry outlined that 'the direction in which Canada would wish to see the United Nations develop is towards a world government with the Assembly presumably evolving towards a democratic world parliament directly representative of peoples on a geographic basis and with direct authority.'[23] All democratic countries had incorporated this principle of representation in their constitution.

But only six months after his statement in the House of Commons, Baratta reports, Bevin had backed away from it entirely. A speech in Moscow's Bolshoi Theatre by the Soviet dictator and mass murderer Joseph Stalin (1878 to 1953) was interpreted as a hidden threat of war against the West. In Fulton, Missouri, in March 1946, the former British Prime Minister Winston Churchill (1874 to 1965) coined the term 'Iron Curtain' for the sealing-off of Soviet-controlled Eastern Europe. As early as June 1945, out of fear of Soviet expansion, he had as Prime Minister authorized an examination of the 'purely hypothetical contingency' of a preventive Anglo-American strike on the Soviet zone in order to drive Stalin back out of Eastern Europe.[24] The looming Cold War was beginning to determine the political agenda.

The issue of a Charter review conference

The elements of the Charter that came in for particular criticism following the San Francisco conference were the right of veto in the Security Council, the principle of the sovereign equality of all states, and the weakness of the General Assembly. Many governments, too, were especially unhappy from the beginning with the right of veto in the Security Council. World federalists complained that even though the Charter opens with the words 'We the peoples', there was no place in the bodies of the UN for delegates elected by popular vote – a fact that has been pointed out time and again since then. On the other hand,

---

23 Ministry on Foreign Affairs and International Trade Canada (ed.). 1946. 'Extracts from the Draft Commentary for the Delegation to the Third Session of the Economic and Social Council of the United Nations, DEA-FAH/7-1946/1, September 1946 (doc. 534)'. In: Documents on Canadian External Relations: 1977. Vol. 12.
24 It has only been known since 1998 that this scenario was explored. See Hastings, Max. 2009. 'Operation unthinkable: How Churchill wanted to recruit defeated Nazi troops and drive Russia out of Eastern Europe'. Mail Online, 26 August 2009 (www.dailymail.co.uk).

it was noted that at least all of the great powers had joined the new organization, in contrast to the League of Nations. Stassen, as a member of the US delegation, had urged strongly in San Francisco that the Charter should at the least be regularly reviewed. In Article 109 of the Charter, it was duly prescribed that after ten years at the latest a proposal for a conference for the purpose of reviewing the Charter had to be on the agenda of the next General Assembly. Thus, the year 1955 became a 'magical date' (Brauer) for world federalists and other advocates of a reform of the UN.

At the urging of the US American lawyer and world federalist Grenville Clark (1882 to 1967), Cuba – at this time under President Ramón Grau – brought a proposal to the second UN General Assembly in 1946 to hold a review conference in 1947. The proposal was rejected by a majority vote, with numerous non-votes and abstentions. In the course of the debate, an issue arose that was to feature repeatedly up to 1955 and beyond, namely that of weighted votes in the General Assembly. The UN Ambassador of the Philippines, Carlos P. Rómulo (1899 to 1985), a 1942 Pulitzer Prize winner who had served as a colonel in the US Army in the Pacific and would later be his country's foreign minister for almost two decades, not only spoke out against the right of veto and in favour of a review conference in 1947 but explained why he would support the introduction of weighted voting in the General Assembly. The principle of 'one nation, one vote' namely served to dissuade the great powers from equipping the General Assembly with 'any power to enact binding world law'. '[M]y nation would be very happy indeed', Rómulo said, 'to trade the fiction of equality in a powerless Assembly for the reality of a vote equal to our actual position in the world in an Assembly endowed with real power.' What was needed was 'a narrowly limited World Federal Government'.[25] Great Britain's UN representative Hartley Shawcross (1902 to 2003), the leading British prosecutor at the Nuremberg trials, agreed that 'some day it might be necessary to devise a weighted form of voting which gave each member State a voting strength in the Assembly consonant with its real influence in world affairs'.[26] But despite this, Great Britain too voted against a Charter review conference. The issue was endlessly deferred from one General Assembly to the next.

---

25 Citation from Baratta, loc. cit., vol. 1, p. 205 (Statement before Committee I, 16 November 1946)
26 Citation from Rusett, Alan de. 1954. 'Large and Small States in International Organization. Present Attitudes to the Problem of Weighted Voting'. Intl. Affairs 30 (4): 463–474, p. 464 (The Times, 12 December 1949).

The foundation of the Council of Europe

The goal of political integration in Western Europe, as a contribution to the creation of an anti-Soviet bloc, was supported by the American Committee for a United Europe, whose founding President was Senator Fulbright, and which in turn was financed in part by the Ford Foundation set up by Ford in 1936. At the European Conference on Federation, possible pathways towards a United States of Europe were examined. In 1949 the Council of Europe was established, initially comprising ten members, with the constitutional aim of achieving 'a greater unity between its members'. Within the structure of this new intergovernmental organization, the idea of an international parliamentary assembly was actually made concrete for the first time in history. Alongside the Committee of Ministers, in which the governments of the member states are represented, the constitution requires an advisory parliamentary assembly whose members are not government diplomats but delegates sent by the member state parliaments. The allocation of seats in the 'advisory assembly' is tiered according to population size. The Union of European Federalists, an umbrella organization for federalist movements in Europe founded in December 1946, pressed for the advisory assembly of the Council of Europe to work on drafting a European constitution to be put forward for ratification by the member states.

Sohn's proposal for a parliamentary assembly at the UN

The creation of this new form of assembly was seized upon as a potential precedent for international organizations in general. 'There is no reason for limiting this interesting development to the countries of Western Europe', wrote the world federalist and lawyer Louis B. Sohn (1914 to 2006), who in 1939 had fled Lemberg in today's Ukraine for the USA, had taken part as a US delegate in the San Francisco conference, and later became a Professor at Harvard University. Using the example of the advisory assembly of the Council of Europe, Sohn proposed in 1949 the establishment of a parliamentary assembly within the United Nations too. Sohn argued that such an assembly, reflecting 'the various shades of world opinion', would increase global public support for the UN and thus contribute to strengthening it. If real statesmen were to emerge in the assembly, capable of representing a global perspective beyond national ambitions, then its decisions, although only advisory in nature, 'might have more effect than the recommendations of the General Assembly or of the Security Council', thought Sohn. As the instrument of international law needed for the creation of this parliamentary assembly, he recommended using a resolution of the General Assembly under Article 22 of the UN Charter which allows the establishment of 'such subsidiary organs as it deems necessary for the performance of its functions'. An alternative would be an international treaty, as long as it were clearly contained within the framework of the UN. These remain today the two options most often cited and debated, and they will be examined in more detail at a later point in this study. In Sohn's view, the allocation of seats should be in line with each country's relative proportion of the world population. For example, one seat could be allocated for each five million inhabitants, albeit no fewer than three for any country and no more than thirty. Altogether, his model at that point produced fewer than 500 seats.[27] At this time, the efforts of world federalists were focused as a rule on radical change, and consequently the proposal to institute a purely advisory assembly within the UN received comparatively little attention. The WFM, for example, principally supported the idea of organising a world constituent assembly.

Models for a world constitution

In order to lend weight to the calls for a world government, which had been increasing at an accelerated pace since the dropping of the atomic bomb, a number of people at the University of Chicago led by the Italian literary scholar and historian Giuseppe Antonio Borgese (1882 to 1952), who had gone into exile to the USA in 1931 as an anti-fascist and later took on American citizenship, formed a study group to draft a world constitution. It was chaired by the Chancellor of the University, the educationalist Robert M. Hutchins (who left to become Director of the Ford Foundation in 1951). It was one of the first such initiatives. Elisabeth Mann Borgese (1918 to 2002), the youngest daughter of Thomas Mann, was one of those who worked on the 'Preliminary draft for a world constitution' published in 1948; she was married to Borgese, and for two years, up to 1950, was Chair of the executive committee of the WFM. Later she was an active supporter of the concept of a 'Common Heritage of Mankind' and contributed substantially to the genesis of the Convention on the Law of the Sea in 1982. G.A. Borgese was a friend of Mann's (who had gone into exile in 1933 and moved to Princeton in the USA in 1938). Together with the theologian Reinhold Niebuhr (1892 to 1971), the philosopher of technology Lewis Mumford (1895 to 1990) and fourteen other prominent figures, they had stated already in 1940 in the jointly written essay 'City of Man' that the fundamental

---

27 Citations from Sohn, Louis B. 1949. 'The Development of International Law'. American Bar Association Journal 35 (October): 860–862.

prerequisite for world-structure today was a 'constitutional order'.[28] The draft of 1948 now contained concrete proposals for a federal world government with responsibility for peacekeeping, the implementation of human rights, arms control, worldwide taxes, currency and credit issues and other areas. The right of legislative initiative and the capacity to pass laws would lie with a council comprised of 99 members appointed by a federal convention, in turn made up of 'delegates elected directly by the people of all states and nations, one delegate for each million of population or fraction thereof above one-half million'.[29]

Other model constitutions, which naturally also dealt with the issues of the structure of a world parliament and the procedures of global legislation, were drawn up and published by many other groups and individuals. One prominent example is the 'Earth Constitution' originally drafted by the World Constitution and Parliament Association at sessions held in 1968 and 1977. The Swiss international lawyer Max Habicht (1899 to 1986), who had opened the founding conference of the WFM in Montreux, counted 13 such texts in the years 1939 to 1971, beginning with Streit's 'Union Now'.[30]

The Clark and Sohn model

The proposals for a comprehensive revision of the UN Charter published (together with a commentary) by Clark and Sohn in the book 'World Peace Through World Law' constituted the model which attracted the most attention. Clark – inspired by Streit – had concerned himself with the subject since 1939, and then joined forces with Sohn. Their book appeared in different versions in the years 1958, 1960 and 1966.[31] 'Of all the twentieth-century proposals for world constitutionalism, however,' wrote the political scientist Samuel S. Kim, "World Peace Through World Law", by Grenville Clark and Louis Sohn, remains the most comprehensive, detailed, rigorous model of world constitutionalism.'[32]

What did this model for the decision-making organs of a reformed UN look like in outline? For a start, the draft Charter proposed that the citizens of all UN

28 Agar, Herbert, Frank Aydelotte, Giuseppe Antonio Borgese, Hermann Broch, Van Wyck Brooks, Ada L. Comstock, William Yandell Elliott, et al.. 1941. The City of Man. A Declaration on World Democracy. New York: The Viking Press, p. 94.
29 Committee to Frame a World Constitution. 1948. The Preliminary Draft of a World Constitution. Chicago: The University of Chicago Press.
30 Habicht, Max. 1980. 'Le droit de l'homme à la paix'. Transnational Associations (2): 84–88, pp. 85f.
31 In the following we only refer to the latest edition: Clark, Grenville, and Louis B. Sohn. 1966. World Peace Through World Law. Two Alternative Plans. 3rd ed. enlarged. Cambridge: Harvard University Press.
32 Kim, Samuel S. 1993. 'In Search of Global Constitutionalism'. In: The Constitutional Foundations of World Peace, Richard Falk, Robert C. Johansen, and Samuel S. Kim (eds.), 55–81. Albany: State University of New York Press, p. 57.

member states should automatically receive an additional and automatic citizenship of the United Nations, thus creating a direct relationship between the UN and the individual. Gradually, following a three-stage plan over 24 years, the members of the General Assembly would be directly elected: by the national parliaments in the first stage; half of them by the parliaments and half directly in the second stage; and from the third stage onwards, entirely by direct election. The allocation of seats would be roughly in line with each country's proportion of the world population, in six tiered categories, whereby none of the then 99 countries would have more than 30 seats, and each at least one. Clark and Sohn wrote that they had also examined proposals for two-chamber and three-chamber systems, but had rejected them. A world legislature consisting of only one chamber was the simplest and most effective option. In their model, the reformed General Assembly would be given the power to pass binding world laws on issues regarding the maintenance and enforcement of peace, disarmament, and the control of nuclear energy. Resolutions in other policy areas would continue to have only the status of recommendations. The former Security Council, now transformed into an executive council without permanent members or a right of veto (it is not possible to go into the full detail of its proposed structure and procedures here), would be subordinate to the General Assembly and would implement its decisions. Clark and Sohn went into considerable detail in their model on plans for disarmament and for the establishment of a permanent UN peacekeeping force, together with a reserve force, which could be mobilized for peacekeeping and when enforcement measures were required. The reasoning behind this model was that general and extensive disarmament can only be achieved through the creation of a supranational armed force, under a shared command, with a monopoly on the use of such force. This is the focus of Clark and Sohn's plan. The Chicago group, by contrast, had supported a 'maximal' option, arguing that a restriction to policing functions only made no sense because it meant that the world organization would have no effective way of dealing with or resolving the social and economic injustice which lay at the root of many conflicts, and which it would then in fact tend to consolidate.[33]

CURE's deliberations and conclusions

The US-based 'Conference Upon Research and Education in world government' (CURE) which since around 1953 organized an ongoing exchange of a wide range of 'students of world affairs' eventually came forward with a set of

---

33 Brauer, loc. cit., p. 133.

charter revisions to illustrate 'that it is possible to strengthen the present Charter so that the United Nations can function as a true federal government in world affairs'. According to CURE's proposal the General Assembly was to be composed of an 'Assembly of Nations', representing governments, and an 'Assembly of Peoples', representing world citizens. This bicameral body was to be vested with the power to 'ratify or revise international conventions', among other things. In a book that summarized CURE's debates and elaborated strongly on the issue of citizen representation at the UN, it was noted that by contrast to Clark and Sohn's idea 'most federalists recognize … the necessity for at least a bicameral legislature'. CURE's participant and prolific world federalist lecturer Vernon Nash is quoted saying that two houses will be created 'since all federal systems have adopted that compromise after long struggle in constitutional convention'. Even if the powers of the UN wouldn't be increased, CURE participants had 'a strong feeling' that the peoples should be more directly represented. 'A popularly elected chamber without power, but with capacity to voice world public opinon,' said renowed political scientist Quincey Wright, 'might assist in the emergence of a world public opinion and a world legislative body.'[34]

Parliamentary cooperation for a world federation

In the years following the Second World War, world federalist parliamentary groups arose in numerous countries. In some parliaments, hearings took place on the question of a world government – for example in the US Congress, where up until 1950 a number of proposals for resolutions on world federalism were considered. Indeed, one of these proposals, with the file number HCR-64, was supported by 111 members, including the future US Presidents John F. Kennedy and Gerald Ford. With the help of the British parliamentary group founded by Labour Party member Henry Usborne (1909 to 1996), an international umbrella association was founded in London in 1951, the World Association of Parliamentarians for World Government. The former British Prime Minister Clement Attlee (1883 to 1967) acted as honorary President. Prime Minister Shigeru Yoshida (1878 to 1967) belonged to the Japanese national group. The purpose of these groups, which existed in more than ten countries, and in some cases – such as Japan – continue to exist, was to provide support for world federalism through the national parliaments. Their activities were closely coordinated with the WFM, which at that time had a presence in over

---

34 Millard, Everett Lee. 1966. Freedom in a Federal World. Rev. 4th ed. Dobbs Ferry, NY: Oceana Publications, pp. 206, 209f., 63f., 65.

50 countries. In a strategy supported by the WFM, it was envisaged that an international committee of parliamentarians would set to work on drafting a world constitution if and when the time came.[35] A highpoint of the movement's international parliamentary activities was the third global conference of the World Association of Parliamentarians for World Government, which took place in the Danish Parliament in Copenhagen, with over 400 delegates participating. A year earlier, the question of whether the IPU should transform itself into a world parliament, or indeed whether it should be pressing for a world parliament at all, had once again petered out in inconclusive internal debates.[36] Looking ahead to the hoped-for UN Charter revision conference in 1955, the conference in Copenhagen passed fourteen revision proposals, including one for the transformation of the UN General Assembly into a world legislature made up of a senate and a chamber of deputies. With respect to the proposed powers for this world legislature, the proposal was 'minimalist', like the later one from Clark and Sohn. Only resolutions passed by both chambers for peacekeeping purposes were to be binding. The concept of UN world citizenship can also be found already in the Copenhagen proposals. 'To ensure that world law can be enforced by the means of the United Nations against individuals breaking the law,' it reads there, 'every citizen of a member state shall be a citizen of the U.N., as well as of his own country. The Charter and the laws enacted thereunder shall bind each individual citizen of the U.N.'[37] Additionally, the conference proposed that the world legislature should have the power 'to raise revenue for UN purposes', whereby a maximum global rate would be fixed in the Charter and levied from the member states proportionately according to their national income. In the Clark and Sohn proposal, the member states would raise specific taxes themselves following a similar model and transfer the sums raised direct to a local UN finance office.

---

35 On the parliamentary activities of world federalists see ibid., pp. 171ff.
36 Cf. Kissling, loc. cit., p. 213.
37 World Association of Parliamentarians for World Government (ed.). 1954. Report of the Third World Parliamentary Conference on World Government held at the Parliament House, Christiansborg, Copenhagen, August 22-29, 1953, p. 132.

6.
Bloc confrontation and
the rise of the NGOs

World federalism caught between the fronts in the Cold War

The authors of the Chicago draft constitution of 1948 were convinced of the rightness of their cause, but at the same time they were not under the illusion that the preconditions for the establishment of a world republic were actually in place. 'Yet World Government shall come', wrote Hutchins and G.A. Borgese, 'whether within five years or fifty, whether without a conflagration or after it.' Their draft should be seen, they said, as 'a proposal to history'.[1] The transfer of sovereignty was rejected not only by the Soviet Union; moreover, internationalism, and more especially world federalism, was slowly but surely being ground between the two fronts of the East-West conflict. In the USA, anti-communist hysteria broke out, personified in the figure of Senator Joseph McCarthy (1908 to 1957). World federalists were suspected by those who succumbed to this hysteria of being communists in disguise. Conversely, in the Eastern bloc they were seen as agents of capitalism. The reaction to Einstein on the Soviet side, for example, was that his idea for a 'world super-state' was 'nothing but a flamboyant signboard for the world supremacy of the capitalist monopolies'.[2] After the IPU put the issue of a world parliament on its agenda in 1949, a number of the 'peoples' republics of Eastern Europe' decided to boycott their conferences.[3]

The federalist movement and the founding of NATO

The Soviet blockade of West Berlin in June 1948 represented the first dramatic crisis of the Cold War. It was not least as a reaction to this escalation that NATO was founded in April 1949, as a military alliance between the Western European countries, the USA and Canada. As the historian and political scientist Ira

---

1   Committee to Frame a World Constitution. 1948. The Preliminary Draft of a World Constitution. Chicago: The University of Chicago Press, p. vii.
2   Citation from Nathan, Otto, and Heinz Norden (ed.). 1960. Einstein on Peace. New York: Simon and Schuster, p. 445.
3   Kissling, Claudia. 2006. Die Interparlamentarische Union im Wandel. Frankfurt: Peter Lang, p. 212.

Strauss notes, it is not widely recognized how decisive the influence of federal thinking originally was on the architects of the Atlantic alliance.[4] 'If it hadn't been for Union Now', wrote the then Director of the Office of Western European Affairs at the State Department, Theodore Achilles, 'I don't think there would have been a NATO Treaty.'[5] The decisive impulse for the creation of the NATO Parliamentary Assembly also came out of the federalist movement. This conference for parliamentarians from the NATO partner countries has been coming together since 1955, and although not a constitutional organ of NATO has been informally recognized since 1967. With the help of Federal Union, the Atlantic Union Committee was set up in New York in 1949, under the leadership of former US Supreme Court judge Roberts, to further the cause of a 'Federal Union of the Democracies'. Numerous prominent figures in the USA joined the committee, including former US President Truman and George C. Marshall (1880 to 1959), who during the war from 1939 to 1945 was chief of staff of the US Army and who received the Nobel Peace Prize in 1953 for the Marshall Plan he devised for European reconstruction. The transatlantic federalists thought that NATO should be more than just a military alliance. The proposal for an Atlantic parliamentary assembly, wrote John A. Matthews, a member of Federal Union, 'stemmed from a more fundamental proposal to create a comprehensive government of democratic nations – most of which have gradually come to be thought of as the Atlantic Community'. [6] In this view, the NATO Parliamentary Assembly was to become the core and the motor of a transatlantic integration project. The renowned British historian Arnold Toynbee (1889 to 1975) argued in an article of 1952 that the assembly ultimately had to become a directly elected common legislature for the western community.[7]

The declining popularity of world federalism and a world parliament

From 1950 and 1951, the political climate - against the backdrop of the Korean War, which is estimated to have claimed 3 million lives - grew ever more difficult. This was the first of numerous so-called proxy wars, including those in Vietnam and Afghanistan, in which the two superpowers and their respective blocs stood on opposing sides as political adversaries, de facto if not officially. The 'Declaration of the Federation of the World' alluded to earlier was actually revoked in thirteen of the US states which had adopted it. And the UN Charter

---

4   Straus, Ira. 1999. 'Atlantic Federalism and the expanding Atlantic Nucleus'. Peace & Change 24 (3): 277–328.

5   Citation from ibid., p. 291 (interview of Achilles by Straus on 18 March 1983).

6   Matthews, John A. 1962. 'Evolution of an Atlantic Assembly', Repr. in: U.S. Congress, Congressional Record, Proceedings and Debates of the 99th Congress, 2nd Sess., Jan. 28, 1986. Ed. by. U.S. Congress, p. 3.

7   Toynbee, Arnold J. 1952. 'Union of Free Inevitable'. Freedom & Union 7 (10): 19–23.

revision conference provided for in Article 109 failed to take place in the key year of 1955 as anticipated. Instead, the General Assembly passed a resolution to the effect that it should take place 'at an appropriate time' and appointed a committee to recommend when that time might be, but which in practice never did so. After 1967 the issue disappeared from the agenda for good.

The question of a world parliament now arose only infrequently until the early 1980s. When the IPU decided in 1965 to review its relations with the apparently indifferent UN, Kissling reports that the British IPU group proposed 'a transformation of the IPU into an advisory parliamentary assembly of the UN by means of simple resolutions of both organisations', but that this met with no support.[8] In 1970, on the 25th anniversary of the founding of the UN, the US American Commission to Study the Organization of Peace (founded in 1939, and influential during the war) submitted a detailed report on the future of the world organization. Sohn was now Chair of the Commission. This report also recommended, as an element of a wider programme to strengthen the General Assembly, the establishment of a UN parliamentary assembly. This was to be the next step in the evolution of international parliamentary institutions. The report also pointed to the examples of the IPU and the NATO Parliamentary Assembly. However, the Commission had passed its zenith and attracted little attention any more, and in 1972 it was quietly wound up.

While world federalism was no longer on the agenda in the Eastern or Western blocs, in India – which had played a leading role in the establishment of the Non-Aligned Movement – it remained a live issue. The Indian activist Vijay Pratap reported that the question of a world parliament was on the agenda of the first Afro-Asian conference of non-aligned states in Bandung, Indonesia in 1955.[9] In any event, it is no accident that the sixteenth world congress of the WFM in 1975 took place in New Delhi, with the support of the Indian Prime Minister Indira Gandhi and the Indian President Fakhruddin Ali Ahmed, and that virtually the entire political leadership of India' took part, as an observer noted.[10]

---

8   Kissling, loc. cit., p. 217.
9   Pratap, Vijay. 'The global political'. In: Global political parties, ed. by Katarina Sehm-Patomäki and Marko Ulvila, 144–150. London, New York: Zed Books, 2007, p. 148. Unfortunately, we couldn't establish more details on this.
10 Logue, John. 'One World, One Family. A Report on WAWF's New Delhi Congress'. Transnational Perspectives 2, no. 1 (1975): 4–8, p. 4.

The World Order Models Project

From 1968 onwards, a new catalyst for world order studies emerged in the form of the academically-oriented World Order Models Project, led by the legal scientist Saul Mendlovitz (b. 1925) of Rutgers University. WOMP served to help build up a transnational framework for the study of issues of world order and of 'preferred future models' oriented on four goals: the minimization of the extensive use of collective force; the maximization of social and economic wellbeing; the implementation of basic human rights and political justice; and the restoration and preservation of ecological stability. The contributors were by no means all committed to the programme of global constitutionalism as advocated by Mendlovitz and his colleague Richard Falk (b. 1930) from Princeton University. In 'A Study of Future Worlds', published in 1975, Falk presented a comprehensive model of a preferred world system at the institutional centre of which was a 'world assembly' with special responsibility for setting standards in the areas of the four WOMP goals. The assembly would consist of three chambers, each with 200 votes, representing respectively the governments, the peoples and civil society organizations. The model does not make clear how the seats are allocated, nor how or by whom the representatives are appointed. This is 'a complicated task of institutional design'.[11] However, it is proposed that decisions endorsed by all three chambers with a four-fifths majority would have binding status, and those endorsed with only a two-thirds majority would have recommendatory status. A world court would be able to subject the decisions to legal scrutiny. Each chamber would elect seven representatives to an executive council charged with implementing the decisions of the assembly and able to call on the services of a coordinating council, whose members would also be elected by the three chambers. So the creation of a broadly-based world legislature was regarded as indispensable within the WOMP, too.

The growing importance of NGOs

A particularly interesting feature of Falk's model is the third 'chamber of organisations'. Other academics working at WOMP were also involved in this initiative. The peace researcher Johan Galtung (b. 1930), for example, recommended not only transforming the General Assembly into a directly elected

---

11   Falk, Richard. 1975. A Study of Future Worlds. Amsterdam: North-Holland Publishing Company, p. 238.

world parliament but also the establishment of a UN chamber for 'nonterritorial actors'.[12] Such proposals reflected the growing significance on the international stage of civil society organizations independent of governments. Anti-Slavery International was one of the first internationally active associations of this kind to be founded, in 1839. They were concerned with the abolition of slavery, with votes for women, with workers' rights and with peace. The International Labour Organization, founded in 1919 and since 1945 continuing under the aegis of the UN, can be regarded as setting the precedent for their inclusion within inter-state organizations. In the structural bodies of the ILO, employees' and employers' associations are represented alongside the governments of the member states, by delegates with equal status. At the annual International Labour Conference, for example, each country has two government representatives and one each representing employees and employers.

After the World Wars, the number of international civil society organizations grew rapidly. Article 71 of the UN Charter stipulated that ECOSOC, the United Nations Economic and Social Council, 'may make suitable arrangements for consultation with non-governmental organizations'. This is the reason for the use since then of the term 'non-governmental organizations', or NGOs. Up to 1975, 650 NGOs had been registered as having consultative status with ECOSOC; today there are more than 3,500, and their exact categorization is a science in itself. Not only did their numbers grow, but the range of topics they address also grew ever broader. Of particular significance was environmental protection. The biologist Rachel Carson (1907 to 1964) stimulated environmental awareness and helped its breakthrough into the popular consciousness with her 1962 book 'Silent Spring', in which she drew attention to the catastrophic impact of chemical toxins like DDT. 'Along with the possibility of the extinction of mankind by nuclear war, the central problem of our age has therefore become the contamination of man's total environment with such substances of incredible potential for harm', she wrote.[13]

In the human rights sector, Amnesty International, founded in 1961, quickly became a prominent and influential group. One of Amnesty's co-founders and international chairs was the Irish politician, former foreign minister and lawyer Seán MacBride (1904 to 1988), who received the Nobel Peace Prize in 1974. In his acceptance speech in Oslo he pointed out that ultimately a world parliament and a world government were needed to achieve world peace. 'Of course, it will

---

12 Cf. e.g. Galtung, Johan. 1975. 'Nonterritorial Actors and the Problem of Peace'. In: On the Creation of a Just World Order. Preferred Worlds for the 1990's, ed. by Saul H. Mendlovitz, 151–188. New York: The Free Press; and the same, 1986. 'International organizations and world decision-making'. Transnational Associations (4): 220–224.

13 Carson, Rachel. 2000. Silent Spring. New edition. London et al.: Penguin Classics, p. 25.

be difficult', he said, 'but what is the alternative? The nearly certain destruction of the human race.'[14]

In 1972, the first UN conference on the environment took place in Stockholm, led by the Canadian Maurice Strong (1929 to 2015). It was shadowed by a parallel gathering of NGOs – a practice repeated at many subsequent UN conferences. Parliamentary associations like the IPU or the Parliamentarians for Global Action, founded in 1978 by the New Zealander Nicholas Dunlop (b. 1956), initially under the umbrella of the WFM, were – in the perspective of the UN – just NGOs like all the others. The Stockholm conference led to the establishment of the United Nations Environment Programme, UNEP, with Strong as its first Director until 1975. In a speech in New York in 1984 Strong advocated a bicameral system for the UN 'in which peoples' directly elected representatives sit in one chamber and representatives of governments in the other'.[15]

The idea of a 'second chamber'

A closer integration of NGOs in the work of the UN was also advocated by the Medical Association for the Prevention of War (now, under the name Medact, the British branch of International Physicians for the Prevention of Nuclear War, IPPNW), set up by the genetic scientist Lionel Penrose (1898 to 1972) and others. At the second special session of the UN General Assembly on disarmament in 1982, this Association proposed the establishment of a 'second chamber' alongside the General Assembly. As one of the initiators, the British doctor Jeffrey Segall (1924 to 2010), explained, this body would concern itself with fundamental global problems, would consist of delegates who were independent of government and not attached to political parties, and would help to give expression to 'world public opinion' within the UN.[16] In the course of the following year the Medical Association formed an international network of NGOs to press for such a chamber - the International Network for a UN Second Assembly, INFUSA. On the 40th anniversary of the UN in 1985, the network appealed to the General Assembly to set up an expert group to examine this proposal. INFUSA's idea had been for an assembly of NGO representatives, but it proposed that each UN member state should itself decide how to select its repre-

---

14 MacBride, Seán. 12 December 1974. 'Nobel Lecture: The Imperatives of Survival'.
15 Citation from Nerfin, Marc. 1993. 'United Nations: Prince and Citizen?' In: The Constitutional Foundations of World Peace, ed. by Richard Falk, Robert C. Johansen and Samuel S. Kim, 147–165. Albany: State University of New York Press, p. 156 (Maurice F. Strong, 'Some Thoughts on the Future of the UN', remarks at a meeting of the New York Chapter, Society for International Development, November 29, 1984).
16 Segall, Jeffrey J. 1982. 'A UN Second Assembly'. Reconciliation Quarterly (June): 35–37.

sentatives. It identified some options, such as direct election by the entire electorate, or a vote taken by electors who had registered specifically for that purpose, or indirect election by an electoral college which might be made up of
representatives of selected NGOs, trade unions, academic establishments and
members of national UN societies. At any event, the spirit of the proposal would
exclude the option of nomination by government. A formula developed by Penrose in 1946 was proposed as the method for calculating the number of seats
per country, namely representation proportional to the square root of the country's population in millions. This formula would automatically result in a graduated distribution.[17]

The issue of weighted voting in the UN General Assembly

Weighted voting in the UN General Assembly remained an issue. As the Canadian peace researcher Hanna Newcombe (1922 to 2011) reported in 1971, the
US State Department carried out a confidential study to calculate the impact
that different systems of weighted voting would have had on past votes in the
General Assembly. The question was which system would have given the best
results for the interests of the United States. The investigation concluded that
'the U.S. does best under the present one-nation, one-vote scheme, because so
many small nations habitually vote in the Western bloc led by the U.S.'.[18] The
State Department therefore decided against supporting any form of weighted
voting. For organizations such as the Center for War/Peace Studies, reor-
ganized by the journalist Richard Hudson (1925 to 2006) in New York, however, the introduction of weighted voting remained an indispensable requirement for a strengthening of the General Assembly. Hudson later wrote that the
General Assembly 'with its absurd one nation, one vote decision-making system ... has no chance to make global laws'.[19] The Center developed its own proposal, the so-called 'Binding Triad'. In this, the voting weight of a country
would be determined by three factors: one nation, one vote (as previously); population size; and the contribution to the regular UN budget (for which a ceiling
would be fixed). Decisions of the Assembly would have to achieve specified
qualified majorities in all three of these areas in order to acquire binding status.

17 International Network for a UN Second Assembly. 1987. 'Appeal to the United Nations General Assembly
    to consider the proposal for a UN Second Assembly'.
18 Newcombe, Hanna. 1971. 'Weighted Voting Formulas for the UN'. Security Dialogue (2): 92–94, p. 92.
19 Hudson, Richard. 1991. 'Should There Be a Global Parliament? What Is the Binding Triad?' In: A New World
    Order. Can It Bring Security to the World's People? Walter Hoffmann (ed.), 32–36. Washington D.C.: World
    Federalist Association, p. 34.

In August 1985, the US Congress then did call for the introduction of weighted voting in the General Assembly. In order to add weight to its call, the Congress held back a portion of the US contribution to the UN budget, and moreover cut it by 20 per cent, thereby drastically aggravating the UN's funding crisis. It took issue both with mismanagement within the UN administration and with what it saw as unacceptable anti-western politicization of the organization by developing countries, who formed a majority. Clearly, the voting arithmetic in the UN bodies had changed. The ruling was brought in by Senator Nancy Kassebaum and Gerald Solomon, a member of the House of Representatives. Voting rights for the member states on issues relevant to the budget of the UN and its specialized agencies, it was argued, should be in proportion to the budget contribution made by each member state.[20] Agreement was then reached with the other member state governments that budget issues would be decided by consensus in order to ensure the assent of the biggest budget contributors without having to formally change the official procedures.

Bertrand's report

Funding crisis, management reform and budget issues were at the very top of the agenda in the UN's 40th anniversary year. The 'Joint Inspection Unit of the United Nations', an independent subsidiary body of the General Assembly established in 1966 to examine the working efficiency of the UN and its specialized agencies, took the opportunity to instruct the outgoing Inspector, Maurice Bertrand (1922 to 2015) from France, to prepare a report with suggestions for reform. The report, delivered in December 1985, turned into a wide-ranging critique. Bertrand lamented the 'extreme fragmentation' of UN activities and their 'extraordinary and unnecessary … institutional complexity'. Most of the organization's problems had structural causes. Resistance to any attempt at improvement was strong. The member states were not interested primarily in efficiency but in political control of the administration. With regard to the allocation of posts, for example, the principal aim was not to find the best qualified person, but rather to get one's own nationals selected if at all possible. Considerations for reform of the UN had to focus 'following the two unfinished experiments of the League of Nations and the United Nations, on a third generation World Organization'. At the conclusion of the report Bertrand recommended, amongst other things, examining proposals for opening up the UN to more non-state actors. However, 'the time had not yet come to think in terms of a

---

20 United States Foreign Relations Authorization Act, Section 143, Fiscal Year 1986-1987, H.R. 2068, P.L. 99-93, August 17, 1985, Reprinted in: International Legal Material, vol. 25 (1986), pp. 17-43.

"World Parliament"'. Over the next few decades, the world organization 'should remain an intergovernmental organization'.[21] The Inspection Unit rushed to distance itself from this devastating report. Bertrand, it stated, had gone beyond his remit and his powers. The Administrative Committee on Co-ordination, which brings together the heads of all the UN specialized agencies, declined for the same reasons to comment on the report at all.

Perestroika and Gorbachev's initiative

The policy of perestroika introduced by Mikhail Gorbachev (b. 1931) from 1986 onwards, involving a step by step democratization and market economy re-forms in the Soviet Union, also ushered in the end of the era of bloc confronta-tion. Since the Cuba crisis of 1962 at the latest, it had been clear to the govern-ments of the nuclear powers that any dispute could potentially spiral out of con-trol and quite possibly lead to an exchange of nuclear strikes and mutual anni-hilation. War, understood in the terms of the Prussian General Carl von Clause-witz (1780 to 1831) as a political instrument for the achievement of one's aims with physical force ('the continuation of politics by other means'), was no longer a realistic option. In his book on Perestroika, in which his stated aim was to 'talk without intermediaries to the citizens of the whole world about things that, without exception, concern us all', Gorbachev described the importance of 'the new way of thinking' for Soviet foreign policy. The core of this new way of thinking lay in the realization that, in view of the dangers of a nuclear war, 'hu-mankind's survival' had to take priority over national interests. All of humankind was in the same boat, and would sink or swim together. Transparency, dialogue and the willingness to cooperate were the maxims required for foreign policy.

In this connection, Gorbachev argued that 'the new style in international relations implies extending their framework far beyond the limits of the diplo-matic process proper. Parliaments, along with governments, are becoming in-creasingly active participants in international contacts, and this is an encourag-ing development. It points to a trend toward greater democracy in international relations'. The increasing role of public opinion and of NGOs in the domain of international politics was a sign of the times, and should be welcomed.[22] In a pathbreaking newspaper article in *Pravda* on disarmament and collective secu-rity among other topics, Gorbachev wrote in September 1987 that a 'world con-sultative council' should be established within the UN to bring together the

---

21   Bertrand, Maurice. 1985. 'Some reflections on reform of the United Nations, Report of the Joint Inspection Unit'. JIU/REP/85/9; A/40/988, pp. 1, 5f., 65f.
22   Gorbachev, Mikhail. 1987. Perestroika. Collins, pp. 9, 146, 158.

world's intellectual elite. Scientists, politicians, public figures, representatives of civil society and the churches, writers, artists and others would be able to 'seriously enrich the spiritual and ethical potential of contemporary world politics'.[23] The proposed body is reminiscent of the 'universal council' envisaged by the philosopher Johann Amos Comenius (1592 to 1670) in the 17th century, a gathering of enlightened 'philosophers, churchmen and politicians of outstanding eminence in wisdom, piety and prudence pledged to introduce plans at long last full enough to secure, establish, and increase the safety of all mankind'.[24]

However, it is far more likely that the four important, independent, international expert commissions of the 1980s will have served Gorbachev as model and inspiration. The Brandt Commission, set up in 1977 and chaired by the former West German Federal Chancellor and Nobel Peace Prize winner Willy Brandt (1913 to 1992), set itself the task 'to study the grave global issues arising from the economic and social disparities of the world community',[25] and it published reports on the 'world crisis' in 1980 and 1982. In 1982 a report also appeared from the Independent Commission for Disarmament and Security chaired by the former Swedish Prime Minister Olof Palme (1927 to 1986). In addition, the following year the UN General Assembly set up an independent World Commission on Environment and Development, chaired by the Norwegian politician Gro Harlem Brundtland (b. 1939). After deliberations taking up several years, at the end of 1987 this body published its concluding report, 'Our Common Future', in which the concepts of sustainable development and intergenerational justice were set out and developed. Finally, in July 1987, the International South Commission was established under the chairmanship of the former President of Tanzania, Julius K. Nyerere (1922 to 1999). Its concluding report was published in 1990, and it later gave rise to the South Centre, a joint think tank today involving fifty governments from the global South.

Gorbachev did not set out his proposal for a 'world consultative council' in detail. But the simple fact that the idea of a permanent advisory body within the UN was now being supported at the very highest political level was seen by advocates of a world parliament as an important development, particularly because Gorbachev welcomed the idea of a role for parliaments in international relations. But the proposal for a consultative body was not met with unalloyed enthusiasm. At a conference of the United Nations Institute for Training and

23 Id. 1987. 'Reality and Guarantees for a Secure World'. International Affairs: A Russian Journal of World Politics, Diplomacy and International Relations 33 (11): 3–11, p. 10 (Pravda, 17 September 1987).
24 Comenius, Johann Amos. 1671. Panorthosia Or Universal Reform, Chapters 19 to 26. Transl. by Archie Dobbie. Sheffield: JSOT Press, p. 129.
25 Independent Commission on International Development Issues. 1980. North/South: A Programme for Survival. London: MacMillan, p. 12.

Research in Moscow in September 1988 attended by 100 people, for example, the topic was discussed with great interest, but there was no agreement in its favour.[26] In a speech to the UN General Assembly on 7 December 1988, Gorbachev affirmed once more, this time in a slightly different formulation, 'that the idea of convening on a regular basis, under the auspices of the United Nations, an assembly of public organizations deserves attention'.[27] However, as far as we know, there followed no concrete diplomatic initiatives for the establishment of such an assembly or of a consultative council. Many other pressing problems and tasks were given higher priority on the political agenda.

26 Kingué, Michel Doo. 1989. 'Report of the Chairman'. In: The Future Role of the United Nations in an Inter-dependent World. Papers of the International Roundtable in Moscow, 5-9 September 1988, sponsored by the USSR Association for the UN and UNITAR, ed. by John P. Renninger, 257–265. Dordrecht: Martinus Nijhoff, p. 264.
27 Citation from Gorbachev, Mikhail. 2006. The Road We Traveled. The Challenges We Face. Ed. by Izdatelstvo Ves Mir. Moscow: Gorbachev Foundation, p. 44.

7.
The end of the Cold War:
the democratization wave and
the revitalization of the debate

The democratization wave

The political turnaround in the Soviet Union, and the accompanying end to bloc confrontation, led to a worldwide wave of democratization. At the beginning of 1989, free elections to the Congress of People's Deputies took place for the first time in the Soviet Union. In Eastern Europe and elsewhere, the yoke of autocratic regimes and their feared security apparatuses was thrown off after decades of oppression. The inhuman apartheid regime in South Africa was peacefully overcome by negotiation, and Nelson Mandela (1918 to 2013) was freed after 27 years in prison. From 1991 onwards, according to the data of the Polity research programme, for the first time since 1930 there were more democracies than autocracies in the world again. Although the process of decolonization had led to a rise in the number of states recognized as independent, from 60 to 120 in the period between 1955 and 1965 alone (and 158 by 1991), and although this brought about an end to heteronomy in the form of colonial rule, self-government in the sense of democratic rule by the people failed to establish itself - at least not durably - in most of these countries. Nevertheless, between 1987 and 1992 the proportion of autocratic regimes in the world halved. Democracy and peoples' right to self-determination seemed to be prevailing at last. The American philosopher Francis Fukuyama announced in 1989 in a widely-read essay, followed shortly by a book with the same title of 'The End of History' that the 'end point of mankind's ideological evolution and the universalization of Western liberal democracy as the final form of human government' had come.[1] An extraordinary summit meeting of the non-aligned Conference on Security and Cooperation in Europe (CSCE), which had been meeting since 1973, declared in the 'Charter of Paris' of 21 November 1990 that the division of Europe was over. The 32 signatory countries pledged, among

---

1 Fukuyama, Francis. Summer 1989. 'The End of History?' The National Interest: 3–18.

other things, 'to build, consolidate and strengthen democracy as the only system of government of our nations'. To mark the beginning of Operation Desert Storm for the liberation of Kuwait from occupation by the Iraqi troops who had invaded five months earlier, on 16 January 1991 US President George Bush welcomed 'the opportunity to forge for ourselves and for future generations a new world order—a world where the rule of law, not the law of the jungle, governs the conduct of nations'.[2]

The revitalization of the debate

On the initiative of Brandt, who had invited the members of his North-South Commission and those of the Commission on Disarmament and Security, the World Commission on Environment and Development and the International South Commission to a joint meeting, and with the support of the Swedish Prime Minister Ingvar Carlsson (b. 1934), the Stockholm Initiative on Global Security and Governance was formed. A year later it published a memorandum. 'We need a new world order, based on justice and peace, democracy and development, human rights and international law', it read. The optimism of the period is reflected in the ambitious proposal to convene 'a World Summit on Global Governance ... similar to the meetings in San Francisco and at Bretton Woods in the 1940s' at which the United Nations and the international financial institutions were established.[3] Brandt, Brundtland and Nyerere then asked Carlsson and the Guyanese Shridath Ramphal (b. 1928), who had been Secretary General of the Commonwealth from 1975 to 1990, to instigate a 'Commission on Global Governance' to develop its own set of proposals.

Meanwhile, motivated especially by Gorbachev's statements regarding a meeting of NGOs and a 'world consultative council', participants in the IN-FUSA network organized three conferences on the democratization of the UN in the years 1990 to 1992, the so-called Conferences on a More Democratic United Nations, CAMDUN. The first of these, in New York, was the most important. It was documented and edited commendably by the nuclear physicist Frank Barnaby (b. 1927), Director of the Stockholm International Peace Research Institute SIPRI from 1971 to 1981.[4] Around one hundred expert participants, including Stassen, Hudson and Newcombe, debated the proposals for a

---

2   Bush, George. 16 January 1991. 'Speech Announcing Commencement of Operation Desert Storm'.
3   Stockholm Initiative. 1991. Gemeinsame Verantwortung in den 90er Jahren. Die Stockholmer Initiative zu globaler Sicherheit und Verantwortung / Common Responsibility in the 1990's. The Stockholm Initiative on Global Security and Governance. Ed. by Stiftung Entwicklung und Frieden. Bonn, pp. 13, 70.
4   Barnaby, Frank (ed.). 1991. Building a More Democratic United Nations. Proceedings of the First International Conference On A More Democratic UN. London/Portland: Frank Cass.

'second chamber' and a parliamentary assembly in the UN in great detail, and also addressed other topics such as reform and strengthening of the General Assembly, the possibility of worldwide referenda and the role of NGOs in the UN system in general.

A UN parliamentary assembly as a strategic concept

The various proposals for a 'second chamber', a citizens' chamber, a world parliament and other models – as also debated within CAMDUN – 'circulated like flies around the margins of the world federalist movement', wrote the Canadian Dieter Heinrich (b. 1954), then head of the political committee of the WFM.[5] The WFM, whose President from 1991 was the actor Peter Ustinov (1921 to 2004), eventually developed a strategy set out by Heinrich in the 1992 pamphlet 'The Case for a United Nations Parliamentary Assembly'. The chances of successfully establishing a directly elected world parliament from a standing start were regarded as very slim. Such a world parliament, capable of creating world law, should therefore remain the ultimate goal, but it should now be pursued in stages, in a long-term evolutionary development. The European Parliament provided the inspiration, having evolved over decades in the course of European integration from a purely advisory assembly of national parliamentarians into a directly elected legislature. The first stage within the UN would therefore be an advisory assembly comprised of national delegates, a 'United Nations Parliamentary Assembly', UNPA. Sohn had already argued for such a body in 1949, but had been unable to arouse much enthusiasm. Now, however, it would no longer be seen as the ultimate destination, but rather as the starting point on the road to that destination. 'What shifted for me', wrote Heinrich, 'was seeing a possible parliamentary body not as a final tree but as something able to be begun from a small seed with the most modest of steps. This made it achievable even in a time of low political will. Once established, it could be its own best advocate, generating its own creative force from within as it all the while drove the process of UN reform itself.'[6]

The prospect that the proposal for a UNPA would fall on fertile ground now looked good. In comparison to a world parliament, the proposal was not overly ambitious. The European Parliament in its early phase and the Parliamentary Assembly of the Council of Europe served as reference points. Moreover, in the 'Charter of Paris', the heads of state and government of Europe, Canada, the

5   Heinrich, Dieter. 2010. The Case for a United Nations Parliamentary Assembly. Extended reprint, originally published 1992. Berlin: Committee for a Democratic UN, p. 42.
6   Ibid.

USA and the Soviet Union had spoken out in support of the establishment of a parliamentary assembly at the CSCE. No doubt this was due to the fact that, on the initiative of the IPU, the CSCE process had been accompanied at the inter-parliamentary level from the beginning. Between 1973 and 1991, seven CSCE parliamentarians' conferences took place independent of the government con-ferences, contributing to the thaw between East and West. The interest shown by the governments and the UN in the IPU altogether increased dramatically after the very first of these conferences in January 1973, according to Kissling.[7] The long slumber into which the IPU had fallen as a result of being perceived as just one more NGO among many was now coming to an end. And in July 1992 in Budapest, the first meeting took place of the new CSCE parliamentary assembly, with delegates from all the countries of the northern hemisphere from Vancouver to Vladivostok, among them four of the five permanent mem-bers of the UN Security Council (i.e. all of them apart from China). The parlia-mentary assembly became a formal organ of what from 1995 was re-badged as the Organization (formerly Conference) for Security and Co-operation in Eu-rope. If a parliamentary assembly made sense as a structural element of the OSCE (or the CSCE), asked Heinrich, then why not of the United Nations? The Cold War was over. Democracy was on the march. In the past, Heinrich argued, the idea of a world parliament had foundered on the existence of so many countries with undemocratic governments. As was seen earlier, Pecqueur had identified this problem as early as 1842. But Heinrich argued that countries with credible parliaments were now increasingly forming the majority. It would therefore be 'a terrible and unjustifiable surrender to these dictatorships if they were allowed to stand as an obstacle to the formation of a UN parliamentary body'.[8]

Support for a world parliament and a UNPA

A committee of the Liberal International (the worldwide federation of liberal parties) led by the then Finnish foreign minister Paavo Vayrynen (b. 1946) seemed to be thinking along the same lines and expressed its support for the long-term goal of a directly-elected world parliament in a report on the federa-tion's ideas for strengthening the UN. This would introduce a 'democratic in-gredient' into the UN. In December 1992, this report was presented to UN Sec-retary-General Boutros Boutros-Ghali (1922 to 2016), who had then been in

7   See Kissling, Claudia. 2006. Die Interparlamentarische Union im Wandel. Frankfurt: Peter Lang, pp. 219, 289ff., 341ff.
8   Heinrich, loc. cit., p. 15.

office for only a year, by the LI President and Chair of the German FDP party Otto Graf Lambsdorff (1926 to 2009). [9]

In Heinrich's analysis, the WFM had published for the first time a detailed description of the concept of a UNPA. The basic approach taken remains relevant today, as do many of the arguments put forward. It will therefore be examined in more detail later on rather than here, in the historical exposition section of the book. The work done by Heinrich and the WFM certainly had some impact. A report from the Standing Committee on External Affairs and International Trade of the Canadian House of Commons, chaired by John Bosley (b. 1947), recommended in the spring of 1993, citing Heinrich's text, 'that Canada support the development of a United Nations Parliamentary Assembly (21) and … offer to host the preparatory meeting of the Assembly in the Parliament Buildings as the centrepiece in [its] celebration of the 50th anniversary of the United Nations in 1995'. [10] In addition, the Committee commissioned the PGA in New York (to which 900 deputies from all over the world now belonged) to carry out a study on the establishment of a UNPA. The study was led by the PGA Secretary-General Kennedy Graham (b. 1946), originally from New Zealand. The report, which appeared in September, concluded that existing international parliamentary institutions, and especially the IPU, were not sufficient 'for the purpose of parliamentary deliberation of UN issues'. [11] Almost all of the PGA members surveyed for the report were in favour of the establishment of a UNPA. However, October 1993 brought a change of government in Canada, and the report was not followed up directly either by the Canadian Parliament or by the PGA.

In February 1994, the European Parliament declared in a resolution on reform of the UN that the possibility of establishing a parliamentary advisory assembly at the UN should be given serious consideration. This was the first time that any parliament had expressed support for the idea. In May, the InterAction Council, an association of former heads of state and government founded in 1983, carried out a consultation on the future of 'global multilateral organizations'. In the report, written under the joint leadership of Andries van Agt (b. 1931) from the Netherlands, Olusegun Obasanjo (b. 1937) from Nigeria and Ola Ullsten (b. 1931) from Sweden, it was stated that 'the feasibility of a parliamentary chamber or assembly complementing the present intergovernmental

9   Liberal International. 1992. Strengthening of the United Nations. Report produced by a Committee headed by Paavo Vayrynen, Foreign Minister of Finland, pp. 11f.
10 House of Commons. 1993. Canada's role in the United Nations. 8th Report of the Standing Committee on External Affairs and International Trade. Parliament of Canada. Penultimate paragraph.
11 Parliamentarians for Global Action (ed.). 1993. 'A United Nations Parliamentary Assembly - Analysis and Parliamentarian Opinion. A Briefing Paper Prepared for the Standing Committee on External Affairs and Trade of the Canadian House of Commons'.

structure should be seriously explored, as it might enhance the political legitimacy of the organizations and strengthen accountability of organizations and
governments'.[12] In an extended study with the title 'The Capacity to Govern',
which was accepted as a Report by the Club of Rome, the Israeli political scientist Yehezkel Dror (b. 1928) suggested that a 'global advisory assembly, composed of from one to six representatives of each country, either directly elected
or elected from the parliaments', should be formed. By this means not only 'the
direct links between the citizens and the coming world government' but also
'an identification of each individual with the whole of humanity' could be furthered.[13] This last point had also been a substantial consideration for Heinrich.

The establishment of a UNPA was then investigated and urgently recommended by Erskine Childers (1929 to 1996) and Brian Urquhart (b. 1919) in
their widely-discussed study 'Renewing the United Nations System'. They cited
Heinrich's study, among others, and also referred to the recent proposals from
Canada and the European Parliament. They came out in favour of a directly
elected UNPA and emphasized that the proposal did not constitute a 'supranational government'. Both had expert inside knowledge of the UN system, which
meant that their initiative could not simply be dismissed. Urquhart had been
working on the development of the UN since 1945, and had been one of the
advisers to UN Secretary General Dag Hammarskjöld (1905 to 1961). Childers,
too, had worked for 22 years in various capacities at the UN. Another who was
convinced by Heinrich's arguments was the Belgian-born Robert Muller (1923
to 2010). From July 1994 onwards he spoke out frequently in support. Muller
had served the UN for 38 years before settling in Costa Rica in retirement and
taking on the role of honorary Chancellor of the UN's University for Peace. The
establishment of a UNPA was one of numerous reform proposals set out in a
dialogue (published as a paperback) between Muller and the Canadian Douglas
Roche (b. 1929), a long-serving parliamentarian, founding President of the
PGA and Chair of the UN commission on disarmament.[14]

A radical restructuring of the world organization was discussed at an expert
panel meeting organized by the Graduate Institute of International and Development Studies in Geneva in the spring of 1995. The starting point was a draft
constitution, drawn up by Bertrand, for a 'world security organization' to replace the UN. The issue of a parliamentary body was also debated. Bertrand's

12 InterAction Council. 1994. Report on the Conclusions and Recommendations of a High-level Expert Group
    on 'The Future Role of the Global Multilateral Organisations'. Chair: Andries van Agt. The Hague, para. 16.
13 Dror, Yehezkel. 1995. Ist die Erde noch regierbar? Ein Bericht an den Club of Rome. Transl. by Hans-Jürgen
    Baron von Koskull. 1st ed. C. Bertelsmann, pp. 271f.
14 Muller, Robert, and Douglas Roche. 1995. Safe Passage into the Twenty-First Century. New York: Contin-
    uum, p. 119.

draft included a directly elected world parliament as one of eight proposed main bodies; it would comprise a maximum of 800 delegates, with seats allocated on the basis of population and GDP of the member states. In the context of the existing system, it was argued, democratic popular representation – for example, by means of an advisory UNPA on the basis of Article 22 – would be of very little practical significance. The key issue was that of competences, and this could only be satisfactorily resolved in the framework of a fundamental transformation of the procedures and structures of the UN. Not until such a transformation was on the agenda would the time be right for it.[15]

The report by the Commission on Global Governance

The Commission on Global Governance under the joint chairmanship of Carlsson and Ramphal published its report – entitled 'Our Global Neighborhood', and, following three years' work, extending to several hundred pages - on the fiftieth anniversary of the founding of the UN. The optimism of 1990 was gone, it found. The United Nations and the members of the Security Council had proved incapable of effectively countering extreme abuses of human rights and genocide, in Bosnia from 1992 and in Rwanda between April and July 1994. The UN-mandated US-led 'Operation Restore Hope' in Somalia had been a disaster. The UN and international law were not up to the challenges they faced. '[T]here is deepening disquiet over the actions--and in some cases the inaction--of governments and of the United Nations', wrote the Commission in its report.[16] US President Bush's proclamation of a 'new world order' had proved an empty slogan, masking what was essentially a continuation of US American great power politics in the new global political conditions. 'It is remarkable how quickly the idealistic formulations of the "transition period" from 1989-1991 were replaced by the classical terminology of power politics once America's position as the sole superpower had gradually become clear and then been consolidated', was the analysis of the Innsbruck philosopher Hans Köchler, co-organizer of the second CAMDUN conference.[17] Unlike after the two World Wars, when the United States took the lead in establishing the League of Nations and the United Nations, now the USA was making no effort at a fundamental restructuring of international relations by means of a reform and strengthening of the world organization. Köchler argued that a new world order as a radical alternative to

---

15 Bertrand, Maurice, and Daniel Warner (ed.). 1997. A New Charter for a Worldwide Organisation? Nijhoff Law Specials 22. The Hague et al.: Kluwer Law International, p. 25. See also p. 217.
16 Commission on Global Governance. 1995. Our Global Neighborhood. Oxford University Press, p. 2.
17 Köchler, Hans. 1998. Neue Wege der Demokratie. Demokratie im globalen Spannungsfeld von Machtpolitik and Rechtsstaatlichkeit. Wien: Springer-Verlag, p. 38.

a simple shift in the power relations between the states required the application of democracy to transnational relations. 'Anyone pressing for a new world order', continued Köchler, 'would have to begin with an amendment to the UN Charter to remove the voting privileges of the permanent members and to institute a second chamber of deputies.'[18]

Alongside other recommendations too numerous to go into here, the Commission on Global Governance recommended exactly that. The drive for reform should find its culmination in a review conference as proposed in Article 109 of the UN Charter. 'Our recommendation is that the General Assembly should agree to hold a World Conference on Governance in 1998, with its decisions to be ratified and put into effect by 2000.' The right of veto in the Security Council should be gradually abolished. Proposals for a UN parliamentary body should also be discussed further. 'When the time comes, we believe that starting with an assembly of parliamentarians as a constituent assembly for a more popular body is the right approach. But care would need to be taken to ensure that the assembly of parliamentarians is the starting point of a journey and does not become the terminal station.' It must not become a substitute for a revitalization of the General Assembly, and a start could be made in the meantime by means of an 'annual Forum of Civil Society'.[19] This approach reveals a fundamental problem with the Commission. 'Its proposals and orientation are too reformist, humanist and populist', Falk comments, 'to be acceptable either to leading states or to the new elites of globalization.' At the same time, however, they were not radical enough to enthuse or even to satisfy civil society.[20] At any event, for world federalists the report was a disappointment. Its categorical rejection of the idea of world government, without even having considered the extensive relevant literature, was downright insulting according to one response - from the economist James A. Yunker, in the foreword to a collection of essays on the topic.[21] For the Commission dismissed the idea in its report with the short and simple remark that global governance did not imply 'world government or world federalism'.[22]

18   Ibid., p. 54.
19   Commission on Global Governance, loc. cit., pp. 258, 351f.
20   Falk, Richard. 1995. 'Liberalism at the Global Level: The Last of the Independent Commissions?' Millennium - Journal of International Studies 24 (3): 563–576, p. 574.
21   Harris, Errol E., and James A. Yunker (ed.). 1999. Toward Genuine Global Governance. Critical Reactions to 'Our Global Neighborhood'. Praeger Publishers, p. ix.
22   Commission on Global Governance, loc. cit., p. 336, see also p. xvi.

The report by the World Commission on Culture and Development

The World Commission on Culture and Development also delivered its concluding report in 1995. It had started its work three years earlier following resolutions by the UNESCO General Conference and the UN General Assembly. It was chaired by the Peruvian Javier Pérez de Cuéllar (b. 1920), who from 1982 to 1991 had been Secretary-General of the UN. International democracy featured prominently in the report. Democracy, it declared, was 'an indispensable principle of a global ethics' and must be universally implemented – in global governance and in the United Nations, too. [23] An international system based solely on relations between governments was no longer adequate for the 21st century. 'The global community should start with a fresh vision that inspires many new generations in the twenty-first century. One bold step could be a General Assembly directly elected by the people of all nations, learning some lessons from the experience of the European Parliament.' The United Nations and all institutions of global governance must become focused on the citizens. The whole range of diverse cultures, and especially marginalized groups, minorities and indigenous peoples, must be given a voice in the international forums. Since a directly elected popular assembly remained only an aspiration at this time, the establishment of a UN world forum of NGOs accredited by the UN seemed a sensible first step in the right direction. [24] In this respect the positions taken by the Commission on Culture and Development and the Commission on Global Governance were very similar. But the issue was given much higher priority in the report of the Commission on Culture and Development: two of the ten concluding recommendations related to this issue.

23 United Nations Educational, Scientific and Cultural Organization. 1995. Our Creative Diversity. Report of the World Commission on Culture and Development, pp. 38, 284ff.
24 Ibid., p. 286.

8.
Democracy in the era of globalization

Globalization and the nation state

The question of whether, or to what degree, increasing international interdependence was taking the traditional nation states beyond the control of politics became an important topic of public debate from at least the middle of the 1990s onwards. The idea that the existing forms of government were incapable of meeting the challenges posed by contemporary global change and therefore had to be transformed was the starting point, for example, of the report by Dror to the Club of Rome cited above. Globalization was undermining 'the effectiveness of territorially-defined democratic control mechanisms', agreed the political scientist Karl Kaiser, Director of the German Council on Foreign Relations.[1] The worldwide bestseller 'The Global Trap: Civilization and the Assault on Democracy and Prosperity' by the *Spiegel* journalists Harald Schumann and Hans-Peter Martin perhaps best expressed the popular perception that governments were increasingly being driven by the inescapable hard realities of international politics and that the democratic state was losing its legitimation. At the national convention of German historians in Munich, Federal President Roman Herzog declared that the nation state 'and the conception of sovereignty associated with it' had outlived its day.[2] The future lay in European integration – a conclusion shared by Schumann and Martin. The influential Egyptian intellectual Samir Amin, writing from a global perspective, said in 1992 that there was 'no solution' to the problems raised by the decoupling of the world economy from the nation states because 'no supranational state is visible on the horizon'.[3] The 'chaos which defines the present situation', according to Amin, was in part a result of the fact that 'new forms of political and social organization transgressing the nation-state' had not been developed. Since then, the idea of a world parliament has surfaced in his writings on several occasions, even if only as a

1   Kaiser, Karl. 1998. 'Globalisierung als Problem der Demokratie'. Internationale Politik (4): 4–11, p. 4.
2   Herzog, Roman. 1996. Speech at the 41st Historikertag in Munich. 17 September.
3   Amin, Samir. 1992. The Empire of Chaos. Transl. by W.H. Locke Anderson. New York: Monthly Review Press, pp. 10f.

catchphrase. 'In many ways, the creation of such a "world parliament" would go beyond the present concept of inter-state institutions.'[4]

As UN Secretary-General, Boutros-Ghali took up some bold positions. For example, he said in a statement of January 1996 that the democratization of international relations was a fundamental requirement in today's world. He understood this to mean the opening up of the UN to new global actors like NGOs, national parliaments and private companies, but also to 'each and every man and woman who feels he or she is a full member of the big human family'. This not only applied to the UN but meant 'the democratization of all places where authority is exercised at the world level'.[5] Boutros-Ghali became the first UN Secretary-General to be denied a second term of office. The USA was the only government against a renewal, and used its veto. In December 1996, in the last week before the expiry of his term of office, and without an explicit mandate to do so, Boutros-Ghali arranged for a report he had written on national and international democratization to be distributed to the members of the UN General Assembly. In it he stressed how, on account of globalization, a growing number of decisions now had to be taken at international level, and how this was hollowing out national democracy. 'Democracy within the State will diminish in importance if the process of democratization does not move forward at the international level', declared Boutros-Ghali.[6] The following year, in the journal *Le Monde Diplomatique*, the French journalist Ignacio Ramonet wrote in an article echoed by many others that the globalization of financial capital 'makes a mockery of national boundaries and diminishes the power of states to uphold democracy and guarantee the wealth and prosperity of their peoples'. The financial markets had long since 'established a separate supranational state with its own administrative apparatus, its own spheres of influence, its own means of action'. This world state was a power with no base in society. 'It is answerable instead to the financial markets and the mammoth business undertakings that are its masters. The result is that the real states in the real world are becoming societies with no power base.' He advocated a Tobin tax on financial transactions and the power to tax unearned income, which was 'a sine qua non of democracy'.[7] Ramonet's specific call for the creation of an NGO entitled 'Attac' (an abbreviation for 'Action pour une taxe Tobin d'aide aux citoyens') to

4   Id. 1993. 'The Future of Global Polarization'. Africa Today 40, no. 4: 75–86, pp. 76, 80.
5   United Nations, 1996. 'Secretary-General says democratization of international relations fundamental requirement for today's world'. Press Release SG/SM/5883.
6   Boutros-Ghali, Boutros. 1996. Supplement to reports on democratization. Report to the 51st Session of the United Nations General Assembly, pp. 19f.
7   Ramonet, Ignacio. 12 December 1997. 'Disarming the markets', Le Monde Diplomatique.

pursue on a broad base the establishment of an international tax on currency transactions was followed up in a number of countries.

The theory of 'cosmopolitan democracy'

In the search for a fundamental answer to these problems, work had been going on already for some time on the theory of 'cosmopolitan democracy', which was also explicitly intended to investigate the possibility of a middle way between the confederal and federal models for an international order. 'The attainment of democracy at the international level requires us to steer between the Scylla of a mass of independent autonomous states and the Charybdis of a planetary Leviathan. To achieve this goal, a new concept of world citizenship must be formulated', wrote the Italian academic Daniele Archibugi (b. 1958) in 1993. A worldwide body representing the interests of individuals as citizens of the world would be a significant step towards overcoming the confederal structure of the global system, Archibugi argued, and in contemplating such an assembly he built on the work of Segall and the CAMDUN conferences.[8] Traditionally, theories of democracy had started from the assumption that there was a direct connection, forged principally through elections, between political decision makers and the people affected by their decisions. 'But the problem is', wrote the British political scientist David Held (b. 1951) in 1992, 'that regional and global interconnectedness contests the traditional national resolutions of the key questions of democratic theory and practice.'[9] Political decisions increasingly affected people across borders who had no power to influence those decisions. He cited as examples the setting of interest rates by a central bank and the economic effects this has on other countries, and the decision to build a nuclear power station near a border with another country.

In an essay from 1992, the philosopher Thomas Pogge (b. 1953), who has also concerned himself with cosmopolitanism, argued along similar lines. Sovereignty, anchored in the nation state, has to be divided vertically between several political decision-making levels through decentralization and centralization. The justification for this is in part democratic. '[P]ersons have a right to an institutional order under which those significantly and legitimately affected by a politi-

---

8   Archibugi, Daniele. 1993. 'The Reform of the UN and Cosmopolitan Democracy: A Critical Review'. Journal of Peace Research 30 (3): 301–315, p. 306, 307ff. His overall discussion of cosmopolitan democracy is included in Archibugi, Daniele. 2008. The Global Commonwealth of Citizens. Princeton University Press.

9   Held, David. 1992. 'Democracy: From City-states to a Cosmopolitan Order?' Political Studies 40 (Special Issue): 10–39, p. 31.

cal decision have a roughly equal opportunity to influence the making of this decision – directly or through elected delegates or representatives.'[10] Growing global
interdependence also requires a 'democratic centralization of decision making'.[11]

The sociologist Ulrich Beck (1944 to 2015) pointed out the transnational
character of the risks associated with modernity in 1986 already in his widely
admired book on the evolution of the 'risk society'. These risks went together
with the industrial system of production and – like the international intertwining of markets and capital – exceeded the reach and powers of the nation state.
They had an immanent tendency towards globalization'.[12] A dramatic historical
event that seemed to confirm this finding was the meltdown and explosion in
the nuclear power plant at Chernobyl, shortly after the book's publication,
which led to a massive release of radioactive material into the atmosphere. The
contamination fallout spread across Europe and ultimately across the entire
northern hemisphere. With the coining of the term 'second modernity', Beck
later sought to identify the characteristics of an epochal change driven in part
by processes of globalization. The institutions established in the course of modernization, above all that of industrial society organized in nation states, were
being dissolved and supplanted by a second modernity.[13] A core challenge for
theory and praxis in all of this was the change of perspective from 'nation state
centrism' to cosmopolitanism. On the occasion of the 150th anniversary of the
1848 revolution, Beck said that what had been going on then, in the Paulskirche
in Frankfurt, was 'the transformation of the religiously-based feudal order into
the nation state democracy'. 'Today', he continued, 'what is going on is the transition from the nation state democracy to the transnational, indeed the cosmopolitan democracy. This entails fundamental institutional innovations, indeed
a detailed working out of the principles of democracy for a world which has
become a danger to itself.'[14]

In his 1995 book 'Democracy and the Global Order', now a standard in the
field, Held explained that the democratic setting of regulatory standards has to
be internationalized in order to remain effective: 'the implementation of a cosmopolitan democratic law and the establishment of a cosmopolitan community

---

10 Pogge, Thomas. 1992. 'Cosmopolitanism and Sovereignty'. Ethics 103 (1) (October): 48–75, pp. 63f.
11 Ibid., p. 66.
12 Beck, Ulrich. 1986. Risikogesellschaft. Auf dem Weg in eine andere Moderne. Frankfurt: Suhrkamp, pp. 48, 310.
13 Id. 1996. 'Das Zeitalter der Nebenfolgen und die Politisierung der Moderne'. In: Reflexive Modernisierung,
ed. by Ulrich Beck, Anthony Giddens, and Scott Lash, 19–112. Frankfurt am Main: Suhrkamp, p. 27. See also
the same, 1994. Reflexive Modernization. Polity Press.
14 Beck, Ulrich. 1999. 'Wie wird Demokratie im Zeitalter der Globalisierung möglich?' (Speech at Paulskirche,
05 May 1998. In: Ende des Staates - Anfang der Bürgergesellschaft. Über die Zukunft der sozialen Demokratie in Zeiten der Globalisierung, ed. by Hans Eichel and Hilmar Hoffmann. Reinbek: Rowohlt, pp. 41f.

... must become an obligation for democrats, an obligation to build a transnational, common structure of political action which alone, ultimately, can support the politics of self-determination.'[15] The cosmopolitan model seeks 'the
creation of an effective transnational legislative and executive, at regional and
global levels, bound by and operating within the terms of the basic democratic
law.' Transnational referenda should be enabled. Regional parliaments should
be created, for example for Africa and Latin America, and should take part in
the setting of regulatory standards. The functional organizations of the international system should be democratized, which could 'perhaps' be done on the
basis of 'elected supervisory boards'. 'But the full implementation of cosmopolitan democracy would also require the formation of an authoritative assembly of
all the democratic states and agencies – a reformed General Assembly of the
United Nations, or a complement to it', Held wrote. As a long-term goal he identified among other things a global parliament with limited taxation powers.[16]

The question of a world parliament was then also taken up by Jürgen Habermas (b. 1929). The key feature of the right of world citizenship sketched by
Kant, he argued, was that it transcended the nation states as subjects of international law and directly endowed the individual legal subject with 'unmediated
membership in the association of free and equal world citizens'. A contemporary reformulation of Kant's idea that cosmopolitanism could pacify the warlike
'state of nature' between the states, Habermas argued in an essay of 1995, 'would
inspire on the one side energetic efforts for the reform of the United Nations,
and more generally for the further development of supranational capacity for
action in the various regions of the world.'[17] Referring to Archibugi, Habermas
wrote that proposals for reform of the UN focused on three points: the establishment of a world parliament, the further development of a world justice system, and the reorganization of the Security Council. If the UN is to cast off its
status as a 'permanent congress of states', then the General Assembly will need
to be transformed into a kind of federal senate and to share its powers with a
second chamber. 'In this parliament', according to Habermas, 'people would
not be represented by their governments but by elected representatives, as the
sum of the citizens of the world.' States that did not allow democratic elections
should be represented by 'non-state organizations appointed by the world parliament itself as representatives of the oppressed population'.[18]

---

15   Held, David. 1995. Democracy and the Global Order. 1st ed. Cambridge: Polity Press, p. 232.
16   Ibid., pp. 272ff.
17   Habermas, Jürgen. 1999. Die Einbeziehung des Anderen: Studien zur politischen Theorie. 1st ed. Frankfurt
     am Main: Suhrkamp, pp. 192-236, pp. 210, 217f.
18   Ibid., p. 218.

The Falk and Strauss essays

In September 1997, Ted Turner (b. 1938), the US American media entrepreneur and founder of the news channel CNN, announced that he would donate 100 million US dollars each year for the next ten years in support of UN activities. This prompted the first in a series (which still continues today) of joint articles advocating the establishment of a global parliament written by Falk together with Andrew Strauss (b. 1958), an international law specialist based at the private Widener University near Philadelphia in the US state of Pennsylvania.[19] In the first of these contributions, which appeared in the *International Herald Tribune*, they wrote that it was only due to globalization that philanthropists like Turner and George Soros (b. 1930) had been able to amass such extraordinary wealth in the first place. Soros is a US American investor of Hungarian extraction who came to international attention in 1992 when he speculated against the British currency and thereby allegedly amassed a billion pounds (the pound crisis cost the British taxpayer 3.3 billion).[20] Soros had been engaged, via his own foundations, in the promotion of an open society in the sense defined by the philosopher Karl Popper (1902 to 1994) since 1984. His Open Society Institute is now active in over 50 countries. In any event, Falk and Strauss suggested that billionaires like Turner and Soros should promote a democratization of the global order and should directly provide money for the creation of a global peoples' assembly elected by universal direct vote, since the governments were reluctant to take this on themselves. The citizens of the world would then have, for the first time, 'a forum to express their planetary aspirations and grievances outside the traditional nation-state context'.[21]

Falk and Strauss proposed a new option for bringing about such an assembly. They suggested that the elections to the global citizens' parliament should be organized independently by worldwide civil society through the agency of an international committee of citizens created for the purpose. This assembly would have only the legal status of an NGO to begin with, but on account of the election process it could claim to speak in the name of the global population and would therefore have considerable moral legitimacy. Formal recognition of this body by governments and the United Nations would then follow sooner or later. It would acquire its own socio-political momentum, leading to an ever

---

19 Collected in the following volume: Falk, Richard, and Andrew Strauss. 2011. A Global Parliament: Essays and Articles. Berlin: Committee for a Democratic UN.

20 Tempest, Matthew. 9 February 2005. 'Treasury papers reveal cost of Black Wednesday'. Guardian (www.guardian.co.uk).

21 Strauss, Andrew, and Richard Falk. 1997. 'For a Global Peoples' Assembly'. International Herald Tribune, November 14. Reprinted in: Falk/Strauss, loc. cit., pp. 177f.

more significant role for it in world politics. It is not clear whether Turner or Soros ever became aware of this proposal, but the latter certainly concerned himself seriously with the problems of globalization in his book 'The Crisis of Global Capitalism', and he concluded that the global capital system was on the brink of collapse. The evolution of a global economy had not been accompanied by the evolution of a global society; the necessary regulatory and political frame-work was lacking. Although it was therefore possible to speak of a global regime for economics and finance, there was no such global regime for politics. Money and credit were intimately bound up with issues of sovereignty, which no coun-try was willing to sacrifice. [22] Yet international law was based on a presumption of the voluntary self-limitation of state sovereignty. A permanent solution, he later wrote, was dependent on a single worldwide currency and a world central bank. But to call for these things was unrealistic.[23]

A community of the democracies?

Soros wanted the democratic countries in the United Nations to join together in an alliance which he hoped would constitute a majority and be able to take over the leadership of the world organization. Thus the UN could be reformed and conduct its business by majority vote. The General Assembly should be-come 'more like a legislature in charge of making laws for our global society'. At the moment it was no more than a talking shop. Any laws would have valid-ity only in those countries which ratified them, so they would not be directly binding. However, the members of this 'open society coalition', as Soros called it, would be free to commit themselves to the automatic adoption of these laws, subject to their being adopted by a specified majority. As a potential model, Soros pointed to Hudson's 'binding triad', which, as mentioned previously, en-tails three conditions: two thirds of the countries, two thirds of the population and two-thirds of the UN budget. Coalition member states that did not accept decisions passed under these conditions would have to leave the alliance. 'In that way', said Soros, 'a body of international law could be developed without infringing on the principle of national sovereignty. The General Assembly could decide what laws are needed and how to enforce them.'[24] An open world society, he argued, could not be created by individuals or by independent citi-zens' organizations; it required cooperation between the states.

22 Soros, George. 1998. The Crisis of Global Capitalism. New York: PublicAffairs, pp. 103, 109, 120.
23 Id. 2005. George Soros on Globalization. New ed. New York: PublicAffairs, p. 130.
24 Soros (1998), loc. cit., p. 287.

Soros was by no means a lone figure in advocating closer cooperation between the democratic countries within the UN. For example, considerable interest was attracted by the book 'Pax Democratica', published by the former US diplomat James R. Huntley in 1998 and firmly in the tradition of Clarence Streit. It argued in some detail for the incremental establishment of an 'intercontinental community of democracies' in which NATO, the OECD, the EU, the Council of Europe and the G7 could gradually be subsumed. This organization would not be set up in opposition to the UN; rather, using the UN delegations of the member states, it could operate within the UN structure. This was perhaps the first and the easiest step of the whole project.[25] One important organ of the community would have to be a parliamentary assembly of the democracies. At the appropriate time, this body could replace other assemblies of parliamentarians such as the NATO assembly or that of the Council of Europe. In June 2000, on the initiative of Madeleine Albright (b. 1937) and Bronisław Geremek (1932 to 2008), at that time foreign ministers of the USA and Poland respectively, a community of democracies was indeed established as an inter-state organization in Warsaw, and in 2010 an associated forum of parliamentarians was formed. However, the community is active only in promoting democracy, and has no brief with respect to integration. Dieter Heinrich has argued that world federalists should seek to strengthen this community, with the goal of supra-national integration in mind. 'Instead of taking a universal organization, the UN, and trying to democratize it, we can now also propose a democratic organization which can be universalized.'[26] The debate around a 'league of democracies' reached a highpoint when the Republican US Presidential candidate John McCain lent his support to this proposal and announced that within a year of taking office he would convene a summit of the democracies to explore practical steps towards this goal. This league was not intended to supplant the UN, but 'could act where the UN fails to act'.[27]

Höffe's federal world republic

Another important contribution to the debate about a world state was made by Otfried Höffe (b. 1943), professor of philosophy at Tübingen, with his 1999 book 'Demokratie im Zeitalter der Globalisierung' (democracy in the age of

25 Huntley, James Robert. 1998. Pax Democratica: A Strategy for the 21st Century. New York: St. Martin's Press. See in particular pp. 109, 153.
26 Heinrich, Dieter. June 2006. 'Uniting the democracies: Let's imagine'. Ed. by World Federalists of Canada. Mondial, 8–9, p. 9.
27 McCain, John. 1 May 2007. 'Address at the Hoover Institution'. Council on Foreign Relations (www.cfr.org).

globalization). In this, as in numerous newspaper articles, he argued for an incremental development towards the ideal of a federal world republic based on subsidiarity and with a 'graduated cosmopolitanism'. Höffe basically followed the theory of the 'state of nature', and argued that every individual possessed a fundamental moral status which took precedence over any statehood. But this relativization applied not only to individual nation states but also and even to the world state; for that reason, the world state must not be accorded the status of an absolute, and must not be allowed to abrogate the nation states. If, and to the degree that, the nation state served the interests of the individual, and acknowledged and accepted the worldwide moral authority of the complementary world republic, then it too had moral status. It follows, according to Höffe, that a 'dual world societal contract' is required as a foundation for a world republic, a contract that encompasses both the wishes and interests of the individual states and those of the global populace. 'The world republic', wrote Höffe, 'acquires its democratic legitimacy through a combination of popular legitimation and legitimation by the states.' In order to reflect these two elements in institutional terms, the supreme body of the federal world state, the global legislature, would therefore have to consist of two chambers, a world council representing the states and a world parliament representing the citizens. While the first would be primarily responsible for issues of international law and inter-state relations, the citizens' chamber would have priority with regard to 'world society' issues. Höffe didn't only touch on the issue of a world legislature at the margin, but was in fact the first person in a long time to consider a little more thoroughly the options for its structure and procedures. He saw the question of how to include both the mini-states and the giant states as a significant area of potential difficulty, and regarded a voting system weighted by population size as being absolutely essential. He brought into the discussion the idea that other, intermediate - regional, continental or sub-continental - political entities positioned between the world republic and the existing nation states might come into play; but he concluded nevertheless that the 'primary states' should in any event be directly represented in the world legislature. He, too, supported the development of a citizens' chamber on the model of the European Parliament as a concrete proposal for reform of the UN. [28]

28 Höffe, Otfried. 2002. Demokratie im Zeitalter der Globalisierung. New ed. Munich: C.H. Beck, pp. 304f., 308ff., 333f.

The call for a WTO parliament and the role of the IPU

Meanwhile, the protests against the third ministerial conference of the World Trade Organization (WTO, founded 1995) in Seattle in late 1999 turned into the birth of the worldwide anti-globalization movement as a media phenomenon. 'No Globalization without representation' was one of the slogans used. It was not only the trade unions and other groups protesting on the streets who felt excluded and marginalized. On the initiative of the US American Senator William V. Roth (1921 to 2003), around 150 parliamentarians who were present in Seattle issued a statement calling for the establishment of a permanent committee of parliamentarians within the WTO by February 2001 in order to improve its transparency and democratic legitimacy. 'Not only have we a crucial role to play in interacting with the citizens and representative organizations of our respective countries to address their concerns', the statement ran, 'but also to approve or legislate on the agreements negotiated under the auspices of the WTO.' The call for a parliamentary assembly within the WTO was then taken up and promoted with particular energy by the European Parliament. However, the proposal quickly ran into the sand, mainly because of the requirement for unanimity at the WTO, which gives every government a veto over all decisions, even though it was supported in principle by the then WTO Director Mike Moore, a New Zealand Labour Party politician, among others.

Furthermore, the efforts of the European Parliament and others in support of a parliamentary assembly at the WTO were opposed by the IPU. Its position was that new structures were neither wanted nor needed, explained Anders Johnsson (b. 1948), the Swede who was Secretary-General of the IPU from 1998 to 2014. 'The legislative function at the WTO', argued Johnsson, 'is undertaken by government negotiators who are held to account in their national governments and parliaments. Providing a parliamentary dimension to the WTO that seeks to mirror the constitutional role that parliaments play at the national level does not make sense.'[29] Eventually, the IPU and the European Parliament agreed to hold regular joint conferences on world trade issues, the first one taking place in 2003. This compromise still remains a matter of regret within the European Parliament today. In 2008, for example, the Parliament continued to stress in a resolution 'the need to create a WTO parliamentary assembly with consultative powers, given the WTO's lack of democratic accountability and legitimacy'.[30]

29　Johnsson, Anders. 2003. 'A Parliamentary Dimension to International Cooperation'. In A Reader on Second Assembly & Parliamentary Proposals, ed. by Saul H. Mendlovitz and Barbara Walker, 20–29. Wayne, NJ: Center for UN Reform Education, p. 28.

30　European Parliament. 24 April 2008. 'Towards a reform of the World Trade Organization'. Resolution P6_TA(2008)0180.

The IPU had at least succeeded in reaching a symbolic agreement on cooperation with the UN in 1996 (it was then awarded observer status at the UN in 2002, since when it has been allowed to distribute its documents at the UN General Assembly). In its own view, the IPU should be the principal forum for all interparliamentary work. In the concluding document of the first world conference of presiding officers of national parliaments in September 2000, it was stated that the so-called 'parliamentary dimension of international cooperation' must be carried out by the IPU, albeit principally by the national parliaments and at the national level. This accords with the definition of the IPU in its Statutes as 'the international organization of the Parliaments of sovereign States'. However, the French parliamentary president Raymond Forni (1941 to 2008) went even further at this world summit. The agreement reached in 1996 could be only a first step, he said. 'The Inter-Parliamentary Union could eventually become a genuine parliamentary assembly of the United Nations, consulted by the General Assembly, the Security Council and the Economic and Social Council and able to make proposals to them.'[31] The Speaker of the Canadian Senate, Gildas Molgat (1927 to 2001), said that the IPU deserved to be recognized as a world parliament and that its status at the UN should be altered accordingly.[32] But in expressing these ideas it is clear that Forni and Molgat represented only a minority within the IPU.

Other initiatives towards a world parliament and a UNPA

The European Parliament declared in the spring of 1999, in a resolution on global governance, that 'transnational economic power … is beyond all democratic scrutiny' and that there was therefore an 'urgent need to create a more consistent institutional structure at world level that is capable of coping with the problems of globalization'. The institutions needed to become both more representative and more democratic. A parliamentary dimension could be introduced to the democratization of the UN system 'by creating parliamentary bodies composed of the chairmen of parliamentary committees of national and regional parliaments, starting e.g. with Environment and Foreign Affairs'.[33] The tenth Human Development Report of the United Nations Development Programme (UNDP), the flagship of its publications programme, also focused on

---

31 Forni, Raymond. 30 August 2000. 'Discours au Conférence des Présidents des Parlements nationaux organisée par l'Union interparlementaire du 30 août au 1er septembre 2000 au siège des Nations Unies à New York', New York.

32 Molgat, Gil. 2000. 'A Parliamentary Vision for International Co-operation'. Canadian Parl. Review 23 (4).

33 European Parliament. 23 March 1999. 'Resolution on the challenges of global governance and the reform of the United Nations'. A4-0077/1999, points T, U and 10.

globalization and its impacts. Like the European Parliament, the Report urged the development of a 'a more coherent and more democratic architecture for global governance'. It recommended 'a two-chamber General Assembly to allow for civil society representation' as one of seven key institutions needed for the 21st century. What exactly was meant by that was not set out in detail, however.[34] As has already been seen, the term 'second chamber' is not very precise and can encompass many variants, from an assembly of NGOs to a directly elected body.

On the initiative of the French politician and entrepreneur Olivier Giscard d'Estaing (b. 1927), a committee was formed in Paris in the year 2000, the 'Comité pour un parlement mondial' (COPAM). This committee was able within a short time to attract a number of prominent personalities as honorary members. They included the former heads of state or government Andreas van Agt from the Netherlands, Felipe Gonzales from Spain, Prince Hassan of Jordan, the Nobel Peace Prize winners Nelson Mandela from South Africa and Shimon Peres from Israel, Mario Soares from Portugal, Gaston Thorn from Luxembourg and from France Raymond Barre, Michel Rocard and Valéry Giscard d'Estaing, Olivier Giscard d'Estaing's brother. Other supporters included the former UN Secretaries-General Pérez de Cuéllar and Boutros-Ghali as well as Jacques Delors, former President of the European Commission, Sonia Gandhi, the Chair of the Indian Congress party, and the Nobel Prize winner for economics Amartya Sen. It proposed the establishment of an advisory body set up on the basis of a separate intergovernmental treaty and with its members initially elected by the national parliaments, though not necessarily themselves parliamentarians. Like Forni, COPAM originally thought that the IPU could form the starting point for global parliamentary assembly. COPAM therefore sought to enter into a dialogue with the IPU about this idea, but in vain. 'After several meetings', d'Estaing told us, 'our idea of transforming this institution met with a categorical rejection.'

Outside the IPU, there were other significant initiatives towards the establishment of a UNPA or world parliament. Thus, the Parliamentary Assembly of the Council of Europe declared in a resolution of September 2000 that the UN should develop, in cooperation with the IPU, a 'parliamentary dimension ... with competencies similar to that of the Parliamentary Assembly of the Council of Europe'.[35] Such a body could contribute to finding solutions to problems where inter-governmental politics had stalled. In May 2000, the Millennium

---

34 United Nations Development Programme. 1999. Human Development Report 1999. Oxford University Press, pp. 12, 111.
35 Council of Europe Parliamentary Assembly. 27 September 2000. 'The United Nations at the turn of the new century'. Recommendation 1476 (2000).

Forum, a body made up of representatives of over a thousand international civil society organizations which had come together at the UN headquarters in New York at the invitation of UN Secretary-General Kofi Annan, had already urged in its concluding declaration, among numerous other recommendations, 'that the UN should consider 'the creation of a UN parliamentary body related to the UN General Assembly'.[36]

At the United Nations Millennium Summit in New York – which, with over 150 heads of state and government participating, was the largest summit meeting in history up to that point – some of the required foundations were laid, above all the agreement of the eight so-called Millennium Development Goals for the year 2015. However, there was no notable progress on UN reform. At the conference of presiding officers of national parliaments which took place shortly beforehand, Annan had stressed the importance of integrating the parliaments into the work of the UN. 'In the age of globalization', Annan said, 'the ancient challenges of poverty and conflict can no longer be met simply by governments working together. Whole societies are affected by international relations, and are playing their part in it. They need to be represented in many different ways.' The national parliaments had a unique role to play in bringing global institutions such as the United Nations 'closer to the peoples they are meant to serve'. Seattle had shown how dangerous it can be when local people are alienated from international organizations.[37] With regard to this issue, however, the concluding declaration of the Millennium Summit contained only a formulaic call for better cooperation between the UN and the national parliaments through the intermediation of the IPU.

But the question of a world parliament was addressed at the world summit. The Czech President Václav Havel (1936 to 2011), a central figure in the Velvet Revolution of 1989, devoted his speech to this issue, which had long concerned him. He argued that the UN should develop from a community of governments and diplomats into a joint institution belonging to all the inhabitants of the planet, not only for the protection of their individual security but for the pursuit of a lasting wellbeing and genuine quality of life for all humanity. 'Such a United Nations', said Havel, 'would probably have to rest on two pillars: one constituted by an assembly of equal executive representatives of individual countries, resembling the present plenary, and the other consisting of a group elected directly by the globe's population in which the number of delegates representing

---

36 Millennium Forum. 26 May 2000. 'Declaration and Agenda for Action: Strengthening the United Nations for the 21st Century'. A/54/959 of 8 August 2000, see section F, point 6.

37 Annan, Kofi. 2000. 'Parliamentary Voices Must Be Heard If Global Democracy Is to Thrive". Address to the Conference of Presiding Officers of National Parliaments. UNIS/SG/2641.

individual nations would, thus, roughly correspond to the size of the nations.'[38] These two bodies, he explained, would create global laws, and a reformed Security Council would be accountable to them. The UN of the future would have its own military and police forces to enforce its laws and decisions. Lech Wałęsa (b. 1943), the former Polish State President and Nobel Peace Prize winner, chair of the trade union Solidarność from 1980 to 1990, later expressed similar ideas. 'Our great grandfathers invented the bicycle, and suddenly the village was too small for them', Wałęsa said for example in one newspaper interview. 'Now we have aeroplanes, and suddenly the nations are too small for us: a jet can cross them in minutes. That's why we have to think globally today. We need a global parliament, a global government, maybe a global ministry of security.'[39]

Finally, the US American humanist and philosopher Paul Kurtz (1925 to 2012) published the 'Humanist Manifesto 2000', which revolved around a worldview guided by secular and philosophical principles, in the tradition of the two humanist manifestoes of 1933 and 1973 (another was to follow in 2003). The Manifesto 2000 explored the need for, and content of, a so-called '*post*-postmodern planetary humanism'. The question of a world parliament was of crucial importance in this. More than ever before, it was argued, a world organization was needed that represented human beings and not just national states. An effective, directly elected parliament should be established for the passing of global laws, perhaps together with the existing General Assembly as a bicameral system. The details were to be worked out by a Charter revision conference, which the Manifesto called for. The document was supported by 140 prominent figures from over 30 countries. The signatories included the British author Arthur C. Clarke (1917 to 2008), who became famous through the film of his science fiction novel '2001: A Space Odyssey'; the biologist Edward O. Wilson; and the British evolutionary biologist Richard Dawkins (b. 1941), the author of the popular science books 'The God Delusion' and 'The Greatest Show on Earth'. Most of the signatories were scientists, among them ten Nobel Prize winners.[40]

---

38 Havel, Vaclav. 8 September 2000. Address of the President of the Czech Republic at the Millennium Summit of the United Nations in New York.
39 Walesa, Lech. 27 August 2005. 'Unser Sieg ist uns teuer zu stehen gekommen' Interview by Konrad Schuller. Frankfurter Allgemeine Zeitung.
40 Barju Benacerraf, Paul D. Boyer, Herbert A. Hauptmann, Harold W. Kroto, Jean-Marie Lehn, Mario Molina, Ferid Murad, José Saramago, Jens C. Skou and Jack Steinberger. A full list of signatories is printed in: Kurtz, Paul. 2000. Humanist Manifesto 2000. A Call For A New Planetary Humanism. Amherst, New York: Prometheus Books.

9.
The 'War on Terror', the role of the IPU, and the campaign for a UNPA

The ban on landmines, the International Criminal Court and the World Social Forum

The beginning of the new century saw some initially very promising developments. A new and successful means of achieving progress in international law seemed to be establishing itself, in the form of cooperation between international NGOs and sympathetic governments. The Ottawa Treaty prohibiting the use of anti-personnel mines came into force in March 1999. The International Campaign to Ban Landmines, founded in 1992 by a group of NGOs and awarded the Nobel Peace Prize in 1997, had contributed substantially to the development of the treaty. Additionally, at a historic United Nations conference in Rome in July 1998, the statute of the International Criminal Court was negotiated and adopted, with 120 votes in favour, nine against and 21 abstentions. Although the statute did not enter into force immediately, the number of ratifications grew rapidly (it came into force following the deposition of the 60th deed of ratification on 1 July 2002). The Coalition for the International Criminal Court, founded by Amnesty International, Human Rights Watch and other big human rights organizations and led by the WFM, played a decisive part in the success in Rome and in the swift ratification of the treaty. The project had long been dismissed as 'unrealistic'. In addition, criticism of globalization was ubiquitous after Seattle. Under the motto 'another world is possible', thousands of initiatives, unionists, activists and NGOs from all over the world gathered in Porto Alegre in Brazil in January 2001 for the first World Social Forum, which has met every year since. Public interest in this counter-event to the elite World Economic Forum in Davos was (initially at least) extraordinarily high. From the very beginning, there has also always been a meeting of the parliamentarians who take part in the World Social Forum. The 'World Parliamentary Forum', it was stated in the first declaration issued by the deputies (who are usually from the left and Green end of the political spectrum), aims to support the movements coming together at the Social Forum in their resistance to the 'inhuman neo-liberal order' and to ensure that their concerns are fed into the national parliaments. According to *Zeit* magazine, the French European Parliament member Harlem Désir, one of the initiators of the parliamentary forum and party leader of the French socialists for two years from 2012, sees it as 'a preliminary stage for its long-term goal, a world parliament'.[1]

New contributions on the idea of a global parliament

Falk and Strauss were encouraged by these developments. Globalization and democratization, they thought, were the two dominant themes of the post-Cold War world. With the aid of a coalition of NGOs and open-minded governments, a global parliament could be established that would bring these two phenomena together and into balance. Alongside the possibility that such a parliament might be organized by civil society itself, they now brought into the discussion the additional option of a new inter-state treaty. An article they wrote in the journal *Foreign Affairs* in early 2001 taking this line of argument attracted considerable attention and probably still remains the most frequently cited publication on this topic.[2] Inspired by Schumann and Martin's critique of globalization, the Australian parliamentarian Duncan Kerr, Australian Justice Minister from 1993 to 1996, then argued in his book 'Elect the Ambassador', also published in 2001, that the process of globalization and the global markets could definitely be brought under political control, namely by democratising and then strengthening the international system. Among the ten proposals he put forward to this end was the establishment of a UNPA. Kerr emphasized that the procedure by which deputies were elected should not be uniformly prescribed. He was sure, though, that it would be the directly elected deputies who would dominate the evolution of the 'second chamber'.[3]

The British journalist and environmentalist George Monbiot, on the other hand, argued in his weekly column in the *Guardian* that 'democracy is meaningless unless ultimate power resides in a directly elected assembly'.[4] Monbiot has contributed a great deal, particularly with his 2003 book 'The Age of Consent', to the growing interest within the anti-globalization movement in the idea of a global parliament. 'As everything has been globalized except democracy', Monbiot wrote, 'the rulers of the world can go about their business without

1   Greve, Christiane. 'Der Internationale'. Die Zeit, no. 06/2002 (www.zeit.de).
2   Falk, Richard, and Andrew Strauss. 2001. 'Toward Global Parliament'. in: Foreign Affairs 80 (1): 212–220. Repr. in the same: 2011. A Global Parliament: Essays and Articles. Berlin: Committee for a Democratic UN, pp. 21-28.
3   Kerr, Duncan. 2001. Elect the Ambassador! Building Democracy in a Globalised World. Annandale: Pluto Press, pp. 144ff.
4   Monbiot, George. 17 July 2001. 'How to rule the world'. The Guardian (www.guardian.co.uk).

reference to ourselves.' 'If we wish to be represented', he continued, 'then let us be represented, and let us no longer accept the evasions, half-measures, impediments, intermediaries and arbiters whose installation masquerades as global democratization. The only genuinely representative forum is a directly representative one, by which, of course, I mean a world parliament.'[5] Anybody working and hoping for a fairer world, he thought, must in all logic speak out in favour of equal rights for all. It was therefore indispensable for everyone to have an equal vote in any election to a world parliament. This could be achieved by having, for the purposes of such elections, 600 roughly equal electoral districts across the world, cutting across national frontiers. Initially, the principal role of the parliament would lie in monitoring the activities of other international organizations and holding them to account. The parliament would derive its power from its moral authority. If it were to lose the support of the people, its authority would decline in proportion. Thus there would emerge a self-regulating system of legitimate exercise of power.

The option of a global assembly as an electronic network, although cost-efficient, can only be in Monbiot's eyes 'a poor substitute for a real debating chamber'.[6] The 'e-Parliament' set up in 2004 by Nicholas Dunlop, the former Secretary-General of the PGA, together with William Ury, the co-founder of the Harvard Program on Negotiation, the then MEP Anders Wijkman and others serves only to link parliamentarians from all over the world via the internet and to support their political communication. Since 2012 the initiative has concentrated on climate policy. The German political scientist and negotiations expert Rasmus Tenbergen, meanwhile, has pursued the idea of a global internet parliament organized by civil society, whose decisions and votes could be participated in by everybody, as an exercise of direct democracy, and which could acquire more than merely moral authority once it reached a critical mass of individual supporters. Tenbergen hopes to demonstrate the validity of this approach through the online project 'World Parliament Experiment', which also involves real conferences as well as representative features.

The Lucknow conferences

In the spring of 2001, the first 'International Conference of Chief Justices of the World' was held in Lucknow, the capital of the Indian federal state of Uttar Pradesh. The conference has been held there every year since, hosted and organized by the City Montessori School, with over 50,000 pupils the biggest school

---

5   Id. 2004. The Age of Consent. Manifesto for a New World Order. London: Harper Perennial, p. 83.
6   Ibid., p. 91.

in the world. This private institution regards itself as the 'self-appointed guardian of the two billion children worldwide and of future generations'. The object of the conference is the strengthening of international law and global governance. The establishment of a world parliament able to pass binding world laws has been called for in every one of the concluding declarations. According to the School, around 700 judges from national supreme courts or constitutional courts have taken part in the eighteen conferences held up to 2017, as well as other judges from over 100 countries. Notable by their absence from this list to date are representatives from Western Europe, the USA and Canada.

9/11 and global democracy

Following the attacks of 11 September 2001, the 'war on terror' ('You are either with us or you are against us', said US President George W. Bush) became the USA's highest priority. Terrorism emerged as the new perceived enemy. The prospect of success for international democratization dwindled rapidly. On the other hand, it was argued that building up a global community based on the rule of law was essential in order over the long term to deprive terrorism of its breeding grounds. Friedrich Merz, leader of the German CDU/CSU parliamentary group, said for example in a keynote speech in October 2001, referring to Höffe, that a world state based on subsidiarity and with a federal constitution was a prerequisite for peace and security, human rights and a fair world economic order. This would entail the creation of a sense of world citizenship, of a cosmopolitan ethos and of democratic institutions such as a world parliament and world courts.[7] It fits with this line of thinking that the conservative German CDU/CSU group in the European Parliament indicated as early as 1999 its willingness to cooperate constructively towards the establishment of a UNPA (a position the group still maintains), as announced on behalf of the group by the MEP Elmar Brok. This notwithstanding, as Brok wrote, a solution still had to be found to the problem of how to deal with dictatorships.[8]

In his book 'Power in the Global Age', Beck warned, in the light of the hegemonic undertones of the war on terror and the accompanying growth of state surveillance, against a 'global anti-democratic populism based on threat prevention' and against a related 'cosmopolitan despotism' – an ostensible worldwide defence of human rights, democracy and peace which has itself been decoupled from those values and thus in reality serves to undermine them. The

---

7   Merz, Friedrich. 10 October 2001. 'Gedanken zur Politik im 21. Jahrhundert'. Speech at the Konrad-Adenauer-Stiftung. Pressedienst der CDU/CSU-Bundestagsfraktion. Mitteilung 1630, pp. 17f.
8   Letter from Elmar Brok to Andreas Bummel, 27 September 1999.

September 11 attacks, Beck thought, had made it clear for the first time in 50 years that the peace and security of the West were not compatible with the continued existence of armed conflicts, and of their root causes, in other areas of the world. In that sense, cosmopolitanism was the appropriate response to the terrorist threat. To be sure, the 'cosmopolitan regime' would have to be conceptually and institutionally conjoined with human rights and democracy and promoted and supported as a reform project at the level of global politics. Among the features that would serve as guarantors of the legitimacy of such a regime, Beck lists making the case for and establishing a world parliament – even if, he writes, an initiative to that end undertaken by sympathetic governments might realistically include initially only a small fraction of the existing states, and even if such a parliament might initially control the levers of symbolic power only.[9]

The report by the German Bundestag's Enquete Commission

The report of the German Bundestag's Enquete Commission inquiry into economic globalization, delivered in the middle of 2002 at over 600 pages long, proved less progressive in outlook. Although it identified the democratization of international institutions as an important task, it did not come out in support of the establishment of a UNPA; rather, it described the proposal as controversial. The initiative met with scepticism, the report said, 'as agreement on the composition of such a parliament presents problems (of demography, for example) that are almost impossible to resolve'.[10] The only recommendations for action in this area were for support for a stronger representation of the global regions in the UN Security Council. Additionally, it was proposed that the right of veto should be subject to a duty to justify its use to the General Assembly. The report did also express the view that the delegates should be given some powers of supervision and influence with regard to processes of globalization, especially in negotiations over agreements under international law. The process of international policy formulation should be monitored and influenced more effectively through the building up and development of interparliamentary networks. To this end, the IPU should be developed and strengthened, and the parliament was encouraged to pursue this. Thilo Bode, the director of Greenpeace International for six years up until 2001, thought it regrettable that there

---

9   Beck, Ulrich. 2009 [2002]. Macht und Gegenmacht im globalen Zeitalter. Frankfurt am Main: Suhrkamp, pp. 425ff., 426, 444, 446.
10 Deutscher Bundestag. 2002. Final Report of the Enquete Commission 'Globalisierung der Weltwirtschaft - Herausforderungen und Antworten', p. 430.

was very little interest in the report even within parliament. He thought Germany had no policy at all on globalization. But, he said, the idea that the nation states were being marginalized by globalization was a myth. All too often, it served national governments as a way of hiding vested interests or their own mistakes. But it was certainly true, he argued, that the nation states had recklessly delegated powers to international bodies without ensuring the maintenance of the necessary democratic controls over those powers. In order to overcome this democratic deficit, Europe should instigate a convention for the creation of a world parliament to take over this supervisory and monitoring role.[11]

The report by the World Commission on the Social Dimension of Globalization

In a resolution on relations between the EU and the UN passed in January 2004, the European Parliament renewed its efforts to this end and called for the creation of a consultative parliamentary assembly in the UN. The following month, the 'World Commission on the Social Dimension of Globalization', set up by the ILO two years earlier under the joint chairmanship of the Finnish President Tarja Halonen and the Tanzanian President Benjamin William Mkapa, delivered its detailed and comprehensive concluding report. The conclusions of the Commission, made up of over twenty prominent international figures, included the following. 'Parliamentary oversight of the multilateral system at the global level should be progressively expanded. We propose the creation of a Parliamentary Group concerned with the coherence and consistency between global economic, social and environmental policies, which should develop an integrated oversight of major international organizations.'[12] The governments of Finland and Tanzania were especially engaged in promoting the report and ensured that it was discussed in the General Assembly. The two governments had already, in early 2003, jointly started the 'Helsinki Process on Globalization and Democracy'. This initiative brought together representatives of government with experts and prominent figures from politics, academia and the NGOs for a dialogue on global problems and possible solutions, and was designed to push forward, in a second phase (running until 2008), the implementation of selected proposals.

---

11 Bode, Thilo. 2003. *Die Demokratie verrät ihre Kinder*. Stuttgart, München: DVA, pp. 11, 205, 192ff.
12 International Labour Organization. 2004. 'A fair globalization: Creating opportunities for all'. Report of the World Commission on the Social Dimension of Globalization. Geneva, p. xiv, see also p. 121.

The Ubuntu Forum campaign

Momentum was building within civil society, too. In April 2001 a world forum of civil society networks, a 'network of networks', had formed in response to a call from the Spaniard Federico Mayor, Director-General of UNESCO from 1987 to 1999, in order to press for a more humane, more just and fairer world. One of its goals was the democratization of decision-making and institutions at all levels, including the global. The name of this forum, Ubuntu, is an African term describing a particular philosophy of life based on togetherness, charity and community. The roll-call of organizations involved in this initiative, which is based in Barcelona and has also participated in the Helsinki Process from the beginning, includes Oxfam, WFM, the South Centre, CIVICUS: World Alliance for Citizen Participation, the Grameen Bank, IPPNW, the International Peace Bureau IPB, the Third World Network and the London School of Economics. The international associations Caritas, Greenpeace, the Red Cross and Médecins Sans Frontières are among the organizations with observer status. In 2002, under the aegis of the Ubuntu Forum, a 'World Campaign for In-Depth Reform of the System of International Institutions' was initiated. The Campaign's London Declaration of April 2004 included a call for comprehensive democratization. 'It is necessary for the world's citizens to be directly represented in the international institutions', it read. To this end, work should go forward on the creation of a parliamentary assembly 'which could play a role in establishing international law, put forward recommendations and exercise control over the other institutions forming part of the system'.[13] The Campaign Declaration was signed by over fifty prominent public figures including Mayor, Soares, Boutros-Ghali, Pérez de Cuéllar, the Nobel Peace laureates Rigoberta Menchú, Adolfo Pérez Esquivel and Joseph Rotblat, Nobel Literature laureates Gabriel García Márquez and José Saramago as well as the future Nobel Peace laureate Muhammad Yunus and Danielle Mitterand, wife of François Mitterrand, French President from 1981 to 1995.

The Cardoso panel report

A report from an independent body of experts on the relationship between the UN and civil society was scheduled for June 2004. The panel had been set up by UN Secretary-General Annan as part of his reform drive, and had worked under the chairmanship of the former Brazilian President Fernando Henrique

---

13 World Campaign for In-Depth Reform of the System of International Institutions, and UBUNTU Forum Ad Hoc Secretariat. 2004. 'Reforms of the System of International Institutions to Make Another World Possible'. London Declaration of 1 April 2004, p. 2.

Cardoso. In addition to investigating how NGOs and other actors could be better integrated into the work of the UN, the panel was also tasked to throw light on the interaction between the UN and parliamentarians and to make recommendations for its improvement. The IPU was also consulted on this issue. However, it was very far from agreeing with the conclusions. In early May, IPU Secretary-General Johnsson went so far as to contact Annan directly to set out the IPU's 'serious misgivings' with regard to the report and to urgently request fresh consultations between the parties involved before the Cardoso report was published.[14] But his request was in vain. The recommendations in this area, drawn up principally by panel member Birgitta Dahl, former President of the Swedish Parliament, were supplemented by a further reference to the IPU but otherwise not amended at all. What was at issue here?

The Cardoso Report found that democracy was becoming problematic, since the substance of politics was globalising rapidly while the most important political institutions such as elections, parties and parliaments remained rooted at the national level. A major factor in the increasing disenchantment with politics was 'the perception that traditional forms of representation are less relevant in this age of globalization. Elected legislators and parliaments', the report continued, 'seem to have little impact on decisions made intergovernmentally or in the supervision and regulation of international markets ... Given that national parliaments are formal and powerful institutions of democracy, the Panel considers it important to link them more structurally with the international intergovernmental process and to explore international parliamentary mechanisms to do so.'[15] Conversely, it is possible to infer an implied criticism of the IPU here. The panel clearly did not believe that the IPU was fulfilling this task, as it would otherwise not be necessary to set up new mechanisms.

The Cardoso Report specifically recommended the establishment – as an experiment initially – of so-called 'Global Public Policy Committees'. These should be organized under the aegis of the UN secretariat ('in consultation with' national parliaments, the IPU and other specialized organizations) and should be made up, in each case, of two to four members from different political parties from up to 30 parliaments for all regions. The idea, just as in the 1999 proposal from the European Parliament, was that the members would be selected from the relevant specialist committees of the national parliaments. The global committees would hold public debates and hearings involving experts from academia, civil society, business and government agencies. The broader aim of the

---

14   Letter from Anders B. Johnsson to Kofi Annan, 4 May 2004.
15   United Nations. 2004. We the Peoples: Civil society, the United Nations and Global Governance. Report of the Panel of Eminent Persons on United Nations–Civil Society Relations. A/58/817. Points 8, 106.

Cardoso panel was to build up overarching participative policy networks, of which these committees would form a substantial constituent part. Gradually, it was hoped, a formalized process could emerge out of these committees. For example, they could be given the right to make recommendations to the UN. The panel stressed that this proposal should be seen by the IPU as an opportunity for closer cooperation with the UN, and expressed scepticism towards the IPU's claim to an exclusive right of representation. Not all parliaments, claimed the report, wanted to be represented exclusively through the IPU, and indeed some were not even members of the organization. This last point was in reference principally to the US Congress. Since the early 1990s, practically no US representatives had taken part in IPU conferences, and in fact the US Congress formally cancelled its membership of the IPU in 1999. Unofficially, the IPU was increasingly seen as a 'talking shop', and moreover as being hostile to the USA.[16]

At a debate in the UN General Assembly in October, Johnsson made it clear that the IPU did not think much of the Cardoso proposals. The report, he said, causes concern 'because it suggests that the United Nations, an intergovernmental institution, should create its own inter-parliamentary structures'. This would duplicate the work of the IPU, and moreover, in Johnsson's view, 'runs contrary to the principle of separation of powers between the legislative and the executive branch of government'.[17] The Cardoso panel, by contrast, had argued that the principle of the separation of powers did not apply so clearly to international intergovernmental institutions as there was no legislative body of elected representatives 'to supervise and oversee the executive function'.[18]

The branch of the Helsinki Process dealing with 'New Approaches to Global Problem Solving' declared itself in agreement with the proposals of the Cardoso panel and the ILO World Commission. The Helsinki Process should support 'the establishment of Global Public Policy Committees (proposed by the Cardoso panel) and ... the development of a Global Parliamentary Group (proposed by the ILO Commission). In order to address these questions, a meeting of representatives from the IPU, other apex bodies of parliaments and parliamentarians, as well as regional parliaments, should be organised.'[19] However, the IPU had no interest in such consultations. The idea was allowed to fizzle out.

---

16 Turner, Fred, and Zlatko Šabič. 2011. 'The US Congress' Participation in NATO and the Organization for Security and Cooperation in Europe (OSCE) Assemblies'. Paper presented at the International Studies Association Annual Conference 'Global Governance: Political Authority in Transition', Montreal, p. 12 (according to an interview of the authors with a high-ranking staff member of the US Congress).

17 Johnsson, Anders. 4 October 2004. 'Statement at the United Nations General Assembly joint debate, agenda items 52 and 54.'

18 United Nations (2004), loc. cit., point 8.

19 Helsinki Process. 2005. 'Governing Globalization - Globalizing Governance. New Approaches to Global Problem Solving'. Finish Ministry for Foreign Affairs, p. 6.

Growing support for a UNPA

Meanwhile, the voices going beyond such moderate proposals and calling for the establishment of a UNPA were growing more numerous. At the 22nd Congress of the Socialist International in São Paulo in October 2003, for example, the worldwide gathering of over 150 social democratic parties and organizations (including the German SPD) declared that 'the time has come to build up efficient democratic structures of global governance'. The text was drawn up by a committee headed by Christoph Zöpel, an SPD member of parliament for many years and former minister of state in the German foreign ministry. 'The goal of the SI must be to parliamentarise the global political system.' At some point, it read, consideration would need to be given to a UN Parliamentary Assembly.[20] At that time, the President of the SI was António Guterres, former Prime Minister of Portugal, who took office as UN Secretary-General in 2017.

With the support of the authors of this study, the Committee for a Democratic UN, or KDUN, was formed in Germany in 2003, a cross-party association whose sole purpose was to lobby for the creation of a UNPA (in 2017, KDUN became Democracy Without Borders). In a strategy paper by Andreas Bummel, the KDUN aligned itself broadly with the argument set out by Heinrich. UN Secretary-General Annan sent a message to let the Committee know that the paper was 'very welcome' at a time when the UN was considering reform options.[21] Among the Committee members was Remo Gysin, a member of the Swiss National Council and one of the initiators of the successful national referendum that led to the accession of Switzerland to the UN on 3 March 2002. With the help of the Committee and of the Society for Threatened Peoples, Gysin organized a cross-party open letter to UN Secretary-General Annan by 108 members of Swiss federal councils, including a majority of the National Council. It stated that Switzerland 'has always promoted international law, democracy and respect for human rights' and that 'on the basis of this tradition' the signatories were asking Annan 'to introduce the idea of a Parliamentary Assembly at the UN into the reform debate and to forward this suggestion to the governments of the UN member states for further discussion'.[22] The letter aroused

---

20 Socialist International. 29 October 2003. Governance in a Global Society – The Social Democratic Approach. Report adopted at the XII. Congress, São Paulo. Chapter III.0.a), and 3.3.
21 Letter from Marta Maurás, Director of the Executive Office of the Secretary-General, to Andreas Bummel, 27 October 2004.
22 Gysin, Remo, Josef Lang, Christa Markwalder Bär, Heiner Studer, and Rosmarie Zapfl. 8 February 2005. 'Establishment of a Parliamentary Assembly at the UN. Open letter of 108 Members of Parliament to the UN Secretary-General'. Swiss National Council.

considerable interest and comment in the Swiss media. In an interview Switzerland's UN ambassador Peter Maurer, who later became President of the International Committee of the Red Cross, stated that the proposal was 'in line with Swiss foreign policy'.[23] Micheline Calmy-Rey, Head of the Federal Department of Foreign Affairs, later agreed that the creation of a parliamentary body within the UN would strengthen its democratic credentials and its proximity to the citizens. However, she claimed it would be difficult to realize this aim, given that an amendment of the UN Charter would require a two-thirds majority of all member states and the assent of all five permanent members of the Security Council. For this reason, other options were also being considered, such as strengthening the role of the IPU within the UN.[24]

In May 2005, the world congress of Liberal International in Sofia declared its support for a UNPA in a resolution, linking back to the LI report of 1992. A UNPA could be established without amending the Charter either as a new body on the basis of Article 22 of the UN Charter or – assuming its agreement – through a transformation of the IPU.[25] The South Centre, whose Chairman from 2003 to 2006 was Boutros-Ghali, also drew attention to the proposal for a UNPA. The reference came in a paper, dating from one year earlier but now made public, submitted to the High Level Panel on Threats, Challenges and Change (another panel initiated by Annan). Subsequently, so this think tank for the developing countries of the global South argued, a World Parliament, directly elected by the people in the style of the European Parliament, could be created.[26]

The issue was also taken up again – for the fourth time now, and more decisively than ever before – by the European Parliament itself. In a resolution on reform of the UN brought in by Armin Laschet, CDU member of the European Parliament and later Prime Minister of North-Rhine Westphalia, the European Parliament called in June 2005 'for the establishment of a United Nations Parliamentary Assembly (UNPA) within the UN system, which would increase the democratic profile and internal democratic process of the organization and allow world civil society to be directly associated in the decision-making process'. This assembly 'should be vested with genuine rights of information, participation and control, and should be able to adopt recommendations directed at the UN General Assembly'.[27]

---

23 Interview with Peter Maurer. 14 Feb. 2005. 'Schweiz muss auf faire Spielregeln achten'. Tages-Anzeiger.
24 Schweizerischer Bundesrat. 18 May 2005. 'Bericht 2005 über das Verhältnis zur UNO und zu den internationalen Organisationen mit Sitz in der Schweiz', pp. 11f.
25 Liberal International. 14 May 2005. 'Strengthening citizens representation on international level through an UN Parliamentary Assembly'. Resolution adopted by the 53rd Congress in Sofia, Bulgaria.
26 Repr. in: South Centre. 2005. What UN for the 21st Century? A New North-South Divide. Geneva, pp. 38f.
27 European Parliament. 6 June 2005. Resolution on the reform of the United Nations, P6_TA(2005). See point 39.

One week later, with the votes of the SPD and the Green Party, the German Bundestag passed a resolution on 'parliamentary involvement in the United Nations system'. Over the preceding six months, following publication of the Cardoso report, the Bundestag had been one of the first national parliaments to investigate the issue in any detail. The text was compiled for the foreign affairs committee by the sub-committee on UN affairs, led by Zöpel, in cooperation with the IPU delegation. There was consensus in the subsidiary committee that the addition of a 'parliamentary dimension' to the UN system was needed, and that its institutional form (and this was the wording in the text then passed by the Bundestag) 'could perhaps be described as a "parliamentary assembly"'. In any event, the delegates thought that the IPU was preferable to alternatives such as 'forming a new parliamentary body within or outside the United Nations, with the IPU remaining in its existing form'.[28] The KDUN by contrast had recommended not putting all of the eggs in one basket and therefore continuing to keep alternative options open in case the further development of the IPU proved impossible. A reference to Article 22 of the UN Charter as a potential vehicle for the construction of a parliamentary assembly was removed from the text at the request of the foreign ministry. The Greens had made it a condition of their assent that an 'agreement' had to be reached with the foreign ministry, at that time headed by Joschka Fischer. Zöpel lamented that it had not proved possible to get the foreign ministry to accept a 'genuine parliamentarization of global politics on the basis of a separation of powers'. The ministry also insisted on the removal of core responsibilities and competences that the lower chamber had proposed should be given to the parliamentary UN assembly, for example participation in the deliberations on multilateral treaties and their ratification, participation in setting and monitoring the budget, a so-called 'right to implement transparency' and the involvement of NGOs. 'There is still a long way to go', Zöpel summed up, 'before the Bundestag understands its role to be that of the German part of a global democratic separation of powers which includes an effective global parliamentarism.'[29] The Green Party manifesto for the Bundestag elections of July 2005 then included the following sentence: 'We also support the establishment of a parliamentary assembly as an advisory body at the United Nations'.[30] The fact that the route through the IPU was a dead end was confirmed shortly afterwards. At the UN summit meeting Millennium+5 in September 2005, the occasion for the second worldwide meeting of presiding officers

---

28 Deutscher Bundestag. 15 June 2005. Für eine parlamentarische Mitwirkung im System der Vereinten Nationen. 15/5690, p. 3.

29 Zöpel, Christoph. 2005. 'Die Vereinten Nationen und die Parlamente (II)'. Vereinte Nationen (4): 145–148, p. 148.

30 Bündnis 90 / Die Grünen. 10 July 2005. 'Eines für alle. Das Grüne Wahlprogramm 2005', p. 107.

of national parliaments, Johnsson – who was not unaware of the growing support
for a UNPA - affirmed once more that the IPU was not in favour of 'the creation
of any parliamentary assembly at the United Nations or elsewhere'.[31] Nor was
there any indication of a possible reform of the IPU in this direction.

This characteristic stance of the IPU failed to convince the Parliamentary
Assembly of the Council of Europe. The Italian delegate Tana de Zulueta explained this as resulting in part from the fact that the IPU was not contemplating 'any structured or systematic participation by parliamentarians in the work
of the UN', nor did it plan to establish links between the parliamentarians and
the functioning of the UN institutions and bodies. To only offer a platform was
not sufficient.[32] Her proposal for a resolution was unanimously accepted in the
relevant committee, and subsequently passed by the assembly. In it, the UN
General Assembly was called upon to develop, together with the IPU, an incremental strategy for the creation of a parliamentary dimension within the UN.
This could include, on a trial basis, the establishment of parliamentary committees that could ultimately lead to the creation of a UNPA. The General Assembly was to institute a panel to work up proposals regarding the exact size, constitution and procedures of a UN assembly of parliamentarians.[33] In October
2006, Andreas Gross, a Swiss National Councillor and member of the Council
of Europe who had also been one of the instigators of the Swiss referendum on
accession to the UN, also spoke out in favour of a UN parliamentary chamber
in a speech to the UN General Assembly. Annan welcomed the idea at a meeting
with the foreign affairs committee of the Swiss National Council. However, at
the same time he doubted whether the governments of the UN member states
would show any interest in it.[34] It was probably this, as well as the negative
stance of the IPU, which explains why Annan never took up the proposal in his
official reports.

The international campaign for a UNPA

The open letter from Switzerland was seen by many world federalists and sup-
porters of a UNPA as a milestone. Shortly afterwards, the Committee for a
Democratic UN – together with the Society for Threatened Peoples, Ubuntu,
WFM and other partners – began planning an international campaign. The

---

31 Johnsson, Anders. 16 Sep. 2005. 'Statement at the High-level Plenary Meeting of the UN General Assembly'.
32 Zulueta, Tana de. 2005. 'Parliamentary dimension of the United Nations'. Report to the Political Affairs
    Committee of the Parliamentary Assembly of the Council of Europe. Doc. 10771, pp. 8f.
33 Council of Europe Parliamentary Assembly. 23 January 2006. 'Parliamentary dimension of the United Na-
    tions'. Resolution 1476 (2006).
34 'Forderung nach UNO-Parlament'. 21 October 2006. sda wire news.

time seemed to have come to join together the various international strands of support for a UNPA in order to make them more effective. In 1996, in one of his first speeches as the new Secretary-General of WFUNA, the worldwide umbrella organization for national UN societies, Childers had encouraged the creation of a coordinated campaign.[35] Now, ten years after his sudden death in 1996, the WFUNA world congress meeting in Buenos Aires passed a resolution officially committing it to support for a UNPA. It called on 'the governments of the United Nations member states, parliamentarians and civil society representatives to jointly examine possible steps and options to create a United Nations Parliamentary Assembly'.[36]

With the publication in April 2007 of an 'Appeal for the establishment of a Parliamentary Assembly at the United Nations', addressed to the UN and the governments of its member states, the international campaign for a UNPA was launched simultaneously in a number of world capitals, including Berlin, Brussels, Berne, Buenos Aires, Dar es Salaam, London, Madrid, Ottawa and Rome. It was an informal network on the model of the campaign for the International Criminal Court. The Appeal created a common political denominator which made it possible to bring together most of the supporters of a UNPA to speak with one voice in a single campaign. 'To ensure international cooperation, secure the acceptance and to enhance the legitimacy of the United Nations and strengthen its capacity to act,' it read, 'people must be more effectively and directly included into the activities of the United Nations and its international organizations. They must be allowed to participate better in the UN's activities. We therefore recommend a gradual implementation of democratic participation and representation on the global level.' The statement saw the establishment of a UNPA as a first and indispensable step in this direction. The assembly 'could initially be composed of national parliamentarians'. But '[s]tep by step, it should be provided with genuine rights of information, participation and control vis-à-vis the UN and the organizations of the UN system. In a later stage, the assembly could be directly elected.'[37]

Boutros-Ghali, who had encouraged the KDUN to undertake the campaign early on, wrote in a message to all its supporters that 'we need to promote the democratization of globalization, before globalization destroys the foundations

---

35 Childers, Erskine. 16 March 1996. 'The United Nations and Global Institutions'. Speech delivered at the 'Conference on The Fate of Democracy In The Era of Globalisation', Wellesley College, Massachusetts.
36 World Federation of United Nations Associations. 10 November 2006. 'A United Nations Parliamentary Assembly'. Resolution adopted at the 38th Plenary Assembly, Buenos Aires, Argentina.
37 Campaign for a UN Parliamentary Assembly. 20 April 2007. Appeal for the Establishment of a United Nations Parliamentary Assembly (en.unpacampaign.org).

of national and international democracy' and that a UNPA was 'an indispensable step to achieve democratic control of globalization'.[38] An international meeting took place in Geneva in October 2007 under the patronage of Boutros-Ghali. It agreed that representatives of regional parliaments such as the European Parliament could also be members of a UNPA, and that the process of parliamentarization must also encompass the Bretton Woods institutions, i.e. the World Bank and the International Monetary Fund. In addition, it was agreed to support regulations that would allow states participating in a UNPA 'to opt for direct elections of their delegates if they wish to do so' from the beginning. Direct elections of the UNPA's delegates were to be regarded as a precondition for vesting the body with legislative rights.[39] It was decided to build up the network further and to continue the campaign by means of the Appeal. The Swiss government, which had been an observer at the meeting, voiced 'sympathy' for the proposal of a UNPA, but emphasized in an official report of the Federal Council that the UN was an inter-state organization.[40] In the following years up to 2015, there were four further international meetings, in the European Parliament in Brussels, in New York and in the Argentinian Senate in Buenos Aires. A particular topic of discussion in Brussels in 2008 was the relationship between the proposed UNPA and the IPU – a topic which kept recurring and for that reason seemed to require a common policy statement. The conclusion was that a UNPA 'would not replace or duplicate the IPU's functions. Quite the contrary, a UNPA would provide a response to the democratic deficit in global governance which the IPU in its current structure is unable to offer'.[41]

The campaign receives international support across all ideological and party political divides. The campaign's appeal has to date been signed by over 1,500 members of parliament and several thousands of other people from 150 countries, including many hundreds of prominent figures from politics, academia and civil society. Only a few can be listed here by name, even if all would deserve to be. They include serving and former heads and ministers of state and government, some presiding officers of parliaments, over 300 university professors, and around twenty winners of Nobel and alternative Nobel Prizes (or 'Right Livelihood Awards'), among them the Nobel Peace Prize laureates the Dalai Lama and John Hume. Among the supporters already named in this section of

---

38 Boutros-Ghali, Boutros. 16 May 2007. 'Message to the Campaign for a UN Parliamentary Assembly'.
39 Campaign for a UN Parliamentary Assembly. November 2007. 'Conclusions regarding policies of the Campaign for a UN Parliamentary Assembly'.
40 Schweizerischer Bundesrat. 21 May 2008. 'Bericht 2008 über das Verhältnis der Schweiz zur UNO und zu den internationalen Organisationen mit Sitz in der Schweiz', p. 39.
41 Campaign for a UN Parliamentary Assembly. November 2008. 'The establishment of a United Nations Parliamentary Assembly and the Inter-Parliamentary Union'.

the book are Daniele Archibugi, Boutros Boutros-Ghali, Elmar Brok, Arthur C. Clarke, Harlem Désir, Richard Falk, Johan Galtung, Bronisław Geremek, Olivier Giscard d'Estaing, Andreas Gross, Remo Gysin, Václav Havel, Dieter Heinrich, David Held, Otfried Höffe, Karl Kaiser, Hans Köchler, Armin Laschet, Federico Mayor, Saul Mendlovitz, Mike Moore, Thomas Pogge, Michel Rocard, Douglas Roche, Harald Schumann, Andrew Strauss, Brian Urquhart, Anders Wijkman, Christoph Zöpel and Tana de Zulueta. In India, important supporters include Shashi Tharoor, an acclaimed writer, parliamentarian and former diplomat as well as Najma Heptulla, a long-time member of parliament and President of the Inter-Parliamentary Union from 1999 to 2002.

Calls for a UNPA since 2007

The campaign helped to maintain the call for a UNPA as an issue for discussion. In Canada, the committee for foreign affairs of the House of Commons recommended in a June 2007 report on the global development of democracy that favourable consideration should be given to the establishment of a UNPA. The Pan-African Parliament, on the initiative of the Mauritian delegate Mokshanand Sunil Dowarkasing, passed a resolution on 24 October 2007 dealing in detail with a UNPA. The first President of the PAP, Gertrude Mongella from Tanzania, who had extensive experience with the UN (for example as head of the UN World Conference on Women in Beijing in 1995), had long been an outspoken supporter of a UNPA. The PAP called on the African Union to develop a common position on the issue. The PAP was founded in March 2004 as an advisory body to the African Union and is made up of 235 national parliamentarians from the member states. According to its founding Protocol it is intended to become a directly elected legislative body for the entire African continent. A UNPA, its resolution stated, could similarly develop step by step. Ultimately, the PAP thought, it would need to be endowed with rights of participation and oversight, and in particular with the right 'to send fully participating parliamentary delegations or representatives to international governmental fora and negotiations'. A UNPA would not run counter to the valuable and highly regarded work of the IPU in any way at all.[42] Almost ten years later, in May 2016, PAP reaffirmed its support in another resolution that was initiated by Ivone Soares from Mozambique and called on the African Union and its member states to support a UNPA.

---

42 Adopted on 24 October 2007, repr. in: Bummel, Andreas. 2010. Developing International Democracy - For a Parliamentary Assembly at the United Nations. 2nd ed. Berlin: Committee for a Democratic UN, 2010, pp. 47ff.

When representatives of the European Parliament and the PAP met in South Africa in May 2008, a common statement of support for a UNPA was removed from the agenda at the urging of the Spanish MEP and honorary President of the IPU Miguel Angel Martínez. The year before, a small advisory group of the IPU Committee on United Nations Affairs had affirmed once more that the IPU should not support the establishment of 'some form of world parliament'. A world parliament, it was minuted, 'would only ever make sense if there was a world government'.[43]

In May 2008, the second Global Congress of all Green parties in São Paulo in Brazil passed the so-called '21 Commitments for the 21st Century', which included the establishment of a UNPA in the section on strengthening democracy. The third Global Green Congress in Dakar, Senegal, in April 2012 passed a resolution calling on 'Greens around the world' to participate in the campaign for a UNPA. The federal board of the German Greens (Bündnis 90/Die Grünen) had decided on the same step two years earlier. 'A global parliament would be well suited to make the United Nations more democratic and more transparent,' commented party chair Claudia Roth at the time.[44]

In Latin America, the call for a UNPA was initially principally carried forward by two Argentinians, the parliamentary delegate Fernando Iglesias from the Coalición Cívica and the Senator Sonia Escudero from the Peronist party. In the book 'Globalizar la democracia: por un Parlamento Mundial', published in Spanish in 2006, Iglesias had dealt in some detail with the question of a world parliament.[45] Argentina had come through a severe economic and financial crisis, including a deep recession, during which the country had descended at some points into chaos and had had to declare itself bankrupt in 2001. There was great controversy over the conditions imposed by the International Monetary Fund, which had been involved as a creditor in determining the country's fiscal policy since the early 1990s, and which therefore was regarded as sharing the blame for the 1999 – 2002 crisis. The IMF seemed to many to be a faceless and undemocratic bureaucracy which was subject to no effective external controls and could not be held to account for its failed policies. A democratization of the international institutions therefore seemed extremely important, and a UNPA was seen as a potential starting point. Iglesias and Escudero took a first step in this direction in the Latin American Parliament, where Escudero held

43 Inter-Parliamentary Union (ed.). 2007. 'Meeting of the Advisory Group of the IPU Committee on United Nations Affairs, 12-13 July 2007, Summary Report', p. 2.
44 'Grüne unterstützen Kampagne für ein UNO-Parlament', 2 July 2010 (de.unpacampaign.org).
45 Iglesias, Fernando. Globalizar la democracia: por un Parlamento Mundial. Buenos Aires: Manantial, 2006.

the office of General-Secretary from 2006 to 2010. The 'Parlatino' is a delibera-tive assembly founded in 1964 with delegates from 23 national parliaments. Currently the assembly has hopes of becoming the legislative organ of the Com-munity of Latin American and Caribbean States (CELAC), which has been in the process of formation since 2010. In December 2008 the Parlatino declared its 'support to efforts towards the creation and establishment of a Parliamentary Assembly of the United Nations Organization'.[46] Similar resolutions followed from the Argentinian Senate and Chamber of Deputies and in December 2011 in the Mercosur parliament, comprising delegates from the Mercosur member states of Argentina, Brazil, Paraguay and Uruguay. If evidence were still re-quired that the call for a UNPA is not a Western but a global project, then it will have been provided by these declarations from Africa and Latin America.

During the global financial crisis, half a year after the collapse of the US American investment bank Lehman Brothers, the leaders of the G20 met in London in April 2009 to discuss what measures could be taken. The campaign took the opportunity to publish a 'Call for global democratic oversight of inter-national financial and economic institutions', which attracted support from many individuals, including the former German finance minister Hans Eichel. 'At this critical juncture we urge the United Nations and the governments of its member states to support the establishment of a United Nations Parliamentary Assembly in their deliberations on the reform of international monetary, finan-cial and economic institutions', said Boutros-Ghali.[47] The assembly could take on a supervisory role vis-à-vis the Bretton Woods institutions, could provide a voice for citizens and could be given a consultative role in the appointment of the executive directors of the institutions.

The Parliamentary Assembly of the Council of Europe, in a resolution drawn up by Gross, emphasized that 'the incorporation of a democratic element in the United Nations system has become even more necessary in response to the process of globalization'. The members regretted that there had been no reform proposal among the many officially brought forward within the UN in recent years 'aimed at improving the democratic character of the United Na-tions'. Their proposal was for a parliamentary assembly within the UN 'com-posed either by representatives of international regional parliamentary assem-blies or directly elected representatives'.[48] But an amendment was also accepted

---

46   Reprinted in: Bummel, loc. cit., p. 45.
47   'Call on world leaders: Global parliament to exert oversight of international system', 30 March 2009 (en.un-pacampaign.org).
48   Council of Europe Parliamentary Assembly. 1 October 2009. 'United Nations reform and the Council of Eu-rope member states'. Resolution 1688 (2009).

acknowledging that, besides a new assembly, the IPU was 'one of the potential options to be considered as the parliamentary branch of the UN'.[49]

The third World Conference of Speakers of Parliament

At the IPU itself, preparations were under way for the third World Conference of Speakers of Parliament, due to take place in Geneva in July 2010. A key question for the further development of the IPU's role within the UN would be the issue of its legal status. Three options were under discussion: maintaining the status quo, aiming for an amendment of the Charter to transform the IPU into an organ of the UN, or putting the IPU onto a different footing through a new intergovernmental treaty. It seems that the Secretariat favoured the third option. But there was unanimity on the point that there should be no additional institution independent of the IPU. The preparatory committee therefore confirmed its rejection of the idea of a UNPA, as such a body, it argued, would be 'incompatible with the strategy for parliamentary interaction with the United Nations'.[50] At the World Conference the differing views within the IPU came out into the open. Abdirahin Abdi, Kenyan Speaker of the East African Legislative Assembly EALA proposed that the parliaments should be formally integrated into the decision-making processes of the UN (the President of the Kenyan Parliament, Kenneth Marende, who was not in Geneva, supported a UNPA). 'It can be made a requirement', said Abdi, 'that every decision of the UN General Assembly or the UN Security Council is subjected to some form of a parliamentary process before it becomes binding. We can do this by strengthening the existing international parliamentary forums like the Inter-Parliamentary Union to co-determine with the UN General Assembly or Security Council the shape of world policies.'[51] Norbert Lammert, President of the German Bundestag, took an opposing position defending the status quo. In his speech he argued that the IPU was 'neither a world parliament nor a subsidiary organization of the UN', and nor should it become either.[52] In contradiction to the resolution of the Bundestag itself, he spoke out against a structural reform. Under

---

49   'PACE: Global governance must be based on democratic principles, debate on UN's parliamentary dimension', 1 October 2009 (en.unpacampaign.org).

50   Inter-Parliamentary Union. 15 February 2010. '122nd Assembly and related meetings: Governing Council Item 13, Preparations for the 3rd World Conference of Speakers of Parliament, Annex I: Summary of decisions of the Second Meeting of the Preparatory Committee'. Document CL/186/13-R.1, p. 2.

51   Abdi, Abdirahin H. 20 July 2010. 'Address of the Speaker of the East African Legislative Assembly on the occassion of the 3rd Conference of World Speakers', Geneva.

52   Lammert, Norbert. 20 July 2010. 'Rede des Präsidenten des Deutschen Bundestages, Prof. Dr. Norbert Lammert, auf der 3. Weltkonferenz der Parlamentspräsidenten in Genf'.

Lammert's aegis, an alliance between Arab and European parliamentary Presidents was successful in maintaining this position (this was still before the Arab Spring). 'The World Conference of Speakers of Parliament', wrote the *Neue Zürcher Zeitung*, 'passed a sober resolution in which Western pressure curtailed the ambitious plan to create a world parliament to realistic dimensions.'[53] However, Abdul Aziz Al Ghurair, the billionaire Speaker of the House of the Federal National Council (FNC) of the United Arab Emirates, spoke out at the same time in favour of IPU support for the creation of a new institution, 'an international independent body representing peoples of the world to act as a parliamentary arm for the United Nations (UN) and hold any country - whatever be big or small - accountable democratically if it flouts its international responsibilities as per principles of international law and legitimacy'. This, he said, would not replace the IPU but complement it.[54] In January 2013, the East African Legislative Assembly passed an official resolution lamenting 'the insufficient formal involvement of elected representatives in the work of the United Nations' and supporting the establishment of a UNPA.[55] In the overview of the report of the World Economic Forum's Global Redesign Initiative, Richard Samans, Klaus Schwab and Mark Malloch Brown explained that a consultative UN Parliamentary Assembly was 'a necessary means for advancing democratic participation'.[56]

The European Parliament resolution of 2011

Meanwhile, in the European Parliament it was now a delegate from the German FDP, Alexander Graf Lambsdorff, who was responsible for UN issues. Before his election as an MEP in 2004 he had worked in the German foreign office. Lambsdorff did not think a UNPA was a good idea. The strongest argument against it, in his view, was that the issue of how to involve undemocratic countries was an insoluble problem. This meant that the drafts drawn up by Lambsdorff for recommendations by the European Parliament to the Council on UN policy always excluded the issue of a UNPA. Its supporters in the Parliament were obliged to propose amendments. In 2011, such a proposal, drawn up by Jo Leinen, Elmar Brok and the two liberal MEPs Alexander Alvaro from Germany and Andrew Duff from Great Britain, was adopted. So the resolution

---

53 Neue Zürcher Zeitung. 22 July 2010. 'Idee für ein Weltparlament gestutzt'.
54 Emirates News Agency (WAM). 20 July 2010. 'UAE calls for world body for democratic accountability'.
55 East African Legislative Assembly. 29 January 2013. 'Resolution of the East African Legislative Assembly on the establishment of a United Nations Parliamentary Assembly'.
56 World Economic Forum. Everybody's Business: Strengthening International Cooperation in a More Interdependent World Report of the Global Redesign Initiative. Cologny/Geneva, 2010, pp. 34f.

passed by the European Parliament on 8 June 2011 included the following recommendation addressed to the Council: 'to advocate the establishment of a
UNPA within the UN system in order to increase the democratic nature, the
democratic accountability and the transparency of global governance and to allow for greater public participation in the activities of the UN, acknowledging
that a UNPA would be complementary to existing bodies, including the Inter-
Parliamentary Union'.[57] This resulted in about 40 societies and associations in
Germany as well as over 150 prominent public figures writing an open letter to
Federal Chancellor Merkel and Federal Foreign Minister Westerwelle asking
them to act on this recommendation and to press for the establishment of a
UNPA at the UN General Assembly. The signatory associations included Attac,
BUND (Friends of the Earth Germany), the United Nations Association of Ger-
many, the Society for Threatened Peoples, Mehr Demokratie e.V., the Senate of
Economy and World Vision Germany. Individual signatories included 40 pro-
fessors, around 70 Members of the Bundestag and of the European Parliament,
from all parties, Chair of the SPD Sigmar Gabriel, former State Premiers Hans
Eichel and Erwin Teufel, numerous former Federal Ministers, the former President of the Bundestag Rita Süssmuth and the former CDU Secretary-General
Heiner Geißler. No response to the letter was received.

In November 2011, in response to a formal parliamentary question in the
European Parliament, the European Council replied succinctly that it '[did] not
have a position on this matter'.[58] A little over two years later, the Belgian Foreign
Minister Didier Reynders listed some familiar arguments in a letter to the Campaign. Following extensive discussions at the level of the EU Council Working
Group on the United Nations in the course of 2012, the conclusion had been
reached that the establishment of a UNPA 'could, for the time being, not be
retained as a priority for the EU'. Reynders pointed to the cooperation between
the UN and the IPU as a reason. Besides, the UN was an intergovernmental
organization whose members were accountable to their national parliaments.
In addition, he claimed that a modification of the UN Charter would be necessary, and that this was 'for the moment, unrealistic'. Finally, the establishment
of a UNPA would entail a high cost that could not be absorbed.[59]

In June 2012, a group of intellectuals from over ten countries led by Fernando Iglesias, who one month later was elected to the chair of the international

---

57 European Parliament. 8 June 2011. '66th Session of the United Nations General Assembly'. Resolution
    P7_TA (2011) 0255. Points (be) and (bf).
58 EU Council/European Parliament. 28 November 2011. 'Reply to a question for written answer. Subject:
    United Nations Parliamentary Assembly'. Doc. P-008768/2011.
59 Letter from Didier Reynders. 26 February 2014. 'Objet: United Nations Parliamentary Assembly'.

council of the WFM, published a joint manifesto 'for a global democracy'. Only a few days after the UN conference on sustainable development in Rio de Janeiro and the G20 meeting in Los Cabos, Mexico, the 25 initial signatories emphasized that the challenges of globalization called for 'the rapid implementation of forms of democratic global governance on all the issues that current intergovernmental summits are evidently incapable of solving'. 'The existing national-state organizations', the manifesto continues, 'have to be part of a wider and much better coordinated structure, which involves democratic regional institutions on all the continents, the reform of the International Court of Justice, a fairer and more balanced International Criminal Court and a United Nations Parliamentary Assembly as the embryo of a future World Parliament.' The signatories included Jacques Attali, Zygmunt Bauman, Ulrich Beck, Noam Chomsky, Susan George, Saskia Sassen and Vandana Shiva. [60] A proposal for support for a parliamentary assembly at the UN brought into the chamber of deputies of the Italian Parliament in November 2013 referred to this manifesto in its rationale. It was initiated by the MP Federica Mogherini of the Democratic Party. Three months later she was appointed Italian Foreign Minister and left the parliament. In November 2014 she took over the office of High Representative of the EU for Foreign Affairs and Security Policy.

The de Zayas recommendations

The proposal for a parliamentary assembly was now also raised in an official context at the UN for the first time. On the initiative of Cuba, the UN Human Rights Council had passed a resolution for the 'Promotion of a democratic and equitable international order' and had mandated an independent expert under UN special procedures to report on this task. The resolution, passed by 29 votes in favour with 12 votes against and 5 abstentions, included detailed consideration of the preconditions for 'a democratic and equitable international order'. Among them were 'the right to equitable participation of all, without any discrimination, in domestic and global decision-making'.[61] The same wording has been used in various resolutions at the UN General Assembly on this topic since 2004, which have been regularly adopted by a two-thirds majority. [62] To date, votes against have come predominantly from Europe and the USA and their

---

60   'Intellectuals call for rapid implementation of forms of democratic global governance'. 26 June 2012 (en.unpacampaign.org).

61   United Nations. 13 October 2011. 'Resolution adopted by the Human Rights Council: Promotion of a democratic and equitable international order'. A/HRC/RES/18/6, point 6 (h).

62   See for example United Nations. 19 December 2016. 'Promotion of a Democratic and Equitable International Order'. A/RES/71/90., point 6 (h).

closest allies. According to the UN Human Rights Council, the newly-appointed independent expert was to 'identify possible obstacles to the promotion and protection of a democratic and equitable international order, and to submit proposals and/or recommendations to the Human Rights Council on possible actions in that regard'. The person elected to carry out this task was Alfred de Zayas, a US American born in Cuba who had worked for over twenty years as a high-ranking UN official in the area of human rights. This expert in international law, who taught in Geneva, announced that he would be looking at the proposal for a parliamentary assembly at the UN. And in a report presented to the UN Human Rights Council on 10 September 2013 he described this proposal as a 'promising initiative' and recommended that the Council commission a study on it. A representative from Egypt said during the debate that his country viewed 'in positive regard the reference to the proposed United Nations Parliamentary Assembly as one instrument of involving the global public opinion in the global decision-making process'.[63] One month later, on 28 October 2013, de Zayas recommended in a report to the UN General Assembly that the UN should hold a conference to discuss proposals such as those for a worldwide assembly of parliamentarians and for a new world court of human rights. At a press conference for the presentation of the report at the UN headquarters in New York, this international law expert said that the establishment of a worldwide assembly of parliamentarians was 'indispensable' if global decision-making was to be made truly representative.

Later developments

Following the fifth international conference on a UNPA, held in the European Parliament in Brussels on 16-17 October 2013 and including a consultation with de Zayas, the latter declared in a press release that the time was ripe for a worldwide assembly of parliamentarians. The Brussels conference was hosted by the MEPs Elmar Brok, Jo Leinen, Isabella Lövin and Graham Watson, from the four largest political groups: the European People's Party, the Progressive Alliance of Socialists and Democrats, the Greens and the Liberals. The meeting of the international campaign signalled at the same time the launch of the first 'Global Week of Action for a World Parliament'. Activists had organized events in more than fifty cities around the world calling for the establishment of a democratically-elected world parliament. In their call to action they expressed their fear 'that our current political system is inadequate to deal with growing global

63 Roshdy, Hussein O. 10 September 2013. 'Statement at the 24th Session of the Human Rights Council'. Permanent Mission of the Arab Republic of Egypt.

challenges'. They argued that the primary concern of governments was to defend what they consider to be in their national interests and not 'the common good of humanity and the environment'. By contrast, a world parliament would be 'an instrument to find and implement solutions that are democratic, accountable and serve the best interest of humanity'.[64] It was decided that the week of action should be held every year in October. In 2014, actions calling for a world parliament were again organized in 40 locations around the world. The aim of the global action week is to increase knowledge of the call and international publicity for it.

At the Commonwealth summit meeting in Sri Lanka in November 2013, the Maltese Foreign Minister George Vella called on the governments of the Commonwealth member states and the Commonwealth Parliamentary Association to support the international campaign for a UNPA. Pointing out that the Commonwealth includes 54 members, Vella said that it could play a major role in bringing about the adoption of an assembly at the UN to strengthen 'representation and parliamentary diplomacy'.[65] To the best of our knowledge, Vella was the first foreign minister in office to speak out in support of the proposal since Ernest Bevin in 1945. With its support for the concept of a 'common heritage of humanity' during the negotiations that led to the Law of the Sea Treaty, Malta had already demonstrated its openness to progressive ideas before.

In a number of papers and monographs published in the last decades, Joseph E. Schwartzberg, now Professor emeritus of the University of Minnesota, put forward various proposals for weighted voting in the UN General Assembly, a World Parliamentary Assembly and other organs of the UN system. Most of these involved the use of simple mathematical formulas. The most comprehensive of these works, 'Transforming the United Nations System: Designs for a Workable World', was published by the United Nations University Press in November 2013 with the warm endorsement of Boutros Boutros-Ghali, among others. A year later Schwartzberg established the Workable World Trust to promote the recommendations included in his book that by now is available in seven languages.

64 Global Week of Action for a World Parliament. 2013 'Let the People Decide - World Parliament Now!' (www.worldparliamentnow.org).

65 'Vella calls on Commonwealth to support creation of UN Parliamentary Assembly'. 16 November 2014 (www.maltatoday.com.mt).

The report by the Albright-Gambari Commission

In 2014, under the co-chairmanship of the former US Secretary of State Madeleine Albright and the former Nigerian Foreign Minister Ibrahim Gambari, and in the tradition of the Commission on Global Governance, a 'Commission on Global Security, Justice, and Governance' was formed. Among the members of the 16-person Commission, whose work was supported by The Hague Institute for Global Justice and the Stimson Center in Washington D.C., was the former Canadian Foreign Minister and President of the WFM Lloyd Axworthy. In the run-up to the 70th anniversary of the founding of the UN, the Commission published a report in June 2015 containing 80 recommendations designed to counter the current 'crisis of global governance'. The recommendations include the establishment of 'a UN parliamentary network'. 'Adopting a pragmatic approach toward strengthening UN-citizen relations and overcoming the world body's democratic deficit, a United Nations Parliamentary Network established under UN Charter Article 22 could wield tremendous potential for expanding public knowledge of and participation in the work of the preeminent global institution', the report stated. A UN parliamentary network made up of deputies from the national parliaments 'would complement the work of the Inter-Parliamentary Union and the longer-term efforts of civil society organizations to develop a transnational democratic culture'.[66] One passage in the report goes into more detail to emphasize the different purposes of the IPU. Whereas the latter concerns itself principally with national issues, the network would focus on the UN and on decision-making at the global level. The report points to the parliamentary conference of the WTO and to the parliamentary network of the World Bank and the IMF, founded in 2000, as models. In contrast with these, however, the UN parliamentary network would be formally linked to the UN. Experts in the field have questioned where exactly the difference would lie between the parliamentary network proposed in this report and the proposal for a parliamentary assembly already on the table for some time.

Unlike with previous panels of this kind, this work is not expected to finish with the publication of the report. Bearing in mind the successful examples of the International Campaign to Ban Landmines and the Coalition for the International Criminal Court, the Commission aims to promote the creation of new coalitions for the implementation of its recommendations involving different actors such as governments, NGOs and businesses. The Commission is thus pursuing a dual strategy. On the one side it will work simultaneously on several

---

66 Commission on Global Security, Justice & Governance. 'Confronting the Crisis of Global Governance'. The Hague Institute for Global Justice and The Stimson Center, Juni 2015, pp. xv, 84.

specific proposals. For example, the report suggests that 'specific UN task forces' made up of permanent representatives from all major world regions could deliberate on reform of the organs of the UN, including the establishment of a UN parliamentary network. At the same time, it is promoting the organization of a 'World Conference on Global Institutions' to mark the 75th anniversary of the UN in 2020, with the purpose of introducing institutional reforms in the system of global governance. This could include the consideration of amendments to the UN Charter, as the report explains.[67]

The election of Trump and ongoing efforts

In a surprise result, Donald Trump won the US election on November 8, 2016, and became 45th President of the United States. This was a blow to the Albright-Gambari Commission, which had probably anticipated that they would be able to work with a Democratic administration under Hillary Clinton to implement their plans. Instead, there was now a nationalist president in the White House who undermined his own State Department's influence, announced massive cuts in US contributions to the UN, and in a symbolic step withdrew US support for the Paris climate agreement, among other things. Trump's presidency was perceived by many as a threat to multilateralism, and indeed to world peace.

Nevertheless, a group of NGOs, among them the Stimson Center, WFM, and the Workable World Trust, started to promote the idea of a UN 2020 reform summit as suggested in the Commission's report. In parallel with this effort, the UNPA campaign in May 2017 managed to bring together representatives of 12 governments at an informal briefing on the UNPA proposal in New York hosted by the Canadian UN mission. Although the meeting was unofficial, the campaign considered it an important step towards an ongoing exchange with open-minded governments, one that eventually might lead to a more substantial initiative.

Another important milestone was achieved when two months later the European Parliament passed its annual resolution on the European Union's policy at the UN. The new rapporteur, Andrey Kovatchev from Bulgaria, supported an amendment introduced by MEPs Jo Leinen, Elmar Brok and Soraya Post. For the first time since 2011, therefore, the document once again referred to a UNPA and called on the Council of the European Union to foster a debate at the UN 'on the topic of establishing a United Nations Parliamentary Assembly with a view to increasing the democratic profile and internal democratic process of the organisation and to allow world civil society to be directly associated in the decision-making process.'[68] In a reply to a parliamentary question, the EU's Foreign Affairs representative Federica Mogherini had told the MEPs on behalf of the Commission earlier in January that the EU 'continues to promote reform of the UN system and of its main bodies and organs', but also that there was still 'no formal position' as regards the creation of a UNPA.[69]

Meanwhile, the Committee for a Democratic U.N., which had been steering the UNPA campaign for ten years since its launch in 2007, decided to continue its work with a new name and an expanded mandate. 'Democratization at the national and global levels is strongly connected. As democracy comes under pressure worldwide, a holistic approach is needed that recognizes this relationship', the group announced, stressing in its new mission statement, among other things, that it would promote a 'strong collaboration between all forces that support the establishment and strengthening of democratic principles at the national, regional, and international levels.'[70]

68 European Parliament. 5 July 2017. 'Recommendation to the Council on the 72nd Session of the United Nations General Assembly'. P8_TA-PROV(2017)0304. See point 1 (bm).
69 European Parliament. 16 January 2017. 'Answer to a written question - VP/HR - United Nations Parliamentary Assembly', E-006879/2016.
70 See www.democracywithoutborders.org.

PART II

Governance and democracy in the 21st century

The phenomenon of industrialization, which began in England in the second half of the 18th century, brought in a period of rapid economic growth, techno-logical innovation and social upheaval which has continued until today and has encompassed the entire globe. These developments could not have been imag-ined when the calls for a world parliament first arose around the time of the French Revolution. 'The evolution of western industrial society', according to the sociologist Georg W. Oesterdiekhoff, 'represents probably the biggest single event in the history of human culture since the emergence of the species, or since the Neolithic era.'[1] Compared with the industrial dynamism of the last two hundred years, writes Oesterdiekhoff, the thousand-year history of Neo-lithic agriculture is 'a slow and boring affair'. Modernity is the story of a con-tinuous striving for ever faster production, mobility, transport and communi-cations. The empirically observable globalization of modernity and industry has meant, according to Oesterdiekhoff, 'that at no point in the history of the world have the living conditions of so many people undergone such drastic changes in such a short space of time.'[2] A periodical visitor from outer space', writes the British diplomat and scientist Crispin Tickell, 'would find more change in the last 200 years than in the preceding 2000, and more change in the last 20 years than in the preceding 200.'[3] The sense that this development is accelerating is not new: H. G. Wells made a similar observation in 1902 already. 'In the past century', he wrote, 'there was more change in the conditions of human life than there had been in the previous thousand years.'[4]

The development of human civilization since industrialization can be gauged with the aid of a few key global statistics. The anthropologist Leslie A.

---

1   Oesterdiekhoff, Georg W. 2005. Entwicklung der Weltgesellschaft: Von der Steinzeit zur Moderne. Münster: LIT, p. 7.
2   Ibid., p. 55.
3   Tickell, Crispin. 2005. 'Are We Pushing Gaia Too Hard?' The 46th Annual Bennett Lecture for the 50th An-niversary of Geology, University of Leicester.
4   Wells, Herbert George. 1913 [1902]. The Discovery of the Future. New York: B.W. Huebsch, p. 58.

White (1900 to 1975), a neoevolutionist in the tradition of Lewis Henry Morgan, emphasized the fundamental role of energy availability in the development of a system. 'Culture', as he put it in his 'basic law of cultural evolution', 'evolves as the amount of energy harnessed per capita per year is increased, or as the efficiency of the instrumental means of putting the energy to work is increased.'[5] The upheavals of the industrial revolution were literally fuelled by the mechanical exploitation of the energy stored in coal, and later in oil and gas. From 1820 to 2010, the *annual* worldwide consumption of primary energy grew by a factor of almost 60, from 220 million tons of oil equivalent to 12.8 billion (a ton of oil equivalent is the sum of energy released by the burning of one ton of crude oil). World population has grown from about one billion people in 1800 to over seven billion today. Finally, *annual* global economic output has increased by a factor of over 70 since 1820. The scale of this increase is clearer if we look at *cumulative* economic output over the whole of human history. Using the data gathered by the economist Angus Maddison, it is possible to observe for example that roughly a quarter of the goods and services ever produced in the history of human activity were produced in this century, i.e. since the year 2000. The proportion produced in the 20th century is around 55 per cent, and that in the 19th century already as little as around 5 per cent.[6]

The rapid rise in world population alone gives us some idea of the concomitant rise in the complexity of the human world and of the world system. For if history is made by people, and if currently there are seven times more people alive than two hundred years ago, then today seven times as much history is being made.[7] In 1965, the futurologist Alvin Toffler diagnosed a 'future shock', meaning the 'dizzying disorientation brought on by the premature arrival of the future' that makes human beings 'progressively incompetent to deal rationally with their environments'. Future shock was 'a time phenomenon, a product of the greatly accelerated rate of change in society'.[8] As the sociologist Norbert Elias explained over 70 years ago, this acceleration is also a characteristic of an ever-thickening, ever-spreading global mesh of interdependence. 'This "tempo"' he wrote, 'is in fact nothing other than a manifestation of the multitude of intertwining chains of interdependence which run through every single social function that people have to perform, and of the competitive pressure

---

5   White, Leslie A. 1969. The Science of Culture. A Study of Man and Civilization. 2nd ed. New York: Farrar, Straus and Giroux, pp. 368f.

6   Cf. Maddison, Angus. 2010. 'Statistics on World Population, GDP and Per Capita GDP, 1-2008 AD'; The Economist Online, 28 June 2011 'Quantifying history: Two thousand years in one chart' (www.economist.com). The percentage share before our time is negligible.

7   The Economist Online, ibid.

8   Toffler, Alvin. 1984. Future Shock. Reissue. New York: Bantam, p. 11

that permeates this densely populated network, affecting directly or indirectly every single individual act.'[9]

A large proportion of the world's population today enjoys historically unprecedented material prosperity. Although there are of course large regional disparities, average global life expectancy is higher than ever. According to UN data it has risen from 47 years in 1955 to 70 years in 2015. Nevertheless, the confident faith in progress of earlier times has for many people given way to fear of the future and disorientation in the face of continual warfare, genocide, nuclear weapons, terrorism, environmental destruction, climate change, dwindling resources, industrial catastrophes, hunger, misery, poverty, unemployment and the growing mountain of public debt. Jürgen Habermas spoke of a 'new obscurity' and of the helpless confusion of the intellectual class.[10] The French philosopher Jean-François Lyotard, in his 1979 book 'La Condition postmoderne', announced the total failure of modernity and the beginning of 'postmodernity'. In the modern era, a very condensed version of his argument might say, there was always an overarching vision of the future, an 'idea yet to be realised', which served as orientation and legitimation. Lyotard meant by this the 'grand narratives' such as progress, enlightenment or socialism. The crime of the Holocaust, he argued, had made it clear in the most tragic terms that such grand legitimating narratives had lost their credibility. The downfall of the meta-narratives, as he also called them, meant the simultaneous destruction of the project of modernity. This left 'capitalist techno-science' as the victor, continuing the process of deligitimation in the name of modernity but in doing so actually furthering to its destruction.[11]

The continuing crisis of modernity provides the wider context in which the project of a world parliament, of a world legal system and a new global enlightenment, must be seen. Although the idea of a world parliament goes back hundreds of years, it is not obsolete, but on the contrary has become ever more topical and more urgent. It is no longer merely about ensuring world peace. Rather, the question being posed is the much wider one of *world governance*, one which reveals at the same time a profound intellectual crisis. The starting point of our deliberations is the influence exerted by human activity on the Earth's ecological balances, which provide the existential basis for the survival of today's global civilization.

9   Elias, Norbert. The Civilizing Process: Sociogenetic and Psychogenetic Investigations. Transl. by Edmund Jephcott. Revised edition. Oxford; Malden, MA: Blackwell, 2000. p. 379
10 Habermas, Jürgen. 1985. Die neue Unübersichtlichkeit. Frankfurt am Main: Suhrkamp, pp. 141, 145.
11 Lyotard, Jean-Francois. 1990 [1984]. 'Randbemerkungen zu den Erzählungen'. In: Postmoderne and Dekonstruktion, ed. by Peter Engelmann and Jean-Francois Lyotard. Stuttgart: Reclam., pp. 49ff.

10.
The Anthropocene, planetary boundaries
and the tragedy of the commons

The era of humankind

A heated debate has broken out in the earth sciences as to whether human activity is now on a geological scale. The introduction of a new geological era is under consideration, to succeed the Holocene, which began twelve thousand years ago.[1] The purpose of such a decision would be to put the spotlight on the influence exerted by humankind. The Dutch meteorologist Paul J. Crutzen, who received the Nobel Prize for chemistry for his contribution to research on the ozone hole, argued in *Nature* magazine in 2002 that the impact of human activity on the global environment had become so significant that the new epoch would have to be called the 'Anthropocene', meaning roughly 'the era of humankind'. The Italian geologist Antonio Stoppani recognized the huge influence of humanity on the environment as early as 1873, and spoke of an 'anthropozoic era'. 'The Anthropocene', Crutzen wrote, 'could be said to have started in the latter part of the eighteenth century, when analyses of air trapped in polar ice showed the beginning of growing global concentrations of carbon dioxide and methane.'[2] The proportion of CO_2 in the atmosphere has risen by more than a third compared with pre-industrial times, and is higher than at any time in the last 2.1 million years.[3] The main cause is the use of fossil energy which was stored up over hundreds of millions of years and is now being released. It will probably still be possible to find the traces of industrial civilization millions of years from now in sediments and fossils. It is likely, too, that from our time forward, many species will rarely be found in fossil form, or even not at all. The Harvard biologist Edward O. Wilson, one of the first to use the term 'biodiversity', spoke in 1992 in his book 'The Diversity of Life' of the sixth great

1   A formal recommendation was made at the 35th International Geological Congress in August 2016, see Zalasiewicz, Jan, et al. 2017. 'The Working Group on the Anthropocene: Summary of evidence and interim recommendations'. Anthropocene 19 (Supplement C):55–60.
2   Crutzen, Paul J. January 2002. 'Geology of mankind'. Nature 415: p. 23.
3   Bärbel Hönisch et al. 19 June 2009. Atmospheric Carbon Dioxide Concentration Across the Mid-Pleistocene Transition, in: Science 324 (5934), pp. 1551–1554.

extinction in Earth history, brought about by human beings.[4] Researchers believe that on the other hand some of the plastic waste now spread all over the
planet will, under certain conditions, be deposited and geologically preserved.
One likely example is the mix of materials referred to as 'plastiglomerate' and
first found on Hawaii.[5] According to Crutzen, the world's strata from 1945 onwards contain tiny but measurable amounts of artificial radionuclides produced
by the detonation of atomic bombs. Up to 1996 over two thousand atomic
bombs had been detonated, more than five hundred of them above ground in the
atmosphere. Crutzen and others believe that these artificial radionuclides could
also constitute a geological marker for the beginning of the Anthropocene.[6]

Earth system boundaries

The concept of the Anthropocene is already in use in practice. It is more useful
than any other term as a means of highlighting the now epochal influence of
human activity on the Earth's natural balancing systems. Its significance lies not
in an anthropocentric approach interested only in the needs and concerns of
human beings; on the contrary, what it acknowledges and emphasizes is the
effects of human activity *on all of life on Earth and on the Earth system as a
whole*. Human beings and their civilization are inseparably embedded in nature
and in the Earth system. The idea that life on Earth is based on a self-regulating
and highly complex integrated system was articulated and popularized by the
British scientist James Lovelock in 1979 in his 'Gaia hypothesis'. In Greek mythology, Gaia was the name of the primeval goddess of the Earth from whom
all life came. This systems-based perspective has found broad acceptance. Thus,
for example, the path-breaking Amsterdam Declaration on Global Change, issued in 2001 by four leading international research networks, speaks of the
Earth system behaving 'as a single, self-regulating system comprised of physical,
chemical, biological and human components'. The scientists from the participating programmes point out in the declaration that Earth system dynamics are
not linear but characterized by critical thresholds and abrupt changes. 'Human
activities', they wrote, 'have the potential to switch the Earth System to alternative
modes of operation that may prove irreversible and less hospitable to humans

4   Wilson, Edward O. 1992. The Diversity of Life. Cambridge: Belknap Press of Harvard Univ. Press, pp. 32, 278ff.
5   Corcoran, Patricia L., Charles J. Moore, and Kelly Jazvac. June 2014. 'An anthropogenic marker horizon in
    the future rock record'. GSA Today 24, no. 6 (www.geosociety.org).
6   Zalasiewicz, Jan, Mark Williams, Will Steffen, and Paul Crutzen. 2010. 'The New World of the Anthropo-
    cene'. Environmental Science and Technology 44 (7): 2228–31, p. 2230.

and other life.'[7] To put it another way: the self-regulating life support system named 'Gaia' could collapse because of human intervention.

Earth system science represents a new interdisciplinary research area focused directly on these issues. It aims to create an understanding of the Earth as an integrated system and to evaluate anthropogenic influences. One important topic of research is the so-called 'planetary boundaries'. 'These boundaries', wrote the Swedish researcher Johan Rockström and his 27 colleagues in 2009, 'define the safe operating space for humanity with respect to the Earth system.' If these boundaries are crossed, then humans could be faced with 'deleterious or potentially even disastrous consequences'. Over the course of the Holocene, lasting more than ten thousand years, the Earth system had been in an exceptionally stable state, they wrote, without which the development of agriculture and complex societies would not have been possible. The aim had to be to preserve this stable state. So far, critical boundaries had been defined in nine areas. They measure climate change (using the concentration of CO_2 in the atmosphere and changes in radiative forcing); biodiversity loss; interference with the nitrogen and phosphorus cycles; stratospheric ozone depletion; ocean acidification; global freshwater use; change in land use; chemical pollution; and atmospheric aerosol loading. In the opinion of the research group led by Rockström, these boundaries have already been exceeded with respect to climate change, biodiversity loss and the nitrogen cycle.[8]

Especially worrying is the concentration of CO_2 in the atmosphere, for which the critical threshold had until recently been regarded by the IPCC (Intergovernmental Panel on Climate Change) as 450 ppm (parts per million), but which in the opinion of Rockström and other scientists such as James Hansen, the former lead climate researcher at NASA, should be 350 ppm. Measurements taken at the Mauna Loa Observatory on Hawaii on 9 May 2013 exceeded 400 ppm for the first time ever, and from 2016 on will probably remain above this level for generations to come. According to data from the World Meteorological Organization, there was a record increase in the average CO_2 concentration of 3.3 ppm from 2015 to 2016 up to a level of 403.3 ppm.[9] This was the largest annual increase in over four decades and represents the highest concentration in the last 800,000 years; it is possible that the forests and oceans are losing their efficacy as carbon dioxide sinks. In its very first report, in 1990, the IPCC came

7   International Geosphere-Biosphere Programme (IGBP), International Human Dimensions Programme on Global Environmental Change (IHDP), World Climate Research Programme (WCRP), and DIVERSITAS. 13 July 2001. 'The Amsterdam Declaration on Global Change'.
8   Rockström, Johan et al. September 2009. 'A safe operating space for humanity'. Nature 461: 472–75.
9   WMO. 30 October 2017. 'WMO Greenhouse Gas Bulletin', no. 13.

to the firm conclusion that the emission of anthropogenic greenhouse gases like CO_2 was increasing the greenhouse effect. Over the course of the last one hundred years, an increase in worldwide *average* air and water temperatures of 0.74 °C has been measured, of which according to NASA two-thirds has taken place since 1975. One of the consequences is a rise in sea level due to melting ice. A rise of 19.5 centimetres has been measured over the period from 1870 to 2004.[10] According to the latest IPCC scenarios, a further rise of between 26 and 98 centimetres can be expected by 2100.[11] The consequences of the rise in temperature for the stability of the Earth system – because of shifts in ocean currents, for example – are uncertain.

The problem of voluntarism

The identification and observance of 'planetary boundaries' is a central and ongoing task for humankind in the Anthropocene. Avoiding the destabilization of the Earth system by human influence is a fundamental prerequisite for the long-term flourishing of human civilization. This task is in the interests of humanity as a whole. Those goods whose exploitation brings us up against 'planetary boundaries' are therefore to be regarded as part of the 'common heritage of humankind'. The responsibility for the management and use of such goods is shared by the whole of humanity. How they are used is everybody's concern. Humankind must wake up, grow up and take responsibility for itself and for all life on earth. This is the deeper meaning of the Anthropocene. However, the appropriate instruments and institutions do not yet exist. And in the current framework of international law it is very unlikely that they can be created. The principle of state sovereignty in international law excludes the possibility of a higher authority above the state – not even humankind itself. States take on commitments only on a voluntary basis. A state can evade its common responsibilities simply by refusing to enter into a treaty, or by withdrawing from one previously entered into. Reference is occasionally made in international law to the common interests of humankind, but the inherent contradiction with the principle of state sovereignty is impossible to resolve.

The United Nations Framework Convention on Climate Change, which was adopted at the Rio Conference of 1992 and which entered into force two years later, states in its opening sentence that 'change in the Earth's climate and its

---

10   Church, John A. and Neil J. White. 2006. A 20th century acceleration in global sea-level rise, Geophysical Research Letters, Vol. 33, L01602.
11   Intergovernmental Panel on Climate Change. Climate Change. 2013. The Physical Science Basis. Working Group I Contribution to the IPCC Fifth Assessment Report. Cambridge University Press, p. 25.

adverse effects are a common concern of humankind'. This wording links back to a resolution of the UN General Assembly in 1988 in which climate change was already described as a 'common concern of mankind'. 'Mankind' (or 'humankind', as would generally be preferred today), however, has remained an abstract concept. The Climate Change Convention in fact reaffirms 'the principle of sovereignty of States in international cooperation to address climate change' and is constructed accordingly. It took five years for the Kyoto Protocol for the reduction of greenhouse gas emissions to be passed in 1997. Eight years later it finally entered into force. It has not been ratified by the USA - before Kyoto already, the US Senate passed a unanimous resolution that the USA would not adopt any resolution which did not include reduction targets for developing countries. And indeed reduction targets were included for only 37 countries in the Kyoto Protocol, for which the first commitment period ended in 2012. China, with roughly a quarter of all emissions the world's biggest emitter today in absolute terms, was one of those not included. Moreover, any country that wishes to withdraw can simply do so. This is what Canada did in 2011 in order to avoid penalty payments for missing reduction targets.

At the Paris Climate Conference in December 2015, an agreement was finally reached which all the states in the world are willing to adopt. The Paris Agreement includes a new target for international climate policy, that of reducing emissions so as to limit the worldwide temperature rise to a maximum of 1.5 degrees Celsius compared to pre-industrialization levels. At the climate conference in Copenhagen in 2009 an initial target of 2 degrees had been agreed. The Paris Agreement was celebrated as a breakthrough in international climate policy. However, the agreement does not include any binding reduction targets for individual states. Instead, they are required to report on so-called 'nationally determined contributions' to the global reduction of emissions every five years. There is an understanding and expectation that these targets will be progressively more ambitious. Yet it is questionable whether this system of voluntary commitment can achieve the reductions required, and the new agreement will only be implemented from 2020. 'By the time the pledges come into force in 2020', commented Steffen Kallbekken, Director of the Centre for International Climate and Energy Policy in Oslo, 'we will probably have used the entire carbon budget consistent with 1.5°C warming. If we stick with the Intended Nationally Determined Contributions we will have warming between 2.7°C and 3.7°C.'[12] In fact, a UN report published ahead of climate talks in Bonn in Octo-

---

12   Chivers, Danny, and Jess Worth. 12 Dec. 2015. 'Paris Deal: Epic Fail on a Planetary Scale'. New Internationalist.

ber 2017 found that national pledges only bring a third of the reduction in emissions required by 2030 to meet climate targets. Without much stronger pledges, a temperature increase of 'at least 3°C by 2100' was 'very likely'.[13]

States remain free anyway, of course, to evade the limitations and costs of international regulatory frameworks, and to reap the benefits of being free riders, if they so wish. Economists speak of 'negative externalities' if third parties suffer negative consequences whose costs are not borne by the party causing them. The 2006 report by the economist Nicholas Stern, commissioned by the British government, on the economic consequences of climate change looks at greenhouse gases from this perspective. 'Those who produce greenhouse gas emissions', the report states, 'are bringing about climate change, thereby imposing costs on the world and on future generations, but they do not face directly, neither via markets nor in other ways, the full consequences of the costs of their actions.'[14] As the emitter doesn't bear the costs, they have no economic incentive to reduce them. But the economic consequences are enormous. Although the Stern report stresses the difficulty of producing an economic estimate, it calculates the costs of stabilising the concentration of greenhouse gases in the atmosphere at 500 to 550 ppm CO_2 equivalent by 2050, subject to certain conditions, at around one per cent of global economic output per year.[15] To this must be added the costs of the damage actually caused by climate change. Stern estimates that in economic terms these costs could lie in a range between five and twenty per cent of annual global GDP. Climate change, the report states, 'must be regarded as market failure on the greatest scale the world has seen'.[16]

The 'tragedy of the commons'

The state is able to counteract the negative effects of emissions, and to create an economic incentive to reduce them, by means of taxation, emissions trading systems and other forms of regulation which set an appropriate price on them. However, the difficulty lies in the fact that the atmosphere is a *global* common good. Regulation at the level of the individual state or the region, for example through the EU, leads to distortion of competition. Experts speak of 'carbon leakage' when higher emissions costs in one country lead to the displacement of emissions to another country where those costs are lower. One study in 2011

---

13 UN Environment. 31 October 2017. 'Emissions Gap Report 2017: Governments, non-state actors must do more to reach Paris Agreement' (www.unenvironment.org).
14 Stern, Nicholas. 2006. The Economics of Climate Change. The Stern Review, pp. 24 ff.
15 Ibid., p. 212ff.; two years later, Stern spoke of 2 percent, see Jowit, Juliette, and Patrick Wintour. 26 June 2008. 'Cost of tackling global climate change has doubled, warns Stern'. The Guardian (www.guardian.co.uk).
16 Ibid., pp. 1, 25.

concluded that although countries with Kyoto commitments reduced their emissions on average by seven per cent, no commensurate reduction in their 'carbon footprint' could be observed. The 'carbon footprint' captures the CO_2 emissions of a country on the basis of the goods consumed there, regardless of where they were produced. The study found that the fact that emissions were reduced while the footprint was not implied a rise in net CO_2 imports. The conclusion to be drawn from the phenomenon of 'carbon leakage' was that unilateral climate policy was not effective in a globalized world. Rather, it argued, effective climate policy required all countries to be bound into a global climate treaty.[17] To be sure, what is meant here is a treaty which is not only worldwide but which includes binding reduction requirements.

The problem here is a form of the 'tragedy of the commons' as described by the biologist Garrett Hardin (1915 to 2003), in an influential article, as a widely-observed phenomenon. Hardin constructed a model showing how the 'rational' users of a limited common resource, in seeking to maximize their short-term utility, thereby exhaust the common resource over the longer term, with the result of ruin for all. Despite the fact that everyone wants to maintain the resource, they are all trapped by the inherent dynamics of the situation. One of the examples Hardin uses is common grazing land on which the individual herds are continuously increasing in numbers. In order to escape the dilemma, Hardin suggests either the transformation of the common goods into private property or setting limits to their common use – that is, managing them.[18] 'Socialism or the privatism of free enterprise', as he later put it, were by this account the only alternatives for their management.[19] In the area of environmental pollution, according to Hardin, comprehensive state regulation is the only possible answer. '[T]he air and waters surrounding us cannot readily be fenced,' he emphasized, 'and so the tragedy of the commons as a cesspool must be prevented by different means, by coercive laws or taxing devices that make it cheaper for the polluter to treat his pollutants than to discharge them untreated.'[20]

According to Mary Wood, the founder of the University of Oregon's Environmental and Natural Resources Law Center, '[r]anking among the most essential purposes of government is the necessity of protecting natural assets for the common benefit of the people and their society.' She argues that the doc-

---

17 Aichele, Rahel, and Gabriel Felbermayr. 2011. 'Auswirkungen der Kyoto-Verpflichtungen auf Emissionen and Carbon Footprints'. ifo Schnelldienst, no. 22: 23–26, p. 26.

18 Hardin, Garrett. 13 December 1968. 'The Tragedy of the Commons'. Science 162 (3859): 1243–1248

19 Id. 1 May 1998. 'Extension of The Tragedy of the Commons'. Science 280 (5364): 682–683.

20 Hardin (1968), loc. cit.

trine of 'public trust' that is to be found in legal systems around the world expands to the atmosphere.[21] In the absence of a global legislature as a primary trustee and a global government that can act as its agent, there is no other way than to make national governments accountable relative to their duty to enforce a reduction of atmospheric emissions.

The management of global common goods

Many instances have been pointed out where the common use of limited resources, at local as well as regional levels, has not led to the scenario described by Hardin because of a system of self-organization among the users, demonstrating the existence of additional alternatives. Moreover, both state management and privatization are also equally capable of failing. This relativizes Hardin's model, and his suggested solutions. The US American political scientist Elinor Ostrom (1933 to 2012) was awarded the Nobel Prize in economics in 2009 for her ground-breaking research in this area. '[T]ragedies of the commons are real, but not inevitable', was how she and four colleagues summarized this finding in the magazine *Science*.[22] However, they expressed themselves more cautiously with regard to *global* common goods, and spoke of the necessity for global institutions. The lessons to be drawn from local and regional examples of self-organization were encouraging, 'yet humanity now faces new challenges to establish global institutions to manage biodiversity, climate change, and other ecosystem services'.[23] It seems that the potential benefits of the kinds of self-organization studied by Ostrom cannot be fully realized in respect of global common goods. In the *Science* article, six reasons were listed why management seemed to be especially problematic in such cases:

- Scale: the huge number of users of global common goods – ultimately, all of humanity – increases the difficulty of organizing, agreeing on rules, and enforcing rules.
- Cultural and economic diversity: growing cultural diversity, along with the stark differences between industrialized and less-industrialized countries, make it less likely that shared interests and understandings can be found.
- Complexity: compared with the management of local grazing land or woodland, the systems of global common goods are more complex, including in

21 Wood, Mary. 2012. 'Atmospheric Trust Litigation Around the World'. In: Fiduciary Duty and the Atmospheric Trust, ed. by Ken Coghill, Charles Sampford, and Tim Smith, 99–163. Ashgate Publishing, pp. 106f., 126ff.

19 Ostrom, Elinor, Joanna Burger, Christopher B. Field, Richard B. Norgaard, and David Policansky. 9 April 1999. 'Revisiting the Commons: Local Lessons, Global Challenges'. Science 284 (5412): 278–282, p. 281.

23 Ibid.

terms of how they intermesh with each other, and it is more difficult to grasp where the common interests in their management lie.

- Rapidity of change: the rate of change continues to accelerate. Ecological thresholds are being exceeded before we even notice them. 'Learning by doing' is increasingly difficult, as past lessons are increasingly less relevant to current problems.
- The principle of voluntarism: the fundamental principle of global resource management is that of voluntary assent to international treaties. National governments can demand special privileges as a price for joining regulatory agreements, 'thus strongly affecting the kinds of resource management policies that can be adopted at this level.'
- No room for experiment: in earlier times, people could migrate to other resources if they made a major error in managing a local resource. In the management of global common goods there is no room for failed experiments.[24]

The problem of the generations

The US American philosophy professor Stephen M. Gardiner has pointed out an additional problematic issue. It is linked to the fact that the *cumulative* effects of greenhouse gases build up over a very long time period. In his view, these delayed effects create an even worse form of the tragedy of the commons. '[C]ontrol of the situation', he writes, 'rests completely with the current generation.' Future generations have no influence whatever on whether the current generation chooses to act as quasi-free riders or not. Normally, all parties in principle have an interest in cooperation. But if the consequences of over-exploitation are not experienced by the current generation, Gardiner asks, why should it forego the benefits? Perhaps the worst aspect of this is that the situation is repeated from generation to generation. Each new generation will find itself in the same situation with regard to the generations to come.[25]

A solution to the problem of the generations lies in a world legal system based on democratic majority decisions. A team of researchers at Harvard University has simulated the use of common resources over several generations using a game theory model. In this, the resource is almost always over-exploited and exhausted when the decisions on its use are made on an individual basis. This is because a minority of users always decides to exploit the resource without regard to coming generations. However, when use decisions are made by

24 Ibid., pp. 281f.
25 Gardiner, Stephen M. 2004. 'The Global Warming Tragedy and the Dangerous Illusion of the Kyoto Protocol'. Ethics & International Affairs 18 (1): 23–39, pp. 30ff.

democratic majority vote, then the usage is always sustainable, and the resource is maintained. What is decisive is that all users have to be bound by the vote. 'Votes that are only partially binding, such as the international Kyoto protocol, have little power', the researchers wrote in *Nature* magazine.[26]

Global majority decision-making

With respect to global common goods, it is our view that Hardin's model still provides the best picture of what is happening at the international level. Alongside the central problem of greenhouse gas emissions, many other unresolved examples of the tragedy of the commons can be adduced. In a critically-acclaimed book on the drastic overfishing of the seas, for example, the Swedish politician Isabella Lövin wrote that the condition of 'most of the world's fisheries are nothing but a shining example of how this theory works in practice'.[27] It needs to be emphasized here that regulation which aims to break the dilemma of over-exploitation can only work if it binds all users equally and if there are no free riders to undermine it. For us, therefore, the principle of voluntarism in international law is among the most serious of the problems identified by Elinor Ostrom for global resource management. The effective management of *global* common goods like the atmosphere and the oceans, or of resources as complex as biodiversity, will hardly be possible on the basis of international law 'à la carte'. The answer lies in a framework provided by a *world legal system*. 'The logic that leads to regulation of the commons is compelling', the world federalist Dieter Heinrich wrote, 'and is one of the main forces driving global political integration at a time of increasing interdependence.'[28] As the Turkish international law specialist Kemal Beslar wrote in 1998, in a study on the concept of the 'common heritage of mankind', 'effective implementation ... can only be achieved by setting up a supranational authority whose power surpasses those of nation-states' and which can 'represent mankind as a whole'.[29]

An international Earth systems research project is currently under way with a specific focus on Earth systems governance, that is, on issues concerning the institutional and regulatory management of the Earth system. In March 2012,

26   Hauser, Oliver P., David G. Rand, Alexander Peysakhovich, and Martin A. Nowak. 10 July 2014 'Cooperating with the Future'. Nature 511 (7508): 220–23, pp. 221f.
27   Lövin, Isabella. 2012. Silent Seas: The Fish Race to the Bottom. Rothersthorpe: Paragon Publishing, p. 72.
28   Heinrich, Dieter. 2010. The Case for a United Nations Parliamentary Assembly. Extended reprint, originally published 1992. Berlin: Committee for a Democratic UN, p. 16.
29   Baslar, Kemal. 1998. The Concept of the Common Heritage of Mankind in International Law. The Hague et al.: Martinus Nijhoff, pp. 92, 94.

a group of around 30 researchers led by Frank Biermann, now at Utrecht University, presented a list of what they consider to be the most important building blocks for a more effective institutional framework. In an article in *Science* magazine, they wrote that 'structural change', a 'major transformative shift' and a 'constitutional moment' were needed in global governance and world politics today - just as in 1945 when the UN was founded. They stressed that the prevailing consensus-based decision-making mechanisms at the international level 'limit decisions to the preferences of the least ambitious country'. International standards setting needed to be based much more on qualified majority decisions and linked weighted voting mechanisms. Governance systems based on majority decision-making, they argued, are quicker to arrive at far-reaching decisions.[30] The negotiations around the UN Framework Convention on Climate Change, for example, are based on consensus, as the governments have been unable since the first Conference of the Parties in 1995 to agree on another system. This is why, for example, the concluding document from the climate conference in Copenhagen in 2009 was only 'to be taken note of' rather than binding. According to a report in the *Observer* newspaper, Bolivia, Venezuela, Nicaragua, Sudan and Saudi Arabia had threatened up until the last minute to use their veto to block a formal deal.[31] Nor has the Paris Agreement changed anything with respect to the consensus principle in climate negotiations. 'Though consent does indeed protect the interests of states and support notions of sovereign equality, it also functions as a barrier to effective cooperation in a world of vastly divergent priorities and concerns', writes the US American professor of international law Andrew T. Guzman on the 'consent problem'. 'We live in a world with nuclear weapons, a warming climate, vanishing fisheries, grinding poverty, and countless other problems whose solutions require a high level of cooperation among states. Unless we change how we view the role of consent, it will be almost impossible to address these problems.'[32] This expresses a view now held ever more widely. '[T]he consent principle is undemocratic', is the judgment of Anne Peters, Director at the Max Planck Institute for Comparative Public Law and International Law. 'It is undemocratic because it allows the tyranny of one member of a political community over the others, and allows a small minority to block collective action.'[33] A world parliament serves the key

---

30 Biermann, Frank, et al. 16 March 2012. 'Navigating the Anthropocene: Improving Earth System Governance'. Science 335 (6074): 1306–1307, p. 1307.
31 Goldenberg, Suzanne, Toby Helm, and John Vidal. 20 December 2009. 'Copenhagen: The key players and how they rated'. The Observer (www.guardian.co.uk).
32 Guzman, Andrew T. 2012. 'Against Consent'. Virginia Journal of International Law 52 (4): 747–90, p. 749.
33 Peters, Anne. 2009. 'Dual Democracy'. In: The Constitutionalization of International Law, by Jan Klabbers, Anne Peters, and Geir Ulfstein, 263–341. Oxford, New York: Oxford University Press, p. 289.

purpose of creating a basis for legitimate, democratic and binding majority decisions at the global level and of overcoming the consensus principle.

The tragedy of international law

The problem emerging here is one of a fundamental nature, affecting all regulation concerned with genuinely global issues. 'Because treaties are often ineffective without the participation of certain, and sometimes most, countries', Andrew Strauss, for example, argues, 'a defiant minority can effectively veto the introduction of treaties that are in the vital interest of the world community.'[34] This makes the system of international law dysfunctional. For in order for a treaty to be effective in terms of its *reach*, it usually needs as many states as possible to sign up to it. But in order to achieve this, the *substance* of the agreement has to be subjected to ever lengthier negotiations and ever more compromises. Heinrich has pointed out how these conditions lead to international treaties representing no more than the lowest common denominator among the treaty partners.[35] This is the case even for the resolutions of the UN General Assembly, which have no universally binding force under international law. In his 2005 report 'In larger freedom', for example, the then UN Secretary-General Kofi Annan lamented the fact that the General Assembly was reaching an increasing number of decisions by consensus. But consensus, he thought, was being interpreted as 'requiring unanimity' and had become an end in itself, yet one which was far from expressing a genuine unity of purpose among the member states. 'Rather', Annan wrote, 'it prompts the Assembly to retreat into generalities, abandoning any serious effort to take action.'[36] It can be concluded as a rule of thumb of international law that a treaty with effective reach will have proportionately less substance, while a treaty with effective substance will have proportionately less reach. This Catch-22 could be termed the tragedy of international law. The loser in every case is both the effectiveness of the regulation and humanity as a whole.

---

34 Strauss, Andrew. 1999. 'Overcoming the Dysfunction of the Bifurcated Global System: The Promise of A Peoples Assembly'. Transnational Law & Contemporary Problems 9 (2): 48–70. Reprinted in and citation from: Falk, Richard, and Andrew Strauss. 2011. A Global Parliament: Essays and Articles. Berlin: Committee for a Democratic UN, pp. 107f.

35 Heinrich, loc. cit., p. 20.

36 United Nations. 2005. 'In larger freedom: towards development, security and human rights for all'. Report of the Secretary-General. A/59/2005, para. 159.

11.
Overshoot, the 'Great Transformation', and a global eco-social market economy

Overshoot and ecological footprint

With the spread of industrialization, an economic system based on ever-increasing and ever-accelerating growth and concomitant consumption has become a global phenomenon. This system's functioning is dependent on a perpetual increase in and re-modernization of material prosperity. If economic output fails to grow, or even worse declines, then loss of income, unemployment, corporate bankruptcies and political, social and economic instability loom. Through the worldwide growth in economic activity and in population, the planet's resources are being put under pressure and used up faster than they can renew themselves. There has been intensive discussion of this problem ever since the 1972 report to the Club of Rome on the 'Limits to Growth'. Specialists in the field refer to the transgression of natural ecological regenerative capacity as 'overshoot'. The concept of the 'ecological footprint', as propounded and developed by the researchers Mathis Wackernagel and William Rees since 1990, serves as a way of measuring and depicting overshoot. According to estimates made by the Global Footprint Network, founded by Wackernagel in 2003, humankind today is using the equivalent of one and half times the biocapacity of the Earth's land and water surface. Thus the ecological footprint of the human race stands at 1.5, and it is rising sharply. According to the Footprint Network, in order for every human being today to enjoy the lifestyle of the average US American would require a fivefold increase in the Earth's biocapacity – which is simply not possible. 'If the present growth trends in world population, industrialization, pollution, food production, and resource depletion continue unchanged, the limits to growth on this planet will be reached sometime within the next one hundred years.'[1] This is the core message of the 'Limits to Growth' study, and it remains as valid as ever.

It is well established that exploitable reserves of oil, gas, coal and nuclear fuel are declining and will eventually be exhausted. The question is only how soon.

---

1   Meadows, Donella, Dennis Meadows, Jorgen Randers, and William W. Behrens III. The Limits to Growth. New York: Universe Books, 1972. p. 23

The data available, and their interpretation, are disputed. As regards conventional oil, the maximum global rate of extraction – known as 'peak oil' – may already have been reached. The extraction of unconventional oil deposits, according to studies carried out at the university of Uppsala, will be able to offset the expected decline in output from already operating conventional oilfields for only a few years.[2] Some studies predict peak production of coal and gas for as early as 2020.[3] Most of the remaining reserves would in any event have to remain where they are for the moment. 'No more than one-third of proven reserves of fossil fuels can be consumed prior to 2050 if the world is to achieve the 2°C goal, unless carbon capture and storage (CCS) technology is widely deployed', stated the annual report of the International Energy Agency in 2012.[4] 'It is a sad fact that humanity has largely squandered the past 30 years in futile debates and well-intentioned, but half-hearted, responses to the global ecological challenge', wrote Donella and Dennis Meadows with Jørgen Randers in a 2004 update of their study. 'Much will have to change if the ongoing overshoot is not to be followed by collapse during the twenty-first century.'[5]

The end of the Utopia of growth

Michael Winter spoke of 'the end of a dream'. In his view, today's highly industrialized countries had largely fulfilled all of the post-Renaissance utopian dreams, namely health, security, prosperity, justice and conviviality.[6] But at what cost? The cost, according to Richard Saage, was equivalent to the failure of the project of modernity. 'The utopian dream of perpetual happiness, guaranteed by the perfect state and the total mastery of nature', this student of utopianism wrote, 'collapsed at the very moment when it seemed to have been realised in the West.'[7] The dream was bought in large part at the expense of the rest of the world, the ecosystem and future generations. 'The Europeans', says Winter, referring to modern affluent societies, 'are to today's world what the aristocracy was to the Ancien régime in France.' This utopia, he thinks, cannot last much longer. A point has been reached when the utopian project itself has to be questioned.[8] An economic system geared for maximum profits, material

2   Aleklett, Kjell. Peeking at peak oil. New York ; London: Springer, 2012, p. 118.
3   Zittel, Werner, Jan Zerhusen, Martin Zerta, and Nikolaus Arnold. 2013. Fossile and Nukleare Brennstoffe – die künftige Versorgungssituation. Ed. by Energy Watch Group. Berlin, p. 14.
4   International Energy Agency. 2012. World Energy Outlook 2012. Paris: OECD/IEA, p. 25.
5   Meadows, Donella, Jorgen Randers, and Dennis Meadows. 2004. Limits to Growth. The 30-Year Update. 1st ed. White River Junction, VT: Chelsea Green Publishing, p. xvi.
6   Winter, Michael. 1993. Ende eines Traums. Stuttgart: Metzler, p. 298.
7   Saage, Richard. 1997. Utopieforschung. Eine Bilanz. Darmstadt: Wissenschaftliche Buchgesellschaft, p. 96.
8   Winter, loc. cit., pp. 297f., 299.

consumption and continuous growth, and the associated values and lifestyles, will be subject to ever closer questioning as it becomes ever more apparent that overshoot is a dead end. In view of the growing gulf between the rich and the poor, the fact that the economic benefits of growth accrue disproportionately to certain sections of the population also plays a role here, alongside the ecological question. Moreover, in the light of diseases of affluence like the obesity epidemic, some people speak of 'the curse of overdevelopment' or of 'overdeveloped countries'.[9] Many people are now asking themselves whether the fixation of the economic system on growth, even on what is called 'green growth', makes sense at all. At any event, the fact that economic growth cannot proceed indefinitely and that development too must stagnate at some point was accepted by no less a figure than the liberal pioneer and philosopher John Stuart Mill 150 years ago in his 'Principles of Political Economy'. 'Towards what ultimate point', asked Mill, 'is society tending by its industrial progress? When the progress ceases, in what condition are we to expect that it will leave mankind?'[10] In fact, Mill expressed sympathy for the idea of a world that has escaped the compulsion of ceaseless growth in population and economic activity, has achieved a state of balance and can concentrate on intellectual, social and cultural progress. The motto must be qualitative and not quantitative growth.

The challenge of global eco-social development

The debate over an economically and socially sustainable order, and the pathways towards it, one which is so important for the future of humankind, should be brought together at an international level in a democratic world parliament. The great challenge is to move as quickly as possible, and *worldwide*, to an economic system which remains within the parameters set by the Earth system and the natural ecological regenerative capacity of the Earth, and which at the same time enables the best possible development and greatest prosperity for all. In the words of the UN High-level Panel on Global Sustainability, led by the Finnish President Tarja Halonen and the South African President Jacob Zuma, 'the long-term vision … is to eradicate poverty, reduce inequality and make growth

9   Worldwatch Institute (ed.). 2012. State of the World 2012: Moving Toward Sustainable Prosperity. Washington D.C.: Island Press, p. 24.
10 Mill, John Stuart. 1909 [1848]. Principles of Political Economy with some of their Applications to Social Philosophy. Ed. by William J. Ashley. 7th ed. London: Library of Economics and Liberty (www.econlib.org). Book IV, Chapter VI, § 1.

inclusive, and production and consumption more sustainable, while combating climate change and respecting a range of other planetary boundaries'.[11]

'Political barriers' as the main obstacle to transformation

The transition to a sustainable global society involves such profound changes that it is often compared to such world-historic shifts as the development of agriculture (the Neolithic revolution) and the Industrial revolution. It is in this sense that the authors of the 'Limits to Growth' speak of the challenge of a 'third revolution' in human history.[12] A fundamental feature of the challenge, one which would in and of itself justify such a comparison, is the shift in energy production to renewable sources accompanied by a simultaneous major increase in energy efficiency. A global energy transition of this kind would transform the existential basis of human civilization and secure it over the long term. Researchers like Ernst Ulrich von Weizsäcker already see the potential today for a five-fold increase in resource productivity.[13] The German Advisory Council on Global Change (WBGU), made up of nine experts appointed by the German Federal Government and established at the time of the UN Environment Conference in Rio in 1992, agrees that the greatest obstacles to the transition are not technological. Rather, according to a very significant 2011 report from this independent body, led by Hans Joachim Schellnhuber, Director of the Potsdam Institute for Climate Impact Research and Dirk Messner, Director of the German Development Institute, the most difficult challenges include 'a global evolutionary leap towards a greater willingness for global cooperation' and overcoming 'political barriers'.[14] Humanity must 'leave the epoch of nation states behind and foster an unprecedented culture of global cooperation'.[15] The transformation to a post-fossil fuel world society would require a new social contract, enabled by 'a new kind of discourse between governments and citizens, both within and beyond the boundaries of the nation state', a 'Social Contract for Sustainability', as it is called in the subtitle of the report.[16]

The need for a 'Great Transformation' had been mooted already in the concluding declarations of the symposia of Nobel prize winners and other leading

11   United Nations High-level Panel on Global Sustainability (ed.). 2012. 'Resilient people, resilient planet: a future worth choosing. Report of the High-level Panel of the Secretary-General on Global Sustainability'. A/66/700, p. 7.

12   Meadows, Donella, Dennis Meadows, and Jorgen Randers. 1992. Beyond the Limits. Chelsea Green, ch. 7.

13   von Weizsäcker, Ernst Ulrich, Karlson Hargroves, and Michael Smith. 2009. Faktor Fünf. Die Formel für nachhaltiges Wachstum. München: Droemer Knaur.

14   German Advisory Council on Global Change. 2011. World in Transition: A Social Contract for Sustainability. Berlin: WBGU, pp. 189f., 203.

15   Ibid., p. 91.

16   Idem. 7 May 2011. 'A Social Contract for Sustainability'. Press release (www.wbgu.de).

figures held in Potsdam, London and Stockholm in 2007, 2009 and 2011, and led by the Potsdam Institute. In the Memorandum of the Potsdam conference, for example, it was stated that humanity was 'standing at a moment in history when a great transformation is needed to respond to the immense threat to our planet'.[17] And a team of scientists linked to the Tellus Institute in Boston and the Stockholm Environment Institute, brought together into the Global Scenario Group, had already presented the scenario of a 'Great Transition' in 2002 in trying to set out a path to a sustainable and solidarity-based world society.[18] The 'Great Transition' approach is still being pursued by the Tellus Institute under the leadership of the US American physicist and futurologist Paul Raskin.

The process of state formation and the rise of the market economy

The 'Great Transformation' is not just a slogan for the project of creating a sustainable world society. The term was introduced by the economist and social scientist Karl Polanyi (1886 to 1964) in his 1944 work of the same title. Behind it lies a complex picture, still widely debated today, of the origins and development of the modern, market economy-based industrial society and of its inherent social, political and economic tensions. In the view of the US American Nobel laureate in economics Joseph Stiglitz, '[e]conomic science and economic history have come to recognize the validity of Polanyi's key contentions'.[19] Polanyi's analysis certainly offers valuable starting points for an understanding of the situation today and for appropriate courses of action.

For Polanyi, born in Vienna but forced into exile in 1933 as a Jew and a socialist, the establishment of the market economy, i.e. the switch from regulated to self-regulating markets at the end of the 18th century, marked the decisive shift in the industrial revolution. Because of the long-term investment needed, the development of mechanized production had only proved economically possible when all the factors involved could be bought and sold as commodities so that it was possible to maintain continuous production. 'The extension of the market mechanism to the elements of industry - labor, land, and money', wrote Polanyi, 'was the inevitable consequence of the introduction of the factory system in a commercial society.' In his view, it has only been possible

---

17   Potsdam-Memorandum. 2007. Conclusions of the sympodium 'Global Sustainability: A Nobel Cause', Potsdam, 8-10 October.
18   Raskin, Paul, Tariq Banuri, Gilberto Gallopín, Pablo Gutman, Al Hammond, Robert Kates, and Rob Swart. 2002. Great Transition. The Promise and Lure of the Times Ahead. A report of the Global Scenario Group. Boston, MA: Stockholm Environment Institute.
19   Stiglitz, Joseph. Foreword in: Polanyi, Karl. 2001. The great transformation: the political and economic origins of our time. Boston, MA: Beacon Press. p. xiii.

to speak of the existence of industrial capitalism as a social system since the abolition of the 'Poor Law', and the minimum subsistence for existence it provided, in England in 1834.[20] Polanyi's study shows how this social system was established step by step through measures undertaken by the state. The 'invisible hand of the market', as the Scottish political economist Adam Smith described in 1776 the self-regulating equilibrium between supply and demand driven by the individual self-interest of the market participants, does not arise automatically, as if by magic. On the contrary: 'free markets', wrote Polanyi, 'could never have come into being merely by allowing things to take their course. Just as cotton manufactures - the leading free trade industry - were created by the help of protective tariffs, export bounties, and indirect wage subsidies, *laissez-faire* itself was enforced by the state.' Paradoxically, the establishment of free markets required an enormous increase in the administrative functions of the state and the growth of a central bureaucracy working ceaselessly to ensure that the system could function.[21] Even the creation of regulated national domestic markets before the market economy itself arose was achieved by means of similar targeted measures. As Polanyi writes, internal trade in Western Europe was actually forced through by 'the *deus ex machina* of state intervention' against the opposition of the 'fiercely protectionist towns and principalities'. This 'commercial revolution' was part of the development of competing centralized nation states. 'In external politics, the setting up of sovereign power was the need of the day; accordingly, mercantilist statecraft involved the marshalling of the resources of the whole national territory to the purposes of power in foreign affairs.'[22] The creation of national internal markets and capitalist deregulation in the course of the industrial revolution can therefore be seen as significant stages in the process of state formation. This went hand in hand with a change in value systems at the level of the individual, namely the rise of the so-called 'Homo oeconomicus', in rational pursuit of his economic interests.[23]

The 'double movement' between market fundamentalism and state interventionism

In the 19th century there then arose within society a struggle over the political control of the state powers established for the regulation or deregulation of the

---

20 Polanyi, Karl. 2001. The Great Transformation: The Political and Economic Origins of Our Time. Boston, MA: Beacon Press, p. 78.
21 Ibid., p. 145.
22 Ibid., pp. 67f., 69.
23 Ibid., pp. 45ff.

markets. Polanyi sets out in his work the concept of a 'double movement' between the forces of market liberalism and those opposing social forces which sought to restrict the market mechanism. This conflict Polanyi saw as 'the one comprehensive feature in the history of the age'.[24] In his view, the First World War, the Great Depression of the 1930s, the rise of fascism and the Second World War were ultimately all symptoms of a single problem: the rise and fall of market fundamentalist capitalism. 'The dissolution of the system of world economy which had been in progress since 1900', wrote Polanyi, referring to the failure of the gold standard and the rise of protectionism, 'was responsible for the political tension that exploded in 1914.'[25] Market fundamentalism, the argument runs, carries within it the seeds of its own failure in the form of the social upheavals it sparks, and at the moment of its collapse it liberates extreme countervailing forces. 'Fascism, like socialism,' wrote Polanyi, 'was rooted in a market society that refused to function.'[26] Fascism and socialism, which both set up a form of state-controlled, centralized command economy, were in Polanyi's reading different examples of an identical countervailing force.

A global eco-social market economy

A prospering and democratic society cannot be maintained at the extreme poles of the double movement described by Polanyi. The art of politics must be that of holding a balance between the forces of free markets and state interventionism. This equilibrium can be achieved by a social market economy of the kind constructed in Western Europe after the Second World War. In the USA, which was badly hit by the Great Depression, a substantial shift was brought about in state welfare and regulation by the economic and social reforms ushered in by President Franklin D. Roosevelt's 'New Deal', beginning in 1933. But the social market economy, which aims at a balance between the forces of laissez-faire and state interventionism, is no longer sufficient today. There is an additional necessity in the form of ecological sustainability. The 'Great Transformation' of the 21st century therefore consists in regulating the market economy so that it operates in a manner that is not only socially but ecologically sustainable. The social concept which emerges from this is that of the 'eco-social market economy'. The economist and mathematician Franz Josef Radermacher and the consultant Estelle Herlyn have summarised this as follows: 'If we want a planet that remains viable for the future, on which people can live prosperously and in

24   Ibid., p. 80.
25   Ibid., pp. 42, 22.
26   Ibid., p. 248.

peace with nature and with each other, then the human race needs a different model. For this we need to combine the dynamism and innovative power of markets, in the Schumpeterian sense, with rigorous protection of the environment and with social equity, above all in terms of promoting universal political participation' – and, as they stress, that means not just on a national but on a global level. Radermacher and Herlyn believe that the economic model required consists of 'a global extension of an ordoliberal approach in the form of a worldwide eco-social regulated market economy, an eco-social market model.'[27] Franz Josef Radermacher, the entrepreneur Frithjof Finkbeiner and many others have been pressing since 2003 - in part as a response to the 1990 proposal for a 'Global Marshall Plan' by Al Gore, the American politician, environmentalist and later Nobel Peace Prize winner, in his bestselling book 'Earth in the Balance' - for just such a Plan as a concrete step towards the construction of a worldwide eco-social market economy.

On account of the intensely competitive international situation and the global common goods involved, the 'eco-social market economy' must of necessity be global. Its chances of success would be small if it were to be implemented via regulation at the nation state level rather than within an international framework. For example, prices in an eco-social economic system would need to include as far as possible all consequential ecological costs, and this in turn would require a functional global taxation system. But the 'tragedy of international law' makes precisely that impossible. For it to happen, an evolutionary step forward is required. The Brundtland Report already made the point that '[t]he traditional forms of national sovereignty are increasingly challenged by the realities of ecological and economic interdependence'.[28] As Stiglitz writes in his book 'Globalization and Its Discontents', we are dealing today, on account of falling transport and communication costs and the removal of barriers to free trade in goods, services and capital, with 'a process of "globalization" analogous to the earlier processes in which national economies were formed. 'Unfortunately', as the former World Bank chief economist continues, 'we have no world government, accountable to the people of every country, to oversee the globalization process in a fashion comparable to the way national governments guided the nationalization process.'[29] That, however, is precisely what is needed if we are to have a sustainable civilization on our planet. The *decisive*

27 Herlyn, Estelle L. A., and Franz Josef Radermacher. 2011. 'Ökosoziale Marktwirtschaft: Ideen, Bezüge, Perspektiven'. FAW/n Report, p. 3.
28 World Commission on Environment and Development (ed.). 1987. Our Common Future. Annex to A/42/427. Ch. 10, point 1.
29 Stiglitz, Joseph E. 2003. Globalization and Its Discontents. W. W. Norton & Company, p. 21.

feature of the new 'Great Transformation' which is on its way must be that the process of state formation described by Polanyi is continued *at the global level*. In the situation that existed after the First World War, Polanyi noted succinctly, the only sensible option would have been 'the establishment of an international order endowed with an organized power which would transcend national sovereignty'. [30]

---

30   Polanyi, loc. cit., p. 43.

12.
Turbo-capitalism, the financial crisis, and countering global deregulation

The contemporary relevance of the 'double movement' and the emancipation question

The newly awakened interest in Polanyi is connected not only to the issue of sustainability, which has now acquired a central importance in the 'double movement' he described. Polanyi's contemporary relevance, in the view of researchers such as the Dublin-based sociologist Ronaldo Munck or the philosopher and feminist Nancy Fraser, who teaches in New York, stems rather from the fact that market forces today have once again been largely released from any constraints - unfettered. The reforms brought in under the British Prime Minister Margaret Thatcher and the US President Ronald Reagan in the 1980s were the beginning of a wave of deregulation which led, after the end of the Cold War and the collapse of 'actually existing socialism' in the Soviet bloc, to what has been called globalised 'turbo-capitalism'. A symbolic highpoint was the 1999 abolition in the USA of the Glass–Steagall Act introduced as part of the New Deal in 1933 to maintain a separation between commercial banking and investment banking. According to the US American government adviser Edward Luttwak, who popularised the term 'turbo-capitalism' via his book of the same title, the protests against the WTO meeting in Seattle were a revolt against the 'unfettered market economy'. 'The capitalism of the 1990s', Luttwak summarised, 'is completely different from that of the preceding decades. That is why I came up with the term 'turbo-capitalism'. It describes a completely deregulated, entirely unfettered market, without any protective barriers.'[1] This is doubtless exaggerated. But it is at least certainly possible to say, using Polanyi's model, that the double movement has swung once again in the direction of laissez-faire. 'What we today call "neoliberalism"', writes Nancy Fraser, 'is nothing but the second coming of the very same nineteenth-century faith in the "self-regulating market" that unleashed the capitalist crisis Polanyi chronicled.'[2] The situation

---

1   Luttwak, Edward. 9 December 1999. 'Wenige Gewinner, viele Verlierer'. Interviewed by Dietmar H. Lamparter and Fritz Vorholz. Die Zeit (www.zeit.de).
2   Fraser, Nancy. 2011. 'Marketization, Social Protection, Emancipation: Toward a Neo-Polanyian Conception of Capitalist Crisis'. In: Business as Usual. The Roots of the Global Financial Meltdown, ed. by Craig Calhoun and Georgi Derluguian, 137–157, 281/2. New York University Press, p. 139.

is so similar, she argues, that it is possible to speak of 'a second great transformation'. Fraser emphasizes that the contrast Polanyi draws between 'good embedded markets' and 'bad disembedded markets' is too simple. The point should be to recognize and question *every form of oppression*, regardless of whether its roots are in economics or in society, in market liberalism or in state interventionism. The struggle for emancipation and for a fairer society can therefore not easily be straitjacketed into Polanyi's double movement model. The capitalist crisis, she contends, has to be understood as a three-sided conflict between market forces, social regulation and emancipation. A descent into authoritarianism and totalitarianism is a possibility which, given historical experience, must always be borne in mind and guarded against.

The financial crisis and the continuing systemic risk

The tendency of 'disembedded markets' towards self-destruction and associated social breakdown postulated by Polanyi seems to have been confirmed in the course of the global financial crisis since 2007. Confronted with the possibility of a collapse of the international financial system, the exact course and results of which were unforeseeable, government and central banks felt themselves compelled to intervene on a massive scale in support of financial institutions and other companies adjudged to be 'too big to fail'. The private commercial risks to which such institutions and their owners were exposed were diverted and passed on to the wider society. Under strict market economy conditions, the institutions concerned would have had to declare insolvency, as Lehman Brothers did. According to figures released by the International Monetary Fund, the G20 countries had promised capital injections totalling 1,160 billion US dollars, and given guarantees up to a further 4,638 billion dollars, by August 2009; this equates to 2.2 per cent and 8.8 per cent respectively of GDP for the year 2008 for all G20 member states together. The IMF figures show furthermore that the sums actually provided up to that point totalled 446 billion dollars in the form of capital injections and 366 billion in the form of credit and equity. Whereas the financial institutions and their owners were rescued, the financial crisis for which they were in part responsible triggered the worst stock market crash since 1929, a worldwide recession, a severe dip in the volume of world trade lasting several years, and job losses and continuing unemployment for many millions of people. The fear of another major global economic crisis spread. Whether this can be successfully resisted by a regulatory counter movement, and how, is the key question.

German Federal President Horst Köhler, Director of the International Monetary Fund for four years before he took office, lamented in an interview that the international financial markets had become a 'monster that has to be locked away'.[3] Even though many years have passed since then, it is impossible to avoid the impression that the 'monster' has certainly not been successfully bound. There was some premature talk of a 'renaissance of the state' in the light of the state interventions that took place. But the measures implemented represented mainly emergency responses for the maintenance of the status quo, and certainly not a systematic eradication of the causes of the crisis. Despite all their promises, governments have relied mainly on improving the regulatory oversight of financial markets. But that is not enough. Neil M. Barofsky – who until early 2011 had been the independent inspector general of the US government's Troubled Asset Relief Program for the purchase of equity shares to shore up unstable financial institutions – complained that one of the purported main aims of the re-regulation prompted by the financial crisis, namely that of ending the dominance of a small number of 'systemically significant' banks, had not been achieved. On the contrary, the top banks in the USA had in fact grown 23% larger in the meantime. The proportion of their contribution to GDP over the period 2007 to 2012 had risen from 43 to 56 per cent. 'The risk in our banking system is remarkably concentrated in these banks, which now control 52 per cent of all industry assets, up from 17 per cent four decades ago', wrote the former inspector.[4] If they get into difficulties, these banks are too big to fail, but at the same time perhaps too big to be rescued.

The Basel Committee on Banking Supervision, a committee of the Bank for International Settlements, drew up the 1,000-page Basel III regulations which entered into force in 2014 and provide new minimum capital requirements. Regardless of how effective these rules might be considered, the uniform implementation of such international standards has proved difficult. The 30 governments belonging to the Basel Committee may have undertaken to implement them in the course of the ongoing international negotiations, but this is not binding under international law. With regard to the regulation of the so-called shadow banking system, which includes hedge funds, the responsible EU Commissioner Michel Barnier made an astonishing statement. More than three years after the collapse of the US investment bank Lehman Brothers, a highpoint of the crisis, Barnier said that it was first necessary to have a 'better

---

3   'Köhler nennt Finanzmärkte Monster', 14 May 2008 (www.stern.de).
4   Barofsky, Neil M. 22 July 2012. 'Bungled Bank Bailout Leaves Behind Righteous Anger'. Bloomberg (www.bloomberg.com).

understanding of what shadow banks actually are and of what kind of regulation and oversight is appropriate for them'. It had to be borne in mind that the
sector was 'innovative' and 'permanently in motion'.[5] Yet shadow banks exert a
decisive influence on the financial system by virtue of their size alone. According to the Financial Stability Council of the G20 countries, their size grew to 34
trillion US dollars in 2015 or 69% of the GDP of the 27 jurisdictions covered in
the assessment.[6] This corresponds to about half of the world's gross domestic
product. There is little progress on regulation. Even with respect to defining
what a shadow bank should be there is disagreement. The systemic traits that
led to the crisis are still in place. It is probably only a matter of time before the
financial systems are out of control again.

State intervention to stabilize the financial system

There is another reason why it is wrong to speak of a 'renaissance of the state'.
For even if the fact is only slowly dawning on the public consciousness, state
intervention to stabilize the financial sector is not an exceptional phenomenon
brought about by the global financial crisis but common practice since decades.
The retreat of the state and the advance of the free market are a myth when seen
in this light. The state has always intervened in the workings of the market to
help investors. Studies show that between the late 1970s and the early 2000s
there were 117 systemic bank crises, in 93 countries, in which taxpayers have
put up on average the incredible figure of 12.8 per cent of national GDP to pay
for state interventions to maintain financial stability.[7] As Jeff Faux of the Economic Policy Institute in Washington D.C. emphasizes, the great financial crises of the 1990s in Mexico, Thailand, Brazil, Bolivia, South Korea, Indonesia,
Russia and Argentina all ended in large investors being protected by public rescue packages while the rest of society was left 'at the mercy of the brutal laws of
supply and demand'. This distorted model of the free market economy is in
Faux's judgement nothing other than 'socialism for the rich'.[8] But the distinctive feature of the global financial crisis was not only that it began in the USA,
a centre of the system, but also that a collapse of the *international* system
loomed, requiring simultaneous massive interventions around the world to
prevent it. On account of the close global interconnections between financial

5   Citation from Mussler, Werner. 19 March 2012. 'Finanzmarkt: EU will Schattenbanken regulieren'. Frank-
     furter Allgemeine Zeitung (www.faz.net).
6   Financial Stability Board. 10 May 2017. 'Global Shadow Banking Monitoring Report 2016', p. 3.
7   Niepmann, Friederike, and Tim Schmidt-Eisenlohr. 2010. 'Bank Bailouts, International Linkages and Coop-
     eration'. London School of Economics and Political Science, CEP Discussion Paper No 1023, p. 2.
8   Faux, Jeff. 2006. The Global Class War. Hoboken NJ: John Wiley & Sons, p. 115ff.

systems around the world, it is increasingly unlikely that crises can be constrained within local borders. '[I]n the absence of appropriate policies,' the IMF wrote, 'highly integrated economies are still susceptible to harmful cross-border spillovers.'[9] The entire world financial system has become unstable.

The financial system as a 'priority global public good'

Before the global financial crisis already, the 'International Task Force on Global Public Goods', initiated by Sweden and France and jointly led by the former Mexican President Ernesto Zedillo and Tidjane Thiam from Ivory Coast, numbered 'enhancing international financial stability' among the *priority global public goods*, alongside five others such as tackling climate change and preventing infectious diseases, strengthening the international trading system and achieving peace and security. In contrast to global common goods, which simply exist, 'global public goods' as defined by this task force are important political goals the achievement of which is in the common international interest, will benefit all states and people, and requires effective international cooperation. By definition they cannot be achieved and maintained by single countries. The same obstacles that impede the management of global common goods also hinder any attempt to ensure the provision of global public goods such as a stable financial system. Governments find it difficult to agree on far-reaching regulation and measures because of differing national interests. Their willingness to subject themselves to binding rules is limited. Since everyone benefits from a public good, there is an incentive to act as a free rider by deferring or leaving to others the investments and efforts needed to maintain that good. Ensuring compliance with the rules agreed on is difficult. Sometimes the provision or maintenance of a public good can be thwarted if only one of the parties involved, the weakest link, fails to observe the rules. The international Task Force found that adherence to the principle of national sovereignty was the 'basic problem [that] underlies all the others'. '[T]he major obstacles', the Task Force wrote in its report, 'emerge from the fact that the international sphere is characterized principally by voluntary interaction between sovereign states.'[10] Here, too, it all comes down to the fact that there is no framework of world law that would enable global regulation.

9   International Monetary Fund. October 2012. Global Financial Stability Report: Restoring Confidence and Progressing on Reforms. Washington D.C.: IMF. Ch. 3, p. 1.
10 International Task Force on Global Public Goods. 'Meeting Global Challenges: International Cooperation in the National Interest. Report of the Intl. Task Force on Global Public Goods'. Stockholm, 2006, pp. 18f.

The anarchic system of international law

It is worth noting at this point that the entire system of international law can be described in terms analogous to those that characterize a disembedded market. Homo oeconomicus, striving - in the doctrine of laissez-faire - to maximize his benefits, equates in international law to the sovereign state seeking advantage. In the final analysis, what concerns the sovereign state is geopolitical interests, that is, the achievement of a position of power relative to rival states. This includes control over territory and resources enforced by military power - the classic instrument of geopolitics; but it goes beyond that. Rivalry between industrialised countries is no longer played out on the battlefield but on economic territory. In what Luttwak calls the 'geo-economy', states intervene in support of specific industries and companies, be it to further their market dominance, to defend them against unwanted competition or to support their conquest of new markets. 'Even when there is no thought of any military confrontation therefore', according to Luttwak, 'even when they cooperate most amicably in all sorts of ways, states are inherently adversarial.'[11] After the end of the Cold War, the influential political scientist Kenneth Waltz, known in the study of international relations as the founding theorist of neorealism, wrote that in spite of the changes 'the basic structure of international politics continues to be anarchic'. 'Each state', according to Waltz, 'fends for itself with or without the cooperation of others. The leaders of states and their followers are concerned with their standings, that is, with their positions vis-à-vis one another.'[12] George Soros has developed this analogy further. The doctrine of geopolitics, he writes, 'has some similarity to the doctrine of laissez-faire in that both treat self-interest as the only realistic basis for explaining or predicting the behavior of a subject. For laissez-faire, the subject is the individual market participant; for geopolitics, the state. Closely allied to both is the vulgar version of Darwinism according to which the survival of the fittest is the rule of nature'. In his view, the idea that the state should represent the interests of *its citizens* rather than being an end in itself does not exist in the world of geopolitics. 'Geopolitical realism', according to Soros, 'may be regarded as a translation of the doctrine of laissez faire into international relations with the difference that the actors are states, not individuals or business units.'[13] We would like to take this line of thought one step further. For if in Polanyi's analysis the state has to intervene in order to control

11   Luttwak, Edward. 1999. Turbo Capitalism. London: Orion, p. 128
12   Waltz, Kenneth N. 1993. 'The Emerging Structure of International Politics'. Intl. Security 18 (2): 44–79, p. 59.
13   Soros, George. The Crisis of Global Capitalism. New York: PublicAffairs, 1998. p. 215.

the disembedded market, then in our analogy it is precisely the option of intervention on the part of the *world state* which does not exist in international law.

Liberalism, Laissez-faire and the question of a world state

However, it should be pointed out here – on behalf of the classical advocates of laissez-faire – that the parallel drawn here with geopolitics and international law distorts and truncates their arguments in important respects. In their doctrine, the point is precisely that the state should *not* get involved in economic affairs, and so for example should not intervene to support specific industries or companies. Moreover, laissez-faire meant for them *not* the *absence* of a superordinate state power, as is the case in the anarchic international order, but precisely its *restriction* to specific tasks. Of course, the state should avoid getting involved in the workings of the market if at all possible, but its active engagement in ensuring peace, liberty and property is taken as given. In their view, the state has to be able to enforce peaceful human cooperation and the observance of common rules when necessary. 'Liberalism is not anarchism, nor has it anything whatsoever to do with anarchism', the influential economist Ludwig von Mises (1881 to 1973) declared in his 1927 work 'Liberalism'. This applies equally to the international order. The international law dogma that 'every single state is sovereign' and represents 'the highest and last instance' was anathema to the proponents of worldwide free trade and movement ('laissez-faire et laissez-passer'). Liberalism is, as Mises attempted to make clear, 'a world-embracing political concept, and the same ideas that it seeks to realize within a limited area it holds to be valid also for the larger sphere of world politics. If the liberal makes a distinction between domestic and foreign policy, he does so solely for purposes of convenience and classification, to subdivide the vast domain of political problems into major types, and not because he is of the opinion that different principles are valid for each'. In the knowledge that it is not enough to ensure peace within the state, liberalism demands 'that the political organization of society be extended until it reaches its culmination in *a world state that unites all nations on an equal basis*' (emphasis added).[14] Friedrich von Hayek (1899 to 1992), a Nobel Prize winner for economics, and together with Mises one of the most important representatives of the Austrian School of economics and for some people a pioneer of neoliberalism, made a clear and simple

---

14 Mises, Ludwig von. 2002. Liberalism. 3rd ed. Mises.org edition; Cobden Press / The Foundation for Economic Education, Inc., p. 37, 105, 148. He later qualified his position under the influence of the Second World War. See idem. 1944. Omnipotent Government: The Rise of the Total State and Total War. Auburn, Alabama: Liberty Fund / Ludwig von Mises Institute, p. 243.

appeal in his 1944 book 'The Road to Serfdom' for a *world federalist* order with a 'super-national authority'. This international political authority should be endowed with precisely defined but fully enforceable powers, including the power to 'hold the economic interests in check, and in the conflict between them [to] truly hold the scales'. It must have the power vis-à-vis the states to implement a set of rules in order to 'restrain the different nations from action harmful to their neighbours'. Hayek thought federalism was 'nothing but the application to international affairs of democracy, the only method of peaceful change man has yet invented. But it is a democracy with definitely limited powers'. 'Wisely used', he wrote, 'the federal principle of organization may indeed prove the best solution of some of the world's most difficult problems.'[15] So differences of opinion, even with those who represent a properly understood form of Laisser-faire, are to do not so much with *whether* there should be a world state as with what form it should take and what exactly its responsibilities should be.

The global race to deregulate

The fact that countries are in a permanent state of 'unrestrained competition' with one another is a source of great advantage for radical free market forces. Once a deregulation has been implemented in a few countries, then international competition means that this leads to a self-propelling deregulatory race. What determines this 'race to the bottom' is where companies and capital can find the most favourable conditions. This puts pressure on wages, social security, environmental standards, workers' rights and fiscal policy. Yet it was precisely this argument that was used to justify the deregulation of the financial system in the USA. At the reading in the US Senate in November 1999 of the 'Financial Services Modernization Act', which among other things abolished the separate banking system, Democratic Senator Chuck Schumer from New York said that what was important above all was 'that US financial firms remain competitive'. 'If we don't pass this bill', said Schumer, 'we could find London or Frankfurt or, years down the road, Shanghai becoming the financial capital of the world'. Important US firms might leave the United States to relocate to other countries where 'these things' are allowed. New York's status as the financial capital of the world and 'millions' of highly-paid jobs were at stake.[16,17] The

---

15 Hayek, Friedrich August von. 2001. The Road to Serfdom. Routledge Classics, pp. 238f., 243.

16 U.S. Congress. 4 November 1999. 'Proceedings and Debates of the 106th Congress, First Session'. Congressional Record 145, no. 154, p. S13880.

17 It is worth noting in passing that the majority of donations to Schumer's campaign funds, according to the Center for Responsive Politics in Washington D.C., ultimately came from investment banks. He seems to illustrate how a politician can soften over time, as in an article in the New York Times of August 1987 he had

New York Times columnist and apostle of globalization Thomas L. Friedman speaks in his bestselling book 'The Lexus and the Olive Tree: Understanding Globalization' of the 'golden straitjacket' created by Thatcher and Reagan. Friedman's metaphor of a straitjacket describes the principles to which a country must adhere in the globalised economy in order to obtain credit and attract capital investment. 'To fit into the Golden Straightjacket a country must either adopt, or be seen as moving toward, the following golden rules: making the private sector the primary engine of its economic growth, maintaining a low rate of inflation and price stability, shrinking the size of its state bureaucracy, maintaining as close to a balanced budget as possible, if not a surplus, eliminating and lowering tariffs on imported goods, removing restrictions on foreign investment, getting rid of quotas and domestic monopolies, increasing exports, privatizing state-owned industries and utilities, deregulating capital markets, making its currency convertible, opening its industries, stock and bond markets to direct foreign ownership and investment, deregulating its economy to promote as much domestic competition as possible, eliminating government corruption, subsidies and kickbacks as much as possible, opening its banking and telecommunications systems to private ownership and competition and allowing its citizens to choose from an array of competing pension options and foreign-run pension and mutual funds.'[18] Friedman calls the straitjacket 'golden' because only this programme, he thinks, is now capable of generating growth. Politics, he argues, has become a mere technical skill with the purpose of implementing a programme demanded by the ratings agencies, the investment funds, speculators and other market forces. They are supported in their demands by the International Monetary Fund and the World Bank, which supply credit only subject to the fulfilment of linked conditions.

The key role of tax havens and anonymous shell companies

As the British journalist Nicholas Shaxson convincingly sets out in his 2011 book 'Treasure Islands', tax havens are a pivot of the unfettered global economic and financial system. Tax havens are sovereign states or territorial jurisdictions under international law which attract businesses by helping people or firms to 'get around the rules, laws and regulations of jurisdictions elsewhere'.[19]

argued entirely in the opposite direction, saying that the separate banking system was actually a competitive advantage because it prevented banking concentration, thus strengthening competition and encouraging innovation-friendly lending. See Schumer, Charles E. 26 August 1987. 'Don't Let Banks Become Casinos'. New York Times (www.nytimes.com).

18   Friedman, Thomas L. 2000. The Lexus and the Olive Tree. New York: Picador, p. 105.
19   Shaxson, Nicholas. 2012. Treasure Islands: Tax Havens and the Men Who Stole the World. London: Vintage, p. 8.

What they offer is high levels of discretion and secrecy, low or even no taxation, and a policy of non-intervention on the part of the local authorities. Around two-thirds of world trade is carried out by companies operating internationally. A presence in offshore territories enables such internationally active companies to choose almost at will, by means of nominal internal costing practices, the location where profits and losses become liable or deductible for tax purposes – a trick which is entirely legal. In combination with the use of holding companies registered in tax havens, to which the rights over brands or other forms of intellectual property are assigned, this often succeeds in its aim of reducing tax liabilities to the lowest possible level. The conditions and financial services on offer in many tax havens play an important role, for example through money-laundering, for criminal enterprises operating at the global level. It is even possible that such money flows rescued the financial system during the financial crisis. The head of the UN Office on Drugs and Crime UNODC, the Italian economic expert Antonio Maria Costa, claimed to the *Observer* that at the height of the crisis, money from the drugs trade and other illegal activities totalling nearly 350 billion US dollars was pumped into the financial system and thereby laundered. For some banks on the brink of collapse, he said, that was the only source of liquid capital available at the time.[20]

It is not only isolated territories like the Cayman Islands in the Caribbean (population 50,000), one of fourteen British Overseas Territories and at the same time one of the world's biggest financial centres, which thumb their noses at the rest of the world in this way. 'The world's most important tax havens are not exotic palm-fringed islands, as many people suppose, but some of the world's most powerful countries', Shaxson reports. The worldwide offshore system involves around sixty shadow finance centres arranged in a network of spheres of influence controlled from Great Britain and the USA. The important roles played by Reagan and Thatcher in the globalization project are well known. Far less attention has been paid to these shadow financial centres, 'the silent warriors of globalization that have been forcing nation states rich and poor to compete through them, and in the process cutting swathes through their tax and regulatory systems and regulations whether they like it or not'.[21] In June 2017, an important study identified 24 so-called 'sink Offshore Financial Centers' (OFCs) which 'attract and retain foreign capital', among them the British Virgin Islands, Cayman Islands, Gibraltar, Hong Kong, Jersey, Liechtenstein, Luxembourg and Malta. In addition, the researchers found a small set

20 Syal, Rajeev. 13 December 2009. 'Drug money saved banks in global crisis, claims UN advisor'. The Observer (www.guardian.co.uk).
21 Shaxson, loc. cit., pp. 21, 24.

of five countries that play a key role as 'conduit OFCs' that 'enable the transfer of capital without taxation': the Netherlands, the United Kingdom, Ireland, Singapore and Switzerland.[22]

The decisive part played by tax havens in this 'damaging tax competition' was clearly identified in 1998 in a ground-breaking OECD report. One problem is tax evasion. In order to track down tax evaders more easily and to increase transparency, a benchmark for bilateral information exchange was developed, to be applied 'on request' and applicable to tax havens. But these efforts, which were taken up by the G20 summit meetings from 2009 onwards, have been ridiculed by many observers. When a tax authority requests information, in every case it has to know in advance fairly precisely what information is sought, according to Shaxson. He sees it as window dressing. In any event, when the fox announces that he has improved the security of the henhouse it should always be taken with a large pinch of salt.[23] Several studies agree in concluding that a patchwork of bilateral agreements on information exchange will in the final analysis achieve nothing anyway. What is needed instead is a 'big bang': *a watertight global agreement.*[24]

In order to successfully close down the offshore system and the associated international money-laundering, corruption and tax evasion, the problem of anonymous shell companies must also be addressed. In April 2016, international reports on the activities of the Panama-based firm Mossack Fonseca, one of the leading service providers for offshore services and shell companies, made massive waves in the media. A study published in 2014 demonstrates that shell companies, meaning companies that cannot be traced back to their true owners, have become one of the most important means of hiding and diverting assets. 'Regulating shell companies', the study found, 'poses a major challenge for many facets of global governance.' While there are of course international standards, drawn up by the Financial Action Task Force on Money Laundering (FATF) at the OECD, these have turned out to be very ineffective. The researchers were most surprised by the finding that it is the incorporation providers based in the OECD countries which are the least rigorous in applying the standards intended to combat anonymous shell companies. 'Incorporation providers in the United States, especially in Delaware, Indiana, Wyoming, and Nevada,

---

22 Garcia-Bernardo, Javier, et al. 2017. 'Uncovering Offshore Financial Centers: Conduits and Sinks in the Global Corporate Ownership Network'. Scientific Reports 7 (1):6246.

23 Ibid., pp. 36, 247ff.

24 Elsayyad, May, and Kai A. Konrad. January 2011. 'Fighting Multiple Tax Havens'. Max Planck Institute for Tax Law and Public Finance, Working Paper 2011-01 (www.tax.mpg.de); Johannesen, Niels, and Gabriel Zucman. 2014. 'The End of Bank Secrecy? An Evaluation of the G20 Tax Haven Crackdown'. American Economic Journal: Economic Policy (6) 1: 65–91.

are among the worst in the world', the report states.[25] In fact, the United States, together with Switzerland and the Cayman Islands, is one of the three world's biggest contributors to financial secrecy, according to the 2018 edition of the Tax Justice Network's Financial Secrecy Index. Next on the list are Hong Kong, Singapore, Luxembourg and the EU's largest economy, Germany.

In the wake of the publication of the so-called Panama Papers, Ecuador called for international efforts to abolish tax havens altogether and launched an initiative for the creation of a UN tax body to deal with the issue once and for all. The idea of a UN Tax Organization, however, has met with resistance from the OECD for a long time. The European Parliament immediately created a committee of inquiry to look into the Panama Papers scandal and its implications. The final report concluded among other things that some EU member states are obstructing the fight against money laundering, tax avoidance and evasion and called for a common international definition of what actually constitutes an offshore financial centre, tax haven or secrecy haven.[26] From a worldwide perspective, a UN Parliamentary Assembly would have been the appropriate place to launch a global investigation. Following the publication of the so-called Paradise papers connected to the offshore law firm Appleby in November 2017, the Financial Transparency Coalition noted that 'this latest in a succession of leaks demonstrates how the global network of tax havens and the secrecy they enable continue to thrive.'[27]

The hidden trillions

The harm done by the offshore system can barely be quantified. The French economist Gabriel Zucman estimates that 8 per cent of households' financial wealth or 7.6 trillion US dollars is held in tax havens.[28] According to a study by Zucman and colleagues based on data leaked from HSBC and Mossack Fonseca, the super-rich with a net wealth of above 40 million US dollars on average evade about 30 per cent of personal taxes.[29] In a widely noted assessment commissioned by the Tax Justice Network, James Henry, former chief economist of the business consultancy McKinsey, described the offshore system as 'the black hole of the world economy'. The *purely financial assets* alone stashed away by

25   Findley, Michael G. Global Shell Games: Experiments In: Transnational Relations, Crime, And Terrorism. Cambridge University Press, 2014, pp. 168ff.
26   European Parliament. 16 November 2017. 'Report on the inquiry into money laundering, tax avoidance and tax evasion'. A8-0357/2017.
27   Financial Transparency Coalition. 9 November 2017. 'Paradise Papers reiterate need for a truly global response to crack down on tax haven abuses' (financialtransparency.org).
28   Zucman, Gabriel. 2015. The Hidden Wealth of Nations. University of Chicago Press, pp. 34ff.
29   Alstadsaeter, Annette, Niels Johannesen, und Gabriel Zucman. 2017. 'Tax Evasion and Inequality'.

private individuals in tax havens have been estimated by him at between 21 and 32 trillion US dollars, which is more than the annual GDP of the USA. Roughly half of this is owned by around 100,000 super-rich people from all parts of the world. Since this money cannot as a rule be captured in official statistics, it distorts survey data on the distribution of wealth. Inequality is even greater than the statistics can possibly reflect. With regard to the money that is siphoned into tax havens by the elites from the developing countries, and invested mainly in assets owned by the industrialised countries, the study concludes that the developing countries are in fact net lenders, since the private wealth that has been moved outside their borders far exceeds their public external debt. 'The problem here', writes Henry, 'is that the assets of these countries are held by a small number of wealthy individuals while the debts are shouldered by the ordinary people of these countries through their governments.' But the super-rich, he adds, are 'one of society's most well-entrenched interest groups'.[30]

Global state formation as the goal of the counter-movement

In his book on 'The Strange Non-death of Neo-liberalism', the British political scientist Colin Crouch writes that the task is not 'to explain why neoliberalism will die following its crisis, but the very opposite: how it comes about that neoliberalism is emerging from the financial collapse more politically powerful than ever'.[31] But this is no longer quite so surprising, given that the counter-movement faces the problem of a lack of world state policy instruments to set against the forces of the market and the global elite. It is effectively neutralised, since there are no global government structures it could use to create globally effective regulation. While initiatives involving a few countries may have some symbolic impact, they cannot achieve much at the level of the system as a whole, and this is even more true of efforts made by states acting unilaterally. 'A third and rather different reason for not seeing the resurgence of the state as a simple strategy for reform', according to Crouch, 'is that political power remains overwhelmingly tied to the level of the nation-state. Not only does this mean that it has problems acting as a truly "public" force on the global stage, but political parties and governments continue to try to define interests in national terms.' In a globalised economy this approach is unrealistic, he argued.[32]

In the end, as we have seen already with regard to the transition to a sustainable economy, it comes down to the fact that the counter-movement will have

---

30   Henry, James S. July 2012. 'The Price of Offshore Revisited'. Tax Justice Network, pp. 3, 5.
31   Crouch, Colin. 2011. The Strange Non-Death of Neo-Liberalism. Cambridge: Polity, p. viii
32   Ibid., p. 173.

to promote a process of global state formation leading to a system of world law. The fundamental principle on which the offshore system stands, for example, is that of the sovereignty of the states and territorial jurisdictions involved. The freedom that these countries enjoy to undermine at will the global fiscal, economic and financial system must be put into question. The fight against the offshore system, Shaxson writes, needs 'an international perspective, to build new forms of international cooperation'.[33] 'A constructive counter-movement', in the view of the Canadian economist Myron Frankman in a rewarding book on world federalism, 'must have on its agenda for serious early consideration the building of democratic institutions at the world level as well as building and strengthening systems at lower levels.'[34] Some critics of globalization may find this a difficult step to take, as the movement has foregrounded a broad and fundamental opposition to international organizations and is characterised by a profound distrust of the state. But without realising it, they have thereby accepted as a premise a vulgar neoliberal conception of the international system. However, there are signs that the weight of opinion is slowly moving in a different direction. Thus, Harald Schumann and Christiane Grefe are now arguing in their book 'The Global Countdown' for 'the further development and democratization of global rules and institutions'. And furthermore, that the challenge is 'to invent a form of world federalism and clear rules for the proper allocation of political responsibility between global, regional and national institutions in order to do justice to the interests of all'.[35] This idea did not feature at all in Schumann's bestselling 'The Global Trap', published twelve years earlier. In a keynote speech at the fiftieth anniversary conference of the International Studies Association in New York in 2009, the then President of the ISA, political scientist Thomas G. Weiss, asked what had happened to the once prominent notion of a federal world government. He argued passionately that the academic community should give serious consideration to the idea once again. 'The market,' noted Weiss, in a striking observation, 'will not graciously provide global institutions to ensure human survival with dignity. Adam Smith's "invisible hand" does not operate among states to solve problems any more than it does within states.'[32]

33 Shaxson, loc. cit., p. 31.
34 Frankman, Myron J. 2004. World Democratic Federalism. New York: Palgrave Macmillan, pp. 37f.
35 Schumann, Harald, and Christiane Grefe. 2008. Der globale Countdown. Gerechtigkeit oder Selbstzerstörung - Die Zukunft der Globalisierung. Köln: Kiepenheuer & Witsch, pp. 31f.

13.
A world currency, global taxation, and fiscal federalism

Within the community of states, potential solutions to the problems in the fiscal, monetary and finance systems have been put forward on numerous occasions. These have included the global coordination of tax policy (especially with regard to corporations) and a world currency. A democratic world parliament ought to play a leading and driving role in the conception and development of such important projects.

A world currency and a world central bank

As early as the 1860s there had been a serious French initiative to introduce an international currency, but it was rejected at the time by Great Britain. Then, during the Second World War, the USA and Britain worked on plans for a world currency as part of their post-war planning. In the USA it had the working title of 'Unitas', while in Great Britain John Maynard Keynes worked on a concept named 'Bancor'. As the Nobel laureate in economics Robert Mundell reports, the intention to launch a world currency was then dropped shortly before the decisive conference of the Allies on currency and financial issues in Bretton Woods in 1944. Concerns had arisen in the USA over a possible consequential loss of sovereignty. 'U.S. reluctance to go forward with a global currency', according to Mundell, 'fits the historical pattern that the leading power resist monetary reform that might interfere with the international role of its own currency.'[1] However, the question continues to be raised regularly and prominently. For example, ten weeks after 19 October 1987 saw the biggest stock market crash in post-war history, the Economist wrote in its cover story that a world currency, at least between the most important industrialised countries, ought to be pursued. The advantages would soon seem 'irresistible to everybody except foreign-exchange traders and governments'.[2] During the global financial crisis twenty years later, the chief economics editor of *Business Week*, Michael Mandel, asked himself what would happen in the not unlikely event that a dollar crisis were to break out which the US American central bank, the Federal Reserve,

1   Mundell, Robert. 2005. 'The case for a world currency'. Journal of Policy Modeling 27: 465–475, pp. 468, 475.
2   'Get ready for the phoenix'. 9 January 1988. The Economist, no. 306: 9–10, p. 9.

was unable to bring under control. In theory it was clear what the answer ought to be, according to Mandel: 'a global central bank, with the ultimate authority to print money and regulate the financial system around the world'.[3]

The external impact of national monetary policy and currency wars

Under the impact of the financial crisis, Russia and China have both put forward proposals for the creation of a world reserve currency. By now, the People's Republic of China has amassed currency reserves of more than 3 trillion US dollars, and feared a severe depreciation in their value through inflation, or even a dollar crash, because of the massive increase in the money supply enacted by the Federal Reserve in the course of its 'quantitative easing' programme. The Governor of the Chinese Central Bank, Zhou Xiaochuan, declared in March 2009, shortly before the G20 summit meeting in London, that the so-called 'Triffin dilemma' had not gone away. Countries that issue reserve currencies, Xiaochuan said in summarising this dilemma, 'may either fail to adequately meet the demand of a growing global economy for liquidity as they try to ease inflation pressures at home, or create excess liquidity in the global markets by overly stimulating domestic demand'.[4] This demonstrates the strong external impact of monetary policy in those countries with the most important worldwide reserve currencies. Reform of the international monetary system should therefore have as its goal, according to Xiaochuan, an international reserve currency disconnected from individual nations.

The US government responded by accusing China of maintaining an artificially low rate for the Renminbi, to the cost of China's trade partners. Monetary policy is an important weapon in geo-economic competition. The American lawyer and investment banker James Rickards, who was jointly responsible for drawing up simulation exercises for economic warfare in the Pentagon, writes in the 2011 *New York Times* bestseller 'Currency Wars' that the Federal Reserve's quantitative easing programme has effectively declared a 'currency war' on the world. The flood of dollars, he argues, prompted higher inflation in China, higher food prices in Egypt, speculative bubbles in Brazil, and above all a devaluation of US external debt, together with other intended and unintended consequences. High-ranking military and secret service personnel have recognised, he claims, that American military dominance is closely linked to the pre-

3   Mandel, Michael. 16 March 2008. 'A Global Bailout?' Businessweek (www.businessweek.com); see also the cover story two years earlier: Mandel, Michael, and Richard S. Dunham. 20 November 2006. 'Can Anyone Steer This Economy?' Businessweek: 57–62.
4   Xiaochuan, Zhou. 23 March 2009. 'Statement on Reforming the International Monetary System'. Foreign Affairs Essential Documents (www.cfr.org).

eminent position of the dollar as the global reserve currency. The international demand for dollars contributes for example to offsetting the USA's huge external trade deficit and financing the US budget (including its military expenditure). According to Rickards, the currency question is therefore now regarded as a 'national security' issue.[5]

Recent proposals for a world reserve currency

By the time of the Russian and Chinese proposals, however, it was no longer possible to put a lid on this highly charged debate. A report from the Department of Economic and Social Affairs of the United Nations Secretariat, for example, stated that 'a new global reserve system could be created, one that no longer relies on the United States dollar as the single major reserve currency. The dollar', it continued, 'has proved not to be a stable store of value, which is a requisite for a stable reserve currency.'[6] The IMF, too, is now approaching the issue more pro-actively. IMF chief strategist Reza Moghadam took up the 'more ambitious reform option' of a global currency in a paper published in April 2010.[7] One idea which has been under discussion for some time is that of gradually building up and transforming the IMF's so-called Special Drawing Rights, an accounting unit based on a basket of currencies, into a world reserve currency. It would also be possible, in Moghadam's view, for the IMF to be authorised to market its own credit instruments, denominated as Special Drawing Rights. Such securities could 'constitute an embryo of global currency'.[8] The President of the 63rd UN General Assembly, the Nicaraguan Miguel d'Escoto Brockmann, set up an expert commission on 'Reforms of the International Monetary and Financial System' under the leadership of Joseph Stiglitz. The commission advocated the adoption of 'a truly global reserve currency'. The current crisis, it argued in its report, provided 'an ideal opportunity to overcome the political resistance to a new global monetary system'.[9]

A single world currency would do away with the possibility of geopolitical currency conflicts, and even the more realistic shorter term options of a global

---

5 Rickards, James. 2011. Currency wars. New York: Portfolio/Penguin, pp. xiv f., 223.
6 United Nations Department of Economic and Social Affairs (ed.). 2010. 'World Economic and Social Survey 2010: Retooling Global Development', p. xxii.
7 Cf. Moghadam, Reza. 13 April 2010. 'Reserve Accumulation and International Monetary Stability'. International Monetary Fund, pp. 26-28.
8 Moghadam, Reza. 7 January 2011. 'Enhancing International Monetary Stability-A Role for the SDR?' International Monetary Fund, p. 12.
9 United Nations (ed.). 21 September 2009. 'Report of the Commission of Experts of the President of the United Nations General Assembly on Reforms of the International Monetary and Financial System', p. 115.

reserve or parallel currency would at least make them much less damaging. Differing monetary policy interests would then have to be discussed and reconciled in the appropriate international bodies. However, one of the lessons of the Euro crisis should be that steps towards a single currency must be seen and implemented within a wider political framework. The US American economist James Tobin pointed this out some time ago. His 1972 proposal for the introduction of a worldwide tax on international currency transactions, aimed at making short-term currency speculation uneconomic, is one of the principal demands of the anti-globalization movement. What is less well known is that this transaction tax was for Tobin only 'a realistic second-best option' after a world currency. 'The mobility of financial capital across currencies is a problem whether exchange rates float freely in markets or are pegged by agreements among governments', he wrote in 1994 in the UNDP Human Development Report. No system in which exchange rates are periodically adjusted can eliminate opportunities for speculation or inhibitions on national monetary policy. Only a 'permanent single currency' can do that. However, Tobin stressed that such a currency could not function without support. 'The United States example', he wrote, 'shows that a currency union works to great advantage when sustained not only by centralized monetary authorities but *also by other common institutions* (emphasis added).' In the absence of such institutions, he thought, a world currency remained many decades away.[10] A world parliament is an indispensable prerequisite for a world currency. It is a cause for concern that in the current debate, the creation of a world currency is presented as a purely technical issue. It is not.

The fiscal race to the bottom

Together with the currency and the armed forces, the raising of taxes has traditionally been at the core of national sovereignty. International cooperation on tax policy has long been largely restricted to coordinating the taxation of private individuals and companies operating trans-nationally, in order to avoid the duplication of taxation in the different countries concerned. Deregulation and globalization have now led to an ever closer interweaving and ever greater mobility of companies and capital. The associated fiscal race to the bottom is evidenced in the decline in the rates of tax levied on company profits. Since 1980, the statutory corporate tax rate has consistently declined on a global basis.[11] The

---

10   Tobin, James. 'A tax on international currency transactions'. In: Human Development Report 1994: New dimensions of human security, ed. by United Nations Development Programme, Oxford University Press, p. 70.
11   Jahnsen, Kari, and Kyle Pomerleau. 2017. 'Corporate Income Tax Rates around the World, 2017', Tax Foundation.

OECD average has fallen from 48 per cent in 1982 to 24.7 per cent in 2016.[12] More important still is the possibility already mentioned of avoiding tax altogether. The US American think tank Citizens for Tax Justice has calculated that 285 of the 500 world's biggest companies on the *Forbes* list for which usable data are available had up until the end of 2011 amassed profits of around 1.5 trillion US dollars which had been stashed away in tax havens and never taxed.[13] Microsoft, for example, whose co-founder and main shareholder Bill Gates now concerns himself mainly with the philanthropic foundation set up with around 35 billion dollars out of his personal assets, has by this account from 2009 to 2011 alone avoided - perfectly legally - US taxes on half of the retail profits it generated in the USA, amounting to 21 billion US dollars, by selling intellectual property rights to subsidiary companies in tax havens, thus avoiding taxes of up to around 4.5 billion US dollars. Complaints were made in the Senate that the proportion of total tax revenue in the USA from corporate income taxes had fallen from 32.1 per cent in 1952 to 8.9 per cent in 2009, while that from payroll taxes had shot up from 9.7 to 40 per cent.[14] However, the downward race will continue for the time being. In the first nine months of 2017, for instance, eight OECD countries reduced their corporate tax rates, with cuts averaging 2.7 per cent.[15] In December 2017, the US Congress approved a tax bill that was presented by the new US administration under Donald Trump which reduced the statutory corporate tax rate in the US from 35 to 21 per cent. According to James Henry, 'the deep corporate tax cuts contained in this bill have already triggered, or at least substantially accelerated, a global tax war.'[16]

In fact, there is a widespread understanding that better international tax law cooperation would be needed to prevent further erosion of the rates of corporate taxation and to counteract the tax avoidance strategies of international companies. The question is how to make it happen. The heads of state and government of the G20 countries have repeatedly voiced their concerns over these problems in their summit declarations. At the G20 meeting of finance ministers in Mexico at the start of November 2012, for instance, the then German and

---

12 Id. 29 June 2012. 'OECD Corporate Income Tax Rates, 1981-2012' (taxfoundation.org). For the 2016 figure see OECD. 2017. Tax Policy Reforms 2017: OECD and Selected Partner Economies, p. 54.

13 Citizens for Tax Justice. 17 October 2012. 'Which Fortune 500 Companies Are Sheltering Income in Overseas Tax Havens?' CTJ Reports (ctj.org).

14 United States Senate. 20 September 2012. 'Subcommittee Hearing to Examine Billions of Dollars in U.S. Tax Avoidance By Multinational Corporations'. The Permanent Subcommittee On Investigations.

15 Houlder, Vanessa. 13 September 2017. 'OECD countries in bout of corporate tax competition'. Financial Times (www.ft.com).

16 Henry, James S. 21 December 2017. 'Ladies and Gentlemen, Take Your Places: The Global Tax Race to the Bottom Is about to Begin'. The American Interest (www.the-american-interest.com).

British finance ministers, in a joint declaration, called for 'concerted international cooperation to strengthen international standards for corporate tax regimes'. They also called for support for the OECD's work on 'identifying possible gaps in the standards'.[17]

Uniform taxation of multinational corporations

How these problems could be decisively tackled had already been set out by a 'High-Level Panel on Financing for Development' convened by UN Secretary-General Kofi Annan in 2001. The members of this body, led by the former Mexican President Ernesto Zedillo, knew what they were talking about. Several senior former finance ministers were involved, in the shape of Robert Rubin from the USA, Alexander Livshits from Russia, Manmohan Singh from India and Jacques Delors from France. Delors had also been a driving force behind European integration for nine years as President of the European Commission. The group's recommendation on this topic was that an international organization for tax issues should be established to take a leading role in curbing international tax competition and countering tax avoidance. In addition to providing statistical information and coordinating and developing multilateral tools for information exchange, this organization should 'in due course seek to develop and secure international agreement on a formula for the unitary taxation of multinationals'.[18]

The prevailing international tax practice at present is for company profits to be split by country and company and then taxed accordingly. What is crucial is where the profit is recorded in accounting terms. By contrast, under a system of so-called 'Unitary Taxation' by proportional allocation, multinational enterprises and groups of companies are treated as single business units. All companies within a group have to submit a report on the whole of the group, across all countries and companies, detailing assets, turnover and numbers of employees. The total profits for the group are then divided up and allocated proportionately to the respective countries and notified to their tax authorities, using a specific formula for working out the respective tax bases based on the factors above, so that the appropriate taxes can be levied. Thus the profits are taxed where the group's real business activities take place. This makes tax avoidance strategies much more difficult.

---

17 Cf. Statement by the Chancellor of the Exchequer, Rt Hon George Osborne MP; Britain & Germany call for international action to strengthen tax standards, 5 November 2012.
18 United Nations (ed.). 2001. 'Report of the High-Level Panel on Financing for Development' (Zedillo report), p. 15.

The Unitary Taxation approach has long been applied, in differing variants, in numerous US federal states in order to divide and allocate the tax base for companies active across state lines. When California made Unitary Taxation calculated on a *worldwide* basis obligatory for multinational companies operating there, governments and companies around the world were up in arms. The US government received over 30 official diplomatic protests, Great Britain threatened counter-measures, and the British Barclays Bank took the issue to the US Supreme Court.[19] According to the Court, a 'battalion of foreign governments' marched to the aid of the bank during the case.[20] These governments stressed that Unitary Taxation was not compatible with internationally accepted principles of corporate taxation. By this time, California had bowed to the political pressure and made the worldwide calculation optional.

Rejection by the OECD

The uncoordinated, unilateral introduction of a worldwide Unitary Taxation could indeed lead to double taxation of companies and to other disadvantages. That is why a global approach with internationally agreed standards, as recommended in the Zedillo report, is the ideal way forward. The fact that this expert group wanted to see this task given to a new 'International Tax Organization', rather than to, for example, the OECD, is entirely consistent. For one thing, the OECD is not properly representative, as it excludes developing countries. For another, the consensus principle that applies at the OECD means that any initiative can be blocked by a single country. Another problem is the fact that most of its decisions do not have legally binding status.[21] And not least of all, the OECD has more or less disqualified itself for this task by its total rejection of the principle of Unitary Taxation. 'The OECD's Committee on Fiscal Affairs', reports the legal and tax expert Sol Picciotto, 'has stubbornly refused even to consider the viability of the approach for over 30 years.'[22] This dogmatic position is somewhat surprising. Or is it? Because ever since the negotiations over an OECD 'Multilateral Agreement on Investment' (MAI for short) in the mid-1990s, if not earlier, the organization has been accused of being too close to multinational corporations and their lobbyists. It was believed that they were given significant input into the draft MAI agreement, while parliaments and the public

---

19   Cf. Rixen, Thomas. The political economy of international tax governance. Palgrave Macmillan, 2008, p. 127.
20   Supreme Court of the United States. 20 June 1994. 'Barclays Bank Plc v. Franchise Tax Board of California'. 512 US 298, para. 40.
21   Horner, Frances M. 29 October 2001. 'Do We Need an International Tax Organization?' Tax Notes: 709–715. See para. 33, 'Condition Five: Governance'.
22   Picciotto, Sol. Nov. 2012. 'Towards Unitary Taxation of Transnational Corporations.' Tax Justice Network, p. 19.

were largely excluded. 'The MAI is unacceptable, because it seeks to privilege the interests of investors in a one-sided manner, whereas social, ecological and other community-based viewpoints play practically no role at all', was a criticism voiced by NGOs about the outcome of the negotiations, which was also rejected by the European Parliament.[23] Eventually, the agreement was dropped due to fierce public protests.

In the concluding document of the 2002 United Nations International Conference on Financing for Development, held in Monterrey, Mexico, and known as the 'Monterrey Consensus', hardly a trace remained of the far-reaching proposals of the Zedillo Commission. There were only generalizations about how international cooperation on tax issues should be strengthened by 'improved dialogue' and 'greater coordination' between the national tax authorities and the relevant multilateral and regional institutions. Once again it was a case of the lowest common denominator. Meanwhile, at the EU level, the European Commission had finally taken a step forward after years of consultation. In March 2011 it presented a proposal for a directive on a 'Common Consolidated Corporate Tax Base' to harmonize corporate taxation in the EU. In the draft, the measure is initially optional and limited to Europe only, but nevertheless it represents, as Picciotto underlines, 'the first formal international proposal for a unitary tax system'.[24] Internationally, it should no longer be so easy from now on to simply ignore the idea of Unitary Taxation.

Global fiscal federalism and the restitution of fiscal sovereignty

It is paradoxical that national governments should express concerns over a possible loss of sovereignty due to deeper cooperation on taxation. On the contrary, it would strengthen their sovereignty. For although it is correct that it would no longer be possible to regulate autonomously in those areas of tax law – such as corporate taxation – included in international cooperation arrangements, on the other hand such arrangements would ensure the full and proper application of the common regulations. The political and economic scientist Thomas Rixen, who teaches in Bamberg, gets to the heart of the matter in his 2008 study of the political economy of the international tax system. 'Only if governments come to share their legislative tax sovereignty, which is becoming ever more fictitious', writes Rixen, 'will they regain de facto sovereignty over their tax systems.'[25]

---

23 Engels, Rainer, Jens Martens, Peter Wahl, and Michael Windfuhr. March 1998. 'Alles neu macht das MAI? Das Multilaterale Investitionsabkommen'. Weltwirtschaft, Ökologie & Entwicklung e.V., p. 34.
24 Picciotto, loc. cit., p. 3.
25 Rixen, Thomas. The political economy of international tax governance. Houndmills: Palgrave Macmillan, 2008, p. 203.

Global federal institutions will be the decisive factor in the further develop-ment of international tax cooperation. In Rixen's view, tax avoidance through the diversion of profits abroad, a result of unregulated tax competition, under-mines mutual solidarity within national societies. A fair solution boils down to a 'worldwide social contract' resembling 'a federal system with a vertical disper-sion of powers over different levels'. This system could be designed in line with the established principles of fiscal federalism, as set out for example in the clas-sic 1972 basic textbook by the US American economist Wallace E. Oates. In such a system, according to Rixen, it could be expected 'that certain taxing rights would be on the central (global) level and others on decentralized (re-gional, nation –state, and substate) levels'.[26] The establishment of an 'Interna-tional Tax Organization' would be a sensible step. The political scientist Dries Lesage summarised another important argument as follows: at the moment, there is still 'no strong political multilateral forum or organization where the developing world has a real seat at the table to discuss and to decide on inter-national tax matters'.[27]

Ideas for global taxes

As with the world parliament and world currency, there is a long history behind the idea of global taxation. The report of the Brandt Commission in 1980 re-ferred already to a whole series of proposals to raise international revenues which were under discussion at the time. On this list were taxes on 'interna-tional trade, on arms trade, on international investment, on hydrocarbons and exhaustible minerals, on durable luxury goods, on military spending, on the consumption of energy, on internationally traded crude oil, on international air travel and freight transport, or on the use of the "international commons" ocean fishing, offshore oil and gas, sea-bed mining, the use of space orbits, radio and telecommunication frequencies and channels'.[28] The philosopher Thomas Pogge, whose specialist area is issues of global justice, has been calling since 1994 for the introduction of a 'global resources dividend'. His proposal envis-ages 'that states and their governments shall not have full libertarian property rights with respect to the natural resources in their territory, but can be required to share a small part of the value of any resources they decide to use or sell'. The

26 Rixen, Thomas. 2011. 'Tax Competition and Inequality: The Case for Global Tax Governance'. Global Gov-ernance 17: 447–467, p. 457.
27 Lesage, Dries. September 2008. 'Global Taxation Governance after the 2002 UN Monterrey Conference'. Ox-ford Development Studies 36 (3): 281–94, p. 292.
28 Independent Commission on International Development Issues. 1980. North/South: A Programme for Sur-vival. London: MacMillan, pp. 243f.

revenues should be used to ensure that all people are able to meet their basic needs in dignity.[29] The French economist Thomas Piketty aroused enormous international interest in 2014 with his book 'Capital in the Twenty-First Century', which concludes with a recommendation for a 'a progressive global tax on capital, coupled with a very high level of international financial transparency'. Otherwise, he argues, democracy will not be able 'to regain control over the globalized financial capitalism of this century'.[30]

In the international community, proposals for international taxes have always been contentious. On one side of the argument is the belief that the right to raise taxes is an expression of national sovereignty; on the other, the fact that the revenues could be used to finance international organizations and global common goods. However, the reservations are perceptibly crumbling. At the UN conference in Monterrey, several heads of government, including France's Jacques Chirac, thought that a serious investigation should be carried out into the introduction of global taxes. This had also been suggested by the expert group led by Zedillo, with a focus on taxes on international currency transactions and on CO_2 emissions. The question of a tax on international financial transactions, a variant on the Tobin proposal but not limited to currency deals, is now on the agenda at the highest political levels. In December 2009, the introduction of such a tax was supported by the European Council, on the condition that it had to be worldwide. Some countries, such as Great Britain, took the position that only worldwide implementation could ensure there would be no distortion of competition. European initiatives to get the G20 summit to adopt the idea have so far been thwarted principally by opposition from the USA. Efforts are continuing, however. As it has also not been possible to get it adopted in the EU or the Eurozone, ten EU countries decided in October 2012 to implement a common financial transaction tax, or FTT, initially by means of an enhanced cooperation procedure, which allows for closer integration within a smaller group of EU member states. In early 2018 it was still unclear if and when the plan will actually come to fruition.

The management, supervision and expenditure of global tax revenues

Further proposals or ideas still currently under consideration can be found in a report on this topic from the Department of Economic and Social Affairs of the United Nations Secretariat. Listed there, in addition to an international tax on

29   Pogge, Thomas. 2008. World Poverty and Human Rights. 2nd ed. Cambridge: Polity, p. 202.
30   Piketty, Thomas. 2014. Capital in the Twenty-First Century. Cambridge: Harvard University Press, p. 515.

financial and currency transactions, are taxes on carbon emissions and on personal assets worth over a billion US dollars and an air transport levy. The UN planners speculate that these and other 'innovative financing instruments' such as IMF Special Drawing Rights could raise up to 400 billion US dollars a year for financing development aid, climate change mitigation or international organizations.[31] This sum is more than eight times as much as the budgets of all UN institutions added together, including UN peacekeeping missions, and three times as much as all the contributions made by the OECD countries to international development work.[32] In fact, the real sum could be even higher. The model proposed by the Harvard economist Richard N. Cooper for a global CO_2 tax, for example, which is based on a rate of 15 US dollars per tonne of CO_2 equivalent, assumes annual revenues of over 500 billion US dollars.[33]

Who manages global tax revenues, who makes the political decisions on how exactly they are used, and what control mechanisms exist, are all issues of the greatest importance, but they are not adequately discussed. The existing international institutions and bodies are not fit for that purpose. As Myron Frankman emphasizes, the British lawyer James Lorimer clearly pointed out as early as 1884 that global taxes have to be part of a world state structure. 'This is a crucial point', says Frankman. '[O]ne can discuss at length the technicalities of global taxes, a global currency, global competition policy, and progressive global income redistribution, but they cannot exist until we are ready to establish a world government.'[34] It is only when this has been recognised and openly acknowledged that the question of democratic legitimation and accountability acquires the appropriate urgency. Anyone who talks about *genuinely* global taxation, and thus about a world tax authority, must in the same breath mention a world parliament with democratic supervisory powers and a share, at the very least, in decisions over the allocation of funds. In open parliamentary debate within a world parliament, where a broader range of political views would be represented, beyond those of the governments, critical questions could be posed and genuinely global political debate could take place. In the course of a workshop on the idea of a global tax on greenhouse gases held at the University of

31 United Nations Department of Economic and Social Affairs. 2012. World Economic and Social Survey 2012: In Search of New Development Finance. New York: United Nations, pp. 29f., 98f.

32 In 2015, the total revenue for the UN system as a whole was US$ 48 billion, see Dag Hammarskjöld Foundation, and The UN Multi-Partner Trust Fund Office (eds.). 2017. 'Financing the UN Development System' (www.daghammarskjold.se); in 2015, the OECD countries' net official development assistance amounted to US$ 131 billion (source: data.oecd.org).

33 Cooper, Richard N. October 2008. 'The Case for Charges on Greenhouse Gas Emissions'. Discussion Paper 08-10. Harvard Project on International Climate Agreements, Belfer Center for Science and International Affairs, Harvard Kennedy School, pp. 5, 12.

34 Frankman, Myron J. 2004. World Democratic Federalism. New York: Palgrave Macmillan, p. 100.

Helsinki in 2011, it was correctly recognised that such a tax 'could be a fundamental building block for the democratization of global governance', as it would
imply the application of the principle of 'no taxation without representation'
through parliamentary representation at a *worldwide* level.[35]

The development and improvement of the international currency and finance system and of international tax cooperation, as a corollary of the specific
proposals above, has to take place within the framework of an overarching institutional reform and democratization of global public policy, rather than sur-
reptitiously and through the back door because of an erroneous assumption
that the existing institutions are adequate to the task. It is notable that this aspect has largely been ignored so far. A pooling of macroeconomic management
at the global level, something desirable in principle, can only be justified if it is
prepared, politically managed, supervised and legitimated by a democratic
world parliament. There should be a global parliamentary assembly now already
with a joint right of decision in the appointment of the executive directors of the
IMF, the World Bank and the WTO, for example. The case for such a right would
be even stronger with regard to the appointment of board members of a world
central bank. And who else but a world parliament should negotiate on the details
of a worldwide uniform rate of corporation tax and possible minimum rates?

A global regulatory counter-movement with the aim of bringing the disembedded finance, currency and tax systems under control is urgently needed.
And a merely technocratic approach has *no emancipatory character*. Ensuring
the emancipatory character of this counter-movement through a democratic
world parliament has to become a main priority for civil society and social
movements.

---

35 Brincat, Shannon. September 2011. 'A Global Greenhouse Tax'. Helsinki Review of Global Governance 2 (2):
    42–44, pp. 42ff.

14.
World domestic policy, trans-sovereign problems, and complex interdependence

'Trans-sovereign problems'

The global civilization of the Anthropocene, which has been developing since the 19th century, has been accompanied by an ever more urgent need for world domestic policy. This need goes well beyond the issues of climate policy and the global economic and financial system addressed above. In addition to the global common goods and matters that touch on the common interests of humanity, world domestic policy covers *all crucial issues and problems with a global dimension*. These are growing rapidly in number and importance on account of the progress of technology and the ever-closer global interconnectedness of all areas of our lives. In an 800-page textbook, the political scientist Volker Rittberger (1941 to 2011) and his co-authors speak of 'Theoretical and Empirical Approaches to Global Governance' and of the increased incidence of 'trans-sovereign problems', which in their definition are 'problems that transgress state borders in a manner over which states have little control, and which cannot be solved through measures taken by states acting alone'.[1] Examples of trans-sovereign problems include the spread of infectious diseases and epidemics, the drugs trade, climate change, weapons of mass destruction and their diffusion, human trafficking, migration and refugee flows, product piracy, terrorism, and 'negative social and ecological externalities of economic globalization' such as 'disparities of wealth and environmental damage'.[2] Furthermore, any problematic situation which initially has no trans-border dimension can quickly escalate and acquire global significance. Thus, in a joint study by the US American National Intelligence Council (the strategic thinktank of the US secret services) and the European Union Institute for Security Studies (EUISS) of the long-term challenges for global governance it was stated that on account of

---

1   Rittberger, Volker, Andreas Kruck, and Anne Romund. 2010. Grundzüge der Weltpolitik. Theorie and Empirie des Weltregierens. 1st ed. Wiesbaden: VS Verlag für Sozialwissenschaften, p. 278 with further references (this definition is from Maryann Cusimano).
2   Ibid., pp. 278, 280.

rapid globalization 'the risks to the international system have grown to the extent that formerly localized threats are no longer locally containable but are now potentially dangerous to global security and stability'.[3]

The concept of interdependence

Since the end of the First World War, the term 'interdependence' has been used to describe the underlying conditions of world politics. The most striking feature of the period between 1870 and 1914 was 'an increasing and irrevocable interdependence of nations', wrote James Louis Garvin, the publisher of the *Observer* in Britain, in 1919 in a book which employs this term repeatedly.[4] 'The world economically has become an interdependent whole', argued the British politician Philip Kerr in 1935 in a text which is central to the history of the federalist movement.[5] 'Our dependence on each other, which is the essence of society, is increasingly also the rule between states. Society is expanding into the society of states. But this means an indissoluble dependence – the interdependence of states', is how this idea was summarised in 1956 by Wilhelm Wolfgang Schütz, a political scientist and adviser on German politics.[6] With the crises of the 1970s, interdependence became a main theme. For the first time since the War, the industrialised countries were hit by recession, high unemployment and inflation. The US government recorded huge budget deficits, not least on account of the galloping costs of the Vietnam war. The money supply and public debt were both increased. The international system of fixed exchange rates and the convertibility of the US dollar into gold (the 'gold standard') could no longer be maintained. When, in October 1973, in connection with the Arab-Israeli Yom Kippur War, eight OPEC countries drastically cut back oil exports in order to exert political pressure on the West, oil prices increased massively, with severe economic impacts experienced all around the world. US American oil production had peaked in 1970 and it was not possible to increase it to compensate for the OPEC embargo. Wall Street's Dow Jones Index fell by almost a half in less than four years. At that time already, Alvin Toffler spoke about the currency and finance markets as a 'global casino' that was out of control and in

3   National Intelligence Council (ed.). September 2010. 'Global Governance 2025: At a critical juncture', p. iii.
4   Garvin, James Louis. 1919. The Economic Foundations of Peace: or world partnership as the truer basis of the League of Nations. London: MacMillan & Co., p. 74, see also pp. 13, 72.
5   Kerr, Philip (Lord Lothian). 28 May 1935. 'Pacifism is not enough nor patriotism either'. Source: Federal Union (www.federalunion.org.uk).
6   Schütz, Wolfgang Wilhelm. 1956. Wir wollen Überleben, Außenpolitik im Atomzeitalter. Stuttgart: DVA, p. 162.

need of a 'new transnational control mechanisms'.[7] Due to insufficient domestic production, the Soviet Union became permanently dependent on grain imports to meet its food supply needs. In spite of the Cold War, it was regularly able to procure huge quantities of grain and animal feeds from the USA and other Western countries for this purpose. The environmental crisis began to enter public consciousness. Against this background, the West German Foreign Minister Hans-Dietrich Genscher chose interdependence as the theme for a speech to the UN General Assembly in 1975. 'The problems', he declared, 'have become global. The unstoppable trend towards ever closer mutual dependence between the states is the hallmark of the new era, it is the direction of World History. For the first time, humanity is travelling together towards a common future: our common survival or our common doom, common prosperity or common decline.'[8] The following year, to mark the 200th anniversary of the American Declaration of Independence, a 'Declaration of Interdependence' was published in the USA, signed by, among others, over 120 Representatives from the US Congress. This remarkable document includes the assertion that 'the economy of all nations is a seamless web, and ... no one nation can any longer effectively maintain its processes of production and monetary systems without recognizing the necessity for collaborative regulation by international authorities'. All people, it states, are part of a global community. If our civilization is to survive, all of mankind must unite.[9]

Transgovernmental networks and the merging of domestic and foreign policy

The American political scientists Robert Keohane and Joseph Nye then introduced in their 1977 book 'Power and Interdependence' the concept of 'complex interdependence'. In using this term, they wanted to make clear that states and their governments do not operate in world politics like coherent entities, and also that they are not the only relevant actors. To see interdependence merely as a phenomenon of inter-state relations was therefore inadequate, in their view. Government departments and agencies, individuals and other actors such as banks and corporations create, in many different ways, their own direct

---

7   Toffler, Alvin. 1975. The Eco-Spasm Report. New York: Bantam, pp. 75f.
8   Genscher, Hans-Dietrich. 1981. 'Außenpolitik im Zeitalter weltweiter Interdependenz. Rede vor der 30. Generalversammlung der Vereinten Nationen am 24. September 1975'. In: Deutsche Aussenpolitik. Ausgewählte Grundsatzreden 1975-1980, 87–104. Stuttgart: Bonn aktuell, p. 89ff.
9   Steele Commager, Henry. 1976. 'A Declaration of INTERdependence'. In: Third Try at World Order. U.S. Policy for an Interdependent World, ed. by Harlan Cleveland, 107–109. Philadelphia: World Affairs Council of Philadelphia, pp. 109, 107.

cross-border links, and thus themselves become actors in world politics. The political scientist Anne-Marie Slaughter has recently investigated the trans-governmental networks and institutions that arise from direct international co-operation between such bodies as the staff of government ministries, legal authorities or parliamentarians. Almost every ministry now practises within its own policy domain a form of 'world domestic policy', whether simply through horizontal networks or through formal negotiating processes and inter-governmental organizations. The state and the world order, according to Slaughter, are now 'disaggregated'. [10]

Trans-sovereign problems and interdependence lead to ever more issues being influenced by consultations and decisions that take place at the international level. Keohane and Nye noted already that 'the distinction between domestic and foreign issues becomes blurred'.[11] The political scientist Harlan Cleveland (1918 to 2008), who was involved in the creation of the 'Declaration of Interdependence' at Aspen Institute in Washington D.C., has similarly spoken of the 'melding' of foreign and domestic policy.[12]

The physicist Carl Friedrich von Weizsäcker (1912 to 2007), in his acceptance speech for the Peace Prize of the German Book Trade in 1963, was one of the first to give substance to the concept of world domestic policy. He said that what had previously been considered foreign policy was gradually turning into 'world domestic policy' because of what he called the 'harmonization of the world'. World domestic policy described two phenomena: 'the development of supra-national institutions and the use of analytical concepts taken from domestic policy to investigate problems of world politics'. He argued that from an evolutionist perspective the fact that the 'foreign policy of smaller entities was turning into the domestic policy of bigger entities' was 'a familiar historical phenomenon'. [13] As Ulrich Bartosch underlines, world domestic policy here must be understood as a continuous process. To begin with, the term – as outlined in Bartosch's study of Weizsäcker's concept of peace – denotes the still 'unfinished' attempt to come up with a solution to global political problems under actually existing conditions. Here, particular interests compete to steer the course of events in a favourable direction, while, according to Bartosch, 'not having to submit to a process of conflict resolution managed and imposed by a

10 Cf. Slaughter, Anne-Marie. 2004. A new world order. Princeton University Press.
11 Keohane, Robert, and Joseph S. Nye. 2011 [1977]. Power and interdependence. 4th ed. Boston: Longman, p. 20.
12 Cleveland, Harlan. 1976. Third Try at World Order. U.S. Policy for an Interdependent World. Philadelphia: World Affairs Council of Philadelphia, pp. 83ff.
13 Weizsäcker, Carl Friedrich von. 'Bedingungen des Friedens'. Dankesrede, Friedenspreis des Deutschen Buchhandels, 1963, p. 11.

higher authority'.[14] This is where the critical element of a 'complete' world do-mestic policy perspective comes in. For instead of favouring the worldwide im-plementation of a particularistic solution, such a perspective will foreground the search for *joint* solutions. World domestic policy must enable a *fair and global harmonization of interests* and must steer the existing system towards an optimal outcome for all, and towards their common interests. As Weizsäcker said with regard to the creation of a peaceful world order, this requires the cre-ation of 'solid supra-national institutions' that include 'all countries and have a lifespan measured in generations'.[15] World domestic policy thus points towards the goal of the resolution of global political issues through global political insti-tutions in a process which is as democratic as possible. This does not of course mean the end of conflict, or the abolition of all political differences (a naive idea in any case), but rather the diversion of such differences into 'a dynamic insti-tutional structure with a firm legal basis whose purpose is to pressurize the par-ties towards a peaceful resolution of conflicts'.[16]

The evolutionary phases of the international order

It is possible to construct a set of sequential phases in the development of inter-state relations based on their degree of interconnectedness. Barry Buzan, for example, an expert on the evolution of the international system who has taught at the London School of Economics among other places, distinguishes between six ideal-typical conditions.[17] The first three phases he proposes are character-ised by war, enmity and power politics, whereas in the following three it is in-creasingly shared values, trustful cooperation and solidarity which predomi-nate. At one end of the spectrum is a hypothetical 'asocial condition' in which genocidal wars of extermination are the norm. It continues with an anarchic phase of pure power politics, followed by a state of coexistence. The latter cor-responds to the Westphalian System, based on Great Power politics, the balance of powers, sovereignty, territoriality, classical international law and warfare. There follow the phases of cooperation, convergence and confederation, each associated with the strengthening of common institutions and rules. Buzan names the EU as an example of an institution belonging to the 'confederative' phase. 'By this stage', he writes, 'restraints on the use of force would have to be

14 Bartosch, Ulrich. 1995. Weltinnenpolitik. Zur Theorie des Friedens bei Carl Friedrich von Weizsäcker. Ber-lin: Duncker & Humblot, p. 254.
15 Weizsäcker, loc. cit., p. 12.
16 Bartosch, loc. cit, p. 263.
17 See Buzan, Barry. 2004. From International to World Society? English School Theory and the Social Struc-ture of Globalisation. Cambridge University Press, pp. 159f., 190ff.

nearly total, diplomacy largely transformed into something more like the process of domestic politics, and international law transformed into something
more like domestic law, with institutions of enforcement to back it up.'[18] The
spectrum, however, needs to be extended by a seventh and decisive phase: the
sphere of inter-state relations is left behind and the participating partners merge
in a new common federal order. A 'comprehensive' world domestic policy
amounts – at least in crucial areas – to this kind of programme of integration.
A world parliament is the most important institutional requirement for a
properly functioning world domestic policy, since it offers the best possible
democratic and supranational framework for the harmonization and successful
management of the particular interests of nation states, for the creation of common rules, and for the representation of the interests of humanity.

The former US American diplomat James R. Huntley speaks in his book 'Pax
Democratica' of four phases in the evolution of the international order: imperial
subjugation, the state-based balance of power system, organised international
cooperation, and supranational community building. In this evolution, the
fourth phase institutions are 'as different from empires, nation-states and intergovernmental bodies as modern *Homo sapiens* was from the Neanderthals'.[19]
The fact that world domestic politics is only possible in a limited or partial degree within the framework of the classical foreign policy model of sovereign
states was pointed out by the philosopher Karl Jaspers (1883 to 1969) in 1953
in his work 'The Origin and Goal of History'. According to Jaspers, technology
had brought about 'the unification of the globe'. Humanity now shared a common fate. He proclaimed the start of 'the history of the one human race' and
looked forward to the transition to a planetary world order. In the coming 'age
of world unity', which he thought would take the form of 'an all-embracing federalism', the *principle of the primacy of foreign over domestic policy would have
lost all meaning*. A federal world order, according to Jaspers, would mean not
only 'the abolition of absolute sovereignty' but with it 'the abolition of the old
concept of the State in favour of mankind'.[20]

Sovereignty and the era of 'implosion'

The influential English political scientist Harold Laski (1893 to 1950), who studied the issue of sovereignty in some depth, pleaded in the 1930s for the term to

18 Ibid., p. 195.
19 Huntley, James Robert. 1998. Pax Democratica: A Strategy for the 21st Century. New York: St. Martin's
Press, pp. 21ff., 35.
20 Jaspers, Karl. 2010. The Origin and Goal of History. Transl. by Michael Bullock. Abingdon, Oxon: Routledge
Revivals, pp. 193, 197f.

be banished from the vocabulary of political science. 'It would be of lasting benefit to political science', he wrote, 'if the whole concept of sovereignty were surrendered.' He argued that its roots lay in an era when it could describe an absolute and ultimate authority. But if one looked more closely at state communities it was impossible in reality to find such a 'sovereign' central point. Sovereignty was always restricted and shared. It was therefore even more questionable, and indeed 'morally dangerous', to assume the existence of state sovereignty in international affairs. 'There are problems of which the impact upon humanity is too vital for any State to be left to determine by itself what solution it will adopt', wrote Laski. 'The notion of an independent sovereign State is, on the international side, fatal to the well-being of humanity.'[21]

The dogma of sovereignty dates back to the era when messages were delivered on horseback. Its genesis is linked to the Reformation and the wars of religion in the rebellion against the rule of kings and popes. The invention of the printing press had a decisive impact. Marshall McLuhan, the theorist of the media, described the 'era of Gutenberg' dominated by the print media as one of *explosion*. From the 16th century onwards, it created the conditions for individualism, nationalism and the fragmentation of the world into sovereign states under international law. Now, however, McLuhan observed with visionary prescience in 1964, 'after more than a century of electric technology, we have extended our central nervous system itself in a global embrace, abolishing both space and time as far as our planet is concerned.'. The 'speed-up' set off by electronic technology, and direct access to a global network in real time, have turned this around into an *implosion*. 'Our speed-up today is not a slow explosion outward from center to margins but an instant implosion and an interfusion of space and functions. Our specialist and fragmented civilization of center-margin structure is suddenly experiencing an instantaneous reassembling of all its mechanized bits into an organic whole. This is the new world of the global village.'[22]

The transformation of the world into a 'global village' on the basis of the 'new electronic interdependence' which McLuhan proclaimed in his book 'The Gutenberg Galaxy' has become a reality thanks to intercontinental glass fibre cables, satellite communications and the Internet they have enabled.[23] In the era of the Internet Revolution, and under the conditions prevailing in the Anthropocene, sovereignty is imploding towards a zero point. No-one has a right to

21 Laski, Harold J. 1938. A Grammar of Politics. 4th ed. London/New Haven: George Allen & Unwin Ltd./The Yale University Press, pp. 44ff., 65ff.
22 McLuhan, Marshall. 1964. Understanding Media. London: Routledge, pp. 4, 39ff., 101.
23 Idem. 1962. The Gutenberg Galaxy. Toronto: University of Toronto Press, p. 21.

unlimited self-determination or to the unlimited exercise of power, or indeed the capacity for either. All states, institutions, bodies and actors are in one way or another accountable to others and bound up with them. None is sovereign over the others in the classical sense, or can act as if they were.

In fact, the sovereignty of nation states is often not as impermeable in constitutional law as a dogmatic interpretation of international law would have us believe. Many national constitutions place limits on state sovereignty and also permit *the transfer of sovereign rights to international organizations*. Joseph Baratta lists 40 national constitutions from Europe, Latin America, Africa and Asia where this is the case.[24] The possibility of the emergence of supra-national political communities was clearly not alien to those who drew up these constitutions.

---

24   Baratta, Joseph Preston. 2004. The Politics of World Federation. United Nations, UN Reform, Atomic Control. Vol. 1. Westport, Connecticut; London: Praeger Publishers, p. 255.

15.
The fragility of world civilization, existential risks and human evolution

The potential for a worldwide collapse

Probably every generation in modern times – indeed, every generation with a consciousness of history – has experienced its own time as a time of decisive radical change. Today however we really are at an unprecedented historical turning point. For the first time in human history there is a single, integrated world civilization that encompasses the whole of the Earth. Not only does human activity now have a significant impact on crucial parameters of the Earth systems, but in addition there is the potential for a *worldwide* collapse of civilization. This stems from the way the potential risks are combined together; that is, the dense interconnectedness and the fragility of the technological, social and economic systems, so that a disruption to one of them can set off a chain reaction with incalculable and unforeseeable consequences. In 2008, an international conference on 'Global Catastrophic Risks' was held at Oxford University. In the published proceedings, the economist and physicist Robin Hanson noted that while humanity could be afflicted by many kinds of catastrophes, 'most of the damage that follows large disruptions may come from the ensuing social collapse, rather than from the direct effects of the disruption'.[1] A habitable Earth will continue to exist for a very long time yet. It will be about a billion years before the radiance and size of the sun have grown so much, and the surface temperature of the Earth has increased so much as a consequence, that life will hardly be possible there any longer. But even from this cosmological perspective, the 21st century could well be 'a decisive moment'; that is the conviction of the British astrophysicist Martin Rees. For the first time in the history of the planet, one species - the human species - is holding the future of the Earth in its hands, and could put at risk not only itself but all of life.[2] In his 2003 book 'Our Final Hour', Rees, a former President of the Royal Society, analysed a number of global risks arising predominantly out of modern technological capacity. 'I think', was his dramatic conclusion, 'the odds are no better than fifty-fifty that

1   Hanson, Robin. 2008. 'Catastrophe, social collapse, and human extinction'. In: Global Catastrophic Risks (ed.). Nick Bostrom and Milan M. Ćirković, 363–377. 1st ed. Oxford, New York: Oxford University Press, p. 375.
2   Bostrom/Ćirković (ed.), ibid, p. xi.

our present civilization on Earth will survive to the end of the present century without a serious setback.'[3] It is true that humanity has survived natural existential risks for hundreds of thousands of years, as Nick Bostrom of Oxford University notes; however, he writes, '[c]onsideration of specific existential-risk scenarios bears out the suspicion that the great bulk of existential risk in the foreseeable future consists of *anthropogenic existential risks* — that is, those arising from human activity'. The consequences to be expected from an existential catastrophe of this kind are so enormous that the objective of reducing such risks has to become a 'dominant consideration' for humanity.[4]

Within the broad concept of a world domestic policy for the Anthropocene, long-term solutions are especially needed for those problems which potentially threaten the functional capacity or even the survival of world civilization as a whole, or those which have a massive impact on the wellbeing of large parts of the world population, or which could bring with them irreversible negative consequences for humanity. The stability of the Earth system and of the economic and finance systems belong to these categories, as do the threat of atomic war, the spread of super-viruses and other epidemics, ensuring food and water supplies, and the possible consequences of bio- and nano-technology, robotics and artificial intelligence.

The genome as the heritage of humanity

The fact that, through genetic engineering and nanotechnology, science is on the verge of endowing us with technical mastery over the fundamental building blocks of life and matter is one of the markers that confirm that this era is a historical turning point. Huge progress in biotechnology, exemplified by the decoding of the human genome in 2003, by cloning technology or genome editing through Crispr-Cas and other systems, has enabled fundamental intervention in the essence of human life. The core of a human being is embodied in her or his DNA sequence. The genome is the construction manual for their entire biological being. The UNESCO General Conference of 1997 stated in the first article of the 'Universal Declaration on the Human Genome and Human Rights' that the human genome 'underlies the fundamental unity of all members of the human family, as well as the recognition of their inherent dignity and diversity', and that '[i]n a symbolic sense, it is the heritage of humanity'. The text of this ancient book, written by evolution itself, will soon be subject to a thoroughgoing interpretation and manipulation the consequences of which

---

3   Rees, Martin. 2004. Our Final Century. 1st ed. Arrow Books, p. 8.
4   Bostrom, Nick. Feb. 2013. 'Existential Risk Prevention as Global Priority'. Global Policy (4) 1: 15–31, pp. 16, 19.

cannot be foreseen. Almost twenty years ago, Jeremy Rifkin, from the Foundation of Economic Trends in Washington, spoke of a technological revolution without precedent in all of history. 'Never before in history has humanity been so unprepared for the new technological and economic opportunities, challenges, and risks that lie on the horizon. Our way of life is likely to be more fundamentally transformed in the next several decades than in the previous one thousand years.[5] Unfortunately, we do not seem any better prepared yet.

Reprogenetics

For example, we can expect that 'reprogenetics' will enable specific genes to be either handed on or blocked at will, and will thus enable choice over the genetic characteristics of children. In 2015, more than 150 experts signed an open letter calling for strengthened prohibitions against heritable human genetic modification. The letter explained that 'genetically modified children who seem healthy at birth could develop serious problems later in life, some perhaps introduced by purported enhancements. Other harmful consequences of germline modification might only present themselves in subsequent generations', but the warning was in vain.[6] In fact, researchers have already started to experiment with Crispr-Cas on human embryos.

In the view of the molecular biologist Lee Silver, who coined the term 'reprogenetics', manipulating the human genome offers us huge opportunities in the first instance. For example, parents could choose to endow their children with a gene that occurs naturally in one per cent of the population and that provides resistance against infection with the HIV virus. 'Reprogenetics will be used to give children better prospects for their physical and mental development and for a longer life', Silver asserts. The problems, in his view, lie not in the misuse or failure of the technology but rather in the far-reaching social consequences of its application. 'The potential of reprogenetics is so great', argues the Princeton University academic, 'that those families and groups unable to afford it run the risk of being seriously disadvantaged.'[7] The social gulf between the rich and the poor would be genetically entrenched and reproduced. A 'genetocracy' could arise. In his book 'Remaking Eden', Silver describes a possible future in which humanity is irrevocably biologically divided into underprivileged 'naturals' and a class of human beings reprogenetically perfected over generations.

---

5   Rifkin, Jeremy. 1999. The Biotech Century. Trade edition. New York: Tarcher/Putnam, p. 1.
6   Center for Genetics and Society. November 2015. 'Open Letter Calls for Prohibition on Reproductive Human Germline Modification' (www.geneticsandsociety.org).
7   Silver, Lee M. 2000. 'Gesündere and glücklichere Kinder mit Reprogenetik'. Novo (44) (www.novo-magazin.de).

'A severed humanity could be the ultimate legacy of unfettered global capitalism', he writes.[8] For under current circumstances it is only the market and technological feasibility that will determine developments in this area. Even if a society were to decide to try to regulate reprogenetics, by whatever means, this would not be able to prevent wealthy parents fulfilling their desire for reprogenetic intervention, abroad if necessary. Only a watertight system of world law could hold out the prospect of successful regulation. 'So long as there are still sovereign states', Silver writes, 'no border will prevent the free movement of cells and genes which are buried deep within a woman's body. Only a world state could control reprogenetics so that its citizens would have access only to what that state allowed.'[9]

Transhumanism and artificial intelligence

Reprogenetics is not the only challenge for human development. For 'transhumanists' like the computer pioneer Ray Kurzweil, the next logical evolutionary leap forward lies in the fusion of human beings with machine and computer technology.[10] The limitations and defects of the human body will finally be transcended in the cyborgs which emerge from this fusion, hybrids of biological organisms and machines. Yet here, too, it seems likely that an unavoidable consequence would be the division of humanity into two species: the naturals and the cyborgs. And once again, as David Rotter writes in an interesting article, 'it would be first and foremost the elites who would have access to these new technologies and who would use the technical advances to become vastly superior to normal people in intelligence, sensory capacity, physical powers, life expectancy and strength'. The 'worker-race', by contrast, would no longer play any significant role in society.[11] Rotter warns us not to dismiss transhumanism as science fiction. The transhumanist agenda, he says, is dictating scientific activity worldwide and is being pushed forward massively by members of the international elites. He cites as an example the 'Human Brain Project', which aims at creating a comprehensive simulation of the human brain using computer technology and which is being funded by the EU to the tune of a billion Euros. In 2016, bil-

8   Id. 6 August 2002. 'Brave New World Dawning'. Project Syndicate (www.project-syndicate.org).
9   Silver (2000), loc. cit.
10 Kurzweil, Ray. The Age of Spiritual Machines: When Computers Exceed Human Intelligence. New York: Penguin Books, 2000.
11 Rotter, David. 2013. 'Transhumanismus. Die Abschaffung des Menschen'. Tattva Viveka (56): 58–67, p. 64.

lionaire and businessman Elon Musk started Neuralink, a company that will develop devices that could merge the human brain with machines and AI.[12] 'Not only do the rich seem to get richer, they may get the benefit of having a computer-enhanced brain', *CNBC*'s columnist Dustin McKissen commented. What will inequality look like if only the very wealthy can afford to get an upgrade, he asked.[13]

In his 2005 book 'The Artilect War', the Australian Artificial Intelligence researcher Hugo de Garis prophesied that it will be possible to create AI superior to human intelligence by a factor of trillions. Further, that the debate over the direction of human evolution and whether it is acceptable to create machines with such unimaginable artificial intelligence will dominate global politics in the later 21st century, and carries within it serious potential for violent conflict. 'However, once these artificial brains really do start becoming smart and threaten to become a lot smarter and perhaps very quickly (a scenario called 'singularity')', writes Garis, 'then humanity should be ready to take a decision on whether to proceed or not.'[14] Elon Musk believes that the big powers' competition for AI superiority may cause a Third World War, echoing a statement by Russian president Vladimir Putin that 'whoever becomes the leader in this sphere will become the ruler of the world.'[15] According to Stephen Hawking, the development of AI may bring about 'the eventual demise of human beings.'[16] With regard to nuclear and biological warfare, environmental problems and AI, the renowned physicist and cosmologist said in an interview with *The Times* that 'we need to be quicker to identify such threats and act before they get out of control. This might mean some form of world government.'[17]

Autonomous weapons

AI is especially problematic with regard to its military applications. Leading military planners think that the armed conflicts of the future will be dominated by unmanned battle systems, which are already increasingly taking the place of soldiers. Drones and robots, they believe, will revolutionize warfare, just as tanks once did. Military robotics is an industry that is already experiencing exponential growth. One major objective currently being energetically pursued is

12   Galeon, Dom. 28 March 2017. 'Elon Musk Just Confirmed That He's Making Tech To Merge Human Brains and Computers'. Futurism (blog) (futurism.com).
13   McKissen, Dustin. 29 March 2017. 'Elon Musk's Neuralink could help rich people get richer'. CNBC.com.
14   Garis, Hugo de. 2005. The Artilect War. Palm Springs, Ca.: ETC Publications, p. 19.
15   Hern, Alex. 4 September 2017. 'Elon Musk Says AI Could Lead to Third World War'. The Guardian (www.theguardian.com).
16   See Caughill, Patrick. 24 Nov. 2017. 'Stephen Hawking believes humankind is in danger of self-destruction due to AI'. Futurism (blog) (futurism.com).
17   Whipple, Tom, and Oliver Moody. 7 March 2017. 'Stephen Hawking on humanity'. The Times.

the development of *fully autonomous* killer robots and battle drones. '[W]e are sleepwalking into a brave new world where robots decide who, where and when to kill', warned the AI researcher Noel Sharkey, co-founder of the International Committee for Robot Arms Control (ICRAC) in 2009. No computer system, he argued, can reliably distinguish between combatants and innocent people.[18] According to *Science* magazine, computer scientists counter that advanced AI may one day even be superior to human judgement in this area. But Mark Gubrud of the Program on Science and Global Security at Princeton University, another member of ICRAC, believes that this risks human beings 'losing control'. "Stupid robots are dangerous, but smart robots are even more dangerous", Gubrud told the magazine.[19] One year before the start of a global campaign against autonomous killer robots, the NGO Human Rights Watch called in a 2012 report for a pre-emptive international ban on such weapons, which recall the dystopian vision of James Cameron's 1984 film 'Terminator'.[20] In this Hollywood blockbuster, intelligent battle robots and information systems have made themselves autonomous and are waging war against humanity. In an open letter to the UN in August 2017, over 100 of the world's leading robotics and AI pioneers, among them Elon Musk and Alphabet's Mustafa Suleyman, backed this demand. The campaign aims to achieve a ban on autonomous weapons systems by getting them included in the 1980 UN Convention on Certain Conventional Weapons. But the technical possibilities now opening up require regulation under world law in the longer term, for as soon as one country pulls out of the Convention and starts to develop autonomous systems, others may well feel compelled to follow. The world-famous science fiction writer Isaac Asimov (1919 to 1992), in his 1950 novel 'I, Robot', was one of the first to address the issues which are raised by robots becoming ever more like humans, and ever more intelligent. There he also set out his famous Three Laws of Robotics. The first of these states that a robot may not injure a human being. A later, 'Zeroth Law' states that robots may not harm humanity. It will be extremely difficult to apply such laws in practise. Asimov held a clear view on dangers that pose a threat to humanity. 'It is important that the world get together and be sufficiently a unit to face the problems which attack us as a unit', he said. '[W]hat we need is some sort of federal world government.'[21]

---

18 Sharkey, Noel. 18 August 2007. 'Robot wars are a reality'. The Guardian (www.theguardian.com).
19 Citation from Stone, Richard. 20 December 2013. 'Scientists Campaign Against Killer Robots'. Science 342 (6165): 1428–1429, p. 1429.
20 Human Rights Watch. 2012. Losing Humanity. The Case Against Killer Robots (www.hrw.org).
21 Asimov, Isaac. 14 January 1989. 'Keynote Address of the Humanist Institute first annual meeting, New York' (www.youtube.com).

Bioterrorism, nanobots und new viruses

Bill Joy, a critic of transhumanism and co-founder of the company Sun Microsystems, sees greater dangers ahead in the combined application of genetics, nanotechnology and robotics than those posed by the 'classical weapons of mass destruction'. He pointed out in a dramatic appeal that within the next thirty years we must expect it to be technically feasible to construct robotic organisms which self-replicate at the molecular level and which could go out of control, or could even be designed from the outset as 'destruction machines'. In the most extreme case, as postulated in his highly controversial thesis, such killer nanobots could lead to the extermination of human beings. The *Frankfurter Allgemeine Zeitung* compared Joy's widely-admired essay in *Wired* magazine in April 2000 with Albert Einstein's letter of 2 August 1939 to US President Roosevelt, in which Einstein called on the President to put the development of the atom bomb under state control and to press ahead with it swiftly, as it had to be assumed that similar research was under way in Nazi Germany. '[W]e are on the cusp of the further perfection of extreme evil', wrote Joy, 'an evil whose possibility spreads well beyond that which weapons of mass destruction bequeathed to the nation-states, on to a surprising and terrible empowerment of extreme individuals.'[22] Later on he added that it would not be long before every computer user with a mind to do so would be able to create their own superviruses using commonly available resources.[23] The only realistic alternative was to abandon the further development of technologies that are too potentially dangerous and to set limits on the search for certain kinds of knowledge.[24] But even *if* such a step were to be decided on, the necessary instruments do not exist in international law. Ultimately, thought Joy, the world's citizens themselves would need to be drawn into taking direct responsibility for the issue.

At the Oxford conference referred to above, nobody doubted that a global pandemic was one of the greatest worldwide risks.[25] The Spanish flu epidemic which raged from 1918 to 1919 and had a case fatality rate of two to three per cent is estimated to have cost the lives of twenty to a hundred million people, though figures are unreliable. The H5N1 bird flu virus, by contrast, has a case fatality rate that can go considerably above 50 per cent. The US American sociologist and writer Mike Davis points out that a H5N1 pandemic similar to the

---

22 Joy, Bill. April 2000. 'Why the Future Doesn't Need Us'. Wired (www.wired.com).
23 Id.. 2000. 'Act now to keep new technologies out of destructive hands'. New Perspectives Quarterly 17 (3): 12–14.
24 Id. (April 2000), loc. cit.
25 Bostrom/Ćirković (ed.), ibid., p. 16.

Spanish flu outbreak could kill up to *one billion* people.[26] This figure makes clear the potential threat posed by new mutations, 'designer viruses' or killer nano-bots. Nobody can know if and when such a dangerous natural mutation of the H5N1 virus, or of another pathogen, might actually occur. However, in highly controversial laboratory trials in the USA and the Netherlands, airborne modified bird flu viruses have already been *artificially created*. The experiments were published in detail in mid-2012 with the backing of the World Health Organization. Following a one-year 'voluntary moratorium', the research was started up again in January 2013. US American microbiologist Richard Ebright criticised the fact that there had been no independent review of the security arrangements or of the balance of risks against potential benefits.[27] International regulations that could be applied to this kind of research simply do not exist.

The need for regulation under global law

In the study by the NIC and the EUISS already referred to in the previous chapter, the dangers posed by bioterrorism, and the broader challenge of biotechnology in general, are judged to be of the greatest significance.[28] 'Rapidly falling costs', it is stated there, 'will bring biotechnology within reach of a hacker community, while a growing number of reputable laboratories will "leak" expertise and, potentially, materials.' The authors believe existing governance mechanisms and regulations in the area of biotechnology are inadequate. Moreover, '[n]o forum currently exists for dealing comprehensively across the scientific community, industry, and governments on measures needed to diminish the risks posed by the biotechnology revolution'.[29] Even if such a 'forum' were to exist, it would not be enough. In the book 'Our Posthuman Future', Francis Fukuyama, who was a member of US President George Bush's Council on Bioethics, came to the conclusion that the development and application of biotechnology and medical science need to be politically regulated by new institutions 'that will discriminate between those technological advances that promote human flourishing, and those that pose a threat to human dignity and well-being'. These institutions must have 'real enforcement powers' and 'international reach'. But leaving aside for a moment the substantive issues, one has to ask how people imagine effective global regulation will come about in this area. De-

26   Davis, Mike. The Monster at Our Door. The Global Threat of Avian Flu. New York: Henry Holt and Company, 2006, pp. 125f.
27   Keim, Brandon. 23 January 2013. 'Ready or Not: Mutant H5N1 Research Set to Resume'. Wired (www.wired.com).
28   National Intelligence Council (ed.). September 2010. 'Global Governance 2025: At a critical juncture', p. iii.
29   Ibid., pp. 35, 69.

cisions over whether the application of biotechnology is legitimate or illegitimate are in essence political rather than technocratic questions, according to Fukuyama. Therefore, and in this we are in agreement with him, it is 'the democratically constituted political community, acting chiefly through their elected representatives' that must be responsible for those decisions.[30] But Fukuyama is thinking here only of arrangements at the nation state level. These need to be brought together and harmonised within an international legal regime. But that in turn would mean that technocrats and not elected representatives would once again ultimately be in charge.

A world parliament, as the political institution representing the world's citizens, should take up all global issues that arise in the fields of biotechnology, nanotechnology and transhumanism and instigate a global public debate on them, leading ultimately to appropriate global regulations. Mario Capanna, President of the Rome-based Genetic Rights Foundation, takes the view that the human genome must be regarded as a global common good. The time is right, he argues, for a world parliament that would represent effectively all the people of the Earth and 'would concern itself with those great questions with a global impact'.[31] How to handle the possibilities opened up by genetic engineering is unquestionably one of those great questions. Another urgent problem that has long been neglected is the threat of growing antibiotic resistance. The Princeton-based Australian bioethicist Peter Singer said with regard to global problems that 'a suitable form of government for that single world' would have to be found on the path to a global ethical community. Institutions for global decision-making would need to be strengthened and made more accountable to the people affected by those decisions. 'This line of thought', said Singer, 'leads in the direction of a world community with its own directly elected legislature, perhaps slowly evolving along the lines of the European Union.'[32]

30   Fukuyama, Francis. 2002. *Our Posthuman Future*. New York: Picador, pp. 182, 204, 211, 186.
31   Capanna, Mario. 2010. 'Towards a World Parliament'. Speech at at the 10th Doha Forum on Democracy and Free Trade (www.fondazionedirittigenetici.org).
32   Singer, Peter. 2004. *One world: the ethics of globalization*. New Haven: Yale University Press, pp. 149, 199ff.

16.
The threat of nuclear weapons, disarmament, and collective security

Nuclear war as the end of all things

The build-up of huge arsenals of nuclear weapons has created the potential to extinguish world civilization and the conditions enabling its existence. The apocalyptic consequences of a nuclear war are well-known. In addition to the direct explosive impact of the nuclear devices themselves, there would be fire-storms and radioactive fallout. Large amounts of radioactive dust would be pro-pelled into the atmosphere. Depending on the quantities involved, a protracted reduction in sunlight would follow, and with it a sharp fall in temperature as well as other weather and climatic impacts. A 'nuclear winter' would seriously reduce global food production and lead to worldwide famine. 'Although a ma-jor nuclear war between the Great Powers would probably not mean the end of humanity', writes the Dutch social scientist Godfried van Benthem van den Bergh, 'it would destroy all the important centres of civilization. The survivors would probably be catapulted back several thousand years in terms of social and political organization; it is likely that a plethora of armed bands would emerge, who would find themselves forced into a wild struggle of all against all.'[1] This destructive capacity is another thing that distinguishes our time from all the historical epochs of the past. The Greek philosopher Heraclitus thought that war was 'the father of all things'. In the Anthropocene, war has become poten-tially *the end of all things*.

The world has once before been a hair's breadth away from 'the abyss of nuclear destruction and the end of mankind', as Robert Kennedy writes in his account of what were perhaps the thirteen most dangerous days in all of history - the Cuba Crisis of October 1962.[2] A few misjudgements could have allowed the conflict between the USA and the Soviet Union to escalate into war. The explosive power of the nuclear weapons in operational readiness spread among the various launch systems is unimaginable. The two hundred intercontinental

---

1 Bergh, Godfried van Benthem van den. 1984. 'Dynamik von Rüstung und Staatsbildungsprozessen'. In: Macht and Zivilisation. Materialien zu Norbert Elias' Zivilisationstheorie. Ed. by Peter Gleichmann, Johan Goudsblom, and Hermann Korte, 217–241. Frankfurt: Suhrkamp, p. 217.
2 Kennedy, Robert F. 1999 [1968]. Thirteen Days. A Memoir of the Cuban Missile Crisis. New York and Lon-don: W.W. Norton & Company, p. 19.

missiles on the American side alone were apparently armed with 635 megatons of explosive, and the forty on the Soviet side with between 108 and 204 megatons – a combined explosive power more than fifty thousand times greater than the atom bomb dropped on Hiroshima. The other operational warheads, especially those of the USA's strategic bomber fleet, represented an additional destructive capacity greater by several multiples. At that point in time it is believed that the USA had 3,500 operational warheads, and the Soviets perhaps 500.[3] The nuclear arms race reached its peak in 1986, at around 65,000 nuclear weapons and an explosive power of over 20,000 megatons. In the course of disarmament negotiations since then, this arsenal has been reduced by more than two thirds. However, taking all warheads into account, the USA and Russia together still have over 18,000 nuclear weapons today, and France, China, Great Britain, India, Pakistan and Israel about another thousand altogether. Whether North Korea possesses operational nuclear weapons is not clear. What is more, the USA and the Russian Federation continue to maintain about 2,000 of their nuclear weapons at the highest level of readiness so as to be able to respond in a matter of minutes to any first nuclear strike by the other side – just as if the Cold War had not ended over twenty years ago. This state of affairs is based on a circular logic, seemingly hard to dispel, according to which one side's nuclear weapons have to be maintained in readiness because those on the other side are as well.[4] 'Nuclear war is seven minutes away, and might be over in an afternoon', wrote the English author Martin Amis.[5] In that respect, nothing has changed yet.

The danger of drifting into nuclear war

The way the states of the world are linked to each other has been fundamentally changed by the existence of nuclear weapons. The possibility of nuclear annihilation has turned direct military conflict between the nuclear Great Powers into a form of suicide. They find themselves in an 'interdependence of destruction', as Wilhelm Wolfgang Schütz called it.[6] However, it would be a fatal error to believe that the obvious insanity of an atomic war makes it impossible. As Norbert Elias pointed out, complex relationships can give rise to an irrational self-perpetuating dynamic from which the partners cannot escape even when they

---

3   Figures from Dobbs, Rachel. 2011. 'What Was at Stake in 1962?' Foreign Policy (www.foreignpolicy.com). See also Norris, Robert S., and Hans M. Kristensen. 12 October 2012. 'The Cuban Missile Crisis: A nuclear order of battle, October and November 1962'. Bulletin of the Atomic Scientists, Nuclear Notebook.
4   Cf. Kristensen, Hans M., and Matthew McKinzie. 2012. Reducing Alert Rates of Nuclear Weapons. New York and Geneva: United Nations Institute for Disarmament Research (www.unidir.ch), p. viii.
5   Amis, Martin. Einstein's Monsters. London: Vintage, 2003.
6   Schütz, Wolfgang Wilhelm. 1956. Wir wollen Überleben, Außenpolitik im Atomzeitalter. Stuttgart: DVA, p. 162.

know that it is harmful to them. And it is precisely in a situation of threat that a spiral of escalation can emerge of a kind Elias called a 'double-bind figuration'. In the face of danger, thought and action become increasingly driven by emotion, which in turn leads to an escalation of the danger, and *vice versa*. In fact, Elias thought the 'drift towards atomic war' was a particularly good example of such an 'unplanned social process'.[7] It would be difficult to disagree with the view of the US American security and nuclear weapons expert Joseph Cirincione that the danger of a global thermonuclear war *at present* is close to zero. But *close to zero* is *not zero*. 'Even a small chance of war each year, for whatever reason, multiplied over a number of years sums to an unacceptable chance of catastrophe', Cirincione points out.[8] What is more, the security situation could deteriorate again in the future. It is only a question of time.

The risk of nuclear accidents

The short response times considerably increase the risk of an order to launch being given on the basis of a misjudgement or human error. Faults can also occur in the command and early warning systems. In a standard work on nuclear safety in the US armed forces, Scott Sagan writes that '[n]uclear weapons may well have made *deliberate* war less likely, but, the complex and tightly coupled nuclear arsenal we have constructed has simultaneously made *accidental* war more likely'.[9]

Dozens of incidents have come to light. In 1979, for example, the North American Aerospace Defense Command centre (NORAD) mistakenly showed as genuine a simulated attack by over two thousand Soviet rockets which had been entered into the system for test purposes. The mistake was spotted one minute before the US President was due to be informed. In 1995, a sounding rocket (a sub-orbital research rocket) launched in Norway was wrongly identified by the Russian early warning system as a possible US American submarine-launched nuclear attack on Moscow. Its flying time was estimated at five minutes. President Boris Yeltsin placed the Russian nuclear armed forces on battle alert. Fortunately, calculations showed just in time that the rocket would land outside Russian borders. And it is worth noting in this context that according to experts the Russian early warning system is in any event in a dangerously run-down condition. Another significant incident occurred in November 2008.

---

7   Elias, Norbert. 1987. Involvement and Detachment. Oxford: Basil Blackwell, pp. 74f.
8   Cirincione, Joseph. 2008. 'The continuing threat of nuclear war'. In: Global Catastrophic Risks (ed.). Nick Bostrom and Milan M. Ćirković, 381–401. 1st ed. Oxford, New York: Oxford University Press, p. 382.
9   Sagan, Scott D. 1995. The Limits of Safety. Organizations, Accidents, and Nuclear Weapons. 4th ed. Princeton University Press, p. 264.

During the extended terrorist attacks and hostage crisis in Mumbai in India, which went on for several days, the Pakistani President received a phone call from the Indian Foreign Minister in which an attack on Pakistan was threatened unless immediate steps were taken against individuals in Pakistan believed to be behind the terrorist attacks. The Pakistani armed forces were placed on the highest level of alert, and planes armed with primed nuclear weapons were sent out on patrol. As it turned out, however, the call was a hoax by an unknown perpetrator. Scientists are convinced that a large-scale nuclear war between India and Pakistan involving the deployment of their one hundred nuclear weapons would result in disastrous worldwide effects over and above the estimated twenty million deaths in the two countries and 'would produce enough smoke to cripple global agriculture'.[10] In the opinion of Tad Daley, a specialist on nuclear disarmament, these and other known incidents are probably only 'the tip of the iceberg'. In his recommended book 'Apocalypse Never', to which we are indebted for a number of ideas and references, he asks rhetorically whether we can 'really expect, if we retain nuclear weapons for another twenty or thirty years, that not a single nuclear crisis will ever descend into nuclear war?'[11]

If just a single nuclear warhead were to be detonated, especially in a big city, the consequences would be devastating, possibly leading to a substantial political and economic destabilization of the world. In his 2013 book 'Command and Control', the journalist Eric Schlosser details numerous, sometimes highly dramatic accidents involving nuclear weapons. In one instance, two W39 hydrogen bombs were released over North Carolina in 1961 following the break-up of a B52 bomber at a height of 3,000 metres. An investigation later uncovered by Schlosser established that the detonation of one of the warheads was prevented only by a simple low-voltage electric switch prone to faults. The explosive power of this bomb was – at four megatons – over three hundred times greater than that of the atom bomb dropped on Hiroshima.[12] Although such a worst-case-scenario accident has fortunately not yet occurred, nobody can give a one hundred per cent guarantee that it will not happen in the future. Moreover, one scenario for nuclear terrorism involves the deliberate detonation of a nuclear weapon which has fallen intact into the wrong hands. It is known that al-Qaida tried to put its hands on a nuclear weapon or on highly enriched uranium for

---

10 Robock, Alan, and Brian Toon. Jan. 2010. 'Local Nuclear War, Global Suffering'. Scientific American: 74–81, p. 76.
11 Daley, Tad. 2010. Apocalypse never. Forging the path to a nuclear weapon-free world. New Brunswick, N.J.: Rutgers University Press, p. 95.
12 Schlosser, Eric. 2013. Command and control: nuclear weapons, the Damascus Accident, and the illusion of safety. New York: The Penguin Press, pp. 245ff.

the construction of an atomic bomb. Cyberterrorism against nuclear installations and systems also poses a serious threat. The US American nuclear weapons expert and disarmament campaigner Bruce Blair has pointed out that hackers could try to manipulate early warning systems in such a way as to provoke an atomic war. It is even possible that a fake order to launch could be fed into the chain of command. According to Blair, this is precisely what the Pentagon identified as theoretically feasible during a security review conducted in 1998. Hackers could have gained back-door electronic access to the U.S. naval communications network, seized control electronically of U.S. Navy radio towers and illicitly transmitted a launch order to U.S. Trident ballistic missile submarines armed with 200 nuclear warheads each.[13] A Third World War, as Mikhail Gorbachev put it in his famous article in *Pravda* in 1987, has been averted not *because of* but *in spite of* the existence of nuclear weapons.[14]

The unfulfilled commitment to general and complete disarmament

As the UN General Assembly has repeatedly and accurately pointed out, 'the only defence against a nuclear catastrophe is the total elimination of nuclear weapons and the certainty that they will never be produced again', as stated in a Resolution of 10 December 1996. This view is now shared by 'realists' such as the former US State Secretaries Henry Kissinger and George Shultz, the former US defence minister William Perry and the former Chair of the defence committee of the US Senate Sam Nunn. In one of a series of jointly written articles published in the *Wall Street Journal* since 2007, they wrote that '[t]he risk that deterrence will fail and that nuclear weapons will be used increases dramatically', and that 'the pace of work [on nuclear disarmament] doesn't now match the urgency of the threat'.[15] In fact, the community of states has been trying to tackle this issue continuously now for more than sixty years. The very first Resolution of the UN General Assembly of 24 January 1946 set up a Commission to make proposals 'for the elimination from national armaments of atomic weapons'. In the so-called Nuclear Non-Proliferation Treaty, which came into force in 1970 and which almost all the world's states have signed up to, those

---

13 Blair, Bruce. 19 Sep. 2004. 'The Wrong Deterrence'. Washington Post (www.washingtonpost.com). Cf. also Rosenbaum, Ron. 2011. How the end begins: the road to a nuclear World War III. London: Simon & Schuster, p. 109.
14 Gorbachev, Mikhail. 1987. 'Reality and Guarantees for a Secure World'. International Affairs: A Russian Journal of World Politics, Diplomacy and International Relations 33 (11): 3–11, p. 4.
15 Shultz, George P., William J. Perry, Henry A. Kissinger, and Sam Nunn. 5 March 2013. 'Next Steps in Reducing Nuclear Risks: The Pace of Nonproliferation Work Today Doesn't Match the Urgency of the Threat'. The Wall Street Journal (www.nuclearsecurityproject.org).

states without nuclear weapons agreed to forego their acquisition or development and to allow inspections to be carried out by the International Atomic Energy Agency to verify this. This commitment is to be matched, according to Article VI, by a commitment on the part of the five officially recognised nuclear weapons states – the USA, Russia, France, Great Britain and China – to pursue negotiations with all other parties 'on a Treaty on general and complete disarmament under strict and effective international control'. When US President Barack Obama announced the aim of 'a world without nuclear weapons' in Prague in April 2009, this was celebrated as a huge breakthrough and rewarded with the Nobel Peace Prize. However, it needs to be acknowledged that *a commitment under international law* to realize this very goal has been in existence already *for more than four decades.* '[T]he obligation involved here', emphasized the International Court of Justice in an Advisory Opinion of 1996, 'is an obligation to achieve a precise result – nuclear disarmament in all its aspects' by negotiating and *concluding* a Treaty.[16] In spite of this, Obama (who was born in 1961) underlined in Prague that a world free of nuclear weapons would not be achieved quickly - 'perhaps not in my lifetime'. It appears that the five recognised nuclear weapons states are determined to remain nuclear powers for the indefinite future. Both in the USA and in Russia extensive modernization programmes are under way. More recently, the two nuclear powers have accused each other of violating the provisions of the Intermediate-Range Nuclear Forces Treaty concluded in 1987. On Twitter US-President-elect Donald Trump declared on 22 December 2016 that in his opinion the 'United States must greatly strengthen and expand its nuclear capability until such time as the world comes to its senses regarding nukes'. When 122 UN member states voted in favour of a Treaty on the Prohibition of Nuclear Weapons on 7 July 2017, this was opposed by all known nuclear powers and many of their allies, including all NATO member states. From the perspective of India, which - like Pakistan, Israel and North Korea - is not a party to the Nuclear Non-Proliferation Treaty, the non-proliferation agreement established in practice a permanent system of 'nuclear apartheid'. India cites the fact that the five official nuclear weapons states ignore their commitments under Article VI of the Nuclear Non-Proliferation Treaty as one of the reasons for not signing up to the Treaty. A particularly grotesque moment in the comedy was played out at a meeting of the UN Security Council chaired by Obama on 24 September 2009. In a unanimous resolution celebrated as historic, the five official nuclear weapons states, all of which have a permanent seat

---

16 International Court of Justice. 1996. 'Legality of the Threat or Use of Nuclear Weapons. Advisory Opinion.' ICJ, para. 99, pp. 41f.

on the Council, in effect called on themselves to meet their obligations under
Article VI.

The architecture of nuclear disarmament

According to Tad Daley, the wording of Article VI of the Nuclear Non-Proliferation Treaty – 'general and complete disarmament under strict and effective
international control' – makes it clear that '[w]hatever nuclear abolitionist architecture might ultimately be created by the conclusion of such negotiations,
that architecture must move beyond pure national sovereignty and exclusive
national control over nuclear weapons ... States must find a way to cede the management, verification, and enforcement of nuclear disarmament to some kind of
international institution, global structure, or mechanism of transnational governance'.[17] In this regard, the new Treaty on the Prohibition of Nuclear Weapons
does not offer any solution. In Article 4 it vaguely says that '[t]he States Parties
shall designate a competent international authority or authorities to negotiate
and verify the irreversible elimination of nuclear-weapons programmes'.

On the initiative of a number of NGOs including the International Physicians
for the Prevention of Nuclear War and the International Association Of Lawyers
Against Nuclear Arms, a number of experts adopted the roles of the various governments in order to draft - from that assumed perspective - a model nuclear
weapons convention, or NWC, that goes into more detail. From a global legal
perspective, a significant element of the draft agreement, first published in 1997,
is that it includes the possibility of criminal proceedings being taken against individuals in cases of a breach of the provisions of the treaty. If none of the treaty
partners is willing or able to instigate such proceedings, then the case becomes
the responsibility of the International Criminal Court. In addition, every individual would be obliged under this treaty to report any infringements to the international authority charged with upholding the treaty. It is explicitly stated that this
reporting obligation overrides any contradictory national regulations. Whistle-
blowers are given international witness protection and where necessary a right of
asylum. This makes it clear that there is an assumption that an approach involving the signatory states alone holds out little prospect for success and that the
creation of a world free of nuclear weapons requires the citizens of the world
themselves to be given direct responsibility. The influential journalist Walter
Lippmann had already made the case for such an approach in 1946.[18]

---

17 Daley, loc. cit., p. 118.
18 Lippmann, Walter. 1946. 'International Control of Atomic Energy'. In: One World Or None, ed. by Dexter
     Masters and Katharine Way, 180–208. New York: The New Press, pp. 187ff.

In one other respect, the draft is less innovative. In the course of the START (Strategic Arms Reduction Treaty) negotiations since 1995, the United States and Russia have established a wide-ranging bilateral inspections system. It is a prerequisite of complete nuclear disarmament that all countries must submit equally to a thorough *international* inspections system. One problem is how to handle the suspected blocking of inspections or other cases of non-compliance on the part of any state. In the draft NWC, such cases are passed to the UN Security Council for further advice and for decisions on measures to be taken if necessary. This obviously was not an option for the countries that negotiated and adopted the prohibition treaty. It is precisely the five nuclear weapons states of the USA, Russia, France, Great Britain and China whose nuclear disarmament is the objective, but who sit on the Council not only as the sole nations with permanent seats but in possession moreover of a right of veto by means of which they can block any decision. They would therefore represent jury, judge and law enforcement at their own hearings. It is clear that such a conflict of interests would make nuclear arms control impossible over the long term. The simple fact of the right of veto of the five permanent members means that the Security Council in its present form cannot play a credible role in the architecture of nuclear disarmament. A multilateral agreement for the abolition of nuclear weapons would either have to involve appropriate reforms to the Security Council or else the creation of a new body better suited to the task. The historical contingency of the special status enjoyed today by the five permanent members of the UN Security Council represents an obstacle to the transition to a world free of nuclear weapons, and will become increasingly hard to justify. We should recall that after the Second World War the US government proposed to renounce nuclear weapons if all other countries would do the same and if at the same time an international inspections system under the control of the UN could be set up to monitor compliance. At that time the USA still had a nuclear monopoly. It was a key element of the US proposal that the right of veto in the Security Council should be abolished in the area of nuclear weapons control. 'There must be no veto to protect those who violate their solemn agreements not to develop or use atomic energy for destructive purposes', explained the US representative Bernard Baruch at a session of the United Nations on 14 June 1946. However, Daley now questions whether it is acceptable at all for the world to be governed by a small group of 'Great Powers', or whether it would not be better if 'our sociopolitical imaginations might someday invent better mechanisms of global governance, and begin to move toward creating something on the world level resembling a parliament of humankind'.[19] 'Unless humanity can someday manage to establish something like a world republic, the logic of anarchy will endure', and with it the danger of self-annihilation.[20]

The link between nuclear and conventional disarmament

The abolition of nuclear weapons once and for all, so important for the survival of world civilization, requires the transformation of the international order into a system of world law. The struggle for political power between the states, which rests ultimately on the institution of war, must be transcended. Although on the one hand the nuclear 'balance of terror' makes military conflict between the nuclear powers impossible as a rational option, on the other hand the danger of drifting into a nuclear war is substantial. But the abolition of nuclear weapons *alone* is not a solution, because then conventional armaments would once again increase in importance in direct proportion. 'Military power would become relative again', argued van den Bergh. Without nuclear deterrence, the likelihood of a military escalation of conflicts, including between great powers, would grow, which would immediately set off in turn a race for nuclear re-armament.[21] Successful nuclear disarmament is therefore directly linked to conventional disarmament and arms control. This became clear already at the tenth special session of the UN General Assembly, on disarmament, which took place in 1978. 'Together with negotiations on nuclear disarmament measures', read the concluding report, agreed by consensus, 'negotiations should be carried out on the balanced reduction of armed forces and of conventional armaments ... These negotiations should be conducted with particular emphasis on armed forces and conventional weapons of nuclear weapons states and other militarily significant countries'.[22] Mikhail Gorbachev highlighted the link at a conference in Rome in 2009, pointing to the US American defence budget, which for a time was equal to those of all the world's other states put together. He said that military predominance such as that enjoyed by the USA represented an 'insurmountable obstacle' to the liberation of the world from nuclear weapons. 'Un-

19 Daley, loc., cit., p. 179.
20 Daley, Tad. 25 October 2013. 'Ban the Bomb!' Foreign Policy in Focus (fpif.org).
21 Bergh, Godfried van Benthem van den. 1992. The Nuclear Revolution and the End of the Cold War. Houndsmills: MacMillan Press, p. 211.
22 United Nations. 1978. 'Resolutions and decisions adopted by the General Assembly during its tenth special session'. A/S-10/4, para. 22, p. 5; see also para. 81, p. 10.

less we discuss demilitarization of international politics, the reduction of military budgets, preventing militarization of outer space, talking about a nuclear-free world will be just rhetorical', the former Soviet President declared.[23]

The problem is closely linked to the origins of modern statehood. As the US American sociologist Charles Tilly (1929 to 2008) has emphasized, the process of state formation was marked by war and war preparations, and the modern state and its administrative and enforcement apparatus developed in large part as 'a by-product of rulers' efforts to acquire the means of war'.[24] 'War made the state and the state made war' was his pithy and subsequently frequently-cited formulation.[25] The possibility of military conflict has always been the decisive factor in the competitive relationship between states. The ability to dispose over armed forces, the capacity to wage war, and the monopoly on force within a defined territory –historically, these constitute core areas of national sovereignty. Nothing makes it plainer than the worldwide existence of national armed forces that the anarchic state of international relations has not in any sense been overcome, but at best overlaid. Even in the European Union, the most advanced example of integration yet, progress towards integrated armed forces is painfully slow, despite the lip service paid to a 'common defence policy' and initiatives like European Corps or the EU Battlegroups. In the wake of Brexit, an important milestone may now have been reached when in late 2017, 25 EU member states agreed on the creation of a new European defence and security cooperation network known as Permanent Structured Cooperation or PESCO. Notwithstanding that, the increasingly multinational composition of armed force units – whether under UN, NATO, EU or AU auspices - reflects a growing acceptance of a general shift in defence policy away from the classical form of defence of the nation and its allies towards global crisis intervention and conflict prevention. The next logical step is fully integrated supra-national armed forces. A sustainable peace order designed to last for generations must consist of more than making war between countries 'unimaginable' and prohibiting it under international law if at the same time the *practical means* of waging war, in the form of national offensive armouries and national decision-making autonomy are *allowed to persist* fundamentally unquestioned. What is needed is a collective security system for the whole of humanity, one that enables the gradual disarmament and ultimately the *total abolition* of national

---

23 Hanley, Charles J. 16 April 2009. 'Gorbachev: US military power blocks ‚no nukes". Associated Press.
24 Tilly, Charles. 2010. Coercion, Capital, and European States AD 990 - 1992. Rev. paperback ed. Cambridge, Mass; Oxford, UK: Blackwell, p. 14, see also pp. 67ff.
25 Id. 1975. 'Reflections on the History of European State-Making'. In: The Formation of National States in Western Europe, ed. by Charles Tilly. Princeton University Press, p. 42.

armed forces. There must be a global treaty on nuclear *and* conventional disarmament. This is precisely what is really meant by the phrase 'general and complete disarmament' in Article VI of the Nuclear Non-Proliferation Treaty, which is constantly invoked.

The McCloy-Zorin Accords

It is worth calling to mind how this phrase came to be adopted as the guiding principle on the path to a global peace order. On 20 September 1961, the USA under President John F. Kennedy and the Soviet Union under Premier Nikita Khrushchev reached agreement on a set of 'Agreed Principles for General and Complete Disarmament', also known as the McCloy–Zorin Accords, after the chief negotiators on each side. An international programme for general and complete disarmament is there set out, step by step: the disbanding of all armed forces and the dismantling of all military establishments around the world; the cessation of the production of armaments, as well as their liquidation or conversion to peaceful uses; the elimination of all stockpiles of nuclear, chemical, bacteriological, and other weapons of mass destruction, and cessation of the production of such weapons and of their delivery systems; the cessation of military training, and closing of all military training institutions; and finally the discontinuance of military expenditures. Only those non-nuclear armaments, forces, facilities, and establishments agreed to be necessary to maintain internal order and protect the personal security of citizens would be allowed to continue in existence. In order to ensure the maintenance of international peace, particularly during the changeover period, the text included provision for a UN peace force Verification of the process of disarmament would be the responsibility of an international authority whose activities would not be subject to veto. Any disputes would be taken before international courts. On 20 December 1961, this programme was unanimously adopted by the UN General Assembly. The programme was intended to ensure that war would no longer be 'an instrument for settling international problems'.[26] After the Cuba Crisis, Kennedy was more determined than ever to press forward with it.[27] On 22 November 1963, Kennedy was murdered in Dallas, and the programme sank into oblivion.

---

26 'Joint Statement of Agreed Principles for Disarmament Negotiations (McCloy-Zorin Accords)'. 20 September 1961. Nuclear Age Peace Foundation (www.nuclearfiles.org).
27 See his speech on peace at the American University Commencement Address, 10 June 1963 in Washington D.C. One month earlier he had also approved a related internal memorandum; see Kennedy, John F. 6 May 1963. 'National Security Action Memorandum Number 239'. John F. Kennedy Presidential Library & Museum.

The unrealised peace concept of the UN Charter, and UN armed forces

The astoundingly radical, inspirational peace programme embodied in the McCloy-Zorin Accords was not plucked out of thin air, but is in fact simply the practical expression of the peace concept proposed in the UN Charter. According to Article 26, the Security Council shall submit plans 'for the establishment of a system for the regulation of armaments'. Article 43 requires binding agreements to be reached for the provision by member states of armed forces at the request and disposal of the Security Council. Under Article 47, a UN Military Staff Committee will take over the 'strategic direction' of all armed forces placed at the disposal of the Security Council and will advise the Security Council on questions of arms control and disarmament. 'The United Nations Organization must immediately begin to be equipped with an international armed force', demanded the former British Prime Minister Winston Churchill in his famous speech at Fulton, Missouri in the spring of 1946. Such an international force was something he had hoped to see come about after the First World War already.[28] In October 1946, US President Truman pressed for the conclusion of the special agreements required in a speech at the UN. The first UN General Secretary, the Norwegian Trygve Lie, floated several more 'trial balloons' up to 1952, as Oxford professor Adam Roberts reports in an historical overview.[29] The peace concept embodied in the UN Charter has still not been realised today.

As no armed forces have been put at the disposal of the UN, it is basically unable to respond consistently, with its own military measures, to breaches of the peace or to acute conflict situations. However, as UN Secretary-General Boutros-Ghali underlined in the 'Agenda for Peace' in 1992, such a capacity, together with the provision of armed forces in accordance with Article 43 of the Charter, is 'essential to the credibility of the United Nations as a guarantor of international security'. The knowledge of the ready availability of UN armed forces on call could serve, in itself, as a means of deterring potential aggressors.[30] Instead, every UN mission has to be painstakingly and slowly put together ad hoc. For this, what is crucial is whether, and if so when, the member states are willing to provide the necessary resources and troops. Whether the prerequisite

---

28 Churchill, Winston. 5 March 1946. 'The Sinews of Peace, Westminster College, Fulton, Missouri'. The Churchill Centre and Museum at the Churchill War Rooms, London.

29 Roberts, Adam. 2008. 'Proposals for UN Standing Forces: A Critical History'. In: The United Nations Security Council and War, 99–130. Ed. by Vaughan Lowe, Adam Roberts, Jennifer Welsh, and Dominik Zaum. Oxford: Oxford University Press.

30 United Nations. 1992. 'An Agenda for Peace. Preventive diplomacy, peacemaking and peace-keeping'. Report of the Secretary-General pursuant to the statement adopted by the Summit Meeting of the Security Council on 31 January 1992, A/47/277-S/24111, para. 43.

political will exists at all is unclear in advance. When between April and July 1994 over 800,000 people were murdered by Hutu extremists in Rwanda and four million more were forced to flee, the Security Council did nothing to intervene in the genocide. It is true that since 1994 there has been a directory where member states can register the availability of troops and equipment for UN peace operations, but it does not represent a fixed commitment and the option of saying 'No' to a specific request always remains open. 'In these circumstances', wrote Boutros-Ghali in 1995 in another report, 'I have come to the conclusion that the United Nations does need to give serious thought to the idea of a rapid reaction force.'[31]

There is another problem resulting from the limitations on the UN's capacity to act: every UN-led multilateral peace operation since 1990 has had to fall back on private security firms, and this trend has in fact been growing.[32] One of the largest of these firms, the security and military enterprise Blackwater, now operating under the name Academi, even 'strives to be an independent army, deploying to conflict zones as an alternative to a NATO or UN force', as the journalist Jeremy Scahill found in a *New York Times* bestseller about the company. However, this army, he adds, would be answerable only to its private owners and not to governments.[33] In view of the fact that the UN does not have its own intervention force at its disposal, the long-serving former UN Deputy Secretary-General Brian Urquhart even opined that private firms could play 'an extremely useful role'. For many tasks, they were better trained and prepared than 'a UN force put together at the last minute'.[34] The idea of the privatization of global security should be met with great scepticism. Indeed, experts from the Global Policy Forum in New York suggest the opposite conclusion: that the UN should cease cooperating with private providers of military services entirely.[35] But if that were to happen, the UN would need a massive upscaling of capacity in order to be able to meet its needs from its own resources.

31 United Nations. 1995. 'Supplement to an Agenda for Peace: Position Paper of the Secretary-General on the Occassion of the Fiftieth Anniversary of the United Nations'. Report of the Secretary-General on the work of the organization, A/50/60-S/1995/1, para. 44.
32 Avant, Deborah. 2005. The Market for Force: The Consequences of Privatizing Security. Cambridge University Press, p. 7.
33 Scahill, Jeremy. 2007. Blackwater. The Rise of the World's Most Powerful Mercenary Army. London: Serpent's Tail, p. 345.
34 'Lateline: Dogs of War'. 18 May 2000. Australian Broadcasting Corp (www.abc.net.au). Interview with Brian Urquhart, Tim Spicer and Abdul Musa.
35 Pingeot, Lou. 2012. 'Dangerous Partnership: Private Military & Security Companies and the UN'. Global Policy Forum and Rosa-Luxemburg-Stiftung, p. 8.

Moreover, military enforcement measures are often only authorised by the UN Security Council in a legal sense, under international law, and not even carried out under a UN banner. This practice, where the use of armed force by member states is authorised on a case by case basis, again illustrates that in the final analysis governments only generally get involved or provide armed personnel in pursuit of their own core interests. Where their own interests are not involved, Security Council decisions tend to lead nowhere. In addition, the right of veto allows any one of the five permanent members of the Security Council to block the implementation of any measures. The right of veto needs to be restrained and eventually it needs to be abolished altogether. If the Security Council is unable to meet the international community's responsibility to protect due to the use of the veto, the General Assembly until then could take charge. Complementing the assembly with a parliamentary body would strengthen its position vis-à-vis the Security Council in such situations. A parliamentary assembly may also be able to mobilize world public opinion in favor of protective measures in face of human rights violations like in more recent times in Darfur or Syria.

And beyond that, when trying to assess a given situation, the UN is substantially dependent on the information provided by governments. All efforts to date to establish an independent UN unit for the collection and evaluation of information on conflict situations and for strategic planning have come to nothing.[36] The governments of the member states, and above all those of the permanent members of the Security Council, are careful to ensure that the UN is unable to break free from the particularistic interests of the nation states.

The four pillars of a world peace order

The system of collective security envisaged in the UN Charter has not yet been brought about, and *even if it were*, it would remain only a first step, albeit an important one. The world had to realise, wrote Albert Einstein in 1947, 'that it is merely a transitional system toward the final goal, which is the establishment of a supranational authority vested with sufficient legislative and executive powers to keep the peace'.[37] What he meant by that was above all the establishment of 'a supranational police force, based on world law'.[38] The liberal British politician David Davies, whom Einstein cited in support, was an influential champion of this proposal. The elimination of rivalry between the states, Davies

---

36   Cf. Lange, Anne. 2012. 'Kein Nachrichtendienst für das UN-Sekretariat'. Vereinte Nationen (6): 257–262, p. 259.
37   Open letter to the United Nations General Assembly. October 1947. Citation from Nathan, Otto, and Heinz Norden (ed.). 1960. Einstein on Peace. New York: Simon and Schuster, p. 440.
38   In a note of May 1947, citation from Nathan/Norden, ibid., p. 407. See also pp. 362, 255, 242, 205f.

argued correctly in his 1930 book 'The Problem of the Twentieth Century', was 'the crux of the disarmament problem'. This could only succeed if ensuring common security were no longer dependent on the whim of one or more Great Powers but had been entrusted to a supranational armed force.[39] And in addition, the jurisdiction of the International Court of Justice in inter-state disputes is not obligatory but optional. An enduring world peace would have to be built on four main pillars: worldwide arms control; democratic global institutions that enable a fair reconciliation of interests and can make binding laws; obligatory recourse to international courts for the peaceful resolution of conflicts; and supranational powers of enforcement through police and military means.

The role of a world parliament

The well-known US American astrophysicist Carl Sagan (1934 to 1996) was one of the first people to study the phenomenon of 'nuclear winter'. In view of the threat of an atomic war between the USA and the Soviet Union, he emphasized in his 1982 world bestseller 'Cosmos' that 'the welfare of our civilization and our species is in our hands'. As a supporter of world government, however, he was painfully aware that 'humanity' as a collective is not represented in the political order. 'We know who speaks for the nations', Sagan wrote. 'But who speaks for the human species? Who speaks for Earth?' he asked, unable to answer his own question.[40] Filling this gap would be the task of a world parliament. The worldwide programme of 'general and complete disarmament' must be accompanied by the formation of a political community. Sixty years after the founding of the United Nations and the destruction of Hiroshima by an atom bomb, the Japanese House of Representatives passed a resolution on 2 August 2005 declaring as a long-term goal the creation of 'a world federation for the whole globe'. On the occasion of the 60th anniversary of Japan's membership in the UN, the upper house adopted a similar resolution in May 2016.

Through cosmopolitan institutions such as a global parliamentary assembly, mutual understanding and a sense of shared community across national and cultural borders can gradually be strengthened, leading to growing levels of the cooperation and trust necessary for progress in demilitarization and disarmament. The assembly itself should play a leading role in the development of a 'comprehensive programme for disarmament', as called for already by the tenth special session of the UN General Assembly, and should contribute to mobilis-

---

39   Davies, David. 1930. The Problem of the Twentieth Century. London: Ernest Benn Limited, p. 271.
40   Sagan, Carl. 2011. Cosmos. Random House, p. 347.

ing the necessary political will. Government bodies like the Conference on Disarmament in Geneva, which also operates on the principle of consensus, are trapped in a dead end. Not the least important of the arguments for a world parliament is that it would constitute in itself one of the essential core institutions of the emerging system of world law. It should participate in decision-making on coercive measures and on peacekeeping missions and should exercise parliamentary control over international armed forces and their operations. Supranational global armed forces must be parliamentary armed forces.

A comprehensive disarmament and peace programme, politically and institutionally secured through a world parliament, would have a positive impact not only in security policy terms but economically as well. It would lead to more prosperity and to greater social justice simply by virtue of making resources free for other purposes through a progressive reduction in military expenditure – for the improvement and modernization of civil infrastructure, for example, or for civil research or social problems. In the long term, there is no way around the fact that the production of weapons of war and the arms trade have to be put under supranational control as part of a programme of disarmament. The Mine Ban Treaty of 1997 and the Arms Trade Treaty of 2013 are the first small steps in this direction.

17.
Fighting terrorism, 'blowback', and data protection

The 'war on terror' as an end in itself

The security dilemma that is continually and endlessly produced by the anarchic international state system represents an important foundation for the demand for armaments and helps maintain the status and power of security and defence establishments around the world. The permanent latent state of war described in George Orwell's novel '1984' constitutes - from the perspective of the military-industrial complex - not a dystopian nightmare but rather an ideal business environment. In fact, the USA is officially in a permanent state of war. Three days after the attacks of 11 September 2001, the US Congress – with only one dissenting voice – voted in the House of Representatives to give the US President the legal authority to take any action he might deem necessary and appropriate, anywhere in the world, to punish the perpetrators or to prevent further acts against the USA by international terrorists. The so-called 'war on terror' conducted on this basis has become a fixed and enduring fact, and the war zone is the entire globe. In the course of a hearing in the US Senate in May 2013, it was stated that this war will continue for *at least* ten to twenty more years. The influential journalist Glenn Greenwald commented in the Guardian that the war clearly 'has no purpose other than its own eternal perpetuation'. The war, he said, is an end in itself, and is also its own fuel: 'it is precisely this endless war - justified in the name of stopping the threat of terrorism - that is the single greatest cause of that threat'.[1]

The USA's covert warfare

Covert operations carried out around the world under the umbrella concept of 'low intensity warfare' have been part of the standard programme of US American foreign policy at least since the foundation of the CIA in 1947. During the Cold War, this included campaigns of disinformation, psychological warfare, the setting up and financing of guerrilla units and political opposition, murder

---

1 Greenwald, Glenn. 17 May 2013. 'Washington gets explicit: its war on terror is permanent'. The Guardian (www.guardian.co.uk).

and assassination, the suppression of revolts, the manipulation of elections, all the way up to supporting coups d'état. Among the many activities of this kind that have now come to light are the involvement of the CIA in the overthrow of the Iranian government under Prime Minister Mohammad Mossadegh in 1953 and in the murder of Patrice Lumumba, the democratically elected Prime Minister of the Congo, in 1961; its support of the putsch against President Salvador Allende in Chile in 1973; its aid to the militant Islamic mujahideen in Afghanistan from the mid-1970s until 1989[2]; and its support of the Nicaraguan Contras in the 1980s. All other aims and values were subordinated to these secret operations. For example, the activities of the Contras were not only financed by illegal arms supplies to Iran, the subject of the so-called 'Iran–Contra affair', but also by the smuggling of cocaine, principally into the Los Angeles area, with the knowledge of the CIA, as revealed by the journalist Gary Webb in 1996. In fact, in spite of the 'war on drugs' proclaimed by the USA, in the course of its covert warfare operations, the CIA was centrally involved in the global drugs trade through making pacts and protection arrangements with important drug dealers. Alfred McCoy, a US American expert on Southeast Asia, set out this situation in detail in his work 'The Politics of Heroin in Southeast Asia: CIA complicity in the global drug trade', first published in 1972 and updated and revised several times since then. Cooperation with criminals and their networks beyond the reach of the law or parliamentary control, according to McCoy, still remains today 'an integral part of the CIA's covert operational capacity'. As the victors of the Cold War, the USA had been able to avoid any kind of critical self-examination of its methods; and while the notorious communist secret services such as the KGB had been swept away, their files opened up and some at least of their leaders convicted in court, the CIA had actually been able to increase its influence through the 'war on terror'.[3]

The consequences of US foreign policy and of the 'war on terror'

Chalmers Johnson described the unintended and unforeseeable consequences of US foreign policy, and especially of its military and secret intelligence operations around the world, as 'blowback'. In his Pulitzer Prize-winning 2004 book 'Ghost Wars', the US American journalist Steve Coll set out how US activities in Afghanistan actually created the conditions for the rise of the Taliban and

---

2   Support for the Mujahedin began six months before the Soviet invasion, cf. Gates, Robert M. 2006 [1996]. From the Shadows: The Ultimate Insider's Story of Five Presidents and How They Won the Cold War. Annotated edition. Simon & Schuster, pp. 146f.

3   McCoy, Alfred W. 2003. The Politics of Heroin. CIA Complicity in the Global Drug Trade. 2nd rev. ed. Chicago: Lawrence Hill Books, pp. 531f.

the emergence of al-Qaida's terrorist network. In this sense, the attacks of 11 September 2001 can be regarded as the most catastrophic backfiring stratagem yet. Nothing can justify terrorist attacks. It goes without saying that they must be defended against. Ultimately, therefore, it was important and in the interests of the world community as a whole that a military offensive was undertaken from October 2001 against the Taliban regime, which had for years allowed al-Qaida to operate on its territory, in contravention of numerous resolutions of the UN Security Council. Lawless territories of this kind, which attract transnationally organised criminality and terrorist groups which then practically merge with local structures of government, are very dangerous for the stability of the interdependent world civilization. Moisés Naím, the Venezuelan former editor of the magazine *Foreign Policy*, called them 'geopolitical black holes' in his book on global crime.[4] But we must not close our eyes to the fact that terrorist acts do not come from nowhere, and besides political or religious motives are usually driven by, or at least justified on the basis of, a desire for retribution for real or perceived injustice.

The so-called 'war on terror' is being conducted in a manner that guarantees further blowback. For example, the multinational coalition which occupied Iraq in 2003, in contravention of international law and on the basis of erroneous information from the CIA on the existence of hidden weapons of mass destruction, was neither prepared nor able to ensure public order and safety in the country. As incredible as it sounds, there really were no plans for the aftermath of the invasion. The country was plunged into chaos. '[T]he U.S. effort resembled a banana republic coup d'état more than a full-scale war plan that reflected the ambition of a great power', is how the US American *Washington Post* journalist Thomas Ricks summarises the totally irresponsible dilettantism of the operation in his book 'Fiasco'.[5] The foreign troops and their private security contractors, at first greeted by the local population as liberators from the despotic regime of Saddam Hussein, soon turned out to be a ruthless occupation force, and this gave a decisive additional impetus to the insurgency that followed. The human rights abuses that took place in the Abu Ghraib prison and came to light in May 2004 became a symbol of the arbitrary and uncontrolled violence of the US troops. In the ten years up to 2013, around 122,000 civilians died as a result of the occupation and the ensuing conflict with insurgents, and

4   Naím, Moisés. 2005. Illicit: how smugglers, traffickers and copycats are hijacking the global economy. 1st ed. New York: Doubleday, pp. 261ff.
5   Ricks, Thomas E. 2007. Fiasco: The American Military Adventure in Iraq. New York: Penguin Books, p. 128.

about a quarter of a million were injured.[6] Corruption, waste, the disappearance of funds, and overexpensive, pointless and failed projects are all-too familiar features of a difficult and drawn-out reconstruction effort. In 2014, the extremist terrorist organization 'Islamic State', which had emerged out of the resistance movement, succeeded in taking control of broad swathes of territory in the north of the country, including Mosul, the second-largest city in Iraq. At times, the organisation was in control of large areas of Syria and its influence extended to Libya.

Human rights abuses and the USA's drone warfare

The USA has now lost all credibility as a political force for democracy, freedom and human rights. From 2001 to 2006, the CIA maintained a worldwide network of secret jails in which kidnapped terrorism suspects were imprisoned without trial and tortured. The inmates of the Guantanamo Bay detention camp were officially declared 'illegal combatants', people without any legal rights whatsoever. Other supposed combatants or terrorists have been the victims of targeted 'extrajudicial' killings, beyond any parliamentary or judicial accountability, carried out by the US administration on the basis of highly suspect and non-transparent decision-making processes. For these killings, the US armed forces are making increasing use of attacks by unmanned drones. According to estimates from the Bureau of Investigative Journalism, by the end of 2017 a minimum of 4,700 such attacks had been carried out in Afghanistan, Pakistan, Yemen und Somalia, resulting in up to 10,000 deaths, including up to 1,500 civilians and 330 children.[7]

Drone warfare is a striking example of the counter-productive effect of the so-called 'war on terror'. 'Drones hover twenty-four hours a day over communities in northwest Pakistan, striking homes, vehicles, and public spaces without warning. Their presence terrorizes men, women, and children, giving rise to anxiety and psychological trauma among civilian communities', reads a report entitled 'Living under Drones' compiled at the universities of Stanford and New York.[8] Under such circumstances, it is hardly surprising that drone attacks are contributing to an anti-American radicalization that in turn creates the con-

---

6   According to estimates by the Iraqi Body Count and the Iraqi Ministry of Human Rights, respectively. Source: 'The War in Iraq: 10 years and counting'. 19 March 2013. Iraq Body Count (www.iraqbodycount.org).
7   See 'Drone Warfare', current statistics, at www.thebureauinvestigates.com.
8   International Human Rights and Conflict Resolution Clinic at Stanford Law School, and Global Justice Clinic at NYU School of Law. September 2012. 'Living Under Drones. Death, Injury, and Trauma to Civilians From US Drone Practices in Pakistan'.

ditions that nurture terrorism. In his 2013 book 'Dirty Wars', on the USA's secret worldwide 'assassination complex', the journalist Jeremy Scahill interviews a Yemeni tribal leader in whose region many civilians have apparently died because of drone attacks. 'The drones are flying day and night, frightening women and children, disturbing sleeping people. This is terrorism', Scahill quotes him directly. He believes there should be compensation for the civilian victims. 'The world is one village. The US received compensation from Libya for the Lockerbie bombing, but the Yemenis have not', he complains.[9] As a result of drone warfare, support for groups like al-Qaida, and the willingness to embrace violent terrorism, are strengthened in groups far beyond that part of the population directly affected.

The root causes of transnational terrorism and the relevance of a world parliament

Military and secret service measures fail to address the real political and social root causes of transnational terrorism, and are therefore effectively only fighting the symptoms. In his influential 1996 book of that title, the US American political scientist Benjamin Barber spoke of a 'clash of "Jihad and McWorld"'. The 'commercial imperialism' of a globalization based on a laissez-faire ideology, encapsulated by Barber in the term 'McWorld', in his view fed the forces of Jihad as a 'dialectical response to modernity'. He saw the democratic institutions of the nation state as being undermined equally by both forces. In his analysis, Barber took Jihad to include not just Islamic extremism, as the term suggests, but any form of religious or political fanaticism that makes a dogmatic claim to exclusivity which it is prepared to back with violent means.[10] Richard Falk and Andrew Strauss similarly see it as an important aspect of transnational terrorism that it also represents a reaction against globalization. Globalization, they argue, increases inequalities within and between societies, and leads to many people feeling that their cultural traditions are under threat. At the same time – and this is the crux of their argument – these people have no opportunity to make their feelings about these impacts and injustices count within the existing international system. 'Presently, with trivial exceptions', the two international law specialists wrote in a joint article, 'individuals, groups and their associations are denied an official role in global political institutions where decision-making is dominated by elites who have been officially

9   Scahill, Jeremy. 2013. Dirty Wars: The World Is a Battlefield. London: Serpent's Tail, p. 466.
10   Barber, Benjamin. 2003. Jihad vs. McWorld. Terrorism's Challenge to Democracy. London: Corgi Books, pp. 219, 157, 31f.

designated by states. ... With the possibility of direct and formalized participation in the international system foreclosed, frustrated individuals and groups (especially when their own governments are viewed as illegitimate or hostile) have been turning to various modes of civic resistance, both peaceful and violent.' In their view, global terrorism is at the violent end of a spectrum of transnational protest. Even when it is driven principally by religious, ideological or regional aims, the political extremism at its core is at least in part 'an indirect result of globalizing impacts'.[11] Tad Daley, too, emphasizes with regard to the threat of nuclear terrorist attacks that in the medium term 'we need to reduce not just the availability of nuclear weapons and materials, but also the motivations for nuclear terror'. Additionally, he says, we must seriously address as causes the globalization of economic inequality and cultural humiliation. People have to be given the hope and opportunity of genuine participation in a peaceful and prosperous global civilization.[12] From this perspective, exclusion from the relevant international decision-making processes also has to be seen as a form of humiliation.

In a global parliament, it would be easier for political frustrations to find expression and to be channelled into a democratic and peaceful process capable of exerting a guiding influence on globalization. For example, when in May 2013 the highest court of the northern Pakistani province of Khyber Pakhtunkhwa classified the US American drone attacks in the region as a violation of Pakistani sovereignty in breach of international law, it called on the Pakistani government at the same time to submit a complaint to the UN Security Council seeking political strictures and other possible measures, and to the UN General Assembly in the event of a US veto in the Council. Although the Pakistani government had in fact already made it clear two months previously to Ben Emmerson, the UN Special Rapporteur on Counter Terrorism and Human Rights, that it did not assent to the drone attacks and saw them as a breach of national sovereignty, cooperation with the USA behind the scenes is probably a little more complicated than that, and moreover the government has to take into consideration, when taking such steps at the UN, the possible wider ramifications for its international network of relationships. In a world parliament, by contrast, the problem could be raised directly by Pakistani representatives without the need to go through the government or for any special diplomatic considerations to be

---

11 Falk, Richard, and Andrew Strauss. 2003. 'The Deeper Challenges of Global Terrorism: A Democratizing Reponse'. In: Debating Cosmopolitics, ed. by Daniele Archibugi, 203–231. London, New York: Verso. Reprinted in and citation from the same: 2011. A Global Parliament: Essays and Articles. Berlin: Committee for a Democratic UN, p. 137.

12 Daley, Tad. 2010. Apocalypse never. Forging the path to a nuclear weapon-free world. New Brunswick, N.J.: Rutgers University Press, pp. 62ff.

taken into account, since the members speak as independent parliamentarians for themselves and their constituents, and not in the name or on behalf of the government, which can therefore not be held responsible for what they say.

Falk and Strauss believe that a global parliament, and efforts towards a fairer and more democratic world order, ought to form part of the political response to the challenges of 'megaterrorism' of the kind seen on 11 September 2001. They rightly do not fall victim to the illusion that extremists like 'the Osama bin Ladens of this planet' will engage in a global parliamentary process, but they do believe the ability of such people to attract a substantial following would be considerably weakened by the existence of a global parliament, 'to the extent that such an institution ... gave the most disadvantaged and aggrieved peoples in the world a sense that their concerns were being meaningfully addressed'.[13] Benjamin Barber also made the point that the forces of Jihad are profoundly undemocratic and can hardly be tamed. He, too, believed that the best prospect for countering the forces of Jihad and 'McWorld' lay in a strengthening of civil society and of democracy at all levels. Barber stressed the importance in this context of a sense of democratic citizenship developed within the framework of a democratic world society. 'If civil society is one key to democracy, then global strong democracy needs and depends on a methodical internationalization of civil society.' A global democratic society was a foundation for 'a global democratic government'. Even though, Barber argued, such a thing might seem no more than 'clever pipe dreams', or 'a distant dream', nonetheless, because international institutions continually came up against the limits to national sovereignty, he thought the case had to be made for 'a gradualist, voluntary, trust-building strategy of supranationality'.[14] What Barber did not address in his book is the question of how the development of a global civil society and of a democratic global public sphere as prerequisites for such a process of integration could be cultivated at the institutional level, that is, 'systematised'. It is precisely here where we see a crucial role for a world parliament. A world parliament, as the direct representative institution for the world's citizens, would be better able than any previous institution to create a democratic world public sphere and to reflect global civil public opinion. Ultimately, as an element of a world legislature, a world parliament should be able to go beyond the role of a political forum so as to take decisions with real practical impact and to be involved in the creation of world law.

13   Ibid., p. 140.
14   Barber, loc. cit., pp. 287f., 229, 277, 290.

The global surveillance system and universal disenfranchisement

However, instead of being strengthened and protected, civil liberties, basic rights and the rule of law are still being undermined under the pretext of fighting terrorism. This applies not only to the direct victims of kidnapping or drone attacks by the United States, but to almost everyone. For example, the partners in the international secret service agreement UKUSA from the immediate post-war period, namely the USA, Great Britain, Canada, Australia and New Zealand, are using various secret surveillance programmes to breach the confidential correspondence, the personal data and the right to privacy of – potentially – everyone around the world who uses telecommunications, without hindrance of any kind. In July 2001, the European Parliament concluded that 'the existence of a global system for intercepting communications … under the UKUSA Agreement … is no longer in doubt'.[15] One of the aims of the Echelon programme is global surveillance of satellite communications. In a history of the US secret service NSA, the journalist James Bamford wrote that '[b]y 2001, the UKUSA partners had become an eavesdropping superpower with its own laws, language, and customs'.[16]

The revelations since June 2013 about surveillance programmes like the NSA's Prism, X-Keyscore and Fairview, and the Tempora programme run by the British intelligence service GCHQ, suggest that the accessing of global internet and telecommunications data, carried out by targeting corporate networks and tapping communications cables, is far more continuous and comprehensive than had previously been thought. Combatting terrorism is now the most important reason put forward to justify these measures. Unlike traditional intelligence gathering, which specifically targeted other states and their agencies, all the millions of users of communications systems without exception or distinction are now automatically being eavesdropped. Progress in computer technology has made it possible to handle 'Big Data'. The premise behind this is that it is no longer only states or genuinely suspect individuals who pose a threat, but potentially *everyone*. In the opinion of Alfred McCoy, who teaches history at the University of Wisconsin-Madison and has studied the history of espionage in the USA, the NSA's global surveillance apparatus exists above all to serve the aims of 'the exercise of global power' and 'global hegemony'. This

---

15 European Parliament. 7 July 2001. 'Report on the existence of a global system for the interception of private and commercial communications (ECHELON interception system) - Temporary Committee on the ECHELON Interception System'. Doc. A5-0264/2001.

16 Bamford, James. 2002. Body of Secrets: Anatomy of the Ultra-Secret National Security Agency. Reprint ed. New York: Anchor Books.

explains why the NSA has monitored EU institutions, the heads of state or government of at least 35 countries, and delegates at the UN, the G20 summit meetings and international treaty negotiations. According to McCoy, this surveillance not only garners intelligence advantageous to Washington, but occasionally also intimate personal information that can be used to provide leverage.[17] He sees the NSA apparatus as part of 'a powerful, global Panopticon that can surveil domestic dissidents, track terrorists, manipulate allied nations, monitor rival powers, counter hostile cyber strikes, launch pre-emptive cyberattacks, and protect domestic communications'.[18] According to the testimony of the whistle-blower Edward Snowden, now fled to Russia, the USA is also conducting industrial espionage. At a hearing held by the committee established by the German Bundestag in 2014 to investigate the actions of the NSA, William Binney, its former technical director, declared that the US secret service was adopting a 'totalitarian' approach, one previously encountered 'only in dictatorships', that was threatening democracy around the world.[19]

Many people only became aware that they themselves were directly affected by the 'war on terror' through the invasion of their privacy following the revelations about the NSA's Prism programme. It had now become clear, commented the *Spiegel* columnist Jakob Augstein, that the drone attacks in Pakistan or the camp in Guantanamo were not simply 'unfortunate incidents at the end of the world', as many people liked to think. 'Those who still believed', Augstein wrote, 'that the torture in Abu Ghraib or the waterboarding in CIA jails had nothing to do with them are now changing their opinions.'[20] The *Spiegel* journalist Thomas Darnstädt spoke of an 'epochal change to international law'. The fact that the people of the world were themselves becoming the objects of US American surveillance threatened to extend the 'erosion of international law which had accompanied the USA's war against people suspected of being terrorists' into the field of espionage.[21] The citizens of other states were being deprived of their legal rights by the governments responsible. Moreover, exactly how which data are being gathered and stored, for what purposes, remains hidden in the fog of secrecy. 'That the US government - in complete secrecy - is constructing a ubiquitous spying apparatus aimed not only at its own citizens,

17   McCoy, Alfred W. 19 January 2014. 'Surveillance and Scandal: Time-Tested Weapons for U.S. Global Power'. TomDispatch (www.tomdispatch.com).
18   Idem. 14 July 2013. 'Surveillance Blowback: The Making of the U.S. Surveillance State, 1898-2020', TomDispatch (www.tomdispatch.com).
19   Deutscher Bundestag. 3 July 2014. 'Binney: NSA-Praxis ist totalitär' (www.bundestag.de).
20   Augstein, Jakob. 17 June 2013. 'Obama's Soft Totalitarianism: Europe Must Protect Itself from America'. Spiegel Online (www.spiegel.de).
21   Darnstädt, Thomas. 10 July 2013. 'Amerikas digitaler Großangriff auf das Völkerrecht'. Spiegel Online (www.spiegel.de).

but *all of the world's citizens*, has profound consequences', writes the *Guardian* journalist Glenn Greenwald, to whom Snowden had entrusted his material. This apparatus, according to Greenwald, 'vests the US government with bound-less power over those to whom it has no accountability [...] It radically alters the balance of power between the US and ordinary citizens of the world. And it sends an unmistakable signal to the world that while the US *very minimally* values the privacy rights of Americans, it assigns zero value to the privacy of everyone else on the planet.'[22]

The fact that the rights to data protection, personal privacy and the confidentiality of personal communications of millions of citizens all around the world are being systematically breached by foreign governments over whom they have no political influence at all highlights the contradiction between the reality of the global communications network and the constriction of democracy within nation state boundaries. On 24 July 2008, in a speech in Berlin during the US Presidential election campaign, Barack Obama addressed 'the peoples of the world' as 'a fellow citizen of the world' and spoke of our common obligations as 'as citizens of Earth'. But this appeal to the 'citizens of the Earth' turns out to be an empty rhetorical device, since as things stand the citizens of the world have neither voice nor rights in that capacity. They can hold neither the US President nor any other foreign government to account for the abuse of their political rights. Data protection, the right to confidentiality of communications and the right to informational self-determination must be embedded at the global level, because internet data streams generally run via international infrastructures, even for inland communications. This illustrates very well the necessity for world law, which in this case needs to place direct obligations not only on states but also on companies and other institutions that handle data.

Global data protection legislation

Following the revelations about the Prism scandal, Peter Schaar, the German Federal Commissioner for Data Protection and Freedom of Information, was among the first people to call for state surveillance and data collection to be subject to international law.[23] The UN High Commissioner for Human Rights, Navi Pillay, pointed out that Article 17 of the International Covenant on Civil and Political Rights stated already 'that no one shall be subjected to arbitrary

---

22 Greenwald, Glenn. 7 July 2013. 'The NSA's mass and indiscriminate spying on Brazilians'. The Guardian (www.guardian.co.uk).
23 Schaar, Peter. 25 June 2013. 'Prism and Tempora: Zügellose Überwachung zurückfahren!' Spiegel Online (www.spiegel.de).

interference with one's privacy, family, home or correspondence, and that everyone has the right to the protection of the law against such interference or attacks'.[24] Schaar suggested as a first sensible step the implementation of a supplementary protocol to Article 17. Clear legal rules, he argued, were essential to enable independent courts and supervisory bodies to verify that security agencies were abiding fully by rules and laws. In the final analysis, however, global legislation for data protection will only be effective if it enables a citizen of country X to protect her- or himself against a possible infringement of their rights by the government of country Y.

The US government rejects any form of international constraints or obligations. It argues that the International Covenant on Civil and Political Rights places obligations on states only with respect to their own citizens, and that the surveillance measures prescribed are neither 'arbitrary' nor 'unlawful' in the sense of the Covenant and fully compatible with US law. A resolution on 'the right to privacy in the digital age' brought before the UN General Assembly in November 2013 by Germany and Brazil conflicted with this position, and in the end could express only 'deep concern' over the 'negative impact' that extra-territorial surveillance measures might have on human rights. It would require considerable pressure from global public opinion for an effective global data protection agreement to succeed. This would involve exerting political pressure not only on governments directly responsible for global surveillance programmes, but also on those - such as Germany - whose security agencies work closely together with the secret services responsible. A world parliament would provide a locus where elected representatives from the USA, Europe and elsewhere could come together to protest against government surveillance apparatuses. Overcoming the inter-governmental nature of the dispute at the international level would strengthen the worldwide opposition. Thus the US government would have to be prepared for the fact that in a global parliamentary assembly critical voices would also be heard from within the USA itself. A draft law to curtail the mass collection of telephone data by the NSA in the United States was only defeated by a narrow majority of twelve votes in the US House of Representatives on 24 July 2013; 205 delegates voted in favour. Much would be gained if parliamentarians like these could be involved in the drafting of a global law on data protection.

---

24 Office of the High Commissioner for Human Rights (ed.). 12 July 2013. 'Mass surveillance: Pillay urges respect for right to privacy and protection of individuals revealing human rights violations'.

18.
A world law enforcement system, criminal prosecution, and the post-American era

The need for world police law and a supranational police authority

The phenomenon of transnational terrorism blurs the boundaries between domestic and external security. Whereas terrorist activities within national borders are subject to police measures, for the prevention of threats to public safety and for the pursuit of criminal justice, which are subject – at least in countries where the rule of law prevails – to the relevant laws and legal regulations, such as the principle of proportionality, dealing with terrorist threats from abroad is more problematic. The comprehensive surveillance of all telecommunications, for example, undoubtedly infringes the principle of proportionality, but this is not applied by governments when dealing with foreign citizens. The targeted killing of so-called 'enemy combatants' by the United States is the most blatant example of a fight against terrorism that has been stripped of all pretence of adherence to the rule of law. 'In the conflicts with terrorism around the world, the unconditional use of violence by the military and the legally constrained enforcement of the law by the police are blurring', writes the *Spiegel* journalist Thomas Darnstädt in his book 'The Global Police State'. The instruments available to the United Nations and international law have proved inadequate to the challenge. 'The threats of violence from non-state sources materialising around the world cry out for a world domestic policy that would transcend all state borders.' Darnstädt argues that 'the no man's land' between legal systems that maintain law and order in the domestic realm and the law of war that characterizes the international level must be safeguarded by a world police law which would put 'the whole of the Earth under the jurisdiction of an internal world security order'. This would make it possible to address the source of any and every threat, regardless of state borders, within the framework of a fair and proper legal system.[1]

The idea underlying this is that it must become possible to treat terrorism, one of the most serious forms of criminality, principally through police powers and the operation of a criminal justice system, even when it manifests itself in transborder activities or entirely within a foreign state. As the problem is trans-

---

1   Darnstädt, Thomas. 2009. Der globale Polizeistaat. 1st ed. München: Goldmann, pp. 294, 46, 326.

national in nature, the solution will also have to be transnational. The implementation and enforcement of world police law dealing with very serious criminal threats from non-state sources is precisely one of those tasks which should come under the province of a supranational police force. In Darnstädt's view, a supranational police authority should step in where states are too weak or too corrupt to guarantee security. 'Only a power higher than the state', the lawyer argues, 'can intervene to restore order in the complex affairs of weak, ineffective or dangerously powerful states, in the disputed no man's lands of the squabbling world family of peoples, without being accused of waging war or at least of pursuing political ends.'[2] As we have seen already, a UN intervention force and a supranational police force are among the necessary elements of a properly functioning, de-militarised world peace order. UN peacekeeping missions already include ever larger policing components to fulfil a variety of different tasks. These include protecting UN facilities, supporting the development of local police forces, or – as in Kosovo and East Timor – taking over all policing functions for a transitional period.

The failure of classical sanctions

Law enforcement follows different guiding principles under a world law framework than it does under international law. What counts is not the implementation of sanctions or the use of military force against states that violate the law, but the targeted enforcement of world law *against individuals by the police or through legal action*. More extreme collective security measures are a secondary option, only to be considered if the first approach fails. The wide-ranging economic embargo decided on by the UN Security Council in 1990 in response to the Iraqi invasion of Kuwait destroyed the country's basic infrastructure, brought a humanitarian catastrophe on the general population, led to a drastic rise in infant mortality, and barely impacted on Saddam Hussein's regime. Since then there has been a paradigm shift in favour of so-called 'smart sanctions', which apply only to selected goods and which target specific people and organizations. To combat terrorism, the UN Security Council holds the so-called 1267 list (named after the number of the original 1999 Resolution), on which, as the journalist Victor Kocher puts it, it identifies on behalf of the community of states 'the enemies of humanity'. All states are obliged to freeze all property and assets belonging to the roughly 500 (at the present time) people and organizations listed there and to refuse them entry or transit. And we can agree with Kocher that '[t]his is all right and proper, as long as they really are

2   Ibid., p. 328.

terrorists'. The problem is that the procedure is untransparent, arbitrary and outside any legal control. If anyone were to end up on the list by mistake, they would have no possibility of defending themselves against the UN through the courts. An Ombudsperson has now been appointed to whom such people can appeal. But the Security Council still takes the ultimate decisions on recommendations from the Office of the Ombudsperson. 'The Security Council is a political authority which makes political decisions. There is no legal recourse against this. That's the way the UN system was constructed'[3], was the laconic comment from Richard Barrett, a high-ranking official of the UN Sanctions Committee. It was for precisely this reason that the European Court of Justice determined in a judgement of 18 July 2013 that UN procedures do not provide 'the guarantee of effective legal protection', and therefore confirmed the suspension of the EU Directive for the implementation of the UN sanctions on the grounds of an infringement of fundamental rights under European law.[4] It can be seen here how the procedural mechanism of classical sanctions has failed to adapt to the new challenges, and thereby also failed to apply in practice those values it is supposed to protect. The rule of law, the separation of powers, and independent accountability must be fundamental principles of the enforcement of world law.

A supranational police force to support the ICC

The International Criminal Court, or ICC, which took up its work in 2002, is a milestone in the development of such a world law. The Court's jurisdiction is unfortunately not universal, as many governments and NGOs had called for it to be, but rather complementary to national criminal justice systems where they are involved, and moreover it applies only if a crime has been committed by a person or in a place belonging to a state which is a party to the ICC treaty. The number of these states is increasing, and in December 2017 stood at 123. However, some important countries such as the USA, Russia and China are not yet among them, and some African countries like Burundi or South Africa have announced that they would withdraw again. In any case, the UN Security Council can refer a 'situation' to the Court, as has already happened in the case of Sudan in 2005 and Libya in 2011. Subject to these conditions, the ICC is responsible for holding individuals to account against charges of war crimes, crimes against humanity, and genocide, irrespective of their offices and notwithstanding any immunities under international law. After long and bitter negotiations,

---

3   Kocher, Victor. Terrorlisten. Die schwarzen Löcher des Völkerrechts. Wien: Promedia, 2011, pp. 13, 139.
4   European Court of Justice. 18 July 2018. 'Judgement of the Court, Kadi v. Council, Joined Cases C 584/10 P, C 593/10 P and C 595/10 P', para. 133

the ICC's jurisdiction over the crime of aggression was activated as of 17 July 2018. For obvious reasons, some governments in Africa in recent times have regretted the fact that state leaders can be indicted as well.

One important task of a supranational police force is to support the work of the ICC. This should include a unit responsible for tracking down, arresting and handing over suspects on behalf of the prosecuting authorities of the Court. The formation of such a unit was proposed already in connection with the International Criminal Tribunal for the former Yugoslavia. When, seven years after the establishment of the Tribunal by the UN Security Council, dozens of those accused of crimes had still not been apprehended, among them Radovan Karadžić and Ratko Mladić, the principal suspects, the Chief Prosecutor Carla del Ponte was at the end of her patience. It was her belief that in spite of numerous opportunities the SFOR military unit for Bosnia-Herzegovina under NATO command and the local authorities had shown themselves to be unwilling or unable ever to carry out many of the arrest warrants.[5] Finally, in 2000, she called for the establishment of a special police unit under the control of the Tribunal. 'Such a police force would not be dependent on the support of other states and would not have to worry about political judgements. Today, we issue an arrest warrant and have to wait for SFOR to carry it out', she complained.[6] As things currently stand, the ICC is also totally dependent on the cooperation of its treaty partner states or on measures taken by the UN Security Council. Its Statute does not permit it to carry out arrests. Nine years after the Security Council referred the situation in Darfur in western Sudan to the ICC, the Chief Prosecutor Fatou Bensouda from Gambia, elected in 2012, complained in strong language that 'no meaningful steps' had been taken by the Security Council to carry out the arrest warrants issued by the Court against those accused of crimes in Darfur, including the President of Sudan, Omar Hassan al-Bashir. 'This reflects badly, not just on the international justice system of which the ICC is only a part, but it also greatly undermines the credibility of this Council as an instrument of international peace and security', declared Bensouda. '[T]he ICC's judicial process cannot take place without arrests', the Chief Prosecutor emphasized.[7] Because of the lack of activity from the Security Council on this issue, she decided in December 2014 to suspend the investigation into the Darfur case 'for the time being'.

---

5 Karadžić was finally arrested in 2008 and Mladić in 2011.
6 Citation from Bummel, Andreas. 2003. 'Für eine ständige Eingreiftruppe der Vereinten Nationen. Ein Memorandum der Gesellschaft für bedrohte Völker' (in an interview published by Allgemeine Schweizerische Militärzeitschrift, no. 11/2001).
7 'Justice for Darfur's victims mired in political expediency – ICC prosecutor'. 17 June 1014. United Nations News Centre (www.un.org).

Extending the prosecuting powers of the ICC

It is perfectly possible to allocate different policing tasks on federal principles to differing public administrative or functional levels, as is in fact the case in federal states. To combat the most serious kinds of transnational criminality, a global criminal investigation police force is needed equipped with its own investigative and executive powers, able to support national authorities or to act independently when necessary and appropriate or when the national authorities are unwilling or unable to do so. The jurisdiction of the ICC should be extended accordingly to cover other offences with global significance. In fact, an additional resolution was already passed at the conference of the states in Rome in 1998 when the ICC Statute came into force confirming that the jurisdiction of the Court should in future encompass terrorism and drug offences as well.[8] Of course, it would also be possible to create more international tribunals for specific offences, but it would be more effective and would help to achieve consistency in the development of global law to extend and strengthen the International Criminal Court instead. However, changes to the ICC Statute require the consent of seven-eighths of the Treaty parties - a high hurdle for this procedural option to clear.

Lawyers point out that the funding of international terrorism is '[o]ne of today's most pressing issues in international financial crimes'. Many states do not have the resources or are unwilling to take action against money laundering.[9] In Moisés Naím's view, fully-fledged 'Mafia states' have arisen which 'integrate the speed and flexibility of transnational criminal networks with the legal protections and diplomatic privileges enjoyed only by states'. National law enforcement agencies are largely powerless against this new 'hybrid form of international actor', and in fact some of them have themselves been infiltrated by criminals.[10] An international form of law enforcement against money laundering is therefore required. It would be possible to extend the jurisdiction of the ICC to include money-laundering offences on the basis of a convention on money laundering to agree the precise details of the offences.[11] According to the UN Office on Drugs and Crime, less than one per cent of the total amounts that are being laundered are detected and seized. 'There is a clear need for universal and stronger participation in international anti-money-laundering efforts at the global level', the UN concluded.[12] Additionally, in the light of the financial

---

8   Final Act of the International Criminal Court. A/CONF.183/10, 17 July 1998. See resolution E.
9   Anderson, Michael. 2013. 'International Money Laundering: The Need for ICC Investigative and Adjudicative Jurisdiction'. Virginia Journal of International Law (53) 3: 763–786, pp. 764, 771.
10   Naím, Moisés. 2012. 'Mafia States'. Foreign Affairs (91) 3: 100–111, p. 109.
11   Anderson, loc. cit.
12   United Nations Office on Drugs and Crime. 2011. Estimating illicit financial flows resulting from drug trafficking and other transnational organized crimes, pp. 11, 119.

crisis and bearing in mind the status of the financial system as a global public good, it would be highly advisable to extend the jurisdiction of the Court to *economic and financial crimes which affect the financial system as a whole*. The French economist Jacques Attali, regularly numbered among the one hundred leading intellectuals in the world by the magazine *Foreign Policy*, has spoken out in favour of regarding 'very serious violations of social and economic rights with global reach' and associated financial offences as 'crimes against humanity' and of including them within the jurisdiction of the ICC.[13] In view of the dominant role played in such offences by companies and especially by financial institutions, Attali believes it should be possible to prosecute not just individuals but also legal persons in such cases. The US American federal law known as RICO, used to combat criminal associations and their leaders, provides an interesting model for consideration in this context.

Other offences for which international criminal prosecution could be considered include ecocide, which has been under discussion in this context since 1970, and forms of cybercrime with a global dimension. Ecocide, according to a definition proposed by the British activist Polly Higgins, involves 'the extensive destruction, damage to or loss of ecosystem(s) of a given territory … to such an extent that peaceful enjoyment by the inhabitants of that territory has been severely diminished'.[14] Cybercrime involves attacks on crucial computer, communications and information systems by criminals or terrorists or by other states. Additionally, as has already been mentioned, it has been proposed that infringements against any bans promulgated by a possible future convention for the abolition of nuclear weapons should be referred to the Court.

Sovereignty and cooperation between law enforcement agencies

When the FBI, the US American federal police force, was founded in 1908, the aim was to create a police authority with the same geographical horizon as the criminals it was supposed to combat, namely that of the entire US American federal territory. In the opinion of an expert from the Defence Academy of the British armed forces who supports a form of 'global FBI', this 'is a direct parallel to the situation facing the world today'. 'Today's international law-enforcement system', he argues, 'is disjointed, fractious, ineffective and, increasingly, is unfit

13 Attali, Jacques. 16 March 2010. 'For an International Financial Court'. L'Express (www.lexpress.fr).
14 Higgins, Polly. Eradicating ecocide: laws and governance to prevent the destruction of our planet. London: Shepheard-Walwyn, 2010, pp. 62f.

to tackle the serious emerging threats of transnational organised crime and terrorism.'[15] The first international report on the threat posed by transnational criminal organizations, published in 2010 by the United Nations Office on Drugs and Crime (UNODC), warned that organized crime – the dark side of globalization - 'has diversified, gone global and reached macro-economic proportions'.[16] At the presentation of the report, the then Director of the Office, Antonio Maria Costa, stated that transnational crime had become 'a threat to peace and development, even to the sovereignty of nations'. 'Crime has internationalized faster than law enforcement and world governance', he said.[17]

One obstacle is that policing and criminal jurisdiction have traditionally been regarded as prominent features of state sovereignty. Domestic security, according to Wilhelm Knelangen, a political scientist based in Kiel, is a 'field of politics laden with sovereignty', in which governments 'jealously defend their formal powers'.[18] But as the UNODC report rightly argues, 'states have to look beyond borders to protect their sovereignty'. 'In the past', the report states, 'they have jealously guarded their territory. In the contemporary globalized world, this approach makes states more, rather than less vulnerable. If police stop at borders while criminals cross them freely, sovereignty is already breached – actually, it is surrendered to those who break the law.'[19] Seen in this light, a supranational police authority would represent a *strengthening* of state sovereignty, even if under shared control. 'We need to consider the possibility that clinging to old ideas about sovereignty may be stunting the evolution of the nation-state and thus weakening the security of its citizens', writes Moisés Naím.[20]

Strengthening international criminal prosecution and a World Parliament

Experts point out that international cooperation between police and judicial authorities is increasing all the time. In their book 'Policing the Globe', the US American political scientist Peter Andreas and the Director of the New York-

---

15   Coffey, Stuart. July 2011. 'The Case for the Creation of a ,Global FBI". Central European Journal of International and Security Studies (5) 2: 23–56, pp. 32, 24.
16   United Nations Office on Drugs and Crime. 2010. The Globalization of Crime: A Transnational Organized Crime Threat Assessment. Vienna: United Nations Office on Drugs and Crime. p. ii.
17   Id. 17 June 2010. 'International criminal markets have become major centres of power, UNODC report shows' (www.unodc.org).
18   Knelangen, Wilhelm. 2008. 'Europäisierung and Globalisierung der Polizei'. Aus Politik and Zeitgeschichte, no. 48 (Beilage) (www.das-parlament.de).
19   United Nations Office on Drugs and Crime (2010), loc. cit., p. iii.
20   Naím, Moisés. Illicit: How Smugglers, Traffickers and Copycats Are Hijacking the Global Economy. 1st ed. New York: Doubleday, 2005.

based Drug Policy Alliance, Ethan Nadelmann, note that '[t]ransgovernmental enforcement networks are more expansive and intensive than ever before, encouraging and facilitating a thickening of cross-border policing relationships'. In their view it is time to abandon the 'popular mythology' of a 'golden age of state control' in the past. On the contrary, the fight against crime is becoming ever more effective, including at international level. Many of the changes driving the globalization of crime, such as the revolutions in transport and in communications, provide just as much of a boost to globalised crime fighting.[21] Examples of this include the increasingly effective options available for manhunts, for surveillance and for information exchange. The crucial next steps are a world police law with a supranational police force, and a strengthened International Criminal Court with an extended jurisdiction. They are an appropriate and logical response to the global security threats emanating from the 'geopolitical black holes' and to the globalization of organised crime.

However, making international criminal prosecution and global security more effective represents only one side of the coin. These developments need to go hand in hand with an appropriate extension and strengthening of democratic legitimation and political accountability. Complaints about substantial democratic deficits can be heard today already. Although there can be no question, writes Wilhelm Knelangen, of 'a global Leviathan replacing national security and criminal prosecution systems', it cannot be denied that 'the legal and institutional foundations for the activities of the criminal prosecution authorities are increasingly being located outside the nation state'. The transfer of decision-making to 'the European or even the global level' is restricting the scope for democratic accountability. 'The fact that security concerns dominate the political debates about international police cooperation, overshadowing the defence of liberty', according to Knelangen, 'is due not least to the fact that intergovernmental networks are further advanced as yet than their parliamentary or civil society equivalents.'[22] Andreas and Nadelmann speak of a 'substantial downside' to international crime fighting. This includes 'growing problems of accountability and transparency', 'a widening "democratic deficit" as police functions become more internationalized and privatized', and 'the emergence of an international crime control industrial complex.'[23]

---

21 Andreas, Peter, and Ethan Nadelmann. 2006. Policing the Globe. Criminalization and Crime Control in International Relations. Oxford, New York et. al: Oxford University Press, pp. 232, 246, 248.
22 Knelangen, loc. cit.
23 Andreas/Nadelmann, loc. cit., pp. 250f., on securitization see also p. 253.

A worldwide parliamentary assembly, by providing a global platform for different political perspectives and critical points of view, would create a counterweight to the governments' one-sided fixation on security issues and their undermining of civil liberties. The Parliamentary Assembly of the Council of Europe provides an example which demonstrates that this is even possible in the absence of specific competences. By means of a Europe-wide investigation, prompted by media reports and beginning in November 2005, into the CIA's secret prisons in the member states of the Council of Europe, the Assembly succeeded in building up considerable political pressure on the governments involved. The investigation contributed to the eventual official acknowledgement by President George W. Bush of the existence of secret CIA prisons abroad on 6 September 2006. A world parliament would have the important task of critically monitoring the activities of and cooperation between police and security authorities, and to this end should establish a committee charged especially with the duty of ensuring that human rights are respected. A world parliament should be given formal rights of supervision over today's most important existing institution for international police cooperation, Interpol, which was established in 1923, and over any new supranational criminal police agency. These should include involvement in the selection and appointment of the head of the organization (of the Secretary-General of Interpol, for example) and the right to call leading executive officers to be questioned before parliament.

Interpol and accountability

Interpol, which is based in Lyon and has two further administrative centres in Buenos Aires and Singapore, is not a supranational police force by any stretch of the imagination. It has no investigative or executive powers. It provides training, coordination, data collection and information exchange services to the national criminal prosecution authorities, and in addition some operational support services. This is not the place to examine whether it would make more sense to develop Interpol into a supranational criminal police force or whether it might be better to create a new agency for that purpose. But the fact that it is not accountable for its actions, neither legally nor politically, to any independent external authority is certainly a problem that needs to be resolved. Interpol's 'Red Notices', for example, are a core instrument of international criminal prosecution. They are issued at the request of national police authorities or international criminal courts and call on all Interpol members for international help in the arrest and extradition of suspects. Although it remains at the discretion of the national authorities how they react to such requests, suspects then generally have to reckon with arrest and extradition proceedings. This is a legitimate and sensible procedure in the international fight against crime. The problem is that it is misused for the persecution of dissidents, political opponents, business competitors, environmental activists and awkward journalists in other countries. Human rights activists have documented countless such cases in recent years. The Parliamentary Assembly of the OSCE has repeatedly expressed concern over the misuse of Interpol's Red Notices by 'Mafia' and autocratic states 'whose judicial systems do not meet international standards'.[24] The British *Daily Telegraph* accused Interpol of providing support to the world's most brutal regimes.[25] In a report published in 2013, the London-based NGO Fair Trials International called for a strengthening of Interpol's internal capacity and procedures with regard to checking requests for Red Notices.[26] Four years later they noted that 'there is still a long way to go in ensuring that Interpol has robust procedural safeguards for the human rights of citizens'.[27] The proposals by Fair Trials deserve to be fully supported. But at the same time, the lack of external accountability which is undermining the credibility of the agency must be addressed.

A World Parliament as an element of world police law

One way of strengthening democratic legitimation would be to give a world parliament a decisive role in the development of the content and procedures of world police law. One of the main issues would be the question of which offences should be criminalised under world law and how exactly they should be defined. This applies to terrorist offences, as identified already in a number of specific UN Conventions, but also to the definition of terrorism itself, on which it has not yet proved possible to reach agreement at the United Nations. A world parliament should concern itself especially with issues such as this, which the governments are inclined to defer; for example, with the definition and criminalization of economic and financial offences of systemic importance. Moreover, a world parliament would serve as a platform where regimes now established under international law could be called into question. International drugs policy, for example, is currently firmly in the hands of the UN conventions on narcotics, which seek a comprehensive global prohibition on drugs in line with the logic of the 'war on drugs'. Due to the need to achieve consensus,

24 See e.g. OSCE Parliamentary Assembly. 2012. Monaco Declaration and Resolutions adopted by the OSCE Parliamentary Assembly at the 21st Annual Session, Monaco, 5-9 July 2012. Para 93 (www.oscepa.org).
25 Oborne, Peter. 22 May 2013. 'Is Interpol fighting for truth and justice, or helping the villains?' The Telegraph (www.telegraph.co.uk).
26 Fair Trials International. November 2013. 'Strengthening respect for human rights, strengthening INTERPOL'.
27 Ibid.. 24 November 2017. 'INTERPOL Four Years On: What's Changed?' (www.fairtrials.org).

a historic reform initiative by several Latin-American states failed at a special UN meeting in April 2016. However, the criminalization of intoxicating drugs has proved to be ineffective, counterproductive and self-contradictory. Millions of users and addicts are pursued under criminal law while at the same time, in spite of all the measures taken to suppress it, the market in illegal drugs continues to produce profits in the billions for transnational criminal networks of the worst kind. According to the latest estimates from the UNODC, the scale of the market in illegal drugs in 2003 was around one per cent of global GDP, or at current values around 300 billion Euros.[28] When in 2012 the major British bank HSBC was forced to admit in the course of proceedings brought in the USA to having laundered billions of dollars of drugs profits for Mexican and Columbian cartels over years, the US public prosecutors were satisfied with a fine and did not press for any other form of criminal sanction. Their rationale, astounding as it may seem, was that criminal proceedings would almost certainly have led to the loss of HSBC's US banking licence and that this in turn would have destabilised the banking system.[29] A new and globally coordinated approach to the problem of the drugs trade and money laundering is urgently needed.

Finally, a world police law has to regulate the responsibilities, powers and limits of a supranational police force. This involves drawing clear lines between measures which can be left to the discretion of the relevant agencies and extraordinary actions which need to be decided and legitimated by political bodies. Whereas a world parliament should involve itself as little as possible beyond its supervisory function in the first category of actions, in the second category – and especially where military sanctions are involved – it has to have a role in decision-making. The *Spiegel* journalist Thomas Darnstädt points out in his book that even a hardliner such as George W. Bush's Secretary of Homeland Security Michael Chertoff has spoken out in favour of an international legal regime that allows the world community to take action against transnational threats emanating from the territory of a state unwilling or unable to do so itself. This arises out of the 'modern obligations of reciprocal sovereignty', Chertoff explained in the magazine *Foreign Affairs*. Although every state had the right to autonomy within its own borders with respect to internal security threats, this also entailed a responsibility to 'take reasonable measures to contain the potentially destructive consequences of these security threats to prevent them from spreading and interfering with other states' sovereign right to exclusive authority

28   United Nations Office on Drugs and Crime. 2005. World Drug Report 2005. Vienna, p. 16f.
29   Rushe, Dominic, and Jill Treanor. 11 December 2012. 'HSBC's record $1.9bn fine preferable to prosecution, US authorities insist'. The Guardian (www.theguardian.com).

over their territories'.[30] The problem with this, in Darnstädt's view, was that it left open the question of who had the authority to decide on such 'peace interventions against terrorists'.[31] The world parliament would have precisely that authority.

Looking at the USA's position in the world following the collapse of the Soviet Union, the neoconservative columnist Charles Krauthammer saw a 'unipolar moment' in 1990; and twelve years later, following the terrorist attacks of 11 September 2001, he thought this moment had become a 'unipolar era'. He argued that the USA should recognize the advent of a 'new unilateralism' in which it could 'explicitly and unashamedly' acknowledge the goal of 'maintaining unipolarity … [and] sustaining America's unrivalled dominance'. The greatest threat was posed by weapons of mass destruction in the hands of rogue states, and '[t]his in itself will require the aggressive and confident application of unipolar power rather than falling back, as we did in the 1990s, on paralyzing multilateralism'. Multilateralists wanted an international order based not on sovereignty but on interdependence. 'The greatest sovereign, of course, is the American superpower, which is why liberal internationalists feel such acute discomfort with American dominance. To achieve their vision, America too— America especially—must be domesticated. Their project is thus to restrain America by building an entangling web of interdependence, tying down Gulliver with myriad strings that diminish his overweening power.'[32] The high water mark of US American unilateralism was the 2003 invasion of Iraq, in breach of international law, by US and British armed forces, supported by a so-called 'coalition of the willing'. However, the operations in Iraq and Afghanistan proved to be disasters rather than the dramatic demonstration of US American dominance that Krauthammer claimed to see in them one year after the invasion of Afghanistan. Despite the enormous quantities of money and military resources put into them, they proved instead to be a demonstration of US American failure in asymmetrical conflicts, a failure already witnessed in Vietnam. To be sure, 11 September 2001 prompted sympathy and cooperation with the USA and suppressed anti-hegemonic tendencies among the world's states. But that was a temporary reaction. By the time of the Iraq War in 2003 already, the USA was unable to pressurize the Security Council into a decision in its favour. The absence of a full and proper mandate under international law – a total absence in the case of the Iraq invasion, and only a weak mandate initially for Afghani-

---

30   Chertoff, Michael. 2009. 'The Responsibility to Contain'. Foreign Affairs (88) 1: 130–147.
31   Darnstädt, loc. cit., p. 334.
32   Krauthammer, Charles. 2002. 'The Unipolar Moment Revisited'. The National Interest (70) Winter: 5–17,
      p. 17, 12. See also the same: 1990. 'The Unipolar Moment'. Foreign Affairs (70) 1: 23–33.

stan – was a factor contributing to the failure of the two missions. Even decisions of the UN Security Council on sanctions, although they may constitute a proper mandate under international law, are similarly hardly legitimate in the sense of being democratically representative, given the current composition of the Council. A world police law and world parliament would provide a solution to these problems, though not of course the solution favoured by US American neoconservatives. It is very much open to doubt that a democratic world parliament would readily give its assent to large-scale military operations. It is far more likely that the bar would be set higher than it is in the UN Security Council because of the more open and more extensive parliamentary working methods, even if – as is to be recommended – there were to be a special parliamentary committee charged with preparing the ground for such decisions. But if the outcome was a mandate, then the legitimacy of the operation could hardly be called into question.

The role and significance of the USA

Ultimately, the construction of a world legal order is in the interests of the United States as well. It would be a means of creating stability and security within a legitimate framework the costs of which would be shared on a global basis. The Polish-American political scientist Zbigniew Brzeziński, who was National Security Advisor to US President Jimmy Carter, declared in 1997 in his book 'The Grand Chessboard' that '[i]n the long run, global politics are bound to become increasingly uncongenial to the concentration of hegemonic power in the hands of a single state. Hence', he argued, 'America is not only the first, as well as the only, truly global superpower, but it is also likely to be the very last.'[33] Contrary to the hope of the neoconservatives, the 'unipolar moment' did not become an era, but passed irretrievably. In the long-term perspective, a relative loss of significance for the USA is apparent, one that will lead ultimately to a post-American age in world politics. This development can be seen most clearly in the shift in relative economic power. In the 1960s, the USA's share of global GDP was around 37 per cent on average according to the World Bank; in the 1970s it was around 30 per cent; and since the 1990s it has been around 28 per cent. Since 2008 it has lain below one quarter. The fact that in 2013 the USA was overtaken for the first time as the world's biggest trading nation by China confirms this trend. Of course, the USA still counts as one of the most innovative, productive and competitive economies in the world, one that is also technologically at the leading edge; but the phenomenon of 'imperial

33 Brzezinski, Zbigniew. 1999. The Grand Chessboard. New York: Basic Books, p. 209.

overstretch' leading to the implosion of hegemonic great powers, as identified by the historian Paul Kennedy in his well-known bestseller 'The Rise and Fall of the Great Powers', now increasingly seems to be the challenge faced by the USA too. Kennedy wrote that the test will lie in whether the United States can find a sensible balance in the area of military strategy between its defence responsibilities and the resources available, and whether the country will be able to 'preserve the technological and economic bases of its power from relative erosion in the face of the ever-shifting patterns of global production'. In 1987 already, when the book first appeared, the British academic had concluded that the decision-makers in Washington had to face the uncomfortable fact that 'that the sum total of the United States' global interests and obligations is nowadays larger than the country's power to defend them all simultaneously'.[34] The USA's enormous public debt fits with the picture of 'imperial overstretch'. In 2017, it stood at over 20 trillion US dollars, more than a hundred per cent of the country's annual GDP. Ironically, about half of this money is owed by the United States to foreign investors. The US's external trade balance has been in the red since 1976, and according to figures from the federal statistics agency the deficit peaked in 2006 at 761 billion US dollars and stood in 2015 at 500 billion. This deficit is financed by inward flows of foreign capital. Unlike the picture drawn by Krauthammer, the US American Gulliver is not tied down to the ground by the rest of the world, but in fact kept alive. It is precisely the fact of interdependence which has made the imperial policies of the USA financially possible.

Paul Kennedy emphasizes that 'the only serious threat to the real interests of the United States can come from a failure to adjust sensibly to the newer world order'. The United States has to evaluate and recognize the limits and the possibilities of its power.[35] Its ruthless striving for global supremacy will not be affordable over the long term and will lead to the social and economic erosion of the nation, provokes anti-hegemonic reaction and anti-Americanism and undermines multilateral cooperation, making the world overall less safe. Unlike the transition from the global predominance of the British Empire to that of the USA, which was concluded by the Second World War, the decline of the USA will not be accompanied by the ascent of a new global hegemon. '[O]nce American leadership begins to fade', writes the geostrategist Brzeziński, 'America's current global predominance is unlikely to be replicated by any single state. Thus, the key question for the future is "What will America bequeath to the world as the enduring legacy of its primacy?"'[36] After the First World War, the

34   Kennedy, Paul. 1989. The Rise and Fall of the Great Powers. New York: Vintage Books, pp. 514f.
35   Ibid., p. 534.
36   Brzezinski, loc. cit., p. 210.

United States supported a League of Nations, and during the Second World War, the establishment of the United Nations. By contrast, the contribution of the USA to the world order since the end of the Cold War looks very bleak so far. Projects such as the International Criminal Court were initially fiercely opposed by the USA. There has not been a 'Third Try at World Order', as called for as early as 1977 by the former US diplomat Harlan Cleveland, along the lines of his 'Declaration of Interdependence'. Even the foreign policy establishment figure Brzeziński believes that 'the U.S. policy goal must be unapologetically twofold: to perpetuate America's own dominant position for at least a generation and preferably longer still; and to create a geopolitical framework that can absorb the inevitable shocks and strains of social-political change while evolving into the geopolitical core of shared responsibility for peaceful global management. A prolonged phase of gradually expanding cooperation with key Eurasian partners,' he continues, 'both stimulated and arbitrated by America, can also help to foster the preconditions for an eventual upgrading of the existing and increasingly antiquated UN structures ... [A] functioning structure of global cooperation, based on geopolitical realities, could thus emerge and gradually assume the mantle of the world's current "regent".'[37] In short: the future lies in the creation of a new *global* power centre.

Following the attacks of 11 September, Paul Kennedy, who teaches at Yale University, wrote that 'even those Americans hostile to the very notion of the sharing of global power and of the U.S. becoming a "normal" country may sooner or later have to accept that it is unavoidable, and is in fact going to happen because of the sort of liberal nation and open society that we are'. In fact, however, the 'war on terror' demonstrates an attitude that could hardly be further removed from such acceptance. Kennedy's belief was that a younger generation of Americans in the 2020s or 2030s might come to the conclusion that it would make more sense for the USA to share the 'power and responsibility and burden' with others and to seek 'a voluntary alteration of America's role from being the hegemonic policeman to being the senior partner in a world of democratic states that work out global problems through international structures and shared policies'. Even more: perhaps they could envision 'a future for this planet in which *real democratic representation*, from local government to *world bodies*, exists; human rights are universally respected; a more equitable prosperity is enjoyed; and the "world community" really is that' (emphasis added).[38]

---

37 Ibid., p. 215.
38 Kennedy, Paul. 2001. 'Maintaining American Power: From Injury to Recovery'. In: The Age of Terror, ed. by Strobe Talbott and Nayan Chanda, 53–79. New York: Basic Books, pp. 77f.

19.
Global food security and the
political economy of hunger

A sufficient and adequate food supply is the basis for every human existence, whether individually or as a society. 'The history of man from the beginning has been the history of his struggle for daily bread', wrote the Brazilian doctor and diplomat Josué de Castro (1908 to 1973) in an influential book on 'The Geography of Hunger' in 1952.[1] The historian Charles Tilly showed that conflicts over control of the food supply played a decisive role in the process of state formation. As he observed, these constitute 'basic processes of state-making as they touch the everyday lives of ordinary people'. Nation-states began to emerge as 'the organization which had finally assumed the responsibility of keeping its population from starving.' Food riots thereby historically marked 'the most frequent form of collective violence setting ordinary people against governmental authorities.' What lay behind the food riots was the struggle of the nascent states to secure a food supply above all for the people 'most inclined to serve their ends', for example in the administration or in the armed forces, or the inhabitants of the capital cities.[2] Famine has burned itself deep into the collective memory of those societies it affected.

The extent of worldwide hunger and the right to adequate nutrition

The sociologist Jean Ziegler, who from 2000 to 2008 was the UN's first Special Rapporteur on the Right to Food, pointed out that hunger 'is by far the leading cause of death and needless suffering on our planet'. According to Ziegler, a quarter of *all deaths* worldwide can ultimately be attributed to hunger and malnutrition. That means over 15 million people every year.[3] The UN report on 'The State of Food Insecurity in the World', published in 2015, calculated that 795 million people in the world were estimated to be suffering from chronic hunger.[4] Yet adequate nutrition has long been recognised in international law

1   Castro, Josué de. 1952. The Geography of Hunger. Boston: Little, Brown and Company, p. 4.
2   Tilly, Charles. 1975. 'Food Supply and Public Order in Modern Europe'. In: The Formation of National States in Western Europe, ed. by the same, 380–455. Princeton University Press, pp. 455, 431, 385, 392.
3   Ziegler, Jean. 2013. Betting on Famine: Why the World Still Goes Hungry. New York: The New Press, p. 6
4   FAO, IFAD, and WFP. The State of Food Insecurity in the World. Rome: Food and Agricultural Organization of the United Nations, 2015.

as one of the most fundamental human rights. In the Universal Declaration of Human Rights adopted by the UN General Assembly in 1948 it is stated that everyone 'has the right to a standard of living adequate for the health and well-being of himself and of his family, including food'. The International Covenant on Economic, Social and Cultural Rights, which came into force in 1976, recognises under Article 11 'the right of everyone to an adequate standard of living for himself and his family, including adequate food', and the right 'to be free from hunger'. In the opinion of Jean Ziegler, '[a]mong all human rights, the right to food is certainly one most constantly violated on our planet'. He described hunger as 'organized crime'.[5]

The rhetoric emanating from officialdom on the fight against hunger has declared for over sixty years that the issue has the highest priority and that a solution is imminent. John Shaw, agricultural economist and former UN official, writes in a historical overview that achieving food security 'has been the subject of countless international conventions, declarations, compacts and resolutions'. Over 120 of them can be listed since the founding of the League of Nations.[6] At the World Food Conference in Rome in 1974, then US Secretary of State Henry Kissinger declared that hunger and malnutrition should and could be overcome 'within a decade'.[7] According to the action plan adopted by the World Food Summit in 1996, food security exists 'when all people, at all times, have physical and economic access to sufficient, safe and nutritious food to meet their dietary needs and food preferences for an active and healthy life'.[8] The summit set a target of reducing the *number* of people suffering from hunger worldwide to around 400 million by 2015, thus halving the figure compared to the reference period of 1990-92.[9] At the UN Millennium Summit in 2000, it was decided for clarification that the actual target was to reduce the *proportion* of people suffering from hunger by half. As the proportion was claimed to have fallen from 23.3 to 12.9 per cent, the report on the Millennium Development Goals in 2015 eventually announced that the goal was almost reached – despite the fact that in *absolute* terms nearly 800 million people still suffered of hunger.[10] The relative fall is of course to be welcomed. But it remains true that it is

5   Ziegler, loc. cit., p. 25.
6   Shaw, D. John. 2007. World Food Security: A History Since 1945. Palgrave, p. 388.
7   Kissinger, Henry. 16 December 1974. 'Address at the World Food Conference in Rome'. The Department of State Bulletin (LXXI) 1851: 821–829, p. 829.
8   Food and Agricultural Organization of the United Nations. 13 November 1996. 'Rome Declaration and Plan of Action', para. 1 of the action plan.
9   Cf. idem. November 2003. Anti-Hunger Programme. Rome: FAO, para 18.
10 United Nations. 2015. 'The Millennium Development Goals Report 2015', p. 20.

intolerable if hundreds of millions of people are starving. As to the second Sustainable Development Goal, worldwide hunger is supposed to vanish completely as part of the 'Agenda 2030'.

According to the United Nations Food and Agriculture Organization (FAO), the minimum energy intake requirement for an adult human being is roughly 1,800 kilocalories per day. The World Health Organization puts the average requirement at a minimum 2,100 kilocalories per day. The FAO estimates that the food available per head of the global population, measured in kilocalories, increased from a worldwide average of 2,200 in the early 1960s to more than 2,800 in 2009.[11] Statistically speaking, and despite the rapid increase in the population from around three billion people in 1960 to more than seven billion today, hunger could therefore indeed have been a thing of the past for decades now. But these figures must not be allowed to obscure the fact that mere energy supply is not the whole story. Two billion people also lack the vitamins and minerals essential for good health.[12]

Population growth and food production

The cause of hunger was long considered to be simply a disparity between the size of a population requiring feeding and the available quantity of food. In 'An Essay on the Principle of Population', first published in 1798, the English political economist and Anglican clergyman Thomas Malthus (1766 to 1834) set out his theory that population growth would always outstrip increases in food production, and that as a consequence there must always be shortages in supply and hence hunger. 'Too many people, too little to eat' would be one way to summarize the Malthusian message. It seemed to Malthus that the reduction of 'overpopulation' by hunger, disease and war was a 'law of necessity'. The problem of 'overpopulation' is a constantly recurring theme. At the time of the Roman Empire, the early Christian writer Tertullian (150 to 220 CE) complained that 'our teeming population' is 'burdensome to the world'. 'In very deed, pestilence, and famine, and wars, and earthquakes have to be regarded as a remedy for nations, as the means of pruning the luxuriance of the human race', he wrote.[13] This view enjoyed renewed attention and influence when the biologist

---

11 Food and Agricultural Organization of the United Nations. 2013. FAO Statistical Yearbook 2013: World Food and Agriculture. Rome: FAO, p. 126.
12 Schutter, Olivier De. 24 January 2014. 'Final report of the Special Rapporteur on the right to food: The transformative potential of the right to food'. A/HRC/25/57, p. 4.
13 Coxe, Cleveland A. (ed.). 1885. The Ante-Nicene Fathers. Translations of the Writings of the Fathers down to A.D. 325, Volume III, Late Christianity: Its Founder, Tertullian. Vol. 3. Buffalo: The Christian literature publishing company.

Paul Ehrlich warned of 'The Population Bomb' in his eponymous world best-seller of 1968. In the light of a rapidly expanding world population, which had almost tripled since the middle of the 19th century and now stood at 3.5 billion, he declared that 'the battle to feed humanity is already lost'. Massive famines, with hundreds of millions of deaths, were inescapable and imminent, and 'could be one way to reach a death rate solution to the population problem' he added, in the style of a true Malthusian. 'Too many people' wrote Ehrlich '- that is why we are on the verge of the "death rate solution".' 'Rapid improvement in public health, advances in agriculture, and improved transport systems have temporarily reduced the efficacy of pestilence and famine as population regulators', he declared.[14] The misanthropic attitude expressed here is shocking. The British historian David Arnold, who teaches global history at the University of Warwick and studies famines, rightly notes that it expresses 'a deeper repugnance and incomprehension, a failure to understand, even to accept the right to exist, of people of another race and culture'.[15] The right to food is based on the recognition that all people are equal. 'The consciousness of our shared human identity lies also at the foundation of the right to food', as Jean Ziegler makes clear. 'No one can tolerate the destruction from hunger of his fellow man or woman without endangering his own humanity, his very identity.'[16]

The unforeseen improvements in agricultural productivity – due to the availability of fossil fuels from the 19th century onwards, for example, and to the use of artificial fertilisers and the 'Green Revolution' – have always kept pace with the rising demand for food from a growing world population, and have always forestalled the occurrence of a global Malthusian crisis. However, this must not be allowed to divert attention from the fact that the race is not yet finished. In his Nobel Peace Prize acceptance speech, for his contribution to the fight against world hunger through the development of high yield crop varieties that led to the 'Green Revolution', the agricultural scientist Norman Borlaug (1914 to 2009) warned against allowing efforts to increase production to slacken. '[W]e are dealing with two opposing forces', he said, 'the scientific power of food production and the biologic power of human reproduction.'[17] Worldwide population growth, meanwhile, is now slowing down, and by the end of the century will in all probability have levelled off. According to the mid-range scenario of the latest United Nations population prognoses, the world

14 Ehrlich, Paul R. 1968. The Population Bomb. New York: Ballatine, pp. 36, 69.
15 Arnold, David. 1988. Famine: Social Crisis and Historical Change. Oxford et al.: B. Blackwell, p. 41.
16 Ziegler, loc. cit., p. 63.
17 Borlaug, Norman. 10 December 1970. 'Acceptance Speech on the occasion of the award of the Nobel Peace Peace Prize in Oslo' (www.nobelprize.org).

population will increase to 8.1 billion people by 2025, 9.6 billion by 2050 and 10.9 billion by 2100. The FAO estimates that food production will have to increase by the middle of this century by 60 per cent against 2005/2007 levels to meet the growing demand. FAO experts are confident that 'at the global level there should be no major constraints to increasing agricultural produce by the amounts required to satisfy the additional demand generated by population and income growth to 2050'. In their estimation, in 2050 there will be 3070 kilocalories available in principle per person per day on a worldwide average.[18] In his book 'Feeding the World', the influential Canadian environmental scientist Vaclav Smil also concludes that there appear to be 'no insurmountable biophysical reasons why we could not feed humanity in decades to come while at the same time easing the burden that modern agriculture puts on the biosphere'.[19]

The fragility of the global food supply

On the other side, Malthusians like Paul Ehrlich do not grow tired of warning of a global hunger crisis. In an article published in 2013, for example, Ehrlich points to the fragility of global food supplies and thence to a potential 'collapse of global civilization'. 'Agriculture', writes Ehrlich, 'has generated miracles of food production. But it has also created serious long-run vulnerabilities, especially in its dependence on stable climates, crop monocultures, industrially produced fertilizers and pesticides, petroleum, antibiotic feed supplements and rapid, efficient transportation.' He argues that the foundations of the agricultural system, and thus of world civilization, are under threat, in particular from the effects of climate change and environmental degradation. He believes that global collapse 'could be triggered by anything from a "small" nuclear war, whose ecological effects could quickly end civilization, to a more gradual breakdown because famines, epidemics and resource shortages cause a disintegration of central control within nations, in concert with disruptions of trade and conflicts over increasingly scarce necessities'.[20] The well-known environment expert Lester Brown, founder of the Worldwatch Institute in 1974, also believes that increasingly, 'food is looking like the weak link in our civilization'. If we continue with business as usual, he argues, then a collapse is 'not only possible

---

18 Alexandratos, Nikos, and Jelle Bruinsma. 2012. 'World Agriculture Towards 2030/2050: The 2012 Revision'. Food and Agriculture Organization of the United Nations, pp. 7, 17, 23.
19 Smil, Vaclav. Feeding the World: A Challenge for the Twenty-First Century. Cambridge, Mass.: MIT Press, 2001, p. xxvii.
20 Ehrlich, Paul R., and Anne H. Ehrlich. 2013. 'Can a collapse of global civilization be avoided?' Proceedings of the Royal Society B 280, no. 20122845, p. 2.

but likely'. He, too, sees failing states as the likely starting-point, where governments lose control and can no longer guarantee the safety of the population and most importantly the security of the food supply. 'If the number of failing states continues to increase', writes Brown in what is now the fourth version of his 'Plan B' to 'save civilization', 'at some point this trend will translate into a failing global civilization.'[21] Rising food prices, he argues, not only lead to protest and revolt, but contribute to the risk of state bankruptcies and thus of failed states.

What is clear is that the ecological challenges posed by global food production are many and complex, including the erosion, degradation and contamination of the soil, water scarcity and falling water tables, temperature rise and the increase in extreme weather conditions, desertification, collapsing fish stocks, and air and water pollution. On the production side, the greatest uncertainty factor seems to be the potential consequences of climate change. The FAO, for example, acknowledges that climate change may 'affect adversely' its projections; and for Vaclav Smil, the possibility of 'a relative rapid global warming induced by higher concentrations of anthropogenic greenhouse gases poses by far the greatest potential threat to future agricultural production'.[22,23] The potential rise in average temperatures illustrates the problem. According to the models used for the IPCC's Fifth Assessment Report, from 2005 to 2035 the Earth's average surface temperature will probably increase within a range from 0.3 to 0.7 °C, and by 2100 by up to 4.8 °C.[24] Disregarding regional disparities, studies show that higher temperatures have a negative impact on crop yields as a rule.[25] A study in the Philippines, for example, found a ten per cent loss in yield for each degree Celsius of increase at the lowest temperature range.[26] Studies in Kansas found that every increase of one degree Celsius in average temperatures reduced wheat yields by around 21 per cent.[27] It also appears that a higher concentration of CO_2 in the atmosphere, as anticipated over the coming decades, has a negative impact on the nutritional value of cereals and pulses.[28]

21 Brown, Lester. 2009. Plan B 4.0. New York and London: W. W. Norton & Company, pp. 3, 4, 185.
22 Alexandratos/Bruinsma, loc. cit., p. 18.
23 Smil, loc. cit., p. xvii.
24 Intergovernmental Panel on Climate Change. Climate Change. 2013. The Physical Science Basis. Working Group I Contribution to the IPCC Fifth Assessment Report. Cambridge University Press, p. 20.
25 Nelson, Gerald C., et al. 2009. Climate Change: Impact on Agriculture and Costs of Adaptation. Ed. by International Food Policy Research Institute, Washington, D.C.
26 Peng, Shaobing, et al. 6 July 2004. 'Rice Yields Decline with Higher Night Temperature from Global Warming'. Proceedings of the National Academy of Sciences of the United States of America (101) 27: 9971–75.
27 Barkley, Andrew, et al. 2013. Impact of Climate, Disease, and Wheat Breeding on Wheat Variety Yields in Kansas, 1985-2011. Ed. by Kansas State University Agricultural Experiment Station and Cooperative Extension Service. K-State Research and Extension, p. 27.
28 Myers, Samuel S., et al. 5 June 2014. 'Increasing CO2 Threatens Human Nutrition'. Nature (510) 139-142.

Dependence on oil and phosphates

More consideration needs to be given over the long term to global agriculture's dependence on fossil fuels and on phosphate-based fertilisers. In an important book on peak oil, the journalist David Strahan points out that the coming fall in oil supplies is likely to have a significant impact on worldwide supply chains in the food sector. Irrigation, the production of fertilisers, agricultural machinery and transport are all dependent on fossil fuels. All of this, Strahan says, raises the question 'whether the onset of the last oil shock threatens to undermine worldwide agricultural production, with potentially disastrous consequences'.[29] In any event, global agriculture in its present form is not viable without fossil fuels, and must be put on a new footing. Moreover, crop yields are heavily dependent on the optimal use of fertilisers. In this context, experts point to dwindling worldwide reserves of phosphates. Together with nitrogen and potassium, phosphorus is an indispensable core element in the nutrition of plants with fertilisers, one for which there is no artificial substitute. Studies suggest that the global maximum rate of supply, or 'Peak Phosphorus', could be reached as early as 2033. It is estimated that without phosphorus fertiliser, wheat yields per hectare could fall by more than half. Shortages would lead in the first instance to a rise in the price of fertilisers. 'We are completely unprepared to deal with the shortages in phosphorus inputs, the drop in production and the hike in food prices that will follow', warns the Soil Association (founded in Britain in 1946) in a report.[30]

Notwithstanding all the challenges and uncertainties involved, overcoming worldwide hunger, in the foreseeable future as well as the long term, is not a problem of inadequate food production. This conclusion is supported not least by the fact that substantial improvements and efficiency gains are possible in irrigation, fertilization, storage and the avoidance of food waste. At present, around a third of all food produced for human consumption worldwide is going to waste.[31]

Hunger as a problem of political economy

To regard hunger as a natural catastrophe or as a problem of insufficient food production is in the vast majority of cases mistaken. It was Josué de Castro who established and spread this insight in the years following the Second World

---

29   Strahan, David. 2008. The Last Oil Shock: A Survival Guide to the Imminent Extinction of Petroleum Man. London: John Murray, p. 126.
30   Soil Association. 2010. 'A rock and a hard place. Peak phosphorus and the threat to our food security', p. 2.
31   Gustavsson, Jenny, et al. 2011. Global Food Losses and Food Waste. Extent, Causes, and Prevention. Rome: Food and Agriculture Organization of the United Nations, p. 4.

War. Just like war, he wrote, hunger is a 'man-made blight' that 'results from grave errors and defects in social organization' and 'always implies society's guilt'.[32] Joseph Collins and Frances Moore Lappé, who founded a think tank on food and development issues in the USA in 1975, pointed out in their bestselling book 'Food First: Beyond the myth of scarcity' that '[t]he poor do not eat no matter how much food there is'. 'Scarcity', they wrote, 'is not the cause of hunger. A production increase, no matter how great, can never in itself solve the problem.'[33] In his influential 1983 study 'Poverty and Famines', the future Nobel Prize winner for economics Amartya Sen showed that famines also occur when there is enough food available. 'Starvation is the characteristic of some people not *having* enough to eat. It is not the characteristic of there *being* not enough to eat', wrote Sen, now teaching economics at Harvard University. What mattered, he argued, was not the availability of food in itself but the *access* to it.[34] As Mike Davis underlines in his book on 'Late Victorian Holocausts', during the worst famines of the 19th century, which cost the lives of up to fifty million people in the three extended global droughts between 1876 and 1902 alone, 'there were almost always grain surpluses elsewhere in the nation or empire that could have potentially rescued drought victims'.[35] But the markets, geared for profit maximization, were unable to give food away. It was hoarded, treated as a speculative commodity, and often exported in large quantities. The FAO concludes that 'the issue whether food insecurity will be eliminated by the end of the century is clouded in uncertainty, no matter that from the standpoint of global production potential there should be no insurmountable constraints'.[36] Hunger is a problem of the global political economy.

The relevance of democracy and the international system

Poverty and underdevelopment are the key causes of hunger. Endemic hunger and malnutrition are often the result of civil wars, failed states or bad or autocratic government. Amartya Sen has speculated that 'in the terrible history of famines in the world, no substantial famine has ever occurred in any independent and democratic country with a relatively free press'. Political and civil rights, he argues, give the citizenship means with which to push the government into

---

32 Castro, Josué de. 1952. The Geography of Hunger. Boston: Little, Brown and Company, pp. 11, 14, 24
33 Lappé, Frances Moore, and Joseph Collins. 1977. Food First. Beyond the Myth of Scarcity. Boston: Houghton Mifflin Co., pp. 19, 112.
34 Sen, Amartya Kumar. 1982. Poverty and Famines: An Essay on Entitlement and Deprivation. New York: Clarendon Press/Oxford University Press, 1982, pp. 1, 7.
35 Davis, Mike. 2001. Late Victorian Holocausts: El Niño Famines and the Making of the Third World. Verso, p. 11.
36 Alexandratos/Bruinsma, loc. cit., p. 21.

action.[37] Whereas, by way of illustration, under British rule in India there were countless famines, which caused millions of deaths and which Mike Davis classifies as genocide, in similar situations after independence, the democratic government has intervened, with great success. For decades now there has been a system of broad food support for the poorest, and in 2013 a right to five kilos of grain per person per month was fixed by law, applying to around seventy per cent of the population. If there is a link between democracy and success in the fight against hunger, then perhaps the key to overcoming hunger throughout the world lies in the creation of a *global* democracy?

As Thomas Pogge writes, people like to present poverty and oppression as 'problems whose root causes and possible solutions are domestic to the foreign countries in which they occur'. And the relevant national policies and institutions are indeed often quite bad; 'but the fact that they are', Pogge writes to underline the key point, 'can be traced to global policies and institutions'.[38] For at the global level we are also dealing with bad or – perhaps even worse – nonexistent governance. One factor to which we have already drawn attention is the illegal flows of capital out of the developing countries, facilitated by the existence of tax havens. In addition, Pogge points to the fact that importing natural raw materials from countries with autocratic regimes provides support to those regimes, and that taking part in such business dealings therefore creates a degree of complicity. Two 'core features of our present global order' are especially significant causes of the persistence of serious poverty: 'the international resource privilege' and 'the international borrowing privilege'. '[W]hoever can gain effective power by whatever means will have the legal power to incur debts in the country's name and to confer internationally valid ownership rights in the country's resources', is how Pogge summarises the problem. This situation breeds corruption, autocracy, coups d'état and civil war. He therefore proposes 'an international treaty declaring that rulers who hold power contrary to their country's constitution and without democratic legitimation cannot sell their country's resources abroad nor borrow in its name'. Thus, in the event of an unconstitutional putsch, any subsequent democratic government could refuse to pay back loans taken out by the putsch leaders and contest any linked sales of natural resources or of extraction licences. Disputes could be handled by 'a standing Democracy Panel under the auspices of the UN'.[39] It would be even simpler to entrust this task to a *world constitutional court*. And in fact the Tunisian President Moncef Marzouki, elected following the revolution, proposed

---

37 Sen, Amartya. 1999. 'Democracy as a Universal Value'. Journal of Democracy (10) 3: 3–17, pp. 7f.
38 Pogge, Thomas. 2008. World Poverty and Human Rights. 2nd ed. Cambridge: Polity, pp. 147, 149
39 Ibid., pp. 29, 148, 162

to the UN General Assembly in September 2012 the establishment of an 'international constitutional court', with the power to decide in cases of doubt whether elections have been conducted democratically and constitutionally.[40] The African Union has already voiced its support for this proposal.

Agricultural subsidies, the WTO, and food security

Agricultural subsidies and protectionism have a direct impact on international trading conditions. The WTO Agreement on Agriculture of 1995 allows the continuation of existing internal price support at a level of 80 per cent, and caps new internal subsidies in developing countries at 10 per cent as a proportion of their total agricultural production. The agreement favours the industrialised countries, as the starting level for them is extremely high. Moreover, they have reformed subsidies in such a way that in strict legal terms they are not classified as a distortion of trade, whereas the developing countries have been persuaded, partly through so-called structural adjustment programmes from the World Bank and the IMF, to reduce import barriers. Producers in the developing countries often cannot compete with the heavily subsidised products from the OECD countries. Where they do have a competitive advantage, they often encounter barriers that make access to the markets in the industrialised countries difficult or impossible. So overall investment in the agricultural sector in developed countries is rarely weak, and productivity is low. The Doha Round of WTO negotiations which began in 2001 has been broken off four times. At the conference of WTO ministers on the Indonesian island of Bali in 2013, the WTO members agreed for the first time on a treaty on trade facilitation, which included some aspects of the Doha Agenda. India was able to get an agreement that price support mechanisms and aid in the context of *already existing* programmes for food security could exceed the limit set in the Agriculture Agreement. It would therefore not be possible in such cases to bring the issue before the WTO's Dispute Settlement Body (DSB) for a final decision. However, new programmes could in principle still represent a breach of WTO rules. The fact that the Bali Ministerial Conference prioritised trade concerns over food security 'provides a textbook illustration of the need to improve coherence of global governance for the realization of the right to food', wrote Olivier De Schutter, Jean Ziegler's successor as the UN's Special Rapporteur on the Right to Food, and like him a supporter of a parliamentary assembly at the UN.[41]

---

40   United Nations. 27 September 2012. 'Statement of H.E. Mr. Moncef Marzouki at the UN General Assembly General Debate of the 67th Session'.
41   Schutter, loc. cit., p. 19, para. 48.

Commodity markets and financial speculation

The commodity markets exert considerable international influence. Prices for agricultural commodities, and hence for staple foods, are set by the important commodity markets like Chicago, New York and London. Trends in international prices impact especially strongly on low earners and on the very poorest people around the world. According to a principle first established by the German statistician Ernst Engel in 1857, the proportion of household income spent on food goes down as income rises. Whereas expenditure on food currently accounts for around 10 per cent of the consumer price index for industrialised countries, in the poorest countries it is often more than two-thirds. Between 1980 and 2000, food prices on world markets were comparatively low in historical terms. Beginning in 2002, a drastic rise then set in, culminating in the food price crisis of 2007 and 2008 which saw at its peak a three-fold increase in the world price of grain. Many millions of people in the global South were plunged into severe difficulty, and protests and riots broke out in dozens of countries. It is now clear that speculators from the financial sector have long been exerting an increasing influence on the price discovery process in the commodity markets, and using the trade in agricultural produce and raw materials for capital investment. This so-called 'financialization' of the commodity markets leads to a de-coupling of prices from the supply and demand of the actual goods themselves. Investors bet on price movements, and also consider other factors, such as portfolio distributions and developments in other markets and in monetary policy, which have nothing at all to do with the fundamental data of trading in commodities. There is broad agreement that financial speculation on the commodity markets was a substantial cause of the extreme fluctuations and price increases.[42] According to a study by the United Nations Conference on Trade and Development (UNCTAD), for example, '[t]he price discovery mechanism is seriously distorted ... leading to an increasing risk of price bubbles'.[43] This is not a new discovery. Joseph Collins and Frances Moore Lappé noted in the 1970s with regard to cocoa prices that '[s]peculative activities are a major cause of extreme fluctuations in price'.[44]

The globalised markets for agricultural commodities result in economies of scale and efficiency gains, and they enable an indispensable international bal-

---

42   Cf. the studies in: Institute for Agriculture and Trade Policy (ed.). 2011. Excessive Speculation in Agriculture Commodities. Selected Writings 2008-2011.
43   United Nations Conference on Trade and Development. June 2011. 'Price Formation in Financialized Commodity Markets: The Role of Information'. United Nations, p. 55.
44   Lappé/Collins, loc. cit., p. 184.

ancing out of supply against demand; but at the same time they lead to a world-wide competition between the basic needs of the poorest and the substantially better resourced needs and wants of the affluent.[45] The growing demand for biofuels and meat, for example, places great demands on available agricultural land. This leads to reductions and price increases in the supply of basic food-stuffs. Energy prices, too, affect the prices of agricultural commodities, mediated via the costs of production and transport. The World Bank estimates the transmission elasticity from world prices for crude oil, natural gas and coal to the price of grain at 0.28.

Food security as a global public good, and the failure of the G20

Global interdependence and interconnectedness is very marked in the food sector. The international trade in food has multiplied by a factor of five since 1960, and has doubled in the period from 2000 to 2010 alone. Worldwide trade is crucial in overcoming local bottlenecks. Production and supply chains are densely meshed and are largely run by globally operating, vertically integrated concerns able to exploit economies of scale. On account of the complexity and the high level of global interdependence of the food sector, and because of its fundamental importance for humanity and for world civilization, ensuring food security should be regarded as one of the global public goods with the highest priority, as indeed is the case in the report of the International Task Force already referred to.[46] Food security is a global responsibility. But here too there is a lack of institutions capable of bringing in effective global regulations and measures. The stability of agricultural markets provides an illustration. As a constituent element of food security, this too is a global public good, as the think tank Momagri, founded in France in 2005, persuasively argues. The argument runs that volatility in the markets unsettles farming activities and food security in countries around the world, that farming is linked to other global public goods such as the environment, that important goals of the international community such as the right to food and the fight against poverty are affected by such volatility, and furthermore that 'the stability of agricultural commodities prices assumes a major strategic and geopolitical character'.[47] In order to limit speculative trading, consistent global rules are needed to prevent loopholes and the displacement of trade into less regulated markets. When France took over

---

45   Schutter, loc. cit., p. 11.
46   International Task Force on Global Public Goods. 2006. 'Meeting Global Challenges: International Cooperation in the National Interest. Report of the Int. Task Force on Global Public Goods'. Stockholm, Sweden, p. 25.
47   Carles, Jacques, and Bastien Gibert. 17 November 2008. 'Financial Stability and Agricultural Markets Stability as Global Public Goods?' (www.momagri.org).

the presidency of the G20 in 2011, it was the declared aim of President Nicolas
Sarkozy to achieve common rules against price manipulation and volatility in
the commodity markets. 'How can we explain that it is normal to regulate the
financial market, but that we have to abstain from any rules on agricultural derivatives?' he asked.[48] In a study for Foodwatch, Harald Schumann criticised the
failure of Sarkozy's project due to the lack of agreement between the G20 governments as 'global governance at rock bottom'. The G20, he complained, was
'nothing more than a kind of discussion group in which decisions could only
be reached by a consensus of all members'. The 'global governmental leadership
that the group is meant to provide', Schumann wrote, 'can therefore only take
place at the lowest possible level and via the lowest common denominator'.[49]
The G20, which is an informal group without even a permanent secretariat, is
in any event unable to pass binding regulation - not for its own members, and
most certainly not for other countries. At best it can achieve agreement on common political goals, which then results in coordinated national policy measures.
The decisive factor for the heads of government is what they perceive as their
priority national interests. For example, when in the course of the financial crisis the banking sector received state guarantees and injections of capital
amounting to billions, at the same time financial aid from the Eurozone for the
World Food Programme was cut drastically. Jean Ziegler has rightly pointed
out that heads of state like Angela Merkel can hardly be reproached for this,
since they 'were not elected to fight world hunger'.[50] World parliamentarians,
by contrast, would actually have a global mandate, and could be held politically
accountable on the issue of world hunger.

The FAO, a World Food Board, and global food reserves

Similarly, the FAO, established in October 1945 as the first UN specialized
agency, with responsibility for food and agriculture, has no global powers, and
the WTO, the World Bank and the IMF have more influence on agricultural
policy. Experts in the field have long complained that the FAO has been downgraded to an 'organ that observes, informs, develops proposals and regularly

---

48   Sarkozy, Nicolas. 24 January 2011. 'Address by the President of the French Republic'. Press Conference to
     present the presidency of the G20 and G8, Elysée Palace, p. 6.
49   Schumann, Harald. 2011. Die Hungermacher. Wie Deutsche Bank, Goldman Sachs & Co. auf Kosten der
     Ärmsten mit Lebensmitteln spekulieren. Ed. by Foodwatch. Berlin: Foodwatch, pp. 66, 70.
50   Ziegler, loc. cit., p. 154.

and repeatedly admonishes'. It would be hard to think of 'a more striking illustration of the deficit in the political management of the world order'.[51] Josué de Castro, who was at one time Chair of the Executive Committee of the FAO, complained that the organization was 'limited to a kind of international consultative function'.[52] The efforts to remedy this made by the first Director-General of the FAO, John Boyd Orr (1880 to 1971), a convinced world federalist, were frustrated by the resistance of the USA and Great Britain. This was the reason he stepped down from the post in April 1948; the following year, he was awarded the Nobel Peace Prize in recognition of his work. The fact that Boyd Orr's concerns continue to be just as relevant and urgent today is underlined by the total lack of progress in international politics over the last decades. At the second FAO conference in Copenhagen in 1946, the Director-General proposed the establishment of a 'World Food Board'. In the opinion of John Shaw, the proposal 'remains one of the boldest and most imaginative plans for international action to achieve world food security'.[53] The Board was to regulate and stabilize prices on the international markets for the most important agricultural commodities by intervening to buy or sell when fixed upper and lower price limits were reached. So it would buy at times when supplies were high, and would sell when supplies were low. It would also build up and manage worldwide food reserves so as to be able to balance out any production bottlenecks and to ensure food security over the longer term. Excess supplies of basic foods which could not be sold on the markets would be used to feed especially needy people at subsidised prices. And finally the World Food Board would give long-term loans for food purchases and for bringing farming practices up to date, as well as supporting measures to increase production.[54]

In addition to combating purely speculative market participation, strategic worldwide food reserves are also particularly important for stability in the markets, as provision against poor harvests and humanitarian crises, and for maintaining and supporting international trade. The British economist John McClintock, who worked in Brussels for the European Commission, sees the management of worldwide food reserves as a potential first step towards worldwide integration. In the book 'The Uniting of Nations', he argues that the management of such reserve provisions is not merely a technical issue but brings

---

51 Donner, Jochen. 2002. 'Ausgegipfelt? FAO: Fünf Jahre nach dem Welternährungsgipfel'. Vereinte Nationen (6): 220–222, p. 222.
52 Castro, loc. cit., p. 306.
53 Shaw, loc. cit., p. xi.
54 Cf. ibid., pp. 24ff;

with it a transfer of national sovereignty to the international level. If supply bottlenecks and unacceptable price rises occur in any country, one possible counter-measure is to put international reserves on the market there at low prices in order to take the pressure out of the situation. In order to prevent these goods being bought up cheaply by traders and then exported, export bans would have to apply. Issuing export restrictions of this kind that can be enforced internationally is a supranational matter.[55] In such a system, McClintock explains, there has to be a parliamentary body so that the citizens are democratically represented.

Free trade, food security, and a world peace order

A trade system which is free and open but at the same time fair is very important for global food security. A 2003 study by the International Food Policy Research Institute based in Washington D.C. identifies as one of the main challenges posed by food security the fact that 'perceived national interest too often leads governments to hoard food stocks, artificially encourage production, and limit imports—ostensibly to buffer consumers from food shortages or swings in market prices and to preserve rural traditions'. Even where the international market offers an alternative and cheaper source of food, the study continues, 'the notion of dependence on external sources is anathema to many politicians and their constituents in both North and South. Food self-reliance and independence from foreign interference ... are extremely popular forms of nationalism'. For the markets and for overall global food security, however, the consequences are counter-productive. Although free and open trade will not of itself guarantee food security, since in some cases the necessary purchasing power has to be ensured, it remains true that '[t]he collective consequence of hoarding and protection is actually to destabilize the international market'. In fact, all countries would benefit from open and free trade, but 'a deeper psychological aversion to dependence on foreign sources of goods' stands in its way. Food security, it is argued, is therefore dependent on a psychological question: whether one is prepared to rely on the existence of an open and free market and on supplies from external producers.[56] The world trading system and the institutional and legal arrangements for global food security have to be able to ensure both factors. What this comes down to is the need to move beyond internationalism within

55 McClintock, John. 2010. The Uniting of Nations: An Essay on Global Governance. 3rd ed., rev. and updated. Brussels et al.: Peter Lang, p. 231.
56 Runge, C. Ford, Benjamin Senauer, Philip G. Pardey, and Mark W. Rosegrant. 2003. Ending Hunger in Our Lifetime: Food Security and Globalization. Baltimore: Johns Hopkins University Press, p. 105-108.

a supranational order. Building up mutual trust is closely linked to the establishment of a world peace order, as we sketched out earlier. Fariborz Moshirian, an economic and financial expert who teaches at the Australian University of New South Wales, writes quite correctly that 'if the UN is not able to establish a global system and a global environment in which all the nations of the world are able to enjoy universal peace and global security, the US, the EU and Japan will continue treating agricultural products as a national security issue and they will keep subsidizing their farmers in order that they do not have to rely on food coming from Africa or Asia, even if these two continents may have natural comparative advantages in agriculture products'.[57]

Concerns over not being able to rely on a free and open market were exacerbated during the food price crisis. Lester Brown identified a newly-apparent 'geopolitics of food scarcity'. Exporting countries such as Argentina, Russia and Vietnam, he noted, had restricted or suspended their exports. In response, importing countries increased their efforts to purchase or lease farmland abroad via bilateral agreements to ensure their own food production.[58] During the price crisis, demand for arable land as a global investment and speculation asset grew strongly. Companies and investors are also concerned to ensure access. Since the relevant contracts are not always released into the public domain, it is hard to calculate the extent of what is called 'land grabbing'. Contracts often cover water rights, too, and apply to land that is already being cultivated by local farmers.

A World Parliament and the democratization of global food policy

Global food policy needs not only to be institutionally strengthened but also to be democratised. The interests of those affected by hunger and malnutrition, and of small farmers, must be given more weight. In this spirit, the UN Special Rapporteur Olivier De Schutter declared at the presentation of his concluding report in March 2014 that '[t]he greatest deficit in the food economy is the democratic one'. The food system, he argued, was efficient only in terms of profit maximization for the agribusiness companies. 'At the local, national and international levels, the policy environment must urgently accommodate alternative, democratically-mandated visions.' In the area of global governance, the efforts undertaken by the Committee on World Food Security (CFS) were

---

57   Moshirian, Fariborz. 2003. 'Globalization and financial market integration'. Journal of Multinational Financial Management, 13: 289–302, p. 293.

58   Brown, Lester R. 2008. 'Jüngstes Gericht. Warum die Nahrungskrise den Anfang vom Ende unserer Kultur markieren könnte'. Internationale Politik, November: 18–35, p. 20ff. and Brown, Lester R. 2012. Full planet, empty plates: the new geopolitics of food scarcity. 1st ed. New York and London: W.W. Norton & Company, pp. 12ff.

'promising'.[59] The CFS was set up at the World Food Conference in 1974, and is an advisory and coordinating body. Following reforms in 2009, the Committee has adopted a multi-stakeholder approach which includes UN institutions, NGOs, research institutes, business associations and philanthropic foundations alongside governments. According to Schutter, perhaps the most immediate success of CFS 'is the fact that it brings together such a wide variety of stakeholders ... thus stimulating a process of collective learning across different constituencies'.[60] The Committee is working on a 'Global Strategic Framework for Food Security and Nutrition' which will bring together all its recommendations in one place. Schutter has called on the other institutions of global governance, such as the WTO, to take account of this strategic framework. In 2012, in response to land grabbing, the CFS passed 'voluntary guidelines on the responsible governance of tenure of land, fisheries and forests' which are aimed principally at ensuring the observance and protection of 'legitimate' leasehold, freehold and usage rights. Although the drawing up of these guidelines represents an important step, there can be no question of their constituting an effective weapon against land grabs. The implementation of these and other 'voluntary guidelines' issued by the FAO is not compulsory. What is needed instead are sufficiently specific and above all *binding* global regulations. The multi-stakeholder approach of the CFS puts global food policy on a broad foundation, and in comparison with the work of other, more insular international bodies it can be considered exemplary. And yet in terms of the democratization of global food policy it does not go far enough. The CFS model needs to be opened up to involve elected parliamentarians, and ultimately its work must feed into a global parliamentary process. According to Hilal Elver, Schutter's successor as special rapporteur on the right to food, 'an elected UN Parliamentary Assembly' may be a means to give those suffering from hunger, the most vulnerable members of our global community, 'a stronger voice so that the systemic international causes of their misery can be more adequately addressed'.

In the area of global food security, a world parliament would represent not only an important supervisory and monitoring authority, with respect for example to the World Food Board as proposed by Boyd Orr, but at the same time it would be a basis for regulation under world law. World law would enable the restriction of futures markets to producers, dealers and buyers of a commodity and the exclusion of speculators. A world parliament should also deal with world trade issues, and as a first step, until such time as it would have acquired

---

59   Schutter, Olivier De. 10 March 2014. 'Democracy and diversity can mend broken food systems - final diagnosis from UN right to food expert' (www.srfood.org).
60   Schutter (24 January 2014), loc. cit., p. 18.

competences in this area under world law, it should take part in WTO negotiations. The world trade committee of the world parliament should be able to send its own delegation, with full participation rights. As a matter of principle, the promotion of a world trade system which is as free as possible is an important objective. But the world trading regime has to be far better aligned with other goals such as global food security, for example with respect to problems such as agricultural subsidies and price dumping. In 1999, during the demonstrations against the WTO conference in Seattle, Luis Cabrera – at that time an AP reporter, today an academic political scientist – was surprised that most of the demonstrators were calling for an end to the word trade negotiations, or even the dissolution of the WTO. 'Why weren't there more groups' he asked in his 'cosmopolitan case for the world state', 'calling for the WTO's supranational powers to be used to help improve the lives of those in less affluent states by linking membership benefits to observance of labor and environmental standards, as well as core human rights?'[61] Members of a world parliament would be able to lobby for precisely such a change. The conference on world trade issues organised by the IPU and the European Parliament since 2003 has proved ineffective and unfit for purpose in this respect.

61 Cabrera, Luis. 2004. Political Theory of Global Justice: A Cosmopolitan Case for the World State. London: Routledge, p. xiii.

20.
Global water policy

The present state of drinking water supply

Along with food, water is fundamental to human survival and to civilization. Our daily drinking water is our most important nutrient, and water is indispensable for agriculture, industry and energy production. 'Basic access to water', according to the Italian social scientist and water rights activist Ricardo Petrella, 'is a fundamental political, economic and social right for both individuals and collectives, since the biological, economic and social security of every human being and every human community depends upon enjoyment of that right.'[1] The first UN conference on water, in Mar del Plata in Argentina, declared in 1977 that '[a]ll peoples, whatever their stage of development and their social and economic conditions, have the right to have access to drinking water in quantities and of a quality equal to their basic needs', and called in an action plan for national governments to commit to a target of full implementation of this right by 1990.[2] The world is still some distance from meeting that target today. In a resolution passed in 2010, the UN General Assembly recognised the human right 'to safe and clean drinking water and sanitation' and at the same time declared that it was '[d]eeply concerned that approximately 884 million people lack access to safe drinking water and that more than 2.6 billion do not have access to basic sanitation'. Every year, it lamented, approximately 1.5 million children under 5 years of age died, and 443 million school days were lost, as a result of water- and sanitation-related diseases.[3] Illness due to contaminated water and lack of hygiene is the biggest health problem worldwide. As the UN interprets the figures, the 2015 target for the Millennium Development Goal of halving the proportion of people in the world without permanent access to hygienic drinking water was reached already in 2010. At that point in time, according to WHO and Unicef figures, that number was estimated at 783 million. The latest estimates, for 2015, show that 663 million people still do not have such access.[4] Without question, progress has been made since 1990, the

1   Petrella, Riccardo. 2001. The Water Manifesto. Transl. by Patrick Camiller. London: Zed Books, p. 58
2   Report of the United Nations Water Conference. 1977. E/CONF.70/29. New York: United Nations, pp. 66, 68.
3   United Nations. 28 July 2010. 'The human right to water and sanitation'. A/RES/64/292.
4   WHO and UNICEF. 2015. 'Progress on drinking water and sanitation. Joint Monitoring Programme update 2015', pp. 4ff.

reference year for the Millennium Development Goals. However, experts regard the UN figures with scepticism. A realistic estimate should not be based on the condition of the spring or water source, but on the water actually used, which is often first contaminated on the way to the user. All in all, a study also cited by the UN itself in the 2014 World Water Development Report concludes that the number of people with unreliable access to water in the reference year 2010 was about *three billion* – i.e. nearly four times as many as given using the UN methodology.[5] A more recent report compiled by the UN and the World Bank Group published in 2018 says that 700 million people are at risk of being displaced by intense water scarcity by 2030, that more than two billion people are compelled to drink unsafe water, and more than 4.5 billion people lack safely managed sanitation services. By 2050, more than half of the world's population 'will be at risk due to water stress', the report predicts.[6]

Water security as a global concern

An investigation by the World Resource Institute found that 68 states suffer from severe or very severe water stress. That is, more than forty per cent of annual available water reserves from rivers, lakes and groundwater (so-called 'blue water') are being used up.[7] About forty per cent of the world's population lives in these countries. In addition, it was stated in a study published in the journal *Nature* that eighty per cent of the world's population is subject to a high level of risk with regard to water security.[8] According to a definition proposed by a UN Water Task Force, water security is 'the capacity of a population to safeguard sustainable access to adequate quantities of acceptable quality water for sustaining livelihoods, human well-being, and socio-economic development, for ensuring protection against water-borne pollution and water-related disasters, and for preserving ecosystems in a climate of peace and political stability'.[9]

The implementation of the right to water and of water security for everyone is a global issue, and this means that water policy, just like food security, is an

5   Onda, Kyle, Joe LoBuglio, and Jamie Bartram. 14 March 2012. 'Global Access to Safe Water: Accounting for Water Quality and the Resulting Impact on MDG Progress'. International Journal of Environmental Research and Public Health (9) 3: 880–94, pp. 887, 892.

6   United Nations, und World Bank Group. 2018. 'Making Every Drop Count. An Agenda for Water Action. High-Level Panel on Water Outcome Document', p. 11.

7   Gassert, Francis, Paul Reig, Tianyi Luo, and Andrew Maddocks. 2013. Aqueduct country and river basin rankings: a weighted aggregation of spatially distinct hydrological indicators. Working Paper. Washington D.C.: World Resources Institute.

8   Vörösmarty, C. J., et al. 30 September 2010. 'Global Threats to Human Water Security and River Biodiversity'. Nature (467) 7315: 555–61.

9   UN-Water Task Force on Water Security. October 2013. 'Water Security and the Global Water Agenda. A UN-Water Analytical Brief'. United Nations University, p. 1.

important topic for world domestic policy in the Anthropocene. All the more so since increasing water scarcity in many regions of the world is feeding the fear of escalating conflicts over water and of a destabilising impact on international relations. 'If we are not careful', declared UN Secretary-General Kofi Annan on a visit to India in 2001, 'future wars are going to be about water and not about oil.'[10] 'Water scarcity', emphasized his successor, Ban Ki-moon, 'is a potent fuel for wars and conflict'.[11] In his book 'Water, Peace and War', the Indian geostrategist Brahama Chellaney of the Center for Policy Research in New Delhi argued that this represented one of the most important security policy challenges for the world community. As world water resources become scarcer and the competition between states to control them intensifies, water wars would become more likely, though without open resort to force. Instead, the use of 'armed militants or irregular forces' was more probable. It was probably not a coincidence, moreover, that many failing states were among those of the world's countries with the poorest water supply. 'The twenty-first century', wrote Chellaney, 'will be a defining epoch for how humanity manages and addresses its grave water challenges. Ensuring adequate freshwater availability to underpin continued progress has become critical to the future well-being of human civilization.'[12]

Global interdependence goes beyond issues of security policy. This is illustrated in the concept of 'virtual water', first introduced in 1993 by the British geographer John Anthony Allan to describe the water used in the production of foods and other goods. As water is directly or indirectly a part of every good produced, the trade in goods results in worldwide 'virtual water flows'. The value of the concept as a starting point for the derivation of policy instruments to improve water security should not be overestimated. Nevertheless, it demonstrates that world trade issues are also water policy issues, and this is especially the case with regard to water-intensive agricultural products. 'The studies on international virtual water trade show that water should be regarded as a global resource', writes Arjen Hoekstra, Professor for Water Management at the University of Twente in Enschede in the Netherlands, who goes on to identify climate change, trade liberalization and privatization in the water sector as the

10 United Nations. 15 March 2001. 'Question and answer session after statement at the Federation of Indian Chambers of Commerce and Industry with UN Secretary-General Kofi Annan '. SG/SM/7742.
11 United Nations. 3 December 2007. 'Secretary-General, in message to inaugural Asia-Pacific Water Summit, warns that scarcity threatens socio-economic gains, could fuel conflicts'. SG/SM/11311.
12 Chellaney, Brahma. 2013. Water, Peace, and War: Confronting the Global Water Crisis. Lanham: Rowman & Littlefield, pp. 47, 54, xiv, 38.

most important factors giving water governance 'a true global dimension'.[13] In the view of Petra Dobner, a political scientist who teaches in Halle in Germany, another factor arguing for the globalization of water policy is the fact that 'the sustainable management of global water resources is beyond the legal and practical capacities of individual states'. 'This applies not only to water systems that cross state borders', Dobner writes in a book on global water policy, 'but also to a multiplicity of social, ecological and economic factors which affect either the global water balance or the global management of water.'[14]

The democratic deficit in water governance and a World Parliament

Since access to water is not a matter of choice but an existential necessity, Ricardo Petrella, in a 'Water Manifesto' published as early as 1999, called for it to be recognised as 'a common global heritage of humanity'. 'The control of water', he wrote, 'must be given to its true owners, to the inhabitants of planet Earth. It does not belong to nation states, nor to markets, corporations or shareholders. It belongs to human communities, from the smallest (villages) to the largest (the global community).' The water problem is above all a problem of democracy and solidarity, he argues. For that reason, a core demand of the manifesto, in addition to the establishment of an international water tribunal, is for the introduction 'as soon as possible' of a World Water Parliament. In its initial phase, the World Water Parliament could provide a kind of global public hearing to produce a comprehensive review of rights and duties with respect to water and to debate scenarios to drive forward sustainable, equitable and mutually supportive solutions. The manifesto suggests that the members could initially be appointed by national parliaments.[15]

Global water policy is only poorly developed to date, and badly fragmented. There is no competent body within the UN, only the network 'UN Water', formed in 2003 and comprising about 30 UN institutions and around two dozen NGOs. As a group of experts pointed out in a critical review of global water governance, UN Water is not there to make binding decisions. 'Existing global institutions addressing water are very weak in terms of regulation, but they are relatively good at agenda setting, sharing information, mobilizing people, and, to a certain degree, in mobilizing resources', it states. That, however, is not enough to meet the challenges in their view. 'In fact, today's reluctance to

13 Hoekstra, A. Y. 2006. The global dimension of water governance: Nine reasons for global arrangements in order to cope with local water problems. Delft: UNESCO-IHE Institute for Water Education, pp. 15, 27.
14 Dobner, Petra. Wasserpolitik. Zur politischen Theorie, Praxis und Kritik globaler Governance. Berlin: Suhrkamp, 2010, p. 16.
15 Petrella, loc. cit., pp. 8, 106-109.

enter into any kind of regulatory framework may generate the need for harsh regulatory measures tomorrow to cope with an aggravated water crisis as the result of present insufficient action.'[16]

As Petra Dobner explains in her book, global water policy is 'an object lesson' illustrating 'the lack of forms, institutions and ideas' of global governance that could 'democratically legitimise the transfer of decision-making away from the state level into transnational forums'. Water policy, she believes, is decisively influenced by a shift in the locus of the political debate and in the referential framework from the state to an elite 'global water network' made up of what she calls 'multi-sectoral and multi-level constellations of actors'. Policy fields such as water thereby fall into what she sees as 'the institutional and legitimational black hole of unripe institutions of global democracy'. For her unambiguous conclusion is that the water network 'has no democratic legitimacy'. One of the bodies that has stepped in to fill the gap or political vacuum created in part by the UN is the non-governmental World Water Forum, which has met every three years since 1997, operating with a broad, participative multi-stakeholder approach that includes representatives of the water industries. In Dobner's view, the one thousand conference participants principally serve to 'act out a performance that mimics legitimation', as the outcomes have already been decided in advance by a small circle of like-minded leading members of the water network who pursue a privatization agenda as favoured by the water industry. Massive resistance towards this agenda has simply been 'brushed aside'. The claim that a consensus has been reached 'can therefore only be considered valid for the participating elites'. The multi-stakeholder participation is thus a form of 'legitimacy phishing'. Dobner sums it up in a nutshell when she writes that '[d]emocratic participation and democratic legitimacy cannot consist merely in attending mega-conferences along with 30,000 other interested parties but remaining excluded from the decision-making process'.[17] Privatization of the water supply as a policy aimed at solving the water crisis is in fact highly controversial, and - as we have seen - the global water balance is hardly convincing evidence of good governance. The manifesto of the first 'alternative water forum', held in Florence in 2003, called by contrast for water to be recognised as a global common good and for privatization to be halted. Additionally, it noted that 'citizens must be able to participate directly in the management of water

16   Dellapenna, Joseph W., Joyeeta Gupta, Wenjing Li, and Falk Schmidt. 2013. 'Thinking about the Future of Global Water Governance'. Ecology and Society (18) 3, p. 3.
17   Dobner, loc. cit., pp. 28, 348f., 283, 329f., 307, 336, 326f., 351.

and ecosystems, at local and global levels'. 'Such participation', ran the manifesto, 'could be furthered by the creation of a world water parliament.'[18] On the need for a world water parliament at least, then, there appears to be agreement. At the fifth official World Water Forum, too, in Istanbul in 2009, over two hundred delegates also declared themselves to be in favour.[19] Dobner, however, is not convinced by the argument for a world water parliament. She fears that it would not differ greatly from the format of the World Water Forum, even if its political orientation might well be different. As a matter of principle, she believes that it is problematic for a parliamentary style body to be restricted to a particular sector. One reason for this is the resulting political and institutional fragmentation. By contrast, she sees a UN parliament as an 'excellent' idea.

The proposal for the establishment of a specialized world water parliament should be combined with the wider goal of a world parliament. A world parliament could be the starting point for regulation in the water sector under world law, and to that end it could create a water committee to take the lead on this and to fulfil exactly the role envisaged for the proposed world water parliament. A global parliamentary assembly could build up political pressure for action simply by acting as a consultative body and by addressing relevant issues such as the desirability of a UN water organization. 'If you are serious about globalising democracy', Dobner says bluntly, 'then the answer can only be to endow the parliament with real powers.'

18 'Manifeste du Forum Alternatif Mondial de l'Eau: Pour une autre politique de l'eau'. *Magazine H2o*, March 2003 (www.h2o.net).
19 5th World Water Forum. 2009. 'Parliamentarians Process: Proposals emerging from Parliaments for Water'.

21.
The elimination of poverty, and
basic social security for all

Poverty as the key problem

The elimination of poverty and of existential misery is the basis for a humane, just, peaceful and safe world, in which all people have the opportunity of education, political participation and self-fulfilment. Poverty is a major cause of hunger and inadequate access to drinking water, poor health care, inadequate education, a lack of family planning, and political instability. As a rule, a higher standard of living is associated with lower birth rates, meaning that overcoming poverty can contribute to slowing down population growth. The political scientist Frank Nuscheler believes that 'the correlation between high population growth and a series of interdependent poverty indicators' suggests strongly that 'poverty is the key problem for population and development policy'.[1] In the view of the Bangladeshi economist Muhammad Yunus, who was awarded the Nobel Peace Prize for his role as a pioneer of microcredit for the poorest, 'poverty is perhaps the most serious threat to world peace, even more dangerous than terrorism, religious fundamentalism, ethnic hatred, political rivalries, or any of the other forces that are often cited as promoting violence and war'. 'Poverty', writes Yunus, 'leads to hopelessness, which provokes people to desperate acts.'[2] At the top of his wish list is the establishment of a global government to see that 'all parts of the world enjoy the similar quality of life' and to 'protect the interest of all living beings on the planet', among other things.[3]

Extreme poverty and the right to an adequate standard of living

Overcoming poverty has been on the international agenda for a long time. At the foundation of the International Labour Organization (ILO) during the Versailles Peace Conference in 1919, it was stated that universal peace 'can be established only if it is based upon social justice'.[4] The Atlantic Charter adopted by the Inter-

1 Nuscheler, Franz. November 2008. 'Armut'. Online-Handbuch Demografie, Berlin-Institut für Bevölkerung and Entwicklung, November 2008 (www.berlin-institut.org).
2 Yunus, Muhammad. 2007. Creating a world without poverty: social business and the future of capitalism. New York: PublicAffairs, p. 105.
3 'Professor Yunus's Wish List' (www.muhammadyunus.org).
4 Versailles Peace Treaty, 28 June 1919, part XIII., ch. 1, before article 387.

Allied Council in 1941 declared as one of its goals 'that all the men in all the lands may live out their lives in freedom from fear and want'. The Charter of the United Nations speaks of international cooperation for the solution of economic and social problems, and elaborates on this in the ninth Chapter to say that 'stability and well-being' are prerequisites for peace. The United Nations should therefore work to promote 'higher standards of living, full employment, and conditions of economic and social progress and development'. As already mentioned, Article 25 of the Universal Declaration of Human Rights and Article 11 of the International Covenant on Economic, Social and Cultural Rights include the right to a standard of living adequate for health and well-being. Everybody should be able to meet their basic needs. A UN summit meeting in September 2015 adopted, as a successor to the Millennium Development Goals, an 'Agenda for Sustainable Development' for the period up to 2030. The first goal of the new 'Agenda 2030' is the elimination of extreme poverty 'for all people everywhere'.

The international poverty line, as used by the United Nations, is based on the World Bank definition. It is reached by calculating an average of the absolute poverty thresholds of 15 of the world's poorest countries, converted into US dollars. Due to variations in the local purchasing power of the US dollar and to changes in the uniform basket of goods on which the calculations are based, since the method was introduced in 1990 the line has been adjusted upwards from one dollar per day in 1990 to 1.25 dollars in 2008 and finally to 1.90 dollars per day in 2015. This last upward adjustment occurred just ten days after the UN summit mentioned above, which is why the concluding document from the summit still refers to 1.25 dollars. Humanity is still a long way from the total elimination of extreme poverty. The target of the first Millennium Development Goal was to halve the proportion of people living in extreme poverty in the developing countries between 1990 and 2015. According to World Bank estimates, that target was achieved in 2010. The proportion is calculated to have fallen from 43.1 per cent in 1990 to 20.6 per cent in 2010 (according to the World Bank figures, by 2011 it was down to only 17 per cent).[5] On average, these people had 0.87 US dollars per day available to them. With the exception of China and India, the economic situation of the poorest people in the low-income developing countries has barely changed over the last thirty years.[6] Half

5   World Bank. 2014. World Development Indicators 2014. Washington D.C., p. 23 (for 2010); World Bank. 2015. World Development Indicators 2015. Washington D.C., 2015, p. 4 (for 2011); the Millennium Progress Report speaks of a decline from 47% in 1990 to 22% in 2010. United Nations. June 2013. 'The Millennium Development Goals Report 2013', p. 7.

6   Olinto, Pedro, Kathleen Beegle, Carlos Sobrado, and Hiroki Uematsu. October 2013. 'The State of the Poor: Where Are The Poor, Where Is Extreme Poverty Harder to End, and What Is the Current Profile of the World's Poor?' World Bank. Economic Premise No. 125, p. 3.

of the people in the developing countries, according to World Bank figures for 2010, had an income of below 2.50 US dollars per day, and 88 per cent had to make do with less than 10 dollars per day.[7] The World Bank defines as the middle class those with an income between ten and fifty US dollars per day. A World Bank report of 2011 gave the number of people living below the poverty line of 1.25 dollars per day as roughly one billion.[8] After the threshold was adjusted to 1.90, the number remained roughly the same. The World Bank says that up until 2013 it then declined to 767 million.[9] If it were possible by magic to raise the income of every person in extreme poverty to the threshold figure, then it would cost 250 billion US dollars per year to eliminate extreme poverty across the world.[10] This is just a fraction of the money made available to rescue the banks during the financial crisis.

However, this mental game is all too easy, and it is fundamentally misleading. Overcoming extreme poverty is not just a matter of daily incomes; it is multi-dimensional, and it is of course linked to many other development parameters. UN-Habitat estimates that more than one-third of city dwellers in the developing countries (about 863 million people) live in slums with inadequate infrastructure.[11] This includes water supply infrastructure and sanitation facilities, as already discussed. Additionally, around 1.3 billion people, according to estimates from the International Energy Agency, have no access to electricity.[12] More than 2.5 billion adults around the world have no bank account and only limited access to banking services.[13] The OECD reports that around 1.4 billion people, including a third of the very poorest, live in the world's fragile states, where basic state functions are only poorly developed.[14] For the very poorest, the basic structures of the rule of law are available only to a rudimentary degree, but they are of crucial importance. The international Commission on Legal Empowerment of the Poor, under the co-chairmanship of the Peruvian economist Hernando de Soto and with the support of the UNDP, stressed in its concluding report in 2008 that 'four billion people around the world are robbed of the chance

7   World Bank. 2013. World Development Report 2014. Washington D.C., pp. 303, 319.
8   Id. 2015. World Development Indicators 2015. Washington D.C., p. 4.
9   World Bank Group. 2016. Poverty and Shared Prosperity 2016: Taking On Inequality. Washington D.C.: International Bank for Reconstruction and Development / The World Bank, p. 3.
10   Cf. Olinto et al., loc. cit., p. 4, based on the threshold of 1.25 US$.
11   UN Habitat. 2013. Streets as Public Spaces and Drivers of Urban Prosperity. Nairobi: United Nations Human Settlements Programme, p. 84.
12   International Energy Agency. 2011. 'Access to Electricity'. World Energy Outlook, 2011.
13   Demirguc-Kunt, Asli, and Leora Klapper. April 2012. 'Measuring Financial Inclusion: The Global Findex Database'. World Bank Policy Research Working Paper 6025.
14   Organisation for Economic Cooperation and Development. 2014. Fragile States 2014: Domestic Revenue Mobilisation in Fragile States. Paris: OECD, p. 16.

to better their lives and climb out of poverty, because they are excluded from the rule of law'. A particular problem is that of weak land property rights which are extremely difficult to enforce. One of the Commission's recommendations was a 'Global Legal Empowerment Compact' that would codify fundamental rights, together with a framework for their enforcement on an international basis.[15]

Moreover, the uniform international monetary poverty line determined by the United Nations and the World Bank is criticised by many as being arbitrary, and the value of the statistics based on it is consequently called into question. Sanjay Reddy and Thomas Pogge, for example, believe the threshold calculated by the World Bank is too low, and regard the calculation method, based on purchasing power parity, as flawed, since the basket includes goods that are irrelevant to the needs of the poor. If income poverty is to be judged on a per capita basis, they argue, then a method must be used that starts from the real local costs of meeting basic needs.[16] Statements made on the basis of World Bank statistics and the monetary line marking extreme poverty in the world are therefore to be treated with caution. A higher threshold for extreme poverty is needed, one based on the real conditions for an 'adequate standard of living', as well as a better way of measuring it. In the long run, it might be useful to depart from a global absolute poverty line and to measure poverty in a relative way, as is already done in the EU and the OECD.

The need for a new approach to international development

A paradigm shift in development policy and in the battle against poverty is indispensable if the goal of the total elimination of poverty is to be reached. Consideration must be given to the political lessons to be learned from the fundamental dispute over the benefits and drawbacks of public development aid, as exemplified and further inflamed in 2009 by the bestselling book 'Dead Aid' by the Zambian economist Dambisa Moyo. As the decades-long experience with state development aid in Africa convincingly shows, wrote Moyo, aid is not part of the solution, but rather part of the problem itself. Her unsparing conclusion was that, in the final analysis, state development aid in in Africa led to corruption and political dependence; fuelled conflicts over the control of state power; undermined the efficiency of public administration; damaged business; and choked off economic development and growth. The former German diplomat

---

15 Commission on Legal Empowerment of the Poor, and United Nations Development Programme (ed.). 2008. Making the Law Work for Everyone. Report of the Commission on Legal Empowerment of the Poor. Vol. I, pp. 1, 10, 34ff., 86.
16 Reddy, Sanjay G., and Thomas Pogge. 2010. 'How Not to Count the Poor'. In: Debates on the Measurement of Global Poverty, ed. by Sudhir Anand, Paul Segal, and Joseph Stiglitz, 42–85. New York: Oxford University Press.

Volker Seitz points out that between 1960 and 2006 up to 2.3 trillion US dollars flowed into Sub-Saharan Africa, six times as much per head as went to Europe under the Marshall Plan, without bringing about any discernible improvement in living conditions.[17] International poverty campaigns and development policy must be brought closer to the people affected. The poor need a voice. Having their interests represented in a parliamentary assembly at the world level would be one way of improving their situation and putting the debate on a new footing. 'The best way to give the poor a real voice is through a world parliament', argued George Monbiot in the *Guardian*, and he added: 'there is a growing recognition in Africa that a world parliament offers the best chance - perhaps the only chance - that the unmediated concerns of the poor will reach the ears of the rich'.[18]

Economic growth is not enough

It is now widely acknowledged that relying on general economic growth and a resultant rise in average incomes to eliminate extreme poverty is not a promising approach. The economist David Woodward extrapolated from the growth figures from 1993 to 2008 that it would take over one hundred years on that basis before extreme poverty – even using the income threshold of 1.25 US dollars – would disappear.[19] Not least in view of its ineffectiveness, but also because of the need to reduce CO_2 emissions and to transition to a sustainable economy, he described the idea of relying on general growth as not only unrealistic but 'dangerous and counterproductive'.[20] In this context it is notable that 73 per cent of the poorest people in the world, those with less than two dollars per day, now live in middle-income countries. In the World Bank's definition, these are countries with an annual GDP per capita between 1,026 and 12,475 US dollars. As Paul Collier, former head of the research division of the World Bank, emphasizes in his book on 'The Bottom Billion', the problem is that growth simply does not reach the poorest.[21] 'Growth alone is unlikely to get the world to the 3 per cent target because as extreme poverty declines, growth on its own tends to lift fewer people out of poverty', as the World Bank itself now states. Growth

17 Seitz, Volker. 2009. Afrika wird armregiert oder wie man Afrika wirklich helfen kann. 2nd ed. München: dtv, p. 65.
18 Monbiot, George. 24 April 2007. 'The best way to give the poor a real voice is through a world parliament'. The Guardian (www.guardian.co.uk).
19 Woodward, David. 2015. 'Incrementum ad Absurdum: Global Growth, Inequality and Poverty Eradication in a Carbon-Constrained World'. World Economic Review, no. 4: 43–62.
20 Woodward, David. 'How progressive is the push to eradicate extreme poverty?' The Guardian (www.guardian.co.uk).
21 Collier, Paul. 2008. The Bottom Billion. Oxford University Press.

policy, it argues, must be designed to be more inclusive, and more resources must be mobilised for the support of the very poor.[22]

Social security as the foundation of a planetary social contract

The key step towards the elimination of extreme poverty in the world lies in guaranteeing basic social security for everyone. In parallel, consideration should be given to the worldwide introduction of a minimum wage that is adjusted on a country-by-country basis but should never be set below 1 dollar per hour.[23] This must form the basis for a new planetary social contract and a global ecosocial market economy. The World Commission on the Social Dimension of Globalization set up by the ILO rightly pointed out that 'a certain minimum level of social protection needs to be accepted and undisputed as part of the socio-economic floor of the global economy'. Global engagement in the elimination of social insecurity, it argued, is crucially important for the continuing legitimation of globalization.[24] In fact, 'social security' is already firmly embedded as a human right, in Articles 22 and 25 of the Universal Declaration of Human Rights and in Article 9 of the International Covenant on Economic, Social and Cultural Rights. Numerous recommendations and conventions have emerged from the ambit of the ILO. The ILO Convention 102 of 1952, for example, ratified (though generally only in parts) by fifty countries, commits them to uphold specified minimum standards in the provision of basic social security benefits. In 1995 the UN held a World Summit for Social Development in Copenhagen. In the 'Declaration on Social Justice for a Fair Globalization' of 2008, unanimously adopted by practically the entire community of states, it is affirmed 'that the ILO has the solemn obligation to further among the nations of the world programmes which will achieve the objectives of full employment and the raising of standards of living, a minimum living wage and the extension of social security measures to provide a basic income to all in need'. The same objective can be found already in the ILO Declaration of Philadelphia of 1944. Seventy years later, in its first report on social protection, the ILO found to its disappointment that, in spite of notable advances in many countries of the world, 73 per cent of the world population, or 5.2 billion people, had either only partial access to public social security systems or none at all. Social protection

22 World Bank. 2014. Prosperity for All. Ending Extreme Poverty. A Note for the World Bank Group Spring Meetings 2014. Washington D.C.
23 Zervas, Georgios, and Peter Spiegel. 2016. Die 1-Dollar-Revolution. Globaler Mindestlohn Gegen Ausbeutung und Armut. München/Berlin: Piper.
24 International Labour Organization. 2004. A fair globalization: Creating opportunities for all. Report of the World Commission on the Social Dimension of Globalization. Geneva, para. 491, p. 110.

is not only a human right, but plays a key role in the view of the ILO in the reduction of poverty, social inequality and hunger and in the promotion of food security, social cohesion, peaceful communities and political stability. It was found to have a positive impact on health care provision, the education system, job creation, consumer demand and economic growth. 'Investing in social protection is investing in a healthy, productive and equitable society', the report states.[25]

A global basic income

Unconditional financial grants have proved successful in the fight against poverty and in development aid, as the political scientist Christopher Blattmann and the economist Paul Niehaus report in the journal *Foreign Affairs*. 'Western officials and organizations are not the best judges of what poor people in developing countries need to make a better living; the poor people themselves are', is how they sum up new study findings.[26] There is no more immediate way of combating poverty than by direct grants. They enable people to decide for themselves which of their needs are the most urgent, from the things needed for day-to-day survival to training and further education or investing in their own small business. The studies analysed by Blattmann and Niehaus confirm that as a rule people are very well able to do this for themselves.

In the EU, the European Parliament confirmed in a 2010 resolution on minimum incomes its belief 'that the various experiments with minimum incomes and with a guaranteed basic income for everyone, accompanied by additional social integration and protection measures, show that these are effective ways of combating poverty and social exclusion and providing a decent life for all'.[27] In the USA, the debate around this idea has a long history. It was proposed, in the form of a so-called negative income tax, by the US American economist Milton Friedman in his book 'Capitalism and Freedom' as early as 1962. If earnings are zero, or below a certain threshold, financial support is given by the state at a level up to a basic income. An advisory commission to the US President recommended the introduction of such a system in 1969. Among the supporters of a basic income were the civil rights activist Martin Luther King and the economists James Tobin and Kenneth Galbraith. 'I am now convinced', wrote Martin Luther King, 'that the simplest approach will prove to be the most effective — the solution to poverty is to abolish it directly by a now widely discussed

25 International Labour Organization. 2014. World Social Protection Report 2014/15. Geneva: International Labour Office, pp. 2, 154ff.
26 Blattman, Christopher, and Paul Niehaus. 2014. 'Show Them the Money'. Foreign Affairs, no. May/June.
27 European Parliament. 20 October 2010. 'Resolution on the Role of Minimum Income in Combating Poverty and Promoting an Inclusive Society in Europe'. Doc. P7_TA(2010)0375, para. 34, 44.

measure: the guaranteed income.'[28] Incidentally, this famous fighter against so-cial oppression and recipient of the Nobel Peace Prize also supported the estab-lishment of a world police and a world government. 'There can be a world gov-ernment where diversity can exist and this would lessen many tensions that we face today,' he noted in 1964.[29]

The issue of an unconditional basic income is becoming an indispensable element of discussion on global development and social policy. Götz Werner, founder of Europe's biggest pharmacy chain, dm, and Adrienne Goehler, for-mer President of the University of Fine Arts in Hamburg, are well-known pro-ponents of the idea. Citing a successful model project in the Namibian village of Otjivero, they question why 'classical development policy, which has deep-ened corruption and enriched the powerful, the despots, dictators, clans and warlords all around the world, is not radically re-routed towards an uncondi-tional basic income'.[30] It also provides an answer to the question that arose ear-lier about what the money raised by global taxes could be used for. A global basic income is perhaps the most sensible use for the bulk of the income from global taxation. Thomas Pogge, for example, believes that 'something like a Global Basic Income may well be part of the best plan for using funds raised through a Tobin Tax or Global Resources Dividend toward poverty eradica-tion'. Projects for the improvement of public infrastructure, he rightly adds, also represent an important component.[31] Werner and Goehler, on the other hand, link basic income to a global CO_2 emissions tax. 'If emissions rights for CO_2 were auctioned today, and the revenues from that were to be paid out as a basic income', they write, 'two fundamental problems of the 21st century would be solved at the same time. CO_2 emissions would be effectively capped, and looming climate change would be slowed down. At the same time, depending on the auction price, everyone would receive between 13 and 14 dollars a month. We in Europe might regard that as "peanuts", but on a worldwide scale this sum can guarantee a minimum subsistence and thus access to clean drink-ing water and an adequate basic diet.'[32]

28 King, Jr., Martin Luther. 1968. Where Do We Go from Here: Chaos or Community? Boston: Beacon Press, p. 162.
29 Id. 1964. 'In a Single Garment of Destiny': A Global Vision of Justice. Ed. by Lewis V. Baldwin. Boston: Bea-con Press. Part V: Statements prepared for Redbook Magazine, 5 November 1964, p. 149.
30 Werner, Götz, and Adrienne Goehler. 2011. 1000 € für jeden: Freiheit. Gleichheit. Grundeinkommen. Berlin: Ullstein, p. 218.
31 Pinzani, Alessandro. June 2005. 'Global Justice as Moral Issue'. Interview with Thomas Pogg. Ethic: Interna-tional Journal for Moral Philosophy (4) 1: 1–6, p. 4.
32 Werner/Goehler, loc. cit., p. 233.

Universal ownership of the global commons

The proposal for a basic income is linked to the idea that everyone has a stake in the commons and a right to share the fruits of civilization. As Myron Frankman explains, 'the essential rationale is quite simple: all earned income takes advantage of pre-existing institutions, knowledge, communication, and transportation nets, which are part of what is commonly regarded as social capital. To the extent that each of us is a common beneficiary of the cumulative global process of civilization, we are entitled to some reasonable monetary dividend.'[33] Thomas Paine, one of the early proponents of this approach, emphasized in 1797, in connection with the issue of ownership of the land, 'that the earth, in its natural, uncultivated state was, and ever would have continued to be, the common property of the human race', and that all those without property should therefore receive compensation from the propertied classes.[34] When global common goods are used, all citizens of the Earth should benefit. A global basic income thus has a strong symbolic dimension. It promotes the idea of the equality of all people and of their global identity. A world parliament should set the framework for practical implementation, should be the highest budgetary authority, and should exercise democratic control. The practical arrangements might involve several different models, all operating within common global guidelines, to suit differing local conditions. In the developed countries, for example, where there are functioning tax and social welfare systems, it might make sense to implement the basic income in the form of a negative income tax. In other countries it might be better to pay it out in full, with the minimum of bureaucracy. In fragile states, and even more so in failing states, there will be severe obstacles to be overcome. What is decisive, however, is that everybody receives it and that it is unconditional - not subject to any compulsion to work or any kind of means test. The latter not only involves considerable bureaucracy and stigmatises the recipients, but it also contradicts the fundamental rationale for a basic income.

The dream of a life free from economic compulsion

The social psychologist Erich Fromm pointed out that throughout human history 'man has been limited in his freedom to act by two factors: the use of force on the part of the rulers (essentially their capacity to kill the dissenters), and,

---

33   Frankman, Myron J. 2004. World Democratic Federalism. New York: Palgrave Macmillan, p. 150.
34   Paine, Thomas. 1995 [1797]. 'Agrarian Justice'. In: Rights of Man, Common Sense and Other Political Writings. Oxford, New York et al.: Oxford University Press, p. 417.

more importantly, the threat of starvation against all who were unwilling to accept the conditions of work and social existence that were imposed on them'. In our age of economic abundance, however, when it is actually possible to satisfy the basic needs of all, everyone could for the first time be made free and independent from economic compulsion by means of a guaranteed income. 'Guaranteed income', wrote Fromm, 'would not only establish freedom as a reality rather than a slogan, it would also establish a principle deeply rooted in Western religious and humanist tradition: man has the right to live, regardless! This right to live, to have food, shelter, medical care, education, etc., is an intrinsic human right that cannot be restricted by any condition, not even the one that he must be socially "useful". The shift from a psychology of scarcity to that of abundance is one of the most important steps in human development.'[35] In that sense, a basic income, for Götz Werner and Adrienne Goehler, is a step towards what is perhaps the most important of all human dreams: a life without existential fear, with the freedom to do what you want. The humanist ideals of the Enlightenment, and the core demands of the French Revolution for 'liberty, equality, and fraternity', would thereby finally be given a 'real foundation'.[36] Guaranteed basic social security for everybody in the world is a human right, and the objective of global social policy. A global basic income can complement national measures and create a financial base that contributes to the elimination of extreme poverty on the planet.

35 Fromm, Erich. 1966. 'The Psychological Aspects of the Guaranteed Income'. In: The Guaranteed Income, ed. by Robert Theobald, 175–84. New York: Doubleday.
36 Werner/Goehler, loc. cit., pp. 11, 25, 265f.

22.
Global class formation, the 'super class', and global inequality

The emergence of global class conflicts and the role of the middle class

The increasing importance of the developing and emerging countries in the world economy, and the associated growth of their middle classes, renders the concept of the so-called 'Third World' obsolete, notwithstanding the continued existence of extreme poverty. Simultaneously, the long predominance in world systems theory of a division of the world into a 'core', a 'semi-periphery' and a 'periphery' is nearly over. This is evidenced by the increase in direct trade links between countries of the South and by their growing share of worldwide consumption. Michael Hardt and Antonio Negri have encapsulated this well in their description of the 'logic and structure of a new form of sovereignty'. 'If the First World and the Third World, center and periphery, North and South were ever really separated along national lines, today they clearly infuse one another, distributing inequalities and barriers along multiple and fractured lines. ... The various nations and regions contain different proportions of what was thought of as First World and Third, center and periphery, North and South. The geography of uneven development and the lines of division and hierarchy will no longer be found along stable national or international boundaries, but in fluid infra- and supranational borders', they state in their book 'Empire'.[1] 'There is a "south" in the North and a "north" in the South', as a UNDP report on human development put it.[2] Seen in this light, a crucial conflict of the future lies not between states, neither on a North-South nor an East-West axis, nor on any other such axis, but *within world society*, between the socially disadvantaged classes and a super-rich global elite.

In an article on 'the globalising security environment', the defence expert Tomas Ries wrote that 'the key political fault lines generating violent conflict have shifted from within the elite peer community to the tensions between un-

---

1 Hardt, Michael, and Antonio Negri. 2000. Empire. Cambridge: Harvard University Press, pp. xi, 335
2 United Nations Development Programme. 2013. Human Development Report 2013. The Rise of the South: Human Progress in a Diverse World. New York: UNDP, p. 2.

equal global socioeconomic classes of society. The drivers of intersocietal violence have shifted from the Westphalian horizontal peer competition towards the vertical asymmetric tensions of the globalised world village, but it is a village on the verge of revolution. While we have an increasingly integrated elite community, we also face increasingly explosive tensions from the poorer strata below'.[3] A study by the UK Ministry of Defence of the strategic defence environment over the next thirty years identified the middle classes as a potential 'revolutionary class'. 'The globalization of labour markets and reducing levels of national welfare provision and employment could reduce peoples' attachment to particular states', the study notes. 'The growing gap between themselves and a small number of highly visible super-rich individuals might fuel disillusion with meritocracy, while the growing urban under-classes are likely to pose an increasing threat to social order and stability, as the burden of acquired debt and the failure of pension provision begins to bite. Faced by these twin challenges, *the world's middle-classes might unite*, using access to knowledge, resources and skills *to shape transnational processes in their own class interest'* (emphasis added).[4] The ambitious middle classes in the developing countries, many of them still living just above the poverty line, demand improved social, political and economic rights, good governance and better public infrastructure, while growing inequality and global structural economic change threaten the grip of the hard-pressed middle classes of the industrialised countries on their precarious relative security. 'The main cause of coming conflicts will not be clashes between civilizations, but the anger generated by the unfulfilled expectations of a middle class, which is declining in rich countries and booming in poor countries', was Moisés Naím's diagnosis.[5]

In a book published in 2011, the economist Branko Milanović of the World Bank, one of the world's leading experts on inequality, expressed scepticism about the possibility of global class solidarity in today's world 'because the underlying material conditions of people are simply too different'. The worldwide proletariat, celebrated by Karl Marx in 1867 as the revolutionary class, had already ceased to exist by the end of the 19th century, he argued. At that time, the income differences between workers in Europe and North America, and in the East and the colonies, had 'exploded' and the solidarity that was assumed to exist 'began to fray and eventually evaporated'. The French social philosopher

3   Ries, Tomas. 2009. 'The globalising security environment and the EU'. In: What ambitions for European defence in 2020?, 61–74. Ed. by Álvaro de Vasconcelos. 2nd ed. European Union Institute for Security Studies, pp. 62f., 67f.

4   UK Ministry of Defense Development, Concepts and Doctrine Centre. 2007. The DCDC Strategic Trends Programme 2007-2036. 3rd ed. Shrivenham: DCDC, p. 80.

5   Naím, Moisés. 5 August 2011. 'The Clash of the Middle Classes'. Huffington Post (www.huffingtonpost.com).

André Gorz thought Marx's proletariat had been no more than a philosophical myth from the beginning. 'For over a century the idea of the proletariat has succeeded in masking its own unreality', he wrote in 1980 in his influential book 'Farewell to the Working Class'.[6] Milanović stresses the point that even the poorest American today is better off than two-thirds of the world population. 'There are many countries in the world', he writes, 'whose top income classes are poorer than the poorest income classes in rich countries.'[7] He, too, concedes nevertheless that there is a 'fragile new global middle class'. The global median income in 2011 was five US dollars per day; so the global middle class consists, he calculates, of people with daily incomes between four and 6.5 dollars. This represents about thirteen per cent of the world population.[8] Taking a different perspective, one could define the global middle class as having an income between two and 16 US dollars per day. The proportion of the world population represented by this income group grew in the twenty years between 1988 and 2008 from 23 to 40 per cent.[9]

As the British study mentioned above suggests, the crucial turning point is the fact that parts at least of the global middle class now recognize the global dimension to the conflict and thus their common global interests. All middle classes, whether in Brazil, Germany, India or the USA, suffer in the same way from the tax avoidance practices of the super-rich and their companies, for example. This creates, the study suggests, a powerful popular basis for support for global regulation, in the sense of Karl Polanyi's concept of a double movement. To take the link to the 'Great Transformation' further, one could speak in this context of the creation of a global 'transformative subject'.

The global precariat

The global middle class is only one of the potential candidates for the role of such a 'transformative subject'. The British labour economist Guy Standing, formerly a senior figure at the ILO and now an academic at the University of London, speaks of the need for 'a new vocabulary, one reflecting class relations in the global market system of the twenty-first century'. A proponent of a basic income, Standing sees a 'new dangerous class' materialising – a 'global precariat', which finds itself at the bottom of the emergent global class structure. The

6   Gorz, André. 1997 [1980]. Farewell to the Working Class: An Essay on Post-Industrial Socialism. Pluto Press, p. 67.
7   Milanović, Branko. 2011. The Haves and the Have-Nots: A Brief and Idiosyncratic History of Global Inequality. New York: Basic Books, pp. 113, 110f., 117f.
8   Id. 28 April 2014. 'How we can strengthen the world's fragile middle class'. Financial Times.
9   Lakner, Christoph, and Branko Milanović. December 2013. 'Global Income Distribution: From the Fall of the Berlin Wall to the Great Recession'. World Bank Policy Research Working Paper 6719, pp. 32, 49.

contours of what Standing also refers to as a 'class-in-the-making' are as yet very unclear. It belongs to neither the middle class nor the traditional, wage labour-based proletariat. Instead, its members live in precarious circumstances, muddling through on temporary jobs, or unemployed with no prospects of a career or of upward social mobility. His description is reminiscent of what André Gorz some time ago called the 'non-class of post-industrial neo-proletarians', 'all the supernumeraries of present-day social production, who are potentially or actually unemployed, whether permanently or temporarily, partially or completely'.[10] According to Standing, they are the people most directly affected by the flexibilization of the labour markets and by cuts to social welfare systems (insofar as these exist and are accessible), have no employment-related social protection, no income from capital, barely any chance of saving money, and live in permanent uncertainty about what the future might bring. They do not feel represented by either the traditional political parties or the unions, and they are largely alienated from the institutions of the state. The precariat, as outlined here, is very inhomogeneous. According to Standing, the largest and most diverse group consists of well-educated people who cannot find regular work suited to their level of qualifications but often have good networks. This is the group from which the recent youth and student protest movements emerged, and which in Standing's view played a leading role in the Occupy movement. Then there are the relatively uneducated former wage labourers, susceptible to populism, who have dropped out of the working class, and the most disadvantaged group, with hardly any rights to fall back on, consisting of migrants (with or without official resident status), asylum seekers and members of ethnic minorities.[11]

The concept of the Multitude

A different approach is illustrated by the concept of the 'Multitude', which was popularised among a wider audience through the eponymous book by Michael Hardt and Antonio Negri. What they mean by 'Multitude' is a 'multiplicity of singular forms of life', woven together in a kind of network, but demonstrating many and varied differences, and which 'can never be reduced to a unity or a single identity'. The term describes 'all those who labor and produce under the rule of capital' in the broadest sense, so encompassing potentially 'all the diverse figures of social production'. This includes the unemployed, for 'just as social production takes place today equally inside and outside the factory walls, so too

10 Gorz, loc. cit., pp. 68f.
11 Standing, Guy. 2011. The precariat: the new dangerous class. London, New York: Bloomsbury Academic, 2011 and the same, 2014. A Precariat Charter: From Denizens to Citizens. London, New York: Bloomsbury Academic.

it takes place equally inside and outside the wage relationship'.[12] Although 'the common conditions of those who can become the multitude' remain relatively broad and unspecified in Hardt und Negri's description, it can be said of them that this 'emerging global class formation' shares 'a common global existence'.[13] The crucial underlying conception of class here is not empirical but determined by politics. Class, they argue, is defined by class struggle, and 'the task of a theory of class in this respect is to identify the existing *conditions* for potential collective struggle and express them as a political *proposition*'. In this instance, therefore, the project consists in bringing the Multitude to life. 'Class is a political concept, in short, in that a class is and can only be a collectivity that struggles in common.'[14] As the cultural theorist Sylvère Lotringer sardonically observes, Hardt and Negri's analysis appears to involve 'an original kind of class struggle', namely 'a struggle looking for a class'.[15]

What is at stake in this struggle, according to Hardt and Negri, is, in short, the resistance to an imperial global apparatus of rule labelled 'Empire', 'composed of a series of national and supranational organisms' including the United Nations, the IMF and the World Bank, which governs the global market and the global circuits of production as a 'sovereign power'. An interesting aspect of this model is that the USA is not regarded as being at its centre. Rather, it is argued that a fundamental principle of the 'Empire' is that its global power has no real centre. The distinction between inner and outer which is so important in the system of nation states is increasingly blurred in the 'Empire'. The 'imperial sovereignty' of the 'Empire' spans the entire globe and 'is both everywhere and nowhere' in Hardt and Negri's metaphysically-tinged analysis.[16] An important element of the 'Empire' is formed by a 'global aristocracy' of multinational corporations and industrialists, supranational institutions, dominant industrial states and influential non-state actors. The Multitude 'is and will remain necessarily antagonistic to these aristocracies', they say. Hardt and Negri see the protests at the WTO summit in Seattle in 1999 as 'the coming-out party of the new cycle of struggles', organised and mobilised now by the Multitude. The aim of the struggles is to 'develop a new framework for the democratic constitution of the world' and to create 'democracy on a global scale'.[17]

12 Hardt, Michael, and Antonio Negri. 2004. Multitude: War and Democracy in the Age of Empire. New York: Penguin, pp. 127, xiv, 107, xv, 135.
13 Ibid., pp. 105, xviii, 127.
14 Ibid., p. 104 .
15 Lotringer, Sylvère. 2004. 'Foreword: We, the Multitude'. In: Virno, Paolo. 2004. Grammar of the Multitude, 7–19. Los Angeles, CA: Semiotext(e), p. 16.
16 Hardt/Negri (Empire), loc. cit., pp. xii, xi, 190.
17 Hardt/Negri (Multitude), loc. cit., pp. 171, 322, 215, 217, 324, xi.

The super-rich and global power structures

While it may be difficult to clearly identify a global 'transformative subject' within a traditional class framework, there is on the other hand no problem in establishing that there is a global elite, economically separated by a large gap from the rest, at the very top of the global class structure. This is the super-rich, a group of about 157,000 people each with a fortune worth over 30 million US dollars. The total wealth of the super-rich adds up to about 22 trillion US dollars, or an average of 140 million each.[18] In reality there is no doubt that the sum is higher, as it can be safely assumed, as already outlined, that further sums totalling trillions are hidden away via obscure investments or in tax havens. This also applies to the wealth belonging to the so-called 'shadow elite' of organised crime, which is not captured in the standard statistics. At any rate, according to another conventional estimate, about 148,200 people across the world have fortunes in excess of 50 million US dollars, 54,800 of them with over 100 million, and 5,700 with over 500 million US dollars.[19] Now we are approaching the very pinnacle of this class at the top of the global wealth pyramid. This is formed of a group that *Forbes* magazine calculated in 2014 as comprising 2,043 people with a combined fortune estimated at 7.7 trillion US dollars.[20] The degree of concentration of wealth this represents is illustrated by the fact that the poorest 3.4 billion people in the world, or 70.1 per cent of the adult world population, together possess – with 7.6 trillion dollars – only slightly more than this group.[21] The 157,000 of the super-rich have more than three times as much. The poorest half of the world population has less than one per cent of global wealth, and the poorest two-thirds less than 2.7 per cent. The richest per centile of the world population, by contrast, holds around 50 per cent of all the wealth. According to Oxfam, the incomes of the poorest 10 per cent of people increased by less than 3 US dollars a year between 1988 and 2011, while the incomes of the richest one per cent increased 182 times as much.[22] Since 1980, the global top one per cent earners has captured twice as much of the growth in global income as the 50 per cent poorest individuals.[23] In terms of climate responsibility it was noted that the poorest half of the global population are responsible for only around 10 per cent of global emissions yet live overwhelmingly in the countries most vulnerable to climate change. In addition, the average footprint of someone in

18   Capgemini, and RBC Wealth Management. 2017. 'World Wealth Report 2017', pp. 7, 10.
19   Credit Suisse. November 2017. 'Global Wealth Report 2017', p. 24.
20   'Forbes 2017 Billionaires List', Forbes Magazine (www.forbes.com).
21   Credit Suisse, loc. cit., p. 21.
22   Oxfam. 18 January 2016. An Economy for the 1%, pp. 10f.
23   Alvaredo, Facundo, et al. 2017. World Inequality Report 2018. World Inequality Lab.

the richest one per cent can be 175 times that of someone in the poorest 10 per cent.[24] 'There's class warfare, all right, but it's my class, the rich class, that's making war, and we're winning', the billionaire Warren Buffet observed in an interview with the *New York Times* a few years ago.[25]

It can be assumed that the members of the class of the super-rich are often, though not always, part of a dominant global power structure composed of a small worldwide elite. The German sociologist Jürgen Krysmanski regards the super-rich as the global 'core of power, in the sense of a ruling class', and speaks of a 'power-money-complex' which has become the basis for 'a new form of global sovereignty'.[26] Krysmanski pictures the 'new planetary ruling structures' as a 'concentric castle'. 'The centre', he writes, 'is formed everywhere by the 0.01 per cent that is the super-rich, a social stratum which has been completely cut loose and is capable of anything, and which our knowledge and information society provides with all the means necessary to establish itself as the new centre of society. Around it, and closest to it, the second ring is formed by the business and financial elites, the specialists in the exploitation and securitization of wealth. The next functional ring is composed of the political elites whose job it is, as far as the empire of the billionaires is concerned at least, to arrange for the distribution of the wealth from the bottom to the top, as inconspicuously as possible. The largest group populates the outer ring of the castle: the administrative and knowledge elites of all kinds, from scientists to technocrats and bureaucrats to the feel-good elites of the media, culture and sport.'[27] David Rothkopf, the former managing director of Kissinger Associates and U.S. Under Secretary of Commerce for International Trade, painted a more diffuse picture in his popular book on the so-called 'Superclass'. There, the 'global power elite' is made up of a circle of 6,000 people, linked to each other by innumerable threads, who are distinguished not by their personal wealth but by their 'international influence'. In his view, this means the highest-ranking officials of the internationally most influential states, the commanders of the most powerful armies, the most important board members of the world's largest companies, richest banks and biggest investment firms, the chairpersons of the biggest NGOs and the most important international organizations, and religious leaders, scientists and other thought leaders.[28]

24   Oxfam. 2 December 2015. 'Extreme Carbon Inequality'.
25   Stein, Ben. 26 November 2006. 'In Class Warfare, Guess Which Class Is Winning'. The New York Times (www.nytimes.com).
26   Krysmanski, Hans Jürgen. 2012. 0,1 Prozent - Das Imperium der Milliardäre. Frankfurt: Westend, pp. 64f.
27   Id. 2013. 'Planetarische Herrschaft'. junge Welt, no. 100.
28   Rothkopf, David. 2008. Superclass: The Global Power Elite and the World They Are Making. London: Abacus.

The transnational capitalist class

For too long, too little attention has been paid by researchers to the super-rich and their influence. And it has often been rightly pointed out that this reticence is in marked contrast to the intensive research carried out into the living conditions of the poor and the middle classes. In C. Wright Mills and William Domhoff, the USA now has two pioneers of serious research into the elites; the global elite is also beginning to attract more attention. However, this is usually focused not on the super-rich in themselves but on the question of the formation of a global class, in which process they play a key role. The sociologist Leslie Sklair, formerly at the London School of Economics, argued in a 2001 study that the increasing significance of transnational concerns had been accompanied by the rise of a 'transnational capitalist class', or TCC for short, 'that is more or less in control of the processes of globalization' as well as of a large part of the worldwide means of production. In his analysis, the dominant group within the TCC is made up of those in control of the most important transnational companies, that is, their owners (the super-rich) and senior executives. This group is supported by three others, consisting of leading bureaucrats, politicians, experts, scientists and media representatives among others. There are numerous overlaps, interrelationships and switches between these groups. 'They are a *transnationalist capitalist class* in that they operate across state borders to further the interests of global capital rather than of any real or imagined nation-state', Sklair emphasizes. Of course there are internal conflicts of interest, but these are 'second order problems'; for 'the global capitalist system as a whole, these intraclass struggles are less important than what binds the members of the class together globally, namely their common interest in the protection of private property and the rights of private individuals to accumulate it with as little interference as possible'.[29]

The sociologist William Robinson of the University of California at Santa Barbara has followed up these studies. In an important work on a 'theory of global capitalism' from 2004, he too emphasizes that the formation of a 'transnational capitalist class' is a central aspect of the process of globalization. It is not simply an outcome of the process, but since the 1970s has also been its driving force. The globalization of capitalism, he argues, replicates at the global level the historical 'Great Transformation' depicted by Karl Polanyi. Capital, embodied and controlled by the TCC, has succeeded in setting itself free from the limitations set by nation states. 'This liberation', says Robinson, 'helped free emergent transnational capital from the compromises and commitments placed on

---

29   Sklair, Leslie. 2001. The Transnational Capitalist Class. Oxford, UK; Malden, Mass.: Blackwell, pp. 5, 17, 295, 12.

it by the social forces in the nation-state phase of capitalism. It dramatically altered the balance of forces among classes and social groups in each nation of the world and at the global level toward an emergent TCC.' The TCC has quite consciously and deliberately circumvented and neutralised at the transnational level those class compromises historically necessitated at the nation-state level by the countervailing movement. As empirical evidence for the rise of the TCC, Robinson cites the growing number and size of transnational corporations, the growth in cross-border fusions and take-overs, rising foreign direct investments, the overlap of personnel on the management boards of transnational corporations, and the evolution of worldwide outsourcing and subcontracting.[30]

A transnational state apparatus

Although a later study by the Canadian sociologist William Carroll found that the TCC has developed furthest in geographical terms in the North Atlantic area, it is a phenomenon by no means limited to the West or the global North.[31] In the developing countries, too, the growing numbers of the super-rich and of members of other sections of the national elites are increasingly integrated into the emerging TCC.[32] As Robinson argues, the state can be understood as a manifestation of certain specific, historically contingent class relations which are reflected in the political institutions. Globalization and the emergence of the TCC have been accompanied by a transformation of the character and structures of the state. National elites and functionaries who have been integrated into the TCC tend to act in the interests of their transnational class and to instrumentalize state institutions and their decisions accordingly. Robinson cites the USA as the most important example of a state dominated by the TCC. And he points to the number of intergovernmental investment protection agreements designed to protect foreign direct investments, now amounting to several thousand around the world, as evidence of the willingness of governments to accommodate the interests of transnational business. These agreements give companies the right to sue governments for compensation outside the national courts, for example at the International Centre for Settlement of Investment Disputes, part of the World Bank Group in Washington D.C. Robinson believes

30 Robinson, William I. 2004. A Theory of Global Capitalism. Production, Class, and State in a Transnational World. Baltimore and London: Johns Hopkins University Press, pp. 41, 54ff.
31 Carroll, William K. 2010. The Making of a Transnational Capitalist Class. Corporate Power in the 21st Century. London and New York: Zed Books.
32 Robinson, William I. 2011. 'Global Capitalism Theory and the Emergence of Transnational Elites'. Critical Sociology (38) 3: 349–63.

that the activities of the TCC taken together represent the formation, now proceeding rapidly, of a 'transnational state'. This is a network-like entity, spread
over several levels, made up of nation state institutions and the leading international economic and political forums and organizations, linked together by the
TCC and without any global institutional centre. The term 'state' applies to a
territory and a social system which are subject to rule or domination from a
specific source. Using this definition, it is certainly possible to describe the
world order dominated by the TCC as a transnational state. 'The TNS com-
prises those institutions and practices in global society that maintain, defend,
and advance the emergent hegemony of this global bourgeoisie', Robinson
writes. The decline of US supremacy is being accompanied by 'the creation of a
transnational hegemony through supranational structures'. The fact that the
nation states persist as part of this structure serves a number of the interests of
the TCC. The dissolution of the class compromise rooted in the nation state,
for example, is based on the power wielded by transnational capital over labour,
which has itself essentially also been globalised but remains structurally imprisoned within the nation state system. In short: 'the nation-state system boxes in
and controls populations within fixed physical (territorial) boundaries so that
their labor can be more efficiently exploited and their resistance contained'.[33]
The nation state system thus prevents, or at least makes considerably more difficult, the horizontal, transnational and political coalescence of any kind of
'transformative subject'.

The interconnections between transnational corporations

An extraordinary concentration of power can be seen in the world of transnational corporations, whose owners and senior executives form the core of the
TCC. Three researchers at the ETH Zurich studied a selection of some 43,000
leading transnational corporations and their interconnecting ownership structures. They found that almost 40 per cent of the economic value of these firms
was under the control of a closely interwoven core group of 147 companies via
a complex network of ownership arrangements. On account of the density of
the controlling power they call this group the 'super-entity'. A larger core of 737
firms in turn controls around 80 per cent of the economic value of the transnational companies in the study group. Over and above the question of what this
degree of concentration means for global financial stability, the study raises the
potential problem of distortion of competition and cartel formation. 'Remarkably', the report states, 'the existence of such a core in the global market was

---

33 Robinson (2004), loc. cit., pp. 99, 91, 77, 100, 88, 94, 101, 135, 106.

never documented before and thus, so far, no scientific study demonstrates or excludes that this international "super-entity" has ever acted as a bloc.' The national competition authorities had not yet concerned themselves with the issue.[34] James Glattfelder, one of the co-authors of the study, believes that 'we may need global anti-trust rules, which now exist only at national level, to limit over-connection among TNCs'. The publication of the report prompted the systems science researcher Yaneer Bar-Yam to suggest that 'firms should be taxed for excess interconnectivity to discourage this risk'.[35]

The need for a global antitrust authority

In spite of the significance of transnational corporations and the strong global interconnections between them, the efforts towards global anti-cartel legislation are making only very slow progress. This is not a marginal issue. The prevention and mitigation of anti-competitive practices is of fundamental importance in the regulation of global markets. As the Chicago law expert David J. Gerber shows in his book on global competition law, the problem of international cartels was already a dominant issue at the First International Economic Conference of the League of Nations in Geneva in 1927. Following the Second World War, the international community agreed in Havana in 1948 to establish the International Trade Organization (ITO), with a Charter which included competition law provisions for the prevention of 'exclusionary practices'. When the US government under President Harry Truman realised that the initiative had no chance in the US Congress, they dropped it from the legislative agenda in 1950. With that, the ITO was doomed to failure. Gerber stresses that the eventual failure of the ITO project 'was the result of numerous geo-political and national developments, none of which were related directly to the competition law project'.[36] However, it was resistance on the part of the USA which also torpedoed a proposal put forward in 1953 by the Economic and Social Council of the United Nations for a specialised international organization to monitor 'exclusionary practices' which was largely based on the relevant provisions of the Havana Charter. An attempt to determine international minimum competition law standards and a dispute resolution process also failed when it proved impossible to reach agreement at the WTO conference in Cancún seven years

34 Vitali, Stefania, James B. Glattfelder, and Stefano Battiston. 19 September 2011. 'The network of global corporate control'. PloS One, no. arXiv:1107.5728v2, p. 8.
35 Coghlan, Andy, and Debora MacKenzie. 19 October 2011. 'Revealed – the capitalist network that runs the world'. New Scientist, no. 2835.
36 See ch. 2 in Gerber, David J. 2010. Global Competition: Law, Markets and Globalization. Oxford, New York: Oxford University Press, pp. 20-54.

later, and was taken up on the WTO agenda after the Cold War was over, as part of the so-called Singapore issues of 1996. The USA did not see the need for it, and feared a restriction of its national sovereignty; many developing countries, on the other hand, with little experience of competition law, suspected that in the WTO framework it might be constructed in a way that would serve the interests of the transnational corporations based in the industrialised countries rather than exercising better control over them. Yet all these proposals were in any event a long way from creating an effective world antitrust authority. International competition law regulation applies only unilaterally, and can be enforced extraterritorially only at the nation state level, and in the case of the EU at the regional level too.

In light of the ongoing deepening of globalization, Gerber sees this situation as 'increasingly precarious' and 'frightening'.[37] The German law expert Dietmar Baetge addresses one of the principal issues in his book on the subject: the task of national antitrust legislation, he writes, 'lies only in protecting national interests, and not the interests of other states or of the international community'. The wellbeing of others is of no consideration. Nearly all countries, for example, exclude export cartels from their competition legislation. In view of the global interconnectedness of the markets, Baetge, who teaches law at the University of Applied Sciences in Wildau near Berlin, calls for 'a globally-based welfare paradigm' to underpin antitrust law, one that would take as its benchmark the optimum outcome for *all* countries involved and would aim to ensure that 'a broad spectrum of the world population', and ultimately the individual consumer, would benefit. Industrial policy concerns must be subordinated to those aims, and the interests of the developing countries must also be taken into account. At the same time, the burden placed on business by the patchwork of national regulations must be reduced. The objective of improving the welfare of consumers around the world which should underlie antitrust law, according to Baetge, is a global public good that can only be delivered by a 'central international authority'.[38] The antitrust experts Robert W. Hahn and Anne Layne-Farrar argue that 'a system that acknowledges the primacy of consumer welfare worldwide is the natural extension of a national antitrust authority aimed at promoting domestic welfare'. They see the international situation as comparable to that in the USA. In antitrust issues taken up by the US government, any US federal states involved will tend to pursue their own particularistic state interests rather than those of the federation, and will therefore tend not only to

---

37 Ibid., p. vii.
38 Baetge, Dietmar. 2009. Globalisierung des Wettbewerbsrechts. Eine internationale Wettbewerbsordnung zwischen Kartell- and Welthandelsrecht. Tübingen: Mohr Siebeck, pp. 103f., 108, 112, 471, 476, 109, 467.

delay and further complicate their resolution but to make the process more ex-
pensive. Furthermore, the individual states are much easier prey for lobbyists
than the federal authorities. Most experts who have studied the problem, they
say, therefore support restricting the role of the federal states in national antitrust proceedings. At the international level, the crucial difference is of course
that there are no global antitrust proceedings. 'The logical solution', the two
experts believe, 'would be a global antitrust authority with enforcement powers.'[39] This is not the right place to discuss whether it would be better to establish
such an authority as a new and independent organization or as, to take one option, a part of the WTO. It is worth stressing, however, that in any event it would
only be possible for it to claim adequate democratic legitimation if it were accountable to a global parliamentary body.

Global inequality and instability

The concentration of power at the very top, the emerging worldwide predominance of a transnational elite class and the unequal distribution of income and
wealth in the world are all of central importance for a detailed understanding
of the new 'Great Transformation'. Reducing global inequality is an important
goal of world domestic policy, and should contribute to political, financial and
social stability and to the creation of a fairer world order. The most frequently
used statistical measure of inequality is the Gini coefficient, which gives a value
between zero for a totally equal distribution (everybody has the same income)
and one hundred for a totally unequal distribution (one person has all the income). The statistical data on incomes, based on household surveys, fails to capture high incomes satisfactorily. If they form the only statistical basis for the
measurement of inequality, the results are disproportionately positive. In order
to obtain more realistic results, in more recent studies the estimated fortunes of
the super-rich are included in the calculations.[40] Research carried out for the
World Bank by Christoph Lakner and Branko Milanović concluded that, when
the fortunes of the super-rich are included, global inequality, contrary to earlier
assumptions, *did not decline at all* between 1988 and 2008. At around 75 on the
global Gini index, it remains at a very high level. The research found that over
the same time period 44 per cent of global growth in income had gone to the
richest five per cent of the world population.[41] A different measure of inequality

39   Hahn, Robert W., and Anne Layne-Farrar. 2002. 'Federalism in Antitrust'. Harvard Journal of Law & Public
     Policy (26) 3: 877–921, p. 917.
40   Vermeulen, Philip. July 2014. 'How Fat is the Top Tail of Wealth Distribution?' European Central Bank
     Working Paper Series No. 1692.
41   Lakner/Milanović, loc. cit., pp. 38, 48, 30.

much discussed recently is the 'Palma ratio', named after its originator, the economist Gabriel Palma. This shows the relationship between the incomes of the top ten per cent and the bottom forty per cent of a population. A Palma value of 5.0 therefore means that the top ten per cent receive five times more in income than the bottom forty per cent. It is seen as a great advantage over the more abstract Gini coefficients that the Palma ratio enables such concrete comparisons to be made. According to Lars Engberg-Pedersen of the Danish Institute for International Studies, the global Palma ratio stands at 32. For the USA, by comparison, the figure given is 1,852.[42]

The link between inequality and social instability has preoccupied thinkers and researchers since antiquity. A pioneering study of development in 71 countries between 1960 and 1985 came to the conclusion that income inequality is causally connected to socio-political instability. 'A large group of impoverished citizens', it found, 'facing a small and very rich group of well-off individuals is likely to become dissatisfied with the existing socio-economic status quo and demand radical changes, so that mass violence and illegal seizure of power are more likely than when income distribution is more equitable.'[43,44] Although this finding may not represent a current scientific consensus, Aristotle already regarded the connection as obvious. He put it in a nutshell more than two thousand years ago: 'everywhere inequality is a cause of revolution'.[45] In the view of Branko Milanović, 'locally, high inequality among communities and individuals is associated with political instability'. In turn, 'national instabilities tend to spill over to neighboring countries and even to the rest of the world'. In other words: 'high levels of global inequality make global chaos more likely'.[46]

Inequality as the cause of the financial crisis

Inequality, combined with factors such as the deregulation and inadequate supervision of the financial markets and systematic fraud on the part of numerous leading financial institutions such as the Bank of America, JPMorgan Chase and Goldman Sachs, also played a role in the financial crisis. The economist James

42   Engberg-Pedersen, Lars. March 2013. 'Development goals post 2015: Reduce inequality'. DIIS Policy Brief, Danish Institute for International Studies, p. 4.
43   Alesina, Alberto, and Roberto Perotti. 1996. 'Income distribution, political instability, and investment'. European Economic Review (40) 6: 1203–28.
44   An overview of the state of research was provided by: Giskemo, Grunhild Gram. 2012. 'Exploring the relationship between socioeconomic inequality, political instability and economic growth. Why do we know so little?' Chr. Michelsen Institute, CMI Working Papers.
45   Aristotle. 'Politics'. Transl. by Benjamin Jowett. The Internet Classics Archive. Book Five, Part I.
46   Milanović, The Haves and the Have-Nots, p. 161f.

K. Galbraith believes that 'in a deep sense inequality was the heart of the financial crisis'.[47] In the opinion of researchers at the IMF, the crisis was ultimately the result of a growing disparity, over several decades, between the income shares of the top earners and the rest of the population. The background to the crisis was largely given, in this view, by the fact that only a small proportion of the growing incomes of the top earners was spent on higher consumption, whereas the bulk went into savings. On the look-out for investment opportunities, this accumulated wealth flowed in the form of loans from the financial sector to the rest of the population, and especially to the low earners, who in this way were able, in spite of a reduction in their earnings, to maintain or even increase their consumption levels, at least for a while. However, as the IMF economists note, a 'large and highly persistent rise of workers' debt-to-income ratios generates financial fragility which eventually can lead to a financial crisis.'[48] This is putting it very cautiously. The growth in defaults on subprime mortgage loans in the USA caused a severe downturn in property prices and is thus regarded as one of the most important triggers of the financial crisis. From a macroeconomic perspective, inequality contributes to a decline in consumption and thus to slowing economic growth. 'The real cause of the crisis', according to Branko Milanović, 'lies in huge inequalities in income distribution that generated much larger investable funds than could be profitably employed. The political problem of insufficient economic growth of the middle class was then "solved" by opening the floodgates of cheap credit. And the opening of the credit floodgates, to placate the middle class, was needed because in a democratic system, an excessively unequal model of development cannot coexist with political stability.'[49]

The growth of capital investments and a global tax on capital

In the analysis put forward by the economist Thomas Piketty, inequality is a characteristic of every capitalist economic system, and the state has to intervene in order to cushion this tendency. According to his research results, which attracted great attention around the world, the rate of return on capital investments over long periods regularly and significantly exceeds the growth rate of general wealth creation in a country. This means that income from capital investments grows faster that that from paid employment. The greater one's

47 Galbraith, James K., Professor. Inequality and Instability: A Study of the World Economy Just Before the Great Crisis. New York: Oxford University Press, 2012, p. 4.
48 Kumhof, Michael, and Romain Rancière. 'Inequality, Leverage and Crises'. IMF Working Paper WP/10/268, November 2010, p. 3, 22.
49 Milanović (2011), loc. cit., p. 196.

wealth, the greater is the growth rate tendency. According to Piketty's data, the income of the top one per cent in the USA more than doubled between 1980 and 2010, while for the top 0.1 per cent it more than tripled, and for the top 0.01 per cent, more than quadrupled. Over the same period, the income of the bottom ninety per cent fell by nearly five per cent.[50] Inequality is thus increasing not only between the wealthy owners of capital and the rest of the population, but within the wealthy class itself. The primary purpose of the global tax on capital that Piketty proposes would be 'not to finance the social state but to regulate capitalism', he says. 'Without a global tax on capital or some similar policy, there is a substantial risk that the top centile's share of global wealth will continue to grow indefinitely.' The aim of the global tax on capital would be 'first to stop the indefinite increase of inequality of wealth, and second to impose effective regulation on the financial and banking system in order to avoid crises. To achieve these two ends, the capital tax must first promote democratic and financial transparency: there should be clarity about who owns what assets around the world.'[51] When critics of the proposal counter that global capital will simply slip through the fingers of such a tax, they have failed to understand its essential feature, which is precisely the introduction of a global and watertight tax system.[52]

The need for global public policy instruments and a World Parliament

A global basic income financed from global taxes, bringing about redistribution in favour of the poorest, is another potential instrument for the reduction of global inequality. In the fight against global inequality, it is a key insight that, without the structures of a world state, there are simply no practical policy options for addressing the problem. 'The political instruments for reducing income inequality between the richest 10 per cent and the poorest 40 per cent of the world's population do not exist. Progressive taxation, provision of social security, etc. are country-level instruments, and official development assistance comes no way near addressing global inequality', notes Lars Engberg-Pedersen.[53] And Branko Milanović writes that 'so long as there is no global govern-

---

50   Piketty, Thomas, and Emmanuel Saez. Table A6: Top fractiles income levels (including capital gains) in the United States (elsa.berkeley.edu/~saez/TabFig2010.xls).

51   Piketty, Thomas. 2014. Capital in the Twenty-First Century. Cambridge Massachusetts: Harvard University Press, pp. 518f.

52   Cowen, Tyler. 2014. 'Capital Punishment. Why a Global Tax on Wealth Won't End Inequality'. Foreign Affairs, May/June.

53   Engberg-Pedersen, Lars. March 2013. 'Development goals post 2015: Reduce inequality'. DIIS Policy Brief, Danish Institute for International Studies, p. 4.

ment, dissatisfaction with the level of inequality cannot be meaningfully expressed or translated into political action, the opinions cannot be conveyed to anyone, and, most important, there is no body who can act upon it'.[54]

A democratic world parliament would enable the discontent over the obscene inequality in the world to be articulated and therefore channelled into constructive pathways. But this can only succeed in defusing global socio-economic conflict if the world parliament is actually equipped with the power to pass serious measures against global inequality, or at least to contribute to passing them. This category certainly includes measures such as global taxes and a basic income, but also *macroeconomic regulation* at the global level. In an appeal for a 'democratic global Keynesianism', Heikki Patomäki, Professor for World Politics at the University of Helsinki, emphasizes that raising the purchasing power of the ordinary population, and thus global aggregate demand, must be a key economic goal. An increase in real wages, above all in the global South, can be achieved by making workers' rights and systematic worker organization 'the central goal of planetary economic policy for states and international organizations'. 'Regulation and maintenance of demand at a universal level', he argues, could be coordinated by a world parliament. 'From the standpoint of regulating global aggregate demand, the key question is how to create the kinds of institutional arrangements that would allow coordination between the economic policymakers of states and international organizations. One possible solution to this is a world parliament.'[55] Supporters of a global basic income, like Guy Standing, also see it as a macroeconomic instrument. In addition to a fixed basic sum, a basic income could include a variable element which could be adjusted in a direction counter-cyclical to trends in the overall economy, i.e. increased during recessions and reduced in boom periods.[56] The economist Mark Blyth and the hedge fund manager Eric Lonergan also made the point in the journal *Foreign Affairs* that direct financial grants made to the population can be a suitable means of stimulating the general economy. 'In the short term, such cash transfers could jump-start the economy. Over the long term, they could reduce dependence on the banking system for growth and reverse the trend of rising inequality', they wrote. Instead of seeking to influence aggregate demand via interest rates, central banks could institute direct cash transfers to the population as a monetary policy instrument. This would be especially effective in

54   Milanović (2011), loc. cit., p. 160.
55   Patomäki, Heikki. 2013. The Great Eurozone Disaster. From Crisis to Global New Deal. Transl. by James O'Connor. London and New York: Zed Books, pp. 179ff.
56   Standing, Guy. 2014. A Precariat Charter: From Denizens to Citizens. London, New York: Bloomsbury Academic, pp. 321f.

reducing inequality if the transfers were restricted to the bottom eighty per cent of households on the income scale. They pointed out that during his time as a professor of economics at Princeton, Ben Bernanke, the future Chair of the US central bank, the Federal Reserve, had recommended direct money transfers as a means of stimulating the Japanese economy in 1998. 'The transfers wouldn't cause damaging inflation, and few doubt that they would work. The only real question is why no government has tried them', they note.[57] Money transfers as part of a wider framework including an unconditional global basic income could be part of the macroeconomic toolbox of a world central bank.

A new global class compromise

From a broader perspective, what is needed is the establishment and institutionalization of *a new global class compromise*. The path to a fairer, a social world order will inevitably require reining in the dominance of the global elite. A world parliament provides the institutional platform for the ongoing task of organising a new settlement between the global elite and the rest of the wold population. David Rothkopf rightly makes the point that the answer cannot lie in a world *without* global elites. This is indeed unrealistic. However, a balance needs to be struck. 'Without the emergence of countervailing power centers to represent and ultimately institutionalize the will of the people at large', Rothkopf also observes, 'we will continue to get only partial solutions.' He argues that such a development ultimately serves the most fundamental interests of the superclass itself. Otherwise, 'crisis is virtually inevitable'; and only in this way might it be possible for them to 'avoid the fate of past elites that were brought down due to their overreaching greed, insensitivity and short-sightedness'.[58]

57   Blyth, Mark, and Eric Lonergan. 2014. 'Print Less but Transfer More'. Foreign Affairs (93) 5: 98–109, pp. 99, 103.
58   Rothkopf, David. 2008. Superclass: The Global Power Elite and the World They Are Making. London: Abacus, pp. 321-323.

23.
The debate on world government,
the age of entropy, and federalism

The global elite and the question of a world government

According to a survey carried out by the World Economic Forum in Davos, the business elite associated with the Forum includes 'severe income disparity' and 'global governance failure' among the ten greatest global risks which it believes need to be countered through 'long-term thinking'.[1] However, it is likely that general opinion in the group is actually closer to what David Rothkopf reports about the attitudes of the global elite. Referring to the idea of 'some global authority' that has 'serious taxing power', he writes that '[v]irtually everyone whom I interviewed about the superclass fell in the range of "not in my lifetime" and "never" on the question of progress toward real and effective institutions of international government'.[2] This is linked to the fact that the majority of the elites clearly regard the idea of a global structure of governance not only as something difficult to bring about but as something that is itself *not desirable*. A democratic world legal order, with a constitution, a clear structure and division of powers, clear rules and decision-making processes, is something that must strike much of the transnational elite as potentially obstructive. Of all the people on the planet, the members of the super-class must be the ones who would be affected last and least by a failure of global governance. They have the means to live wherever and however they please, entirely shielded from the existential problems that affect everyone else.

The economist Jeff Faux has accurately described the dilemma faced by the global elite gathered at the World Economic Forum, whom he terms the 'Party of Davos'. 'Having found a way to escape the social contract of the national community through the creation of a global economy, the Party of Davos is confronted with the "catch-22" of how to govern that economy in the absence of a legitimate global government', he writes. The problem is that promoting the 'freedom of capital' requires global rules, whereas a democratically constituted global government established for that purpose would restrain the 'freedom

---

1   World Economic Forum. 2014. Global Risks 2014. Geneva, p. 9.
2   Rothkopf, David. 2008. Superclass: The Global Power Elite and the World They Are Making. London: Abacus, p. 497.

of capital'. 'So the vacuum created by the absence of global government is being filled by transnational bureaucratic networks aimed at supervising the global market in a way that maximizes corporate investor freedom', according to Faux.[3]

One example of this is the transgovernmental networks of 'complex interdependence' described by Princeton University Professor Anne-Marie Slaughter, among others. She welcomes the fact that these networks 'perform many of the functions of a world government – legislation, administration, and adjudication – without the form', since a world government is 'both infeasible and undesirable'. 'The size and scope of such a government presents an unavoidable and dangerous threat to individual liberty', she writes, repeating an argument that has been advanced, in several variants, for over two hundred years. 'Further, the diversity of the peoples to be governed makes it almost impossible to conceive of a global demos. No form of democracy within the current global repertoire seems capable of overcoming these obstacles', she states. According to Slaughter, 'directly elected legislative assemblies at the regional level may yet have a valuable role to play in the world. Similar bodies on a global scale may also have a future, though it is hard now to imagine any that would be taken seriously.'[4]

One important regular meeting of the transnational class is the annual Bilderberg conference, which began in 1954. The participants always include more than one hundred prominent leading figures from the worlds of finance, business, international organizations and politics, mainly from the USA, Canada and Europe. Not much is known about the meetings, since the conferences are not public, no reports are published, and the participants mostly maintain a discreet silence. Speculation about them is therefore all the more rife. In 1976, in one of the first reports published about the Bilderberg conferences in Germany, it was stated that 'the Bilderbergers' discussed 'questions about the state of the international financial system, about the worldwide dismantling and removal of customs barriers and the free movement of capital and labour', and in addition they expressed a wish for 'some kind of world police, and also an international parliament'.[5] Whatever is actually discussed at the Bilderberg conferences, it surely does *not* include the creation of a world police or a democratic world parliament. What the transnational elite thinks of the project of a world parliament became apparent at a meeting of the Trilateral Commission in London in 2001. This body was founded in 1973 at the instigation of leading Bild-

3   Faux, Jeff. 2006. The Global Class War. Hoboken NJ: John Wiley & Sons, pp. 169f.
4   Slaughter, Anne-Marie. 2004. A new world order. Princeton University Press, pp. 4, 8, 124.
5   Wagner, Hans. 1976. 'Internationale Hochfinanz im Zwielicht: Der unheimliche Kreis um Prinz Bernhard'. Quick, no. 9, February, p. 27.

erberg participants such as the billionaire banker David Rockefeller. The commission brings together leading representatives of academia, business and politics from North America, Western Europe and Japan. For William Robinson, the establishment of the commission represents a marker of the 'politicization' of the 'transnational bourgeoisie', which ultimately led, through the 'Washington Consensus', to the creation of a programme for global liberalization of the markets.[6] At the core of one of the commission's first reports, in 1975, was a critique of democracy. Its authors bemoaned the fact that an 'excess of democracy' and of political participation, and an accompanying 'delegitimation of authority', was diminishing the governability of the USA, the countries of Europe and Japan.[7] At the conference in London there was agreement that a global parliament was 'quite obviously nonsense', as one of the participants put it. In particular, it was said that the European Parliament was not a suitable model for the global level. The UN, it was argued, was not a supranational project, and governments were of course already under the supervision and control of the national parliaments. It was explicitly stated that 'there is (and should be) room for institutions that are outside the realm of direct popular control'.[8] Joseph Nye, one of the co-chairs of the commission, is one of the originators of the concept of 'complex interdependence' and has done much to popularize it, and it is hardly surprising if he believes that a world government or federal power at the global level is no answer to the problem of how the globalised world ought to be governed. 'Rather than thinking of a hierarchical world government', Nye believes, 'we should think of networks of governance crisscrossing and coexisting with a world divided formally into sovereign states.'[9]

The spectre of a global Leviathan

In a critique of Karl Jaspers' observations on the question of a world state, Hannah Arendt (1906 to 1975), whose own research focus was on totalitarianism, wrote that a sovereign world state would represent the greatest threat to human freedom. She was thinking of sovereignty in the classical sense, which presumes

6 Robinson, William I. 2004. A Theory of Global Capitalism. Production, Class, and State in a Transnational World. Baltimore and London: Johns Hopkins University Press, pp. 113f.
7 Crozier, Michael, Samuel P. Huntington, and Joji Watanuki. 1975. The Crisis of Democracy. Report on the Governability of Democracies to the Trilateral Commission. New York University Press, pp. 113, 161ff.
8 Nye, Joseph S., Jessica P. Einhorn, Béla Kádár, Hisashi Owada, Luis Rubio, and Soogil Young. 2003. The 'Democracy Deficit' in the Global Economy: Enhancing the Legitimacy and Accountability of Global Institutions. Report to the Trilateral Commission, The Triangle Papers Vol. 57. Washington, Paris, Tokyo: Trilateral Commission, pp. 33ff., 37.
9 Nye, Joseph S. 2002. The Paradox of American Power. Oxford, New York et al: Oxford University Press, pp. 104f.

a monopoly on force. 'No matter what form a world government with central-ized power over the whole globe might assume', Arendt wrote, 'the very notion of one sovereign force ruling the whole earth, holding the monopoly of all means of violence, unchecked and uncontrolled by other sovereign powers, is not only a forbidding nightmare of tyranny, it would be the end of all political life as we know it.'[10] However, at the same time she acknowledged that simply pointing out the dangers of such a world state was not a solution. Arendt be-lieved that the classical concept of sovereignty had to be abandoned, as she set out in 'On Revolution', since 'in the realm of human affairs sovereignty and tyranny are the same'.[11] Like Jaspers, she arrived finally at the conclusion that the solution lay in a *federal world order*. 'Politically, the new fragile unity [of mankind] brought about by technical mastery over the earth can be guaranteed only within a framework of universal mutual agreements, which eventually would lead into a world-wide federated structure.'[12]

However, the image of a global Leviathan is often used as a quick and easy way to brush aside the idea of a world state. Nothing is less desirable, wrote UN Secretary-General Kofi Annan in his report to the Millennium Assembly in the year 2000, than 'images of world government, of centralized bureaucratic behe-moths trampling on the rights of people and states'.[13] But this is to attack a straw man, as there is nobody who seriously advocates a global centralized state. 'It is absurd to conceive a world government as a form of state endowed with the same characteristics that the sovereign, independent and mutually competing individual states had', as the federalist and political scientist Lucio Levi pointed out.[14] What is really going on here, however, is the rejection of *any form of over-arching hierarchical order* at the global level. In response, political scientists like Volker Rittberger speak of 'heterarchical world governance', meaning some-thing between anarchy and hierarchy. The term describes 'a dense net of insti-tutions of world governance which are created and maintained by public and private actors to deal in a regulated way with trans-sovereign problems by means of *horizontal* political coordination and cooperation' (emphasis added).[15]

10 Arendt, Hannah. 1995. Men in Dark Times. San Diego, New York, London: Harcourt Brace & Company, pp. 81f.
11 Id. 1965. On Revolution. London: Penguin Books.
12 Arendt (1995), loc. cit., p. 93.
13 Annan, Kofi. 2000. We the Peoples. The Role of the United Nations in the 21st Century. Report of the Secre-tary-General. A/54/2000. New York: United Nations, para. 42, p. 7.
14 Levi, Lucio, Giovanni Finizio, und Nicola Vallinoto (ed.). 2014. The democratization of international insti-tutions: first international democracy report. Milton Park et al.: Routledge, p. 20.
15 Rittberger, Volker, Andreas Kruck, and Anne Romund. 2010. Grundzüge der Weltpolitik. Theorie und Em-pirie des Weltregierens. 1st ed. Wiesbaden: VS Verlag für Sozialwissenschaften, p. 315.

'[T]he very notion of centralizing hierarchies', Annan's report continued, 'is it-self an anachronism in our fluid, highly dynamic and extensively networked world — an outmoded remnant of nineteenth century mindsets.'[16] This kind of thinking may be consistent with the ruling ideology of 'complex interdependence' and global governance, but that does not make it any the less disconcerting.

Hierarchical order and complexity

A key insight offered by the history of evolution is that hierarchies developed as a natural way of *governing complexity*. The influential social scientist and Nobel laureate for economics Herbert A. Simon (1916 to 2001) noted that '[i]t is a commonplace observation that nature loves hierarchies'.[17] Simon was an early pioneer of the study of the architecture of complex biological, physical and social systems. 'Empirically,' he wrote, 'a large proportion of the complex systems we observe in nature exhibit hierarchic structure. On theoretical grounds we might expect complex systems to be hierarchies in a world in which complexity had to evolve from simplicity. In their dynamics, hierarchies have a property, near decomposability, that greatly simplifies their behavior.'[18] What Simon terms 'near decomposability' indicates that subsystems can be almost independent, and that the interaction of elements within the subsystems is more intensive than that between them. The nub of the matter, however, is that despite this there is an ordered hierarchical nesting of systems and their interactions, as well as an overarching governance.[19]

Different types of hierarchies

The philosopher and author Arthur Koestler suggested in his 1967 book 'The Ghost in the Machine' that the constituent parts of the nested hierarchies found everywhere should be called 'holons'. The term is intended to make it clear that the elements of a hierarchical order are always simultaneously both a part and a whole. 'Organisms and societies', Koestler wrote, 'are multi-levelled hierarchies of semi-autonomous sub-wholes branching into sub-wholes of a lower

16 Annan, loc. cit., para. 42, p. 7.
17 Simon, Herbert A. 1973. 'The Organization of Complex Systems'. In: Hierarchy Theory. The Challenge of Complex Systems, ed. by Howard H. Pattee, 1–27. New York: George Braziller, p. 5.
18 Id. 1962. 'The Architecture of Complexity'. Proceedings of the American Philosophical Society (106) 6: 467–82, pp. 481f.
19 Id. 2002. 'Near decomposability and the speed of evolution'. Industrial and corporate change (11) 3: 587–99, pp. 595f.

order, and so on. The term "holon" has been introduced to refer to these intermediary entities which, relative to their subordinates in the hierarchy, function as self-contained wholes; relative to their superordinates as dependent parts. This dichotomy of "wholeness" and "partness", of autonomy and dependence, is inherent in the concept of hierarchic order.'[20] To emphasize this connection, the term 'holarchies' is sometimes used for hierarchies.

The scepticism towards hierarchies derives in part from the experience of higher levels having a tendency to become too dominant or even oppressive towards lower levels. Totalitarian systems are characterised by a monopoly on power at the highest level, meaning that all lower levels are in principle downgraded to mere recipients of orders. The US American author Ken Wilber, however, emphasizes that '[t]he existence of pathological hierarchies does not damn the existence of hierarchies in general'.[21] He cites in support the distinction drawn by the systems scientist and lawyer Riane Eisler between domination and actualization hierarchies. 'The term *domination hierarchies* describes hierarchies based on force or the express or implied threat of force. Such hierarchies are very different from the types of hierarchies found in progressions from lower to higher orderings of functioning – such as the progression from cells to organs in living organisms, for example. These types of hierarchies may be characterized by the term *actualization hierarchies* because their function is to maximize the organism's potentials', Eisler writes in the book 'Chalice and the Blade'.[22] The challenge lies in creating a *planetary actualization hierarchy*. The key to this is a federal and democratic structure. One organizational principle of the functional relationship between socio-political holons on different levels is that of subsidiarity. This requires that tasks and competences should be located at the lowest possible level where they can still be effectively carried out. For the main challenges of world domestic policy, however, on account of their global character, only the planetary level will do.

The principle of subsidiarity

The philosopher Christoph Horn, who teaches at the University of Bonn, believes that 'a tiered system of powers based on the principle of subsidiarity' is a 'key means of nullifying the fear that a world state holds for people'. 'Consideration should for example be given to a decentralization arranged in tiers from World State – continental units – national and regional units – finally down to

20 Koestler, Arthur. 1967. The Ghost in the Machine. London: Pan Books, p. 76.
21 Wilber, Ken. 2000. Sex, Ecology, Spirituality: The Spirit of Evolution. 2nd ed. rev. Boston Mass.: Shambhala, p. 30.
22 Cit. from ibid., pp. 30f.; see also Riane Eisler, 1987. Chalice and the Blade. San Francisco: Harper, p. 205.

local units. The bulk of current competences could thus remain at the national, regional and even local levels; and thus a considerably stronger degree of delegation of decision-making competences down to small units could be considered than is presently the case in contemporary states. In this way, the structure of a world state – far from requiring a massive bureaucracy – could be precisely what leads to a transformation of political decision-making along participatory and democratic lines', Horn argued. A world state could thus, and perhaps better than any other structure, 'by means of an appropriate division into federal sub-states and the protection of minorities ensure adequate legal protection for group interests and identities'.[23]

The fragmentation of global governance and of international law

The system of global governance and international law is marked by a fragmentation unmitigated by any form of overarching hierarchy, harmonization, governance or coordination. This also broadly applies to the United Nations, with its dozens of programmes, specialised agencies, commissions, secretariats, funds and other 'entities'. Its coherence and governability have always been considered inadequate. As Thomas G. Weiss reports, the UN's development work was described in 1969 already as a 'prehistoric monster' in an official evaluation. Even forty years later, this 'lumbering dinosaur' was no better suited to the conditions prevailing in the 21st century. It would be difficult, Weiss thought, to imagine 'a better design for futile complexity'.[24] More recently, the UN High-level Panel on Global Sustainability noted in a report that '[w]hile institutional fragmentation may begin at the national level, it is endemic at the international level'. In order to achieve sustainable development, the report said, '[w]e must overcome the legacy of fragmented institutions established around single-issue "silos"'.[25] The German law expert Dieter Grimm, a former member of the constitutional court, gave an accurate description of the characteristics of world governance with regard to the issue of putting the international use of force by states on a constitutional footing. 'There is no coherent form for the exercise of force by the world community', he wrote. 'Rather, there

23 Horn, Christoph. 1996. 'Philosophische Argumente für einen Weltstaat'. Allgemeine Zeitschrift für Philosophie 21: 229–51, p. 244.
24 Weiss, Thomas G. 2009. 'What Happened to the Idea of World Government?' International Studies Quarterly 53:253–71, p. 255.
25 United Nations High-level Panel on Global Sustainability (ed.). March 2012. 'Resilient people, resilient planet: a future worth choosing. Report of the High-level Panel of the Secretary-General on Global Sustainability'. A/66/700, pp. 8, 74.

are individual, functionally specific, publicly authorised bodies which are un-connected to each other and which possess only ad hoc powers. Their legal ba-ses are equally ad hoc and do not add up to a systematic and coherent world legal order. The currently prevailing world order', according to Grimm, 'is in-stead reminiscent of the medieval order with its widely dispersed forms of ad hoc powers delegated to independent holders, which similarly did not add up to a basis for a constitutional order.'[26]

The fragmentation of the international system of states is mirrored in the system of international law. In an influential report commissioned by the UN International Law Commission, the Austrian international law expert Gerhard Hafner warned in the year 2000 against its increasing fragmentation. '[E]xisting international law does not consist of one homogenous legal order, but mostly of different partial systems, producing an "unorganized system"', he wrote, and referred to a 'disintegration of the legal order'. He identified the causes as being specialization in differing autonomous legal regimes, differing norm structures, parallel or competing regulations within the same area of law, the extension of the application of international law to new areas, and overlapping and contradic-tory subsystems of secondary law. But the first and perhaps most important cause identified by Hafner, at that time a member of the International Law Commis-sion, was *the lack of centralised organs*. 'Fragmentation stems from the nature of international law as a law of coordination instead of subordination as well as from the lack of centralized institutions which would ensure homogeneity and con-formity of legal regulations', he wrote.[27] For Tomer Broude, an international law specialist teaching in Jerusalem, the problem of norm fragmentation is directly linked to the problem of 'authority fragmentation'. '[They] are the warp and weft of the complex fabric that is international law', he writes. '[L]egal principles of normative integration are not merely technical, lawyerly methods for producing consistent legal outcomes. They have a political meaning for the entire interna-tional system's structure of authority and governance', he writes. Their result 'is a trend towards greater centralization and/or harmonization of authority.'[28] But the use of the term 'fragmentation' here should not be taken to mean that a once uniform and coherent system is now falling apart. International law has by its

---

26 Grimm, Dieter. 2006. 'Transnationale Macht - konstitutionalisierbar?'. In: Vernunft oder Macht: zum Verhältnis von Philosophie and Politik, ed. by Otfried Höffe, 161–70. Tübingen: Francke, p. 168.

27 Hafner, Gerhard. 2000. 'Risks Ensuing from Fragmentation of International Law'. In: Report of the Interna-tional Law Commission on the work of its fifty-second session, Official Records of the General Assembly, Fifty-fifth session, suppl. no. 10, A/55/10, 143–50, pp. 143, 147, 145.

28 Broude, Tomer. 2008. 'Fragmentation(s) of International Law: On Normative Integration as Authority Allo-cation'. In: The Shifting Allocation of Authority in International Law, ed. by Tomer Broude and Yuval Shany, 99–120. Oxford and Portland, Oregon: Hart Publishing, pp. 104, 110.

nature always been fragmentary. The international law specialist Walter Jenks, later Director-General of the ILO, pointed out as early as 1953 that '[i]n the absence of a world legislature with a general mandate, law-making treaties are tending to develop in a number of historical, functional and regional groups which are separate from each other and whose mutual relationships are in some respects analogous to those of separate systems of municipal law'.[29]

Coherent world law and a World Parliament

It is precisely such a world legislature that must form the starting point and the centre of a coherent and harmonised world legal system which can establish clear and universally binding hierarchies of norms and prioritization rules. A hierarchization into constitutional primary law and secondary or delegated legislation is indispensable. An essential basic principle will be that world law takes precedence over international law. In areas regulated by world law, it must therefore be able to intervene directly in international law. This will involve bringing together in the world legislature hitherto disconnected and divergent political regulation processes within network governance and international institutions, and applying to all of those processes a system of global political balancing, preference-setting and prioritization. Using Anne-Marie Slaughter's terminology, one could speak of the world parliament having the responsibility to 'aggregate' the existing but fragmented elements into a coherent world order. From the elevated vantage point of a historian, Charles Maier of Harvard University attacked the concept of 'governance' as 'a utopia of the academic administrative elite', and emphasized this point in connection with a lack of state control. 'The concept of governance, which enjoyed such popularity at the end of the 20th century and which still today holds such a fascination for social scientists and foundations, was and is testament to the hope for a government without "statehood" – as if politics in future could be relieved of the task of gathering together different preferences and finally opting for one or the other, and could instead function via consensus and the power of rational debate.'[30]

The bewildering world order and the 'age of entropy'

Politically, too, the world order is characterised by confusion and complexity. Samuel Huntington wrote in 1999 that global politics 'has thus moved from the

---

29 Jenks, Wilfred. 1953. 'The Conflict of Law-Making Treaties'. Brit. Yearbook of Int. Law 30: 401–53, p. 403.
30 Maier, Charles S. 2012. 'Leviathan 2.0: Die Erfindung moderner Staatlichkeit'. In: Geschichte der Welt. 5, Weltmärkte and Weltkriege 1870-1945, ed. by Akira Iriye and Jürgen Osterhammel, 34–286. München: Beck, p. 285.

bipolar system of the Cold War through a unipolar moment - highlighted by the Gulf War - and is now passing through one or two uni-multipolar decades before it enters a truly multipolar 21st century'.[31] Richard Haass, President of the Council on Foreign Relations, noted ten years later that we would have to *completely abandon* the concept of geopolitical polarity as the main explanatory model for the world order. At first sight, according to Haass, the world may appear to have become multipolar, with China, the EU, India, Japan, Russia and the USA as the most important powers. In fact, however, there are far more centres of power, some of which are not even nation states. The power and pre-dominance of the states is being challenged in the course of globalization by regional and global governmental organizations as well as a multitude of NGOs and companies. 'The principal characteristic of twenty-first-century interna-tional relations is turning out to be nonpolarity', writes Haass; that is, 'a world dominated not by one or two or even several states but rather by dozens of ac-tors possessing and exercising various kinds of power.' If left to itself, this 'non-polar world' would become ever more chaotic with time.[32] The political scientist Ian Bremmer, founder of the Eurasia Group consultancy, speaks of a 'G-Zero world' to describe the disappearance of any single state or even group of states with the capacity to provide effective leadership for the international system. 'Who will lead?' he asks rhetorically, only to immediately provide the answer himself. 'No one.' Neither the G7, nor the G20, nor any other forum.[33] For Stew-art Patrick of the Council on Foreign Relations, 'what really marks the contem-porary era is not the absence of multilateralism but its astonishing diversity'. In the world of the 'G-X', as Patrick calls it, collective action 'is no longer focused solely, or even primarily, on the UN and other universal, treaty-based institu-tions, nor even on a single apex forum such as the G-20. Rather, governments have taken to operating in many venues simultaneously, participating in a be-wildering array of issue-specific networks and partnerships whose membership varies based on situational interests, shared values, and relevant capabilities'.[34]

The US American political scientist Randall L. Schweller believes that the world order is transitioning into an 'age of entropy'. In contrast to Stewart Pat-rick, however, he finds little positive to say about the associated 'multilateralism à la carte' and disaggregated network governance. 'What some call global gov-

31 Huntington, Samuel P. 1999. 'The Lonely Superpower'. Foreign Affairs (78) 2: 35–49, p. 37.
32 Haass, Richard N. 2008. 'The Age of Nonpolarity - What Will Follow U.S. Dominance'. Foreign Affairs (87) 3: 44-56.
33 Bremmer, Ian. 2012. Every Nation for Itself: Winners and Losers in a G-Zero World. London: Portfolio Pen-guin, p. 4.
34 Patrick, Stewart. 2014. 'The Unruled World'. Foreign Affairs (93) 1: 58–73, p. 62.

ernance', says Schweller, 'is little more than a spaghetti bowl of clashing agreements brokered within and among thirty thousand or so international organizations of varying significance.' It is practically impossible for states to find out where international responsibility for any given problem actually lies. The reason for this, according to Schweller, is that as a consequence of growing entropy there is no central international authority over anything any longer. 'No one will know where international authority resides because it will not reside anywhere; and without authority, there can be no governance', writes Schweller. And he complains that 'the labyrinthine structure of global governance is more complex than most of the problems it is supposed to be solving'.[35] As Dirk Messner long ago established, 'it must not be overlooked that the architecture of global governance can itself become a global problem on account of its complexity'.[36] This point has undoubtedly now been reached.

The entropic decline of world civilization?

The current system of 'heterarchic' world governance is highly ineffective and inefficient. It adds to the complexity of the world system rather than guiding or reducing it. This could lead to entropic decline, as described by the US American futurologist Hazel Henderson in 1978, writing about industrial societies. She believes that on account of increasing complexity industrial societies could at some point reach an 'entropy state'. 'The entropy state', she writes, 'is a society at the stage where complexity and interdependence have reached the point where the transaction costs that are generated equal or exceed the society's productive capabilities. In a manner analogous to the phenomenon that occurs in physical systems, the society slowly winds down of its own weight and complexity.' This is linked in her view to the fact that the unproductive costs of social governance and coordination, and the costs of the externalities arising, become too large. 'We seem unwilling to come to terms with the fact that each increase in the order of magnitude of technological mastery and managerial control requires and inevitably leads to a concomitant order of magnitude of government coordination and control.'[37] This reasoning can be applied to world civilization as a whole. Ten years later, in an influential study of 'The Collapse of Complex Societies', the US American anthropologist and historian Joseph Tainter also came to the conclusion that the growth of complexity brings

35 Schweller, Randall L. 2014. Maxwell's Demon and the Golden Apple: Global Discord in the New Millennium. Baltimore, Maryland: Johns Hopkins University Press, pp. 118, 23.
36 Messner, Dirk. 1998. 'Architektur der Weltordnung'. Internationale Politik, November: 17–24, p. 23.
37 Henderson, Hazel. 1996 [1978]. Creating Alternative Futures. The End of Economics. First Kumarian Press Printing. West Hartford CT: Kumarian Press, 1996, p. 83f.

with it a fundamental problem. According to his analysis, it lies in the nature of human societies that mastering problems inevitably involves an increase in socio-political complexity. This is brought about by the cumulative expansion of bureaucracy and organizational structures, or perhaps by ever-increasing social and hierarchical differentiation. This brings in turn a growing burden of costs and taxes for the productive population. The economic benefits that accompany this growth in complexity steadily decrease, and beyond a certain point of social development they can tip over into the negative. This means that what Henderson describes as 'the entropy state' has been reached. In this phase, a collapse in the form of socio-political disintegration is – despite its disastrous consequences – an economically explicable and even inevitable development in Tainter's view, unless new sources of productivity growth can be tapped. A collapse of civilization would consist in a forced return to less complex organizational stages. Tainter emphasizes in his study that under the prevailing conditions of a complex world civilization, the isolated collapse of a single society is no longer possible. Should another collapse happen, it will be *on a global scale*. 'World civilization will disintegrate as a whole.' Tainter fears that today's world civilization, like earlier societies that did collapse, does not have the capacity to solve its problems. 'If we are to escape nuclear annihilation, if we control pollution and population, and manage to circumvent resource depletion, will our fate then be sealed by the high cost and low marginal return that these things will require?' he asks.[38]

World federalism as a means of reducing complexity

However, the question arises whether these costs would really be so high at a higher socio-political level of organization – that is, at the level of world-state structures – or whether they might not in fact be lower than they are today. One important objective of the global programme of integration that would accompany a world parliament is the harmonization, reorganization and de-fragmentation of today's system of global governance within a democratic world-state framework. A world federal order with a global legislative system would contribute to *a reduction in complexity* and to *lower transaction costs*. It represents a hierarchical consolidation of the civilizational process at a higher systemic level. The reason why world civilization is threatening to reach the 'entropy state' is that the current, inter-state based system by its very nature *cannot* de-

38 Tainter, Joseph A. 1988. The Collapse of Complex Societies. Cambridge University Press, p. 213, see also pp. 118, 123, 127, 195.

liver efficient global solutions to problems at low transactional cost. The fragmented 'heterarchical' structure of global governance, based on the paradigm of national sovereignty without any central control, is inherently incapable of it. One example of transaction costs that also lower productive capacity is the immense expenditure on the military and on armaments, which arises not least out of the structure of the system. It is a result of the fact that it has not yet proved possible, in spite of all the accretion of subsequent social layers, to entirely move beyond the phase of anarchism. The creation of a world peace order, as sketched out in this book, would make it possible to do without much of this expenditure. The increase in inequality coupled with the growing accumulation of capital by the super-rich, a process facilitated by the system, represents an additional illustration of how productive forces are being held back without any possibility of effective central countervailing policies.

A world state as a taboo topic

Few people are willing to speak openly about the need for world state structures. It is not rare for us to hear from academics that, although they find the idea of a world parliament interesting and in principle right, they don't want to risk opening themselves up to criticism. The horizon of the debate over the form of world governance has narrowed sharply. In the keynote speech already referred to by the political scientist Thomas G. Weiss on the fiftieth anniversary of the International Studies Association, he observed that 'the idea of world government has been banned in sober and sensible discussions of global affairs and certainly is absent from classrooms'. In drastic words, he bemoaned before the assembled representatives of the discipline 'the abject poverty of our current thinking'. Following the Second World War, an intensive engagement with the issue had been part of the mainstream, he argued; however, 'currently a world federal government or even elements of one is not only old-fashioned, it is commonly thought to be the preserve of lunatics'. Yet Weiss reminds his audience that even realists such as Hans Morgenthau and Reinhold Niebuhr believed that a world state was 'logically necessary'.[39] In his 2011 book 'The Realist Case for Global Reform', the political scientist William E. Scheuerman set out the argument that there was an 'important programmatic overlap' between leading representatives of the realist school of international relations and world federalism.[40]

---

39   Weiss, loc. cit., p. 261ff.
40   Scheuerman, William E. 2011. The realist case for global reform. Cambridge: Polity Press.

The teetering paradigm of intergovernmentalism

The mainstream today suffers from its readiness to content itself with describing the state of things as they are. The modern nation state, and the associated idea of sovereignty, remains the hub around which mainstream thinking revolves. The resulting conception of the necessarily intergovernmental nature of world governance can be classified in line with Thomas S. Kuhn's theory of scientific revolutions as a paradigm. Deviations from the paradigm are neither conceived, recognised or desired by the mainstream. Long-term reflection on alternative ways of organising world governance is therefore of no interest. 'It is not a diagnosis which is lacking; what needs to be explained is the timidity towards a perspective which would open up a path, however difficult to pursue, towards a transnational world domestic policy', Jürgen Habermas wrote, referring to the social sciences. 'A discipline of sociology which almost always considers 'society' as a unit defined by the nation state, that is, as a national society, will have severe conceptual difficulty in dealing with an entity as weakly structured politically as the "world society".'[41] It may be correct that the 'heterarchical model', as Volker Rittberger and colleagues write, 'is best placed to explain many of the empirically observable forms of world governance'.[42] However, the dominant paradigmatic framework will struggle to recognize and explain the characteristic processes of the formation of a global state. Although Rittberger regards a world state as an unlikely outcome of the socio-evolutionary process, and opposes it anyway, he himself wrote in 1973 that 'the world-state model must be exposed to tentative empirical testing at least insofar as there may or may not exist discernible trends in present-day world politics that point toward the eventual establishment of a world state'.[43]

In his famous work 'The Civilizing Process', published first in 1939 and then in a revised edition in 1969, Norbert Elias adopted a long-term perspective on the development of the structures of personality and society since about the 8th century CE. The 'forces of social interweaving' he describes there, which ever since the 'point of utmost feudal disintegration' have created pressure for the integration of ever larger socio-political associations, are seen as still operating today and now spanning a system of interdependence 'embracing the entire inhabited earth'. 'The competitive tension between states,' wrote Elias, 'given the pressures which our social structure brings with it, can be resolved only after a

---

41 Habermas, Jürgen. 1998. 'Jenseits des Nationalstaats? Bemerkungen zu Folgeproblemen der wirtschaftlichen Globalisierung'. In: Politik der Globalisierung, ed. by Ulrich Beck, 67–84. Frankfurt: Suhrkamp, p. 79.
42 Rittberger et al., loc. cit., p. 711.
43 Rittberger, Volker. 1973. Evolution and International Organization. Toward a New Level of Sociopolitical Integration. Den Haag: Nijhoff, p. 47.

long series of violent or non-violent trials of strength have established monopolies of force, and central organizations for larger dominions, within which
many of the smaller ones, "states", can grow together in a more balanced unity.'
Although it was impossible to foresee the timeframe and the make-up of the
'larger hegemonial units', the direction of the processes of interweaving was
clear: the creation of 'a worldwide monopoly of physical force' and 'a single
central political institution' for the Earth.[44] Referring to long-term processes of
state development, Elias bemoaned the fact that these were obviously 'developmental processes of such duration as to be beyond the reach of the contemporary sociological imagination, which is focused on much shorter-term perspectives'.[45] Not much has changed with regard to this finding. Yet in view of the
ever more apparent failure of global governance, doubts continue to grow over
whether the dominant perspective will be adequate. The model of a paradigmatic crisis as described by the philosopher of science Thomas S. Kuhn can be
clearly seen here. 'Political revolutions', he wrote, 'are inaugurated by a growing
sense, often restricted to a segment of the political community, that existing
institutions have ceased adequately to meet the problems posed by an environment that they have in part created. In much the same way, scientific revolutions are inaugurated by a growing sense, again often restricted to a narrow
subdivision of the scientific community, that an existing paradigm has ceased
to function adequately in the exploration of an aspect of nature to which that
paradigm itself had previously led the way. In both political and scientific development the sense of malfunction that can lead to crisis is prerequisite to revolution.'[46] In this instance, modern international law and the existing Westphalian international order are without doubt a product of the idea of the sovereign
nation state, of that idea which continues to serve the discourse as paradigm.
This paradigm is no longer sufficient for an understanding of the world order
or the direction in which it might develop. In addition, the failure of the Westphalian order to meet the global challenges is the source of ever growing criticism. In an article published in 1999, the British social scientist Susan Strange
encapsulated this in the pithy term 'Westfailure System'. 'We have to escape
and resist the state-centrism inherent in the analysis of conventional international relations', she wrote. 'It is not our job, in short, to defend or excuse the
Westphalian system.'[47]

---

44 Elias, Norbert. 2000. The Civilizing Process: Sociogenetic and Psychogenetic Investigations. Transl. by Ed-
    mund Jephcott. Rev. ed. Oxford; Malden, MA: Blackwell, pp. 436-438, 446.
45 Id. 1984. What Is Sociology. Rev. ed. New York: Columbia University Press.
46 Kuhn, Thomas S. 1970. Structure of Scientific Revolutions. 2nd ed. Chicago: University of Chicago Press, p. 92.
47 Strange, Susan. 1999. 'The Westfailure System'. Review of International Studies (25) 3: 345–54.

2015 saw the founding of the international World Government Research Network. It was joined by leading academics in the field including Daniele Archibugi, Richard Falk, Thomas Pogge, William E. Scheuerman, Thomas G. Weiss and Alexander Wendt. The two coordinators of the network, Luis Cabrera of Griffith University in Brisbane, Australia, and James Thompson of Hiram College in Ohio, wrote on the website that there had not been so many academics giving serious thought to global integration since the 1940s. The founding of this network underlines the fact that the debate over a world government is beginning to acquire a new quality, and can no longer simply be dismissed.

The standard reactionary arguments

However, the problem is not just academic or intellectual. It would be a mistake to believe that the debate over the form that world governance should take is conducted entirely free of influence by interest groups. Rather, the debate reveals distinct traits of what might be termed a *hegemonic discourse*. It is not of course mere coincidence that the paradigm of intergovernmentalism and the fiction of the sovereignty of the nation state are defended most vigorously precisely by the members of the transnational elites. The rhetoric that emanates from that quarter against the idea of a world democracy ultimately serves the purpose of making it appear that there is no alternative to the current system and condition of world governance. This is often accompanied by recourse to the perversity thesis and the jeopardy thesis. Fear of the supposed danger of a tyrannical world state is thus instrumentalized and extended to *any* form a world state might take. A democratic, federal world state, so the argument runs, may be a noble aim, but it always bears within it the potential to degenerate into tyranny, which would pose a *much greater threat* to democracy and freedom than existed before. As the sociologist Albert O. Hirschman showed, this line of argumentation – the perversity and jeopardy theses – is among 'the major polemical postures or maneuvers likely to be engaged in by those who set out to debunk and overturn "progressive" policies and movements of ideas'. Reactionary rhetoric of this kind, according to Hirschman, has been used since the 19th century to oppose individual human rights, the universal franchise and democracy, as well as the development of the welfare state. Now it is being directed against a globalization of these hard-won achievements through a world state. In his book 'The Rhetoric of Reaction', Hirschman examined the typical rhetorical devices of reactionary argumentation. 'According to the *perversity* thesis', he explains, 'any purposive action to improve some feature of the political, social, or economic order only serves to exacerbate the condition one wishes to remedy. The *futility* thesis holds that attempts at social transformation will be unavailing, that they will simply fail to "make a dent." Finally, the *jeopardy* thesis argues that the cost of the proposed change or reform is too high as it endangers some previous, precious accomplishment.'[48] The fact that hundreds of millions of people, if not the majority of the world population, are *already now* subjected to structural violence embedded in the global system, and that the failure of global governance puts at risk the existing level of world civilization, is simply disregarded in this line of argument. The concept of structural violence was introduced by Johan Galtung. Following Galtung, structural violence is violence which cannot be attributed directly to one single actor and which, on account of its permanent presence and 'noiselessness', is often not recognised as such even by its victims. This violence, Galtung sums up, 'is built into the system and expresses itself in unequal power relations and consequently in unequal life chances ... When people starve at a time when it could objectively be avoided, then violence is being committed, regardless of whether a clear subject-object relation obtains.' The enabling condition of structural violence, according to Galtung, is social injustice, and particularly the unequal distribution of power.[49] A democratic world state and a world parliament are intended to serve the goal of *eliminating the existing global barbarity.*

48 Hirschman, Albert O. 1991. The Rhetoric of Reaction. Cambridge, London: The Belknap Press of Harvard University Press, pp. 6f.
49 Galtung, Johan. 1975. Strukturelle Gewalt. Reinbek: Rowohlt, pp. 12f., 19.

24.
The third democratic transformation
and the global democratic deficit

'In perusing the pages of our history', wrote the lawyer and historian Alexis de Tocqueville in the introduction to his 1835 work 'Democracy in America', 'we shall scarcely meet with a single great event, in the lapse of seven hundred years, which has not turned to the advantage of equality.' He saw before his eyes the long arc of history, tracing the continual decline of the aristocracy and the rise of the bourgeoisie from the Crusades via the Reformation to the revolutions of the 18th century. He pointed out how the invention of firearms and the printing press, along with improvements in education, science and literature had contributed to this development. A 'great democratic revolution' was going on, he wrote.[1] At that time, the revolution was just beginning.

The waves of democratization

The spread of democracy around the world, and of the civil and political rights associated with it, is among the most important political trends of the last two centuries. This development can be divided up into historical waves of democratization, as first proposed by the US American political scientist Samuel Huntington. A 'wave of democratization' means that over a given period considerably more non-democratic states become democracies than vice versa. When considering different attempts to capture such developments, it is important to bear in mind that the evaluation of a democracy in a given country is often determined by subjective judgements, starting with the choice of indicators. However, the overall picture is not affected by such small imperfections. The first wave identified by Huntington begins in 1828 and lasts until about 1926. It had its roots in the American and French Revolutions and involved a gradual extension of suffrage and the subordination of the executive to parliament. In the one hundred years of the first wave, Huntington reports, over 30 countries established at least a minimum level of democratic institutions.[2] Using the data and definitions of the Polity research programme, at the end of the first wave

---

1 Tocqueville, Alexis de. 1899. Democracy in America. The Colonial Press, pp. 3, 5.
2 Huntington, Samuel. 1991. The Third Wave: Democratization in the late Twentieth Century. Norman: University of Oklahoma Press, pp. 15ff.

twenty-one countries, or at least 30 per cent of all states surveyed, qualified as democracies.[3] Some 17 per cent of the world population lived in these countries at that time.[4] After the setbacks of the 1920s and 1930s, a second democratization wave took place in the period roughly between 1943 and 1962. By the end of this wave, 35 of the countries analysed for the Polity programme, or one-third of the growing total number of states in the world, holding 36 per cent of the world population, were now classified as democracies. After some further setbacks, in 1974, following Huntington's categorization, the third wave of democratizations began with the 'Carnation Revolution' in Portugal. Other researchers place the beginning of the third wave in 1987, as in their view the movements towards more and towards less democracy among states balanced each other out.[5] At any rate, from 1989 onwards, with the onset of the reform programme in the Soviet Union, the peaceful revolutions in Eastern Europe and the end of the Cold War, democratization acquired unprecedented momentum throughout the world. Between 1974 and 1989, the number of democracies counted by the Polity programme grew from 34 to 49, which was an increase from 25 to 35 per cent. Over just the next three years to 1992, the number shot up to 75, representing 47 per cent of all states. Since that point, for the first time ever more than half the world's population has been living under democracy. The third wave reached a high point in the year 2006, when Polity counted 95 democracies around the world, or 58 per cent. According to the Lexical Index of Electoral Democracy used by the new Global State of Democracy report first presented in 2017, as of 2016 in 68 per cent of the world's countries, home to 62.2 per cent of the world population, government power was determined by 'genuinely contested elections.' In 1970, the figure was a little under 30 per cent of countries or 40 per cent of the world population. 'A closer look at the last 10 years reveals that there is little support for the proposition of a substantial, global decline in democracy', the report states.[6]

The Washington D.C. based NGO Freedom House estimates each year the level of civil and political rights in the world. As the democracy expert Larry Diamond of Stanford University in California highlights, on a scale ranging from one for the greatest freedom to seven for the worst repression, a worldwide average of 4.38 was assumed for the year 1974. After the fall of the Wall, the

3   Polity IV Annual Time-Series 1800-2010 (www.systemicpeace.org/inscrdata.html).
4   These figures and the ones which follow on population proportions were put together by Max Roser based on Polity IV, US Census and Gapminder (ourworldindata.org).
5   Inglehart, Ronald, and Christian Welzel. 2005. Modernization, cultural change, and democracy: the human development sequence. Cambridge University Press, pp. 176f.
6   International Institute for Democracy and Electoral Assistance (International IDEA). 2017. The Global State of Democracy: Exploring Democracy's Resilience. Stockholm: Int. IDEA (www.idea.int/gsod/), pp. 2ff.

average broke the threshold of 4.0 and reached a peak of 3.22 in 2005.[7] Since then, further large advances have not been recorded, neither with respect to the number of democracies nor to the evaluation of rights and liberties. Experts are therefore debating whether the third wave is still continuing or whether a reaction has set in. In Diamond's view, since 2006 at the latest the world has been in a 'mild but protracted democratic recession', and there is a danger that this could develop into 'something much worse'.[8] Others say that the relatively small swings shown by the different surveys of democracy, like those of Polity and Freedom House, do not justify talk of a reversal. They attribute such pessimistic interpretations to the fact that many observers had been hoping for much clearer progress. The disappointed hopes are perceived as setbacks. 'In effect, nondemocratization in China, the Middle East, or Central Asia is treated as a setback', was the verdict of Steven Levitsky and Lucan Way, for example.[9] According to Polity, the number of democracies has varied since 2005 within a range between 91 and 95, and in 2015 stood at an all-time high of 96. The figures from Freedom House vary at a slightly higher range, between 115 and 125, and in 2014 and 2015 a new peak was reached with 125 'electoral democracies'. In 2017, the number stood at 123. It was only due to more rigorous criteria introduced with the 2018 report that the number then fell to 116. Following the Arab revolutions in Tunisia, Egypt and numerous other countries, after 2011 there was also talk of a possible fourth wave of democratizations. At the same time, Freedom House has been registering a decline in political rights and civil liberties in a majority of countries since 2006. Based on its own data, the international research project V-Dem concluded in its 2017 report that although there was a global democratic backslide since 2013 'the average levels of democracy in the world are still close to their highest ever recorded level.' They argue that 'that alarmist reports about a global demise of democracy are not warranted.'[10]

Economic development and democracy

Whether there is a link between economic development and democracy has been debated for decades. The debate was set off by the sociologist and political scientist Seymour Lipset (1922 to 2006), who argued in 1959 that 'the more

7   Diamond, Larry. 2015. 'Facing Up To The Democratic Recession'. Journal of Democracy (26) 1: 141–55, pp. 141f.
8   Ibid., pp. 144, 153.
9   Levitsky, Steven, and Lucan Way. 2015. 'The Myth Of Democratic Recession'. Journal of Democracy (26) 1: 45–58, p. 53.
10   V-Dem Institute. 2017. Democracy at Dusk? V-Dem Annual Report 2017. Gothenburg, pp. 12, 14.

well-to-do a nation, the greater the chances that it will sustain democracy'.[11] A distinction is drawn between the 'endogenous' theory, which holds that the likelihood of democratization in poor countries is increased by development, and the 'exogenous' theory, which holds that development makes it less likely for established democracies to relapse into dictatorship. Recent studies have confirmed these hypotheses. The political scientists Carles Boix and Susan Stokes, for example, demonstrate both effects over the period from 1850 to 1990. In contrast to earlier studies, theirs also covered the first wave of democratizations.[12] The political scientists Ronald Inglehart and Christian Welzel, on the other hand, investigated whether economic development brought with it more regime changes to democracy than to autocracy, as might be expected from the assumptions. 'The balance of regime changes shifts strongly and monotonically in favor of democracy as income rises', they report. With each increase in per capita income of 1,000 US dollars, they found that the relative number of changes to democracy as against autocracy *doubled*. 'Socioeconomic development does contribute to the emergence of democracy and it does so dramatically', was their conclusion.[13] Above a per capita income of 4,000 US dollars, the likelihood of a democracy collapsing is practically nil.[14] These results do not mean, however, that poor countries cannot democratise. Economic development only makes democratization *more likely*, and democratic systems more stable. Conversely, the oil states of the Arab world demonstrate that wealth alone is no guarantee of democratization. A crucial factor is *cultural* change linked to economic development.

The post-industrial transformation in values

The worldwide forward march of modernization and the post-industrial structural transformation to an information and knowledge society is being accompanied in the better-off population segments of an increasing number of countries by a shift in values and culture. Continuing economic prosperity and higher levels of education encourage the turn towards post-material values, which foreground individual self-realization and the search for quality of life, freedom and happiness over issues of economic survival and betterment. This development was captured in the large-scale project World Values Survey, or

11 Lipset, Seymour Martin. 1959. 'Some Social Requisites of Democracy: Economic Development and Political Legitimacy'. The American Political Science Review (53) 1: 69–105, p. 75.
12 Boix, Carles, and Susan C. Stokes. 2003. 'Endogenous Democratization'. World Politics 55: 517–49.
13 Inglehart/Welzel, loc. cit., p. 169.
14 Przeworski, Adam, and Fernando Limongi. 1997. 'Modernization: Theories and Facts'. World Politics (49) 2: 155–83, p. 165.

WVS. Representative survey data on socio-cultural and political views were collected in six waves between 1981 and 2014 in over ninety countries, covering all regions of the world and almost ninety per cent of the world population. Ronald Inglehart, the programme director, concludes that 'rising self-expression values play a central role in the trend toward democracy'. 'Postindustrialization', according to Inglehart and his colleague Welzel, 'brings even more favorable existential conditions than industrialization, making people economically more secure, intellectually more autonomous, and socially more independent than ever. This emancipative process gives people a fundamental sense of human autonomy, leading them to give a higher priority to freedom of choice and making them less inclined to accept authority and dogmatic truths.' They explain that 'the shift from survival to self-expression values linked with postindustrialization brings emancipation from authority' and produces 'increasingly powerful mass demands for democracy, the form of government that provides the broadest latitude for individuals to choose how to live their lives.'[15] Not for nothing are the ambitious middle classes regarded as the 'potential revolutionary class'.

Of course, post-industrial structural change is not the only driver of democratization. After the end of communism, democracy is now without an ideological competitor as a form of government. Authoritarian and repressive regimes are subject to an ever stronger pressure to justify themselves, one that cannot remain hidden from their own populations. Despite their attempts to control the internet, for example, these regimes can have only limited success in trying to cut their people off from the global flow of information. 'There is hardly a dictatorship in the world', writes Larry Diamond,, 'that looks stable for the long run. The only truly reliable source of regime stability is legitimacy, and the number of people in the world who believe in the intrinsic legitimacy of any form of authoritarianism is rapidly diminishing. Economic development, globalization, and the information revolution are undermining all forms of authority and empowering individuals. Values are changing, and while we should not assume any teleological path toward a global "enlightenment," generally the movement is toward greater distrust of authority and more desire for accountability, freedom, and political choice.'[16] We see the fact that autocratic regimes are turning the screw as evidence that the desire and pressure for democracy in their populations is growing ever stronger.

15 Inglehart/Welzel, loc.cit., p. 209, 29, 1.
16 Diamond, loc. cit., pp. 153f.

Democracy as a universal value

The question of whether democracy is a universal value can now be considered settled. Representative surveys around the world attest to very high approval rates in the world population. Harvard professor Pippa Norris, concludes, based on the empirical data from the WVS and other surveys, that 'overt approval of democratic governance is widespread and universal'. Average worldwide approval rates in the fifth WVS survey wave, carried out between 2005 and 2009, stood at *92 per cent*. As Norris emphasizes, although there is a variety of motivations for the approval for democracy, the respondents' cultural background or region of origin, or the political regime under which they lived, *made no real difference*. Their level of education had an influence on the attitude of the respondents, but interestingly enough the level of economic development of their country did not play a role. 'No statistically significant contrasts in democratic aspirations or in satisfaction with democratic performance can be observed when comparing affluent post-industrialized societies, emerging manufacturing economies, or poorer developing nations', she reports. Moreover, the empirical data were *not* able to confirm a general trend towards a growing loss of faith in democracy. The widespread theory of a 'democratic crisis' is in her view an 'oversimplification' based on 'over-simple claims' and isolated anecdotes, one which 'needs revising'.[17] The opposite is true, according to Ronald Inglehart and Christian Welzel. 'Contrary to often-repeated claims that social capital and mass participation are eroding, the publics of postindustrial societies are intervening in politics more actively today than ever before', they write.[18] Precisely because democracy is held in such high regard, there is also considerable dissatisfaction in some quarters. An important distinction here is that between approval for democracy as an *abstract ideal* and satisfaction with the implementation of democracy *in practice*. Norris sees the democratic deficit as arising from the gap between expectation and reality.

At the international level, too, democracy is established as a universal value. Democracy is seen today as practically the only legitimate form of government. In the Millennium Declaration of the year 2000, adopted by the heads of state and government of the world, for example, the talk is of strengthening democracy, the rule of law and human rights in all countries. At the world summit that followed five years later, it was 'reaffirmed' in the concluding statement 'that democracy is a *universal value* based on the freely expressed will of people to determine their own political, economic, social and cultural systems and

17 Norris, Pippa. 2011. Democratic Deficit: Critical Citizens Revisited. Cambridge Univ. Press, pp. 92, 129, 110, 58, 4.
18 Inglehart/Welzel, loc. cit., pp. 44, 117.

their full participation in all aspects of their lives' (emphasis added).[19] When the UN General Assembly in 2007 declared the 15th September as the 'International Day of Democracy', it was emphasized once more that democracy is a universal value, and moreover that it belongs to 'the universal and indivisible core values and principles of the United Nations'.[20] As UN Secretary-General, Boutros Boutros-Ghali argued that with the opening words of the UN Charter – "We the peoples" – 'the founders invoked the most fundamental principle of democracy, rooting the sovereign authority of the Member States, and thus the legitimacy of the Organization which they were to compose, in the will of their peoples'.[21]

This development is reflected in other regions of the world besides Europe, where promotion of democracy became a key regional concern after the end of the Second World War, especially through the Council of Europe. A 'right to democracy' is embedded in the first article of the Inter-American Democratic Charter adopted by the Organization of American States in 2001, and the governments of the member states 'have an obligation to promote and defend it'. Representative democracy is declared to be fundamental and indispensable. In the 2008 Charter of the Association of Southeast Asian Nations (ASEAN) 'strengthening democracy' is named as one of the purposes of the organization. In the Charter of Democracy of the South Asian Association for Regional Co-operation (SAARC), passed in 2011, the member states undertake to 'promote democracy at all levels of the Government and the society at large' and to 'uphold participatory democracy characterised by free, fair and credible elections, and elected legislatures and local bodies'. And the African Charter on Democracy, Elections and Governance, which entered into force in 2012, commits the treaty partners to adhere to 'the universal values and principles of democracy'.

The right to democracy

There are of course different views as to what exactly defines democracy and a democratic system. There is no universally recognised model that could be used as a yardstick. Nevertheless, certain requirements have been defined under international law. For example, Article 21 of the Universal Declaration of Human Rights of 1948 stipulates that '[t]he will of the people shall be the basis of the authority of government; this will shall be expressed in periodic and genuine elections which shall be by universal and equal suffrage and shall be held by

---

19   United Nations. 24 October 2005. '2005 World Summit Outcome'. A/RES/60/1, para. 135.
20   Id. 13 December 2007. 'Support by the United Nations system of the efforts of Governments to promote and consolidate new or restored democracies'. A/RES/62/7.
21   Boutros-Ghali, Boutros. 20 December 1996. Supplement to reports on democratization. Report to the 51st Session of the United Nations General Assembly. A/51/761, para. 28.

secret vote or by equivalent free voting procedures'. According to Article 25 of the International Covenant on Civil and Political Rights, which entered into force in 1976 and has been ratified by 176 states, 'every citizen shall have the right and the opportunity ... to take part in the conduct of public affairs, directly or through freely chosen representatives [and] to vote and to be elected at genuine periodic elections which shall be by universal and equal suffrage and shall be held by secret ballot'. The US American lawyer Thomas M. Franck (1931 to 2009) argued in an influential article in 1992 that democratic governance was becoming an international norm and an entitlement under international law.[22] In essence, the right to democracy means that everyone who is affected by the exercise of public authority must have the right to influence it, at the very least through the free election of representatives.

The level at which the decision-making process of the public authority takes place must not play a role. To restrict this right to the nation state level would be - in view of the migration of important decision-making processes to the intergovernmental level – to hollow out the right to democracy and to make it ineffective. Democratization cannot be allowed to advance no further than the nation state level. The right to democracy demands the democratization of international decision-making and organizations as well. Article 28 of the Declaration of Human Rights can be read in this light. 'Everyone', it is stated there, 'is entitled to a social and *international order* in which the rights and freedoms set forth in this Declaration can be fully realized' (emphasis added). In a number of resolutions passed since 2004, the UN General Assembly has declared, repeatedly using identical wording, that a 'democratic and equitable international order' requires the realization of 'the right to equitable participation of all, without any discrimination, in domestic and *global* decision-making' (emphasis added).[23] How that can be institutionally ensured is answered by the right to democracy itself, namely through the involvement of *freely elected representatives of the people*. The democratic exercise of public authority within the framework of the international order is only possible if parliamentary representation is extended to the global level. Only in this way can the 'will of the people' – here, the will of the world population - be given effect as pluralistically as possible. Ultimately, worldwide parliamentary representation must be based on *worldwide elections*. Franck proposed in 1995 a parliament directly elected by

22 Franck, Thomas M. 1992. 'The Emerging Right to Democratic Governance'. The American Journal of International Law 86: 46–91.
23 United Nations. 19 Dec. 2016. 'Promotion of a Democratic and Equitable International Order'. A/RES/71/90.

the world population, with seats allocated according to population size, in order to institutionalize the 'democratic entitlement'.[24]

The undermining of democracy by intergovernmentalism

Even if all the countries in the world were perfect democracies, that would not alter the fact that the intergovernmental system of international law is undemocratic. The democratic process of policy formulation and promotion has to date been extremely difficult in the international arena. The political scientist Klaus Dieter Wolf has posited that the 'de-democratization effect' which has accompanied the internationalization of governance is in fact one which is positively desired. Wolf argues that 'the parallelism of voluntary intergovernmental commitment and structural democratic deficit which is characteristic of governance beyond the state is *the intended result* of strategic interaction between state governments' (emphasis added). The executive, he believes, can strengthen 'its tactical position in the domestic power struggle' by shifting decisions into the intergovernmental arena and thereby 'removing them from domestic political control and accountability'. According to Wolf, what is termed the 'Politics of the new Raison d'état' consists in 'the cartel-like attempt to safeguard state authority by means of intergovernmental ties and reciprocal voluntary commitments. Its purpose is to create a space in which substantive decisions can be made beyond the reach of social disputation and thus also beyond the possibility of domestic political challenge'.[25]

There is something to be gained by looking at it in this way. Intergovernmental treaty negotiations, for example, are usually conducted by government officials away from public scrutiny, even though related domestic policy matters are very often also touched upon and decided on. Recent examples are the negotiations on the Anti-Counterfeiting Trade Agreement (ACTA) or on the Transatlantic Trade and Investment Partnership (TTIP). The parliaments are seldom involved, and often do not know what their governments are even discussing. Representatives of trade associations and large corporations by contrast are frequently consulted. The principle of the separation of powers is effectively suspended, and the executive promotes itself to the role of legislature. After the conclusion of the negotiations, the parliament is usually only able to accept or reject the treaties presented to it by the government in their totality. The supervisory rights of the parliament are 'curtailed in the field of foreign

---

24 Franck, Thomas M. 1995. Fairness in International Law and Institutions. Oxford: Clarendon Press, pp. 482ff.
25 Wolf, Klaus Dieter. 2000. Die Neue Staatsräson - Zwischenstaatliche Kooperation als Demokratieproblem in der Weltgesellschaft. 1st ed. Baden-Baden: Nomos, pp. 13, 17f., 67.

policy, or in fact in all cross-departmental areas of international politics, especially when it comes to the specific rules for parliamentary influence on treaties under international law' was a criticism made in the report of the Enquete Commission of the German Bundestag on 'The Globalization of the World Economy' in 2002. Parliamentarians needed to play 'a supervisory as well as a policy-making role also with regard to processes of globalization'.[26] The arbitrary involvement of individual parliamentarians in selected government delegations, as practised in some states, is irrelevant in this context. 'Modern parliamentarism demanded in many states the ratification of foreign policy treaties', writes Klaus von Beyme. 'But in practice, not even the opposition were prepared to withhold their approval from most treaties so as not to put at risk the continuity of external relations'.[27] This applies all the more to the parliamentary groups of governing parties, who certainly were not willing to stab their own executive in the back. In most cases the parliaments give straightforward majority approval to the international law treaties laid before them, if only not to destabilize their own governments either domestically or in terms of foreign relations. The governments can take the easy position that international guidelines have to be followed – guidelines that they themselves of course have negotiated. In addition, in intergovernmental relations in practice, treaties under international law can be developed and expanded in an organic process without the parliaments being able to have any appreciable influence on them.

The Harvard sociologist and political scientist Robert D. Putnam speaks of 'two-level games'. The first level is that of inter-governmental negotiations, the second that of national approval for the outcomes of those negotiations. 'The motives of the chief negotiator include ... [s]hifting the balance of power at Level II in favor of domestic policies that he prefers for exogenous reasons', Putnam notes.[28] To strengthen its position, the executive can invoke 'the national interest' or 'national security'. These concepts can be employed repeatedly as rhetorical figures to suggest actions taken for the greater public good, on the basis of broad public consensus, to the point where they lose all substance. 'The pervasive phrase "the national interest" is one of the cloudiest concepts in our political environment', writes Jeff Faux. 'It hides more than it reveals, and has the effect of giving the ordinary citizen the false impression that a democratic consensus has been reached and therefore no longer has to be debated.'[29]

26 Deutscher Bundestag. 16 June 2002. Schlussbericht der Enquete-Kommission 'Globalisierung der Weltwirtschaft - Herausforderungen and Antworten', pp. 446, 445ff.
27 Beyme, Klaus von. 1998. 'Niedergang der Parlamente'. Internationale Politik 4: 21–30, p. 21.
28 Putnam, Robert D. 1988. 'Diplomacy and domestic politics: the logic of two-level games'. International Organization (42) 3: 427–60, pp. 436, 457.
29 Faux, Jeff. 2006. The Global Class War. Hoboken NJ: John Wiley & Sons, p. 50.

The influence of transnational corporations

The current state of the world order constitutes an advantageous environment for action not only for the officials of national governments but also for the transnational capitalist elite. Transnational corporations and the business interests they represent are skilled at instrumentalising all the elements of the fragmented international system – the confusing tangle of international actors, sectoral organizations, agencies, officials, committees, negotiators, jurisdictions, agreements and legal regimes - to their own best advantage. Transnational corporations are the key institutions of so-called 'post-democracy'. They have the means required to exercise influence in the right places, at the national and the international level. In important international bodies like the Codex Alimentarius Commission, company representatives take part in the discussions on an equal footing with government officials. They are often integrated into intergovernmental treaty negotiations by governments, and invited to comment on drafts and to make proposals. Other bodies such as the International Accounting Standard Board (IASB) are entirely in their hands. 'The IASB', says the MEP Sven Giegold, 'decides on international accounting regulations without any effective democratic accountability. The Board is dominated by so-called experts from international corporations.' The standards drawn up by the IASB are regularly adopted into EU law.

The example of the Codex Commission

With regard to the Codex Alimentarius Commission, Leslie Sklair is critical of the fact that representatives of transnational corporations like Nestlé, Unilever and Monsanto make up a large proportion of the delegates.[30] These companies have direct influence on the formulation of standards that apply to their products and business activities. In this respect, the Codex Commission is a good illustration of the complicated and distant way global governance functions. The Commission, set up in 1963 by the FAO and WHO, is the most important body for the setting of international standards in the food sector. This covers many important issues directly affecting consumers, such as rules on food labelling, limits on additives and toxins, and safety assessments for feed additives. In principle, the standards set by the Codex Commission or by the International Organization for Standardization (ISO) were not binding. However, the 1994

---

30   Sklair, Leslie. 2002. 'Democracy and the Transnational Capitalist Class'. Annals of the American Academy of Political and Social Science 581: 144–157, pp. 148f.

WTO agreements on food safety and plant protection measures and on technical barriers to trade state that international standards must be taken into account and that their observance is regarded as evidence of compliance with the agreements. The Codex standards have thus acquired substantial legal significance in the area of food safety. In the prominent trade dispute between the USA and the EU over the European ban on imports of hormone-treated meat, the standing Appellate Body of the Dispute Settlement Body concluded in 1998 that WTO members are able to set higher standards of health and consumer protection than the Codex standards.[31] Despite this, however, uncertainty remains over the status of the Codex standards, since according to business lawyers any deviation from standards requires justification and increases the risk of proceedings being brought at the WTO.[32] For that reason they speak of a 'de facto compulsion' to apply the standards and of a 'hidden supranationality' embedded 'in the underlying structure'. International standardization is sensible and necessary. But what is problematic, given its far-reaching influence, are the 'legitimational deficits with which the respective organizations are tainted'. It is argued that the interests of industry 'often predominate', as the appointment of personnel to the standardization bodies 'is neither democratic nor balanced'.[33] This also applies to the ISO, which has drawn up over 15,000 standards since its founding in 1947. Its members, the national standards organizations, are civil associations open to everyone who wants to work with them. It is of course essential that industries and businesses that are directly affected should be able to take part in their work. However, the fact that crucial standards and rules which indirectly acquire legal effect can be created without the involvement of parliaments or parliamentarians and without any accountability to parliament is problematic. It is also characteristic of 'post-democracy' that parliaments and deputies allow themselves to be treated in this way, though it must be conceded that they are trapped within their respective national political frameworks, where they have only limited opportunity to exert any influence.

31 Eggers, Barbara. 1998. 'Die Entscheidung des WTO Appellate Body im Hormonfall - Doch ein Recht auf Vorsorge?' Europäische Zeitschrift für Wirtschaftsrecht 5–6: 147–151.
32 Veggeland, Frode, and Svein Ole Borgen. 2005. 'Negotiating International Food Standards: The World Trade Organization's Impact on the Codex Alimentarius Commission'. Governance: An International Journal of Policy, Administration, and Institutions (18) 4: 675–708, pp. 690f.
33 Herrmann, Christoph, Wolfgang Weiß and Christoph Ohler. 2007. Welthandelsrecht. München: C.H. Beck, 2nd ed. §12 no. 591, p. 258.

Fragmentation as a problem of democracy

In the view of Armin von Bogdandy, Director of the renowned Max Planck Institute for Comparative Public Law and International Law, ensuring the continuing global development of parliamentarism is 'one of the greatest contemporary challenges'. An expert in international law, he believes that 'in the light of the requirement for universality' the fragmentation of the 'international level of policy formation' must be regarded as 'problematic in terms of democratic theory'. The 'requirement for universality' with respect to the process of legislation means that the democratic legislature must be the principal locus of regulation and legitimation, where all possible perspectives are carefully assessed openly and impartially. 'The starting point', according to von Bogdandy, 'is the individual as a whole and multidimensional person, one who is not divisible in accordance with the logic of functionality but instead claims the right to a representational mechanism in which competing perspectives can be weighed up against each other.' The setting of particularistic priorities by international regimes therefore undermines 'the requirement for universality as a core element of the principle of democracy'.[34] Against this background, the 'aggregating' function of a world parliament assumes a key significance for democracy. The world parliament is directly integrated at the level of international standard-setting. The world parliament must be directly linked into existing processes via committees, or where necessary or appropriate it must completely take over the discussions and relevant regulatory competences. So, for example, it should have to take part in the deliberations of the Codex Commission and to sanction their outcomes. In addition, the right for a UNPA 'to send fully participating parliamentary delegations or representatives to international governmental fora and negotiations' has already been called for.[35] In 1954, the British philosopher, Nobel Prize winner and world federalist Bertrand Russell made the interesting proposal that agreements under international law should require approval by a federal 'Central Authority' within the framework of a constitutional federal world order.[36] Insofar as matters of world law are affected by international law treaties, this is an idea worth considering. In any event, the only institution that ought to come into question here as the relevant responsible authority is a world parliament.

---

34 Bogdandy, Armin von, and Ingo Venzke. 2010. 'Zur Herrschaft internationaler Gerichte: Eine Untersuchung internationaler öffentlicher Gewalt und ihrer demokratischen Rechtfertigung'. Zeitschrift für ausländisches öffentliches Recht und Völkerrecht (70) 1: 1–49, pp. 21, 25f.
35 Pan-African Parliament. 24 October 2007. 'A United Nations Parliamentary Assembly'. Resolution adopted at the 8th Ordinary Session, Midrand, South Africa, para. 16.
36 Russell, Bertrand. 28 August 1954. 'A Prescription for the World'. The Saturday Review: 9–11, 38–39, p. 10.

The dilemma of scale

Considerable attention has been given to the view of the influential political scientist Robert Dahl that an honest acknowledgement and expression is required of the fact that international organizations, institutions and processes simply *cannot be* democratic *when measured by the yardstick of proximity to the citizens*, since of necessity they require the delegation of decision-making powers to international elites who by their very nature are distant from the ordinary citizen. A 'fundamental dilemma' of democratic theory and practice, according to Dahl, is the fact that 'a smaller democratic unit provides an ordinary citizen with greater opportunities to participate in governing than a larger unit. But the smaller the unit the more likely that some matters of importance to the citizen are beyond the capacity of the government to deal with effectively'. Larger units are needed to solve such problems. While the capacity to govern is then improved, the individual's opportunities for influence are conversely reduced. At the international level, the acceptable upper limit for what can still be considered democracy is thereby exceeded.

Nevertheless, it is clear to Dahl that international organizations are indispensable. It might be possible to agree with him that democracy cannot be realised at the international level *in any ideal form* (insofar as this is possible at all). However, that is no reason to give up on the possibility of steady democratic progress towards that objective. 'If we judge that important human needs require an international organization, despite its cost to democracy, we should not only subject its undemocratic aspects to scrutiny and criticism but also try to create proposals for greater democratization and insist that they be adopted', Dahl himself noted. In order for even just an approximation of the level of democratic control that exists in democratic states to be achieved at the international level, 'political institutions that would provide citizens with opportunities for political participation, influence, and control roughly equivalent in effectiveness to those already existing in democratic countries' would be needed.[37] Dahl is thinking here, entirely in line with the 'right to democracy', of an 'international citizen body' with elected representatives and international parties.[38]

The concept of a chain of legitimation

The concept of a 'chain of legitimation' is often employed as a way of demonstrating that international organizations are democratically accountable. This idea

37 Dahl, Robert. 1999. 'Can international organizations be democratic? A skeptic's view'. In: Democracy's Edges, ed. by Ian Shapiro and Casiano Hacker-Cordón, 19–36. Cambridge University Press, pp. 22, 34, 31.
38 Id. 2000. On democracy. New Haven: Yale University Press, p. 116.

originated with the German lawyers and former constitutional court judges Roman Herzog and Ernst Wolfgang Böckenförde. It posits that democratic legitimation comes from the electorate and is then transferred from one level to the next. The voters elect the parliament, the parliament elects the government, the government appoints representatives to international bodies, and these may elect the leading functionaries of the relevant organizations. It must be borne in mind that there is therefore not one chain of legitimation, but a number of such chains running in parallel for all the states. However, according to Anne Peters, 'the democratic link between international institutions and citizens' it is supposed to supply 'is a legal fiction that has little to do with reality'.[39] With each successive link in the chain, proximity to the citizen and legitimation both become weaker, and the democratic deficit larger. The political scientists Frank Nullmeier and Martin Nonhoff do not believe the theory works at all for inter- and supra-national political constellations. 'As there are no direct electoral relationships between the world population, i.e. a world citizenship, and the ruling bodies of international organizations there can be no question of direct legitimation. From this perspective, talk of a "democratic deficit" is almost an understatement, as these systems are fundamentally democratically illegitimate.'[40] The political scientist Giovanni Sartori, who also speaks of 'macrodemocracies', 'got to the heart of the dilemma when he compared the legitimation chain to a swimmer. Just because he can swim does not automatically mean he is able to cross an ocean'.[41] The gulf that separates the citizens from intergovernmental processes has grown too wide. Popular awareness and criticism have increased, and democratic expectations have grown, at the same time as the significance of the intergovernmental level. In any case, at least there is a 'socially constructed transnational awareness of a problem' that requires political participation at the global level, to use the terminology of Volker Rittberger and his co-authors.[42]

Output legitimation

The idea of the legitimation chain belongs to the field of what political scientists call input legitimation. 'The input-oriented perspective emphasizes "government *by the people*". Political decisions are legitimate if and when they reflect the "will

---

39 Peters, Anne. 2009. 'Dual Democracy'. In: The Constitutionalization of International Law, by Jan Klabbers, Anne Peters, and Geir Ulfstein, 263–341. Oxford, New York: Oxford University Press, p. 294.
40 Nullmeier, Frank, et al. 2010. Prekäre Legitimitäten: Rechtfertigung von Herrschaft in der postnationalen Konstellation. Frankfurt: Campus Verlag, p. 21.
41 Petersen, Niels. 2008. 'Demokratie and Grundgesetz'. Max Planck Institute for Research on Collective Goods, p. 3.
42 Rittberger, Volker, Andreas Kruck, and Anne Romund. 2010. Grundzüge der Weltpolitik. Theorie und Empirie des Weltregierens. 1st ed. Wiesbaden: VS Verlag für Sozialwissenschaften, p. 616.

of the people" – that is, if they have their roots in the genuine preferences of the members of a community', wrote the political scientist Fritz Scharpf. With regard to international organizations, where input-legitimation is poorly developed, an 'output perspective' is applied in order to provide legitimation. The 'output-oriented perspective', Scharpf explains, 'places the aspect of "government *for the people*" in the foreground. Political decisions are thereby legitimate if and when they effectively promote the general wellbeing of a community'. But who should judge whether that is the case, using which criteria? Ultimately, the output perspective, too, leads us back to the electorate. 'In all constitutional democracies, output legitimacy is primarily ensured through universal, free and equal elections', Scharpf notes. Regular elections, he asserts, maintain and strengthen the orientation of the office holders toward the public interest. The anticipation of public debate, and its potential repercussions for the political career of the office holders, creates the conditions for output legitimacy.[43]

The global governance system is increasingly discredited within civil society on account of both perceived inadequate output and the democratic deficit. 'Global governance isn't working. Global problems still lack global people-oriented solutions', is the succinct summary in the 2014 annual report on the state of civil society published by CIVICUS, a global alliance of civil society organizations. 'Many of the institutions and processes by which international decisions are made, and by which norms are set and diffused, are out of date and unable to meet present-day, entrenched challenges', the report says. But the crisis is more than one of efficiency. It is also one of democracy, as the report points out. 'The institutions of international governance are not open enough. It is hard for people to relate to them or indeed to understand them. They are less democratic even than the states that make up their membership, and it is naive to expect citizens' voices to be filtered through their states to be heard at the global level', the report concludes.[44] Thus, when it comes to assessing progress on the new Sustainable Development Goals in pursuit of the Agenda 2030, this should not be left in future to governments and their international agencies. Ideally a global parliamentary assembly should play a major role.

This dissatisfaction is also revealed by representative surveys. The United Nations regularly receives very high approval ratings in comparison with other institutions. In a 2013 survey conducted in 39 countries, about 58 per cent of respondents on average said they had a 'favourable view' of the UN, and only

43 Scharpf, Fritz W. 1999. Regieren in Europa. Effektiv and demokratisch? Frankfurt: Campus, pp. 16, 22f.
44 CIVICUS: World Alliance for Citizen Participation (ed.). 2014. 'Towards a Democratic Multilateralism: Civil Society Perspectives on the State of Global Governance'. In: State of Civil Society Report 2014: Reimagining Global Governance: 39–69, p. 39.

27 per cent had a negative attitude.[45] Approval ratings were similarly high in earlier years. However, a more differentiated picture emerges if one looks at surveys that question in more detail. In a survey of eight countries conducted from 2006 to 2007, respondents were asked to mark their *feelings* toward the UN on a scale from 0 to 100, where 0 is very cold and negative and 100 very warm and positive. The international average was a warm 66 degrees. By contrast, in the fifth WVS survey wave, respondents in 52 countries were asked to mark their level of *trust* in the organization. An average of 46 per cent reported that they had *no trust* in the UN, while 42 per cent reported at least some level of trust. The results are interpreted as evidence that there is a high level of approval for the mission and vision of the UN, but not for its performance in practice.[46]

Accountability to the world's citizens

In his book 'Independent Diplomat', the former British diplomat Carne Ross observes that even the connection between the governments in the capitals and their own diplomats sitting on international bodies is often unsatisfactory. And indeed, in today's massively networked world '[i]t is ridiculous to pretend that the wishes and needs of an entire country can be embodied in a single diplomat'.[47] We have already described the disconnection between governments and parliaments on intergovernmental issues and the associated 'de-democratization effect'. Like Ross, Anne Peters points out that government representatives in international organizations must be accountable not only to their national electorates but to *the citizenry of the world as a whole*, since their interests must also be taken into account. 'The sum of national constituencies does not make a proper global constituency. Thus the parallel chains of accountability to parallel domestic constituencies do not generate an appropriate accountability to the combined citizenry of all the states involved, the global constituency. This also means that the sum of national mechanisms for monitoring and controlling respective national representatives acting in international bodies does not result in full oversight', she argues.[48] The point here is not how effectively a national parliament can monitor the stance and actions of its own government and officials within international organizations, but the supervision of the international organization itself, and of its bureaucracy. A world parliament charged

45   PewResearchCenter. 17 September 2013. 'United Nations Retains Strong Global Image' (www.pewglobal.org).
46   Council on Foreign Relations. 2012. 'Chapter 2: World Opinion on International Institutions'. In: Public Opinion on Global Issues. New York: Council on Foreign Relations, pp. 1, 2f.
47   Ross, Carne. 2007. Independent diplomat: dispatches from an unaccountable elite. Ithaca N.Y.: Cornell University Press, p. 210.
48   Peters, loc. cit., p. 295.

with this task would create *an additional and significantly shortened* legitimation chain, since there would be no need in this case for mediation via the government executives and their representatives. Moreover, the members of the world parliament would themselves in principle be accountable to the entire world citizenry.

Equality and representation in international law and world law

In intergovernmental bodies, all states as a rule have one vote and equal rights, in accordance with the fundamental international law principle of 'sovereign equality'. But the countries of the world are anything but equal. The world's population is divided extremely unequally between the states. Compared with the heavyweights, most countries are tiny dwarfs with respect to their population size. This imbalance, which can also be seen with respect to economic power and to the size of their UN budget contributions, in conjunction with the principle of equality under international law, is a significant problem in the political reality of intergovernmental organizations. According to Mark Malloch Brown, who served as UN Deputy Secretary-General, Chef de Cabinet to the Secretary-General, and for six years as administrator of the UN Development Programme, 'the intergovernmental gridlock between the big contributors and the rest of the membership concerning governance and voting is the core dysfunction'.[49] The sociologists Patrick Nolan and Gerhard Lenski take the same view, and noted that '[t]he greatest obstacle to the effectiveness of that organization is probably the system of representation in the General Assembly, which provides an equal vote for the People's Republic of China, with its population of 1.3 *billion*, and for Tuvalu with its population of 10 *thousand*'.[50] Pascal Lamy, former EU Commissioner for external trade and at one time Director-General of the WTO, believes that the principle of equal voting rights for the states 'is a long-standing fiction dating back to a distant period when democracies did not exist. It was a useful fiction in its day, but it is completely out of step with contemporary geopolitical realities. It can represent neither the diversity of the world nor the variety of its actors.'[51]

Notwithstanding this, the international law principle of the equality of states is often celebrated as a key element of international democracy. From the perspective of world law, it is in fact just the opposite – a symptom of the undemocratic nature of the intergovernmental order. The principle of equality underlying international law, which applies to *states* ('one state, one vote'), stands in

49 Brown, Mark Malloch. 2008. 'Can the UN Be Reformed?' Global Governance 14: 1–12, p. 8.
50 Nolan, Patrick, and Gerhard Lenski. 2006. Human societies: an introduction to macrosociology. 10th ed. Boulder Colo.: Paradigm Publishers, p. 352.
51 Lamy, Pascal. 2005. Towards World Democracy. London: policy network, pp. 24f.

contrast to the principle of equality underlying world law, in which people as world citizens are the key element. Thus, the 100 countries with the smallest populations represent about 265 million inhabitants and *4 per cent* of the world population, but they make up *more than half* of the total votes in the UN General Assembly with its 193 member states. The 128 least populous countries, which can constitute *a two-thirds majority* in the General Assembly, have 565 million inhabitants, or roughly *8.5 per cent* of the world population. By contrast, the 10 most populous countries, with some *4 billion* inhabitants, have a voting strength of *5 per cent*. The members of the G20 represent about *two-thirds* of the world population and almost 90 per cent of global GDP, but have a voting strength of only *10 per cent*. In the light of these figures, it is no surprise that the heads of state and government of the biggest industrialised and newly industrialising countries decided to coordinate their response to the global financial crisis within the framework of the G20 summit meetings and not at the UN. As the social scientist Geoffrey McNicoll noted some time ago, the powerful states always have an 'exit option'. 'Powerful states', he wrote, 'have a de facto option of exit: they can shrug off Lilliputian efforts to trammel them and conduct their business elsewhere.'[52] In reality, the least populous countries do not vote together in blocs. When it really counts, the bigger economic powers are quite prepared to try to influence their votes. But that does not alter the fact that the votes of the world's citizens in the intergovernmental bodies are extremely unequally weighted, subject as they are to their national citizenship.

It must also be considered that the political opposition and (in most cases) ethnic minorities have no voice at all under this system. Although it is true that almost 100 per cent of all states are represented by diplomats in the General Assembly, these do not represent 100 per cent of the world population if internal national arrangements are taken into account. In democratic states, in addition to the governing majority there is generally an opposition - which, however, has no access at all to the intergovernmental level. Its voters are not represented there. There are around 5,000 indigenous peoples in the world with a combined population of up to 350 million people. Although their global population size is larger than that of the 100 smallest countries, the latter have 100 votes at the UN and the former none at all. Thomas M. Franck explained the situation with regard to minorities as follows: 'there are some fifty nations in which an indigenous minority has identified itself: Hmong, Inuit, Lap, Sorb,

---

52 McNicoll, Geoffrey. 1999. 'Population weights in the international order'. Population and Development Review (25) 3: 411–42, p. 422.

Mauri, etc. Nowhere do these indigenous peoples form a majority. Taken together, however, they form a constituency larger than the respective populations
of half the states represented at the UN'. Yet, he says, 'the global system as now
constituted affords them little opportunity to be heard.'[53] The South Asian ethnic
group of the Hmong, for example, numbers 4 to 5 million people. That is roughly
equivalent to the aggregate total population of the 27 to 30 least populous countries. To be represented under the current Westphalian system, Franck observes,
such peoples would have no other choice but to try to found their own state.

The principle of equality underlying world law requires a form of political
representation for the world population in which ideally the vote of every person on the planet would have equal weight. This must be the guiding principle
for the design of elections to a world parliament and for the allocation of seats
within it. A world parliament would thus be made up of independent delegates
who should reflect the whole spectrum of political opinion of the world citizenry.
So the best way of allocating seats would be in proportion to their share of the
vote. This would be a means of enabling political and other minorities to be represented who take no part, or only a limited part, in national governments.

The third democratic transformation

Robert Dahl believes that three 'great transformations' can be observed in the
history of democracy.[54] Each of these transformations involves a step up in the
scale of democratic governance. The first transformation, he believes, began
around 500 BCE and consisted in the metamorphosis of the autocratic Greek
city states into the first communities with democratic features. Their central
institution was the assembly of the people, in which all male citizens who had
completed military service could take part. The Australian political scientist
John Keane locates the roots of this 'self-government by assemblies of people
who regard each other as equals' two thousand years earlier in the Syrian-Mes-
opotamian region.[55] How far one can speak here of democracy from a modern
perspective is open to question. Individual rights were not protected. Women
were excluded, and the commonwealth of the Greek polis was based to a significant degree on slavery. As the French philosopher Christian Delacampagne reports, there arose here 'for the first time in history a society in which slavery

---

53 Franck (1995), loc. cit., pp. 480f.
54 Dahl, Robert. 1994. 'A Democratic Dilemma: System Effectiveness versus Citizen Participation'. Political
    Science Quarterly (109) 1: 23–34, pp. 25ff.
55 Keane, John. 2010. The life and death of democracy. London: Pocket Books, pp. 89ff., 111

was no longer one economic resource among others but became the most important means of production'.[56] Nevertheless, it has to be conceded that the idea of rule by the people was first put into practice in the Greek city states, albeit restricted to male 'free citizens'. 'For the next two thousand years', according to Dahl, 'the idea and practice of democracy were associated almost exclusively with small scale city-states.'[57] This changed in the course of the second transformation. The process of state formation had advanced, and had created relatively large territorial dominions. In the nascent nation states, the idea of representative democracy established itself through resistance to and rebellion against monarchical rule. An exemplary and revolutionary instance was the federal constitution of the USA adopted on 17 September 1787. This was followed by the establishment of the nation state system around the world and the three waves of democratization described above.

The spread of democracy at the nation state level is not, however, the 'end of history', as Francis Fukuyama suggested. The idea that the territorial state and the system of international law represent the end of ten thousand years of the political development of humanity is absurd and ahistorical way of looking at things. Just as very few people in the 18th century, before the second democratic transformation, were able to picture representative democracy in the territorial states, so today the idea that there can be democracy at the world level is still beyond many people's imagination. But that is precisely what the *third transformation* is about, and it is already happening. 'Just as earlier city-states lost much of their political, economic, social, and cultural autonomy when they were absorbed into larger national states, so in our time the development of transnational systems reduces the political, economic, social, and cultural autonomy of national states', is how Dahl describes the situation at the start.[58] As in the second transformation, the development is part of a process of state formation, but one that now encompasses the entire world system. It is the vehicle for a new 'Great Transformation' in Karl Polanyi's sense, leading towards the establishment of a global eco-social market economy. The future of democracy depends on the success of this third transformation, as it will be increasingly marginalised within the framework of the nation state system. At the same time, continuing democratization within the community of states is an important prerequisite for global democratization. The two processes are intertwined. As the Swedish philosopher Torbjörn Tännsjö argued in a book on the need of a democratic world government, 'without the establishment of global democracy, the process towards local

56   Delacampagne, Christian. 2004. Die Geschichte der Sklaverei. Artemis & Winkler, p. 51.
57   Dahl (1994), loc. cit., p. 25.
58   Ibid., p. 26.

democracy will be slowed down'. What is needed, he concluded, 'is nothing less than a world parliament, elected in a representative manner'.[59]

The third transformation involves the globalization not only of democracy but also of government. Democracy is a form of government. The history of democracy is a history of the *transformation of government*. Participation and representation, unless they feed into government, ultimately lead nowhere. If the necessary instruments do not exist, as is the case at the global level, then they have to be created. The call for global democracy is thus at the same time a call for global government. As Otfried Höffe argues, the third democratic transformation means 'the formation of a democratic, constitutional state at the global level, under the rule of law and justice, a world republic based on subsidiarity and federalism'.[60] During the second transformation, the assumption of a right to self-determination for all peoples was of the greatest importance for overcoming foreign rule and oppression and for the development of democracy at the nation state level. The dense interdependence of the world system and the planetary-level tasks and challenges are now insistently raising the question of a *right to self-determination for humanity*. Global democratic structures of government are needed now so that the global government vacuum can be ended and foreign rule by an elite, imperial, transnational order – one based paradoxically on the perpetuation of the Westphalian system of states - can be thrown off. The core institution of democracy is the parliament. The creation of a world parliament is thus at the centre of the third transformation. What is needed first of all is to gradually link the various existing forms and processes of public authority at the global level to a global parliamentary body so that they can be made subject to effective democratic supervision and participation by the world population. The parliament is both the starting point and the motor for the formation of a supra-national community at the global level.

International parliamentary institutions

The rapid growth in the number of international parliamentary institutions, or IPIs, is a precursor of the incipient third transformation. They represent a variety of forms of democratic representation and cooperation beyond the nation state, that is, not mediated through the governments but delivered directly by elected delegates. The oldest of these institutions is the Inter-Parliamentary Union, founded in 1889, which has so far played an ambivalent role in the efforts

59 Tännsjö, Torbjörn. 2008. Global Democracy: The Case for a World Government. Edinburgh Univ. Press, pp. 29, 95.
60 Höffe, Otfried. 2002. Demokratie im Zeitalter der Globalisierung. New ed. Munich: C.H. Beck, p. 428.

to establish a world parliament. The foundation in 1949 of the Council of Europe and its Parliamentary Assembly, PACE for short, represented the creation of an important IPI and was immediately taken as an opportunity to propose a UNPA. As the directly elected legislative organ of the European Union, the European Parliament is today the IPI that has evolved the furthest. The Andean Parliament and the Central American Parliament represent two further directly elected regional IPIs. Direct elections are also planned for the Mercosur Parliament and the Pan-African Parliament. Amazingly, the state of research into the important phenomenon of IPIs remains very weak. Claudia Kissling, an academic expert in public administration and law, undertook a critical survey and legal classification of all IPIs in existence at the time in 2011.[61] She found 40 such institutions in 1990, and around 160 already, with the trend increasing, twenty years later. One of the newest IPIs is the Parliamentary Assembly of the South-East European Cooperation Process, established in 2014. The establishment of a parliamentary assembly for the BRICS states (Brazil, Russia, India, China and South Africa) is one of several others currently under discussion. As Kissling writes, '[c]onsidering the growing acceptance and importance of IPIs throughout the world, it is remarkable that major international intergovernmental organizations do not yet possess any formal parliamentary organ, even in an advisory capacity'. This is especially true of the UN, the WTO, the World Bank Group and the IMF. 'Those parliamentary institutions that do exist and relate to the activities of these IGOs, such as the Inter-Parliamentary Union, the Parliamentary Conference on the WTO, or the Parliamentary Network on the World Bank, are not willing – and not legally able – to exert any considerable influence on their agenda and decision-making, let alone exert formal oversight', she writes. Kissling emphasizes however that not every one of these organizations needs its own parliamentary organ. A UNPA could be structured as a common parliamentary body with appropriate committees. 'In any case', she notes, 'an UNPA would contribute significantly to overcoming an ever-growing legitimacy gap at the international level.[62] To this end, a great deal can be learned from the existing IPIs.

---

61 Kissling, Claudia. 2011. The Legal and Political Status of International Parliamentary Institutions, Committee for a Democratic UN.
62 Ibid., p. 53.

25.
The development of a planetary consciousness, and a new global enlightenment

The social evolution of the human race can be described as a continual coming together and breaking apart of human communities.[1] Oscillating between co-operation and rivalry, they competed since the dawn of history for settlements, raw materials and food, and finally for geopolitical control. Through technological progress and population expansion, the social units have grown ever more intricate, and their interconnections ever closer and more complex. Within the communities, rules evolved to make living together as free of conflict as possible, albeit that this was primarily in the interests of a ruling class which controlled the use of force and the distribution of resources. Mistrust was the predominant attitude towards other units, and the willingness to use force was high. War, forcible displacement, oppression, slavery and assimilation were characteristic of such circumstances. Democracy, human rights and humanitarian international law are in historical perspective very recent developments. Over the long term, the number of autonomous social units has steadily decreased. Their maximum size and degree of organization have increased. Hunter-gatherers, nomadic shepherds and settled communities have evolved into city states, principalities, dynastic kingdoms, continental empires and today's territorial states. Setbacks such as the fall of the Western Roman Empire were followed eventually by new consolidation processes. Around 1500 BCE, when the world population is estimated to have been 50 million, there were perhaps 600,000 units.[2] Today the 193 states of the world are inhabited by nearly seven billion people, and it is more than questionable whether these states can be seen as autonomous units at all. In reality, we are dealing already with *one* integrating world system.

---

1   This section is based in part on Bummel, Andreas. 2011. 'Soziale Evolution, Weltparlament und Bewußtsein'. Tattva Viveka 48: 64–69.
2   Carneiro, Robert L. 2004. 'The Political Unification of the World: Whether, When, and How—Some Speculations'. Cross-Cultural Research (38) 2: 162–77, p. 175.

War and socio-political evolution

Historically, wars of conquest and the use of force have played a key role in the emergence of larger social units and the structures of state. 'Force, and not enlightened self-interest, is the mechanism by which political evolution has led, step by step, from autonomous villages to the state', wrote the anthropologist Robert Carneiro in an influential essay in 1970. From small villages to great empires, in the whole of history there could not be found 'a single genuine exception' to 'the demonstrated inability of autonomous political units to relinquish their sovereignty in the absence of overriding external constraints'.[3] However, the socio-political dynamic of development is undergoing a fundamental change, one which increasingly excludes the use of force. The English sociologist Herbert Spencer established in 1897 already that wars of conquest had outlived their day as a means of bringing about lasting integration. 'That integration of simple groups into compound ones, and of these into doubly, compound ones, which war has effected, until at length great nations have been produced, is a process already carried as far as seems either practicable or desirable', he wrote. He recognised the human urge to emancipation. Rule by oppression would not work any longer. 'Empires formed of alien peoples habitually fall to pieces when the coercive power which holds them together fails; and even could they be held together, would not form harmoniously-working wholes: *peaceful federation* is the only further consolidation to be looked for.'[4] (Emphasis added.)

Nevertheless, wars of conquest continued to be pursued. The anthropologist Robert Bates Graber cited the two world wars as the most important examples. Territorial conflicts played a significant part in the outbreak of the First World War, and the Second World War was conducted by Nazi Germany as a war of annihilation and conquest. As Graber notes however, the final outcome of both wars was an increase, not a decrease, in the total number of states. 'In terms of political evolution, this suggests disintegrative rather than integrative overall effects for conquest warfare', was his summing up for the 20th century.[5] After 1945, maintaining the territorial integrity of states became a key international principle which can be found in Article 2, Paragraph 4 of the UN Charter. Even the artificial colonial borders remained intact in the course of decolonization. Since 1976 there have been no significant instances of the successful annexation of territory over a

---

3   Id. 1970. 'A Theory of the Origin of the State'. Science 169: 733–38, p. 734.
4   Spencer, Herbert. 1897. The Principles of Sociology. Vol. II, Part 2. New York: D. Appleton and Company, p. 664.
5   Graber, Robert Bates. 2006. Plunging to Leviathan? Exploring the World's Political Future. Boulder Colo.: Paradigm Publishers, p. 67.

longer term.[6] The takeover of Crimea by the Russian Federation in 2014, against the wishes of the Ukraine, therefore represents a worrying retrograde step.

The prohibition against the use of force in Article 2, Paragraph 4 of the UN Charter documents the fact that the use of force is no longer acceptable between states. From 17 July 2018, wars of aggression will be added to the list of crimes that can be prosecuted by the ICC, as was originally planned. The prohibition against war under international law, as first laid down in the Kellogg–Briand Pact of 1928, reflects a growing change in attitudes. The desire to wage war or to conquer is a relic of an archaic mentality that is gradually being overcome.[7] The demonstrations against the USA-led Iraq War in 2003, to give one illustration, were in many countries the biggest such demonstrations in their history. On one day alone, 15 February 2003, more than 10 million people are believed to have gone out on the streets in an internationally coordinated protest. The protest was directed not only against the war but against the hegemonic conduct, in defiance of international law, of the USA. The *New York Times* commented apropos of these protests that world public opinion was now a new 'superpower'.[8]

The 'interdependence of destruction' (Schütz) between the nuclear great powers means that the consolidation of the system of states into a single world state entity by the exercise or threat of military force by a hegemonic power is practically impossible. A third world war would destroy world civilization. It is simply wrong to assert, as Rittberger and his co-authors do, that the establishment of a world state 'would require the exercise of military force, in the worst case even a global war of elimination' between the states in existence today'.[9] Just like the process of economic and political integration in the regions, the global process of state formation will not be driven today by the use of force between states. Contrary to Carneiro's assumption, the example of European integration demonstrates that it is perfectly possible for states to relinquish their rights of sovereignty in a gradual, peaceful and cooperative process. How else but in this way could a world federation committed to human rights and democratic principles come about? On several major issues today already, sovereignty at the international level is no more than a façade; a world state framework would offer the possibility of a collective restoration of genuine political control. It may be true, though, that the *rapid* establishment of a global federal state under

6   Zacher, Mark W. 2001. 'The Territorial Integrity Norm: International Boundaries and the Use of Force'. International Organization (55) 2: 215–50.
7   Cf. Oesterdiekhoff, Georg W. 2012. Die Entwicklung der Menschheit: Von der Kindheitsphase zur Erwachsenenreife. VS Verlag für Sozialwissenschaften, pp. 509ff.
8   Tyler, Patrick E. 17 February 2003. 'A New Power In the Streets'. The New York Times (www.nytimes.com).
9   Rittberger, Volker, Andreas Kruck, and Anne Romund. 2010. Grundzüge der Weltpolitik. Theorie und Empirie des Weltregierens. 1st ed. Wiesbaden: VS Verlag für Sozialwissenschaften, p. 317.

present conditions is unrealistic. We have already pointed out, for example, how the democratization processes at the nation state and global levels are mutually dependent. However, as William E. Scheuerman points out, this is no reason 'to preclude more or less a priori' (as he accuses those belonging to the contemporary cosmopolitan school of thought of doing) 'that a global federal state might proffer a worthwhile eventual goal, whose bases could potentially be *carefully and gradually constructed via responsible and peaceful political means*' (emphasis added).[10]

The decline of violence

An important precondition and driver of the changing dynamics of socio-political development lies in a changing global mindset. In a very influential book published in 2011, the Harvard psychologist Steven Pinker argued with the aid of a multitude of statistics that human recourse to violence had decreased over the centuries: for example, that, relative to total population, the numbers of murders, rapes, war deaths and genocide victims had gone down sharply. This development is especially clearly observable in the period since 1945. According to Pinker, '[t]he decline of violence may be the most significant and least appreciated development in the history of our species', and 'nostalgia for a peaceful past is the biggest delusion of all'. Following Norbert Elias, Pinker believes that the single most important factor in the reduction in violence may be the rise of the state, which 'uses a monopoly on force to protect its citizens from one another'. As bands and tribes came under the control of the state, something Pinker describes as a 'pacification process', the rate of violent death fell by a factor of five. As the fiefs of Europe coalesced into kingdoms and sovereign states, 'the consolidation of law enforcement eventually brought down the homicide rate another thirtyfold'.[11] Further progress in the 'humanitarian revolution' was brought about by the era of the Enlightenment, the decline in violent conflict between states and the revolution in human rights following the Second World War.

The development of reason, empathy, and morality

Among the *psychological* factors responsible for the declining use and acceptability of force Pinker includes the rise of empathy, self-control, morality and rationality. The New Zealand political scientist James R. Flynn found that intelligence as measured by IQ tests has increased steadily and significantly over the

---

10   Scheuerman, William E. 2014. 'Cosmopolitanism and the world state'. Rev. of Int. Studies (40) 3: 419–41, p. 425.
11   Pinker, Steven. 2011. The Better Angels of Our Nature. New York: Viking, pp. 692f., 681.

course of the last century from generation to generation. In his view, 'the greater complexity of everyday life in the modern world' promotes classificatory, logical, abstract and hypothetical thought of a kind which is valorised in intelligence tests.[12] This refers to the 'formal operational' stage of cognitive development as described by the developmental psychologist Jean Piaget (1896 to 1980). According to Piaget's research, human intellectual development from birth to adulthood, in all cultures, can be divided into up to four consecutive stages - the sensorimotor, preoperational, concrete operational and formal operational periods. Extended modern school education is a precondition for a successful formal operational stage, roughly between the eleventh and sixteenth years.[13] 'Thinking now draws the appropriate conclusions from arbitrary assumptions and premises, without necessarily believing in them', is the summary put forward by the sociologist Georg W. Oesterdiekhoff. This is what first enables the formation and testing of hypotheses, for example.[14] He argues that modern culture and modern education have enabled the diffusion of formal operational thinking 'throughout the entire industrial population'. This is how the scientific-technical civilization arose over the course of the 19th and 20th centuries. 'The 20th century can be understood not just as the age of the industrialization and modernization of the world, but also as the epoch of the worldwide expansion of formal operational thinking, or as the era of the maturation of humanity', writes Oesterdiekhoff.[15]

Advances in cognitive development create the conditions required for a maturation of human empathetic capability and moral judgement. Research shows that the cognitive stages identified by Piaget represent a prerequisite for the parallel development of stages of social perception and role performance, which in turn form a prerequisite for a parallel maturation of moral judgement. While cognitive development leads to a progressively better understanding of the objective world, the development of the capacity to adopt others' perspectives brings with it a progressively better understanding of how and why people as subjects think and behave in certain ways. Moral judgement then represents a further step in which a judgement is made as to how we, and others, *ought to* think and behave.[16] The developmental psychologist Robert Selman distinguishes between four stages in the evolution of social perception which relate to Piaget's stages. With regard to individual moral development, the psychologist Lawrence

---

12 Flynn, James R. 2012. Are We Getting Smarter? Rising IQ in the Twenty-First Century. Cambridge Univ. Press, p. 96.
13 Oesterdiekhoff, Georg W. 2006. Kulturelle Evolution des Geistes. Die historische Wechselwirkung von Psyche and Gesellschaft. Münster: LIT, pp. 65ff.
14 Ibid., p. 45.
15 Id. (2012), loc. cit., pp. 324, 59.
16 Walker, Lawrence J. 1980. 'Cognitive and Perspective-Taking Prerequisites for Moral Development'. Child Development (51) 1: 131–39, p. 137.

Kohlberg (1927 to 1987) identified three cognitive levels, each with two stages, which are linked to Piaget's and Selman's stages: the preconventional, conventional and postconventional levels.

At the first stage of Kohlberg's preconventional level, morality is situation specific and aligned with punishment and obedience. Whether an act is viewed as right or wrong depends on its consequences. At the second stage, an action is right if it serves to satisfy the self's needs and occasionally others'. Moral evaluation on the conventional level is then aligned with the expectations of others, regardless of consequences. The third stage here is linked to people, while the orientation of the fourth is towards law and authority. 'There is orientation toward authority, fixed rules, and the maintenance of the social order', wrote Kohlberg. 'Right behavior consists of doing one's duty, showing respect for authority and maintaining the given social order for its own sake.'[17] On the postconventional level, moral values and norms are generally applied regardless of the authority of the groups or persons advocating those principles. It is also irrelevant whether one identifies with these groups oneself. At the fifth stage of the 'social-contract legalistic orientation', the relativity of one's own behaviour is recognised, and an action is regarded as right if it is in accordance with laws and standards agreed by the whole society following democratic rules and procedures. The sixth stage involves an orientation towards self-selected ethical and moral principles with the personal conscience as a guiding agent. Kohlberg summed this up as follows: '[a]t the heart, these are universal principles of *justice*, of the *reciprocity* and *equality* of the human *rights* and of respect for the dignity of human beings as *individual persons*'.[18]

Kohlberg's theory is not good at explaining *why* people decide to take account of others' wellbeing and to act selflessly. As the psychologist Martin Hoffman emphasizes, the formation of the relevant cognitive capacities alone is not enough. For him it is the *emotional* aspect of empathy and morality which is the decisive factor. A tendency towards empathising and caring is *innate* to human beings, he believes, and can be observed already in small children. On the preconventional level already, children spontaneously demonstrate empathetic reactions and an intuitive, pro-social moral attitude. According to Hoffman, human empathetic maturation develops in five steps, beginning in infancy.[19] It is

---

17 Kohlberg, Lawrence, and Richard Kramer. 2009. 'Continuities and Discontinuities in Childhood and Adult Moral Development'. Human Development 12: 93–120, p. 101.
18 Ibid.
19 Hoffman, Martin L. 2000. Empathy and Moral Development: Implications for Caring and Justice. Cambridge University Press, pp. 6, 63ff.

only at the more advanced stages of empathetic development that emotional reactions are linked to cognitive processes.

The origin of morality in group selection

In evolutionary psychology, a whole new branch of research has arisen focused
on the evolutionary origins of human psychology. The constant and ubiquitous
human disposition to empathy seems to be a feature with deep evolutionary
roots. The picture of human beings as egotistical and asocial creatures which
underlies the thinking of Thomas Hobbes, to name one example, 'is untenable
in light of what we know about the evolution of our species', writes the prima-
tologist Frans de Waal. Human beings 'have been group-living forever' and are
'social to the core'.[20] In his famous work 'The Descent of Man', published in
1871, Charles Darwin (1809 to 1882) asked how social instincts, altruism and
actions for the benefit of the community might be explained by his theory of
natural selection. The solution, he argued, might lie in prehistoric group selection. Individuals who were prepared to take risks for others and died in the process would on average have fewer descendants, and the leaning towards selfless-
ness should therefore gradually disappear. 'It must not be forgotten', he explained, 'that although a high standard of morality gives but a slight or no advantage to each individual man and his children over the other men of the same
tribe, yet that an increase in the number of well-endowed men and an advance-
ment in the standard of morality will certainly give an immense advantage to
one tribe over another. A tribe including many members who, from possessing
in a high degree the spirit of patriotism, fidelity, obedience, courage and sympathy, were always ready to aid one another, and to sacrifice themselves for the
common good, would be victorious over most other tribes; and this would be
natural selection. At all times throughout the world tribes have supplanted
other tribes; and as morality is one important element in their success, the
standard of morality and the number of well-endowed men will thus everywhere tend to rise and increase.'[21]

In what is perhaps one of the most important recent research contributions
to this topic, the economists Samuel Bowles and Herbert Gintis confirm the
significance of group selection to the early origins of social behaviour, altruism
and morality in the harsh conditions that characterised the Pleistocene, beginning roughly 2.5 million years ago and ending about 10,000 years BCE. In the

20   Waal, Frans de. 2006. Primates and Philosophers and How Morality Evolved. Princeton University Press, pp. 4f.
21   Darwin, Charles. 1874. The Descent of Man. 2nd ed. New York: Clarke, Given and Hooper, p. 150.

2011 book 'A Cooperative Species', they explain that 'between-group competition for resources and survival was and remains a decisive force in human evolutionary dynamics'. They ascribe the decisive role to the extremely violent and deadly conflicts between Palaeolithic hunter-gatherers. 'Groups with many cooperative members tended to survive these challenges and to encroach upon the territory of the less cooperative groups, thereby both gaining reproductive advantages and proliferating cooperative behaviors through cultural transmission. The extraordinarily high stakes of intergroup competition and the contribution of altruistic cooperators to success in these contests meant that sacrifice on behalf of others, extending beyond the immediate family and even to virtual strangers, could proliferate.'[22] Since altruism and selfless behaviour are extended to a much wider circle than just direct genetic relatives, the theory of kin selection is not sufficient to explain the phenomenon. Forms of reciprocity on the other hand, which can explain the cooperative behaviour of individuals, are ineffective for larger groups, and apart from that they are not truly altruistic, as they include an expectation of reward in return. Edward O. Wilson has now also endorsed this school of thought. In his 2012 *New York Times* bestseller 'The Social Conquest of Earth', the founder of sociobiology and the world's leading researcher on ants supports a multi-level selection interpretation. 'At the higher level of the two relevant levels of biological organization,' he writes, 'groups compete with groups, favoring cooperative social traits among members of the same group. At the lower level, members of the same group compete with one another in a manner that leads to self-serving behavior.' Thus, individual selection favours selfishness and group selection favours altruism – the latter, however, not with respect to the members of *other* groups, but only of *one's own*.[23] As Frans de Waal writes, '[m]orality likely evolved as a *within-group* phenomenon in conjunction with other typical within-group capacities, such as conflict resolution, cooperation, and sharing' (emphasis added). 'In the course of human evolution', he goes on, 'out-group hostility enhanced in-group solidarity to the point that morality emerged.'[24]

In-group morality and humanity's crisis of adolescence

So not only is it important that the individual's emotional and cognitive moral capacity is able to develop progressively through the different stages; the degree

22 Bowles, Samuel, and Herbert Gintis. 2011. A Cooperative Species. Human Reciprocity and its Evolution. Princeton University Press, p. 4.
23 Wilson, Edward O. 2012. The Social Conquest of Earth. New York: Liveright Pub. Corporation, pp. 289, 241.
24 Waal, loc. cit., pp 53f.

to which the empathy and morality that result are group-oriented or universal is also key. It is routinely the case that a different moral yardstick is applied to members of the same social group from that applied to those outside the group. In-group and out-group morality can differ sharply. Aspects of group identity and group membership therefore play an important role in practical moral assessments. In the most extreme cases, this can go so far that outsiders are denied the status of human beings. Such a dehumanization means that the minimum moral consideration naturally due to every human being is taken away from them. According to Gregory Stanton, an expert on genocide who teaches in the USA, dehumanization of a previously recognised group of persons is a key precondition for genocide. 'Dehumanization overcomes the normal human revulsion against murder', Professor Stanton explains.[25] The industrialised genocide carried out by Nazi Germany against the Jews was based not only on a 'law and order' morality on the conventional level, in which obedience of authority represents an end in itself, but also on just such a dehumanization.

On the postconventional level, in terms of moral judgement, an emancipation from group memberships should take place, since it is on this level that values and norms begin to be guided by principles and to take on a universal character. As Peter Singer has argued, in a coherent ethical system the same standards must be applied to everyone – to oneself, one's family, one's own group and to other groups. As a matter of principle, one's own interests cannot be more important than another's simply because they are one's own.[26] A postconventional morality as pure in-group morality is a contradiction in terms. Thus, the German philosopher Karl-Otto Apel has pointed out that the integration of universalist moral principles into 'European post-Enlightenment morality' cannot be equated with 'the successful transformation of the *purely conventional* in-group morality of the tribes, nations and militant faith communities into a *postconventional* morality that now extends into the institutions and conventions'. Apel sees the 'universalist transcendence of any pure "in-group morality"' as an 'unfinished project of humanity' – 'the overcoming of the collective crisis of adolescence of the human race'. The adolescent crisis of the human race is 'a problem on a world-historical scale' that can be observed in the transition from the conventional to the postconventional level of morality.[27] If the ethical principle of impartiality is taken to its logical conclusion, according to Singer, then we would have to treat all people with the same compassion that

---

25 Stanton, Gregory H. 2013. 'The Ten Stages of Genocide." Genocide Watch (www.genocidewatch.org).
26 Singer, Peter. 2011. The Expanding Circle. Princeton University Press, pp. 118f.
27 Apel, Karl-Otto. 1990. Diskurs and Verantwortung. Das Problem des Übergangs zur postkonventionellen Moral. Frankfurt am Main: Suhrkamp, pp. 410, 429, 474

we extend to our own wider family. 'The ideal of the brotherhood of human beings has now passed into official rhetoric; turning that ideal into reality, however, is another matter. There can be no brotherhood when some nations indulge in previously unheard-of luxuries, while others struggle to stave off famine.'[28] From the perspective of postconventional morality, structural violence and the underlying governance and democracy deficits afflicting the international system cannot be justified.

According to Karl-Otto Apel, modern western democracies manifest in their constitutions and their recognition of human and civil rights 'a representation of postconventional morality at the level of law and of cultural revolution'.[29] For Georg W. Oesterdiekhoff, the emergence of formal operations, which is of course a precondition for postconventional thought, should be regarded as 'the only cause' of the emergence of the democratic state and the rule of law. 'Democratic institutions are direct products of the spirit of liberty and of humanism. These ideas only arise in the formal operational stage', he writes.[30] The capacity to adopt other social perspectives and for empathy is another precondition. Jeremy Rifkin stresses this aspect in a book on the 'empathic civilization'. 'Empathy', he writes, 'is the soul of democracy ... The evolution of empathy and the evolution of democracy have gone hand in hand throughout history. The more empathic the culture, the more democratic its values and governing institutions. The less empathic the culture, the more totalitarian its values and governing institutions. While apparent, it's strange how little attention has been paid to the inextricable relationship between empathic extension and democratic expansion in the study of history and evolution of governance.'[31]

The challenge of 'humanity's crisis of adolescence' lies in giving objective form to the principles of postconventional morality in a *democratic world legal order*. The current international system is the expression of a morality which contains elements from both the preconventional and the conventional levels. On the one side, although the main features of a legal order are absent, at the same time the states are most certainly bound to each other by complex legal ties which make behaviour foreseeable and regulate interactions and which all of them therefore have an interest in maintaining. On the other side, the actions of the governments are largely directed towards the pursuit of their own interests and as far as possible towards the instrumentalization of the system to that purpose.

28 Singer, loc. cit., p. 119.
29 Apel, loc. cit., p. 433.
30 Oesterdiekhoff (2012), loc. cit., pp. 392f.
31 Rifkin, Jeremy. 2010. The Empathic Civilization: The Race to Global Consciousness in a World in Crisis. Cambridge: Polity Press, p. 161.

Sociogenesis and psychogenesis

As Norbert Elias demonstrated, there is an indivisible connection between the development of the human psyche and that of the social institutions, between psychogenesis and sociogenesis. Psychological change and structural change are mutually dependent. It was only after a given level of complex social inter-dependence was reached, characteristic of the state formation process and modernity, that greater control of the emotions, rationality and a fully developed sense of shame were able to develop. 'Psychological developments contingent on sociogenetic or institutional factors in turn effect institutional transformations', Oesterdiekhoff summarises. 'Civilization and the civilising of human beings is a psychogenetic process which totally transforms the cognitive, emotional and habitual structures of the population. Industrialization, modernization and state formation are the result of this civilising of the population. The civilising of psychological functions is a movement away from 'natural', instinctive, egocentric, childish, undifferentiated and primitive states to more differentiated, more rational and more intellectual psychological states. This gradual increase in cognitive sophistication and emotional self-control is what gave rise to nation-building, modernization and industrialization', he explains. In human history, there can thus be observed 'a sequentially proceeding, unilinear and increasing sophistication and integration of *social and psychological structures*' (emphasis added).[32] The continuing growth of global interdependence, complexity and modernity should lead us to expect both a deepening psychological transformation and an accompanying transformation of the social structure. As formal operational thinking, empathy, postmaterialist values and postconventional morality spread and deepen through the world population, so the issue of a world legal order and a global state will present itself ever more insistently and inescapably. As Immanuel Kant wrote during the era of the stage-coach already, while 'gradually approaching' the goal of a world state, cosmopolitan law becomes a 'necessary complement' of public and international law as soon as 'a violation of right in *one* part of the world is felt *all over* it.'[33]

The widening circle of empathy

In Peter Singer's view, it is an unavoidable consequence of postconventional rationality that altruistic concern for people's wellbeing will be extended to the entire human race. Ultimately, all living creatures capable of pain and pleasure

---

32 Oesterdiekhoff, Georg W. 2000. Zivilisation and Strukturgenese. Norbert Elias and Jean Piaget im Vergleich. Frankfurt: Suhrkamp, pp. 48f., 29.
33 Kant, Immanuel. 1903 [1795]. Perpetual Peace, transl. by Campbell Smith. London: George Allen & Unwin, p. 142.

will be included within this circle.[34] It has been a recurrent observation since the 18th century that, as the size of social units grows, so too does the circle of those to whom feelings of empathy, moral equality and solidarity are extended. Kant's contemporary David Hume (1711 to 1776), for example, pointed in his 'Enquiry Concerning the Principles of Morals' to the 'natural progress of human sentiments, and ... the gradual enlargement of our regards to justice'. Beginning with the family, the circle of those to whom the same rules apply, and thus of those deserving to be treated with justice and fairness, grows steadily and continuously *as interaction with them increases.*[35] 'As man advances in civilization, and small tribes are united into larger communities,' wrote Charles Darwin, 'the simplest reason would tell each individual that he ought to extend his social instincts and sympathies to all the members of the same nation, though personally unknown to him. This point being once reached, there is only an artificial barrier to prevent his sympathies extending to the men of all nations and races.'[36] According to Carl Sagan, '[h]uman history can be viewed as a slowly dawning awareness that we are members of a larger group. Initially our loyalties were to ourselves and our immediate family, next, to bands of wandering hunter-gatherer, then to tribes, small settlements, city-states, nations. ... If we are to survive, our loyalties must be broadened further, to include the whole human community, the entire planet Earth'.[37]

Jeremy Rifkin has traced this development and sees a link between increasing global interconnectedness and the extension of human 'empathic consciousness'. Globalization has created an 'ever more boundaryless social space', bringing hundreds of millions of people into permanent contact with each other and enabling their empathic capacity to grow and reach beyond national cultures, beyond continents, oceans and other traditional barriers. The 'cosmopolitanization of the human race' has begun, he believes.[38] Over fifty years ago, Marshall McLuhan noted that '[e]lectric speed in bringing all social and political functions together in a sudden implosion has heightened human awareness of responsibility to an intense degree. ... The aspiration of our time for wholeness, empathy and depth of awareness is a natural adjunct of electric technology'.[39] Following McLuhan, who always emphasized the point that the technological medium changes our perception and awareness independently of its content ('the medium is the

---

34 Singer, loc. cit., p. 120.
35 Hume, David. 1912. An Enquiry Concerning the Principles of Morals. Chicago: The Open Court Publ. Co., p. 25.
36 Darwin, loc. cit., p. 138.
37 Sagan, Carl. 2011. Cosmos. Random House, p. 361.
38 Rifkin, loc. cit., pp. 425, 428.
39 McLuhan, Marshall. 1964. Understanding Media. London: Routledge, p. 5.

message'), we should expect the increasing interconnectedness of global communications to lead to a planetary consciousness and ultimately to planetary integration. Rifkin perceives in his fellow human beings 'a journey to mature empathic consciousness' leading to a 'universal consciousness'. This consciousness gives one 'the ability to experience an entire group of people or even other species as if their distress were one's own'. Since in Rifkin's view the empathic circle is widening as the societal structures of world civilization grow ever more complex, and since these in turn entail an ever greater use of resources, he believes the great paradox of human history lies in the fact that the price of our growing empathic consciousness is the ever more piratical plundering of our home planet. Just at the moment when the human race is so close to achieving global empathic consciousness, it stands simultaneously on the brink of self-destruction through climate change or weapons of mass destruction. 'We are at a decisive moment in the human journey', he writes, 'where the race to global empathic consciousness is running up against global entropic collapse.'[40]

In his 1979 book 'The Imperative of Responsibility', the philosopher Hans Jonas declared global empathy to be the ethical imperative of the technological age. On account of modern technology, he argued, the consequences of individual actions now had the potential to affect every other person on the planet and the survival of the human species. For this reason, there was no longer a duty to love only one's neighbour, i.e. those in the immediate vicinity of one's actions, but also to love the most distant strangers, including *all people* and *all life* on Earth, now and in the future. From the responsibility for the survival of the human species Jonas derived the so-called 'ecological imperative: 'Act so that the effects of your action are compatible with the permanence of genuine human life'; and 'do not compromise the conditions for an indefinite continuation of humanity on earth'.[41] Based on his theory of universal stages of evolution, the British author Richard Barrett argues that human evolution 'will only continue to progress if we, the members of the species known as Homo sapiens, can learn how to bond with each other to create human group structures that cooperate with each other to solve the problems of humanity.'[42]

40 Rifkin, loc. cit., pp. 127-128, 42.
41 Jonas, Hans. 1985 [1979]. The Imperative of Responsibility: In Search of an Ethics for the Technological Age. University of Chicago Press, p. 11.
42 Barrett, Richard. 2015. The Metrics of Human Consciousness, p. 34.

The transition to integral consciousness

There are numerous models for the categorization of human consciousness and its development, under the most diverse aspects. Ken Wilber has tried to provide a comparative overview within the theoretical framework of an 'integral psychology'.[43] From the perspective of world history, the description by the philosopher of culture Jean Gebser (1905 to 1973) has proved especially influential. He distinguishes in his groundbreaking work 'The Ever-Present Origin', the first volume of which appeared in 1949, between four structures of consciousness: the magical, the mythical, the mental and the integral, all of them deriving from an underlying fundamental structure he terms 'archaic'. According to Gebser, humanity finds itself now in a transitional phase in which the integral structure is beginning to form. Each structure of consciousness is characterised by its own perception of time, space, self and external world, by different forms of thinking and feeling, discourse and language, and by certain social and societal features. The magical structure, for example, is instinctive and impulsive, experiential and natural, self- and timeless, and prerational-analogical. Gebser believes that power politics, and the lust for power, have their roots in the wish, located deep within the nature-embedded magical consciousness, to rule the external world (in order not to be ruled by it).[44] The mythical structure is based on a pictorial imagination, sensibility, irrationality, and interpreted experience, and is ego-less/'we-oriented' and focused on the past. The awakening of nature here reaches its conclusion, and the awakening of the world of the soul begins. The future-oriented mental structure, which according to Gebser was first manifested in Greece around 500 BCE, is then marked by an individual consciousness, reflection, abstraction, volition, rationality, directive thought, three-dimensionality and conceptual imagination. It is presumably no mere accident that it coincides with the rise of the first democratic state forms.

Finally, the integral structure arises out of a holistic realization (or 'presentation'), perception and integration of the other structures. Gebser describes the integral consciousness as present in the now, ego-free/amaterial, aperspectival, arational and four-dimensional. All the structures are 'still present in more or less latent and acute form' in every person. If one structure or any element of it begins to predominate, it becomes destructive, or to use Gebser's term 'deficient'. The significance of the integral structure is that 'the various structures that constitute [a person] must have become *transparent* and conscious to him;

---

43   Wilber, Ken. 2000. Integral Psychology: Consciousness, Spirit, Psychology, Therapy. Shambhala Publications.
44   An English edition of this groundbreaking work finally appeared in 1985: Gebser, Jean. The Ever-Present Origin. Transl. by Noel Barstad. Athens, OH: Ohio University Press, cf. pp. 51ff.

it also means that he has perceived their effect on his life and destiny, and mastered the deficient components by his insight'.[45] Whereas the magical and mythical structures are associated with clan and tribal consciousness, and the mental with nationalism, the integral structure stands for 'a consciousness of the whole, an integral consciousness encompassing all time and embracing both man's distant past and his approaching future as a living present'.[46] The integral consciousness is *planetary and mankind-oriented.*

The third democratic transformation is happening in conjunction with an internal revolution. '[W]ith the rise of the integral worldview, a world federation becomes realistic and even inevitable', writes the US American author Steve McIntosh. 'The mechanism of a world federation', he continues, 'is the practical way that integral consciousness can take greater responsibility for the problems of the world.' The link between sociogenesis and psychogenesis can also be found in his work. He argues that every new worldview has developed around a political project, and that the integral worldview will not be an exception. The creation of 'a new level of human political organization' will be the political project that enables the integral worldview 'to produce lasting cultural evolution'.[47] As Jürgen Habermas observed, each new evolutionary push is marked by contributing institutions in which the rationality structures of the next higher stage of development are already embodied.[48] An assembly of democratically elected representatives of the world population would be the first political body in the history of humankind to establish a direct connection between every single person and the planet as a social unit. It would be the most powerful symbolic embodiment of a postconventional, integral and planetary consciousness. Two months after his election to the presidency of Czechoslovakia, Václav Havel, a believer in the vision of a world parliament, gave a remarkable speech in Washington D.C. 'Consciousness precedes Being, and not the other way around, as Marxists claim', he declared before the US Congress. 'For this reason', said Havel, 'the salvation of this human world lies nowhere else than in the human heart, in the human power to reflect, in human humbleness and in human responsibility. Without a global revolution in the sphere of human consciousness, nothing will change for the better in the sphere of our Being as humans, and the catastrophe toward which this world is headed, whether it be ecological, social, demographic or a general breakdown of civilization, will be unavoidable.'[49]

---

45   Ibid., pp. 42, 99.
46   Ibid., p. 6.
47   McIntosh, Steve. 2007. Integral Consciousness and the Future of Evolution. St. Paul, Minnesota: Paragon House, pp. 115f.
48   Habermas, Jürgen. 1976. Zur Rekonstruktion des Historischen Materialismus. Frankfurt: Suhrkamp, p. 37.
49   Havel, Vaclav. 21 February 1990. 'Address to the Joint Session of the U.S. Congress, Washington D.C.'.

Group narcissism and the Promethean gap

More than six decades ago, Jean Gebser wrote that the world was heading for a catastrophe 'of decisive finality for life on earth'. The span of time separating us from that event, he continued, 'is determined by an increase in technological feasibility inversely proportional to man's sense of responsibility'.[50] Albert Einstein's theory of relativity links space and time in a four-dimensional structure, and is regarded by Gebser as a striking manifestation of integral consciousness. However, it was used to construct the atom bomb. The world crisis is characterised by a destructive excess of rationality and egoism within the framework of the mental structure, combined with the lust for power of the magical level. Humanity and the Earth in their present forms could disappear, and the transition to an integral consciousness could be delayed by 'two millennia', Gebser thought.[51] Nevertheless, he assumed that many people today were already capable of developing an integral consciousness. 'Mutations have always appeared when the prevailing consciousness structure proved to be no longer adequate for mastering the world', he wrote. 'This was the case in the last historically accessible mutation which occurred around 500 B.C. and led from the mythical to the mental structure. The psychistic, deficient mythical climate of that time presented a threat, and the sudden onset of the mental structure brought about a decisive transformation. In our day the rationalistic, deficient mental structure presents an equal threat, and the breakthrough into the integral will also bring about a new and decisive mutation.'[52]

The gulf between humankind's emotional-moral maturity and its technological abilities was something that also preoccupied the humanist Erich Fromm. In his book 'The Heart of Man', he investigates the connections between narcissism and destructiveness, nationalism and war. 'We live in a historical period', wrote Fromm, 'characterized by a sharp discrepancy between the intellectual development of man, which has led to the development of the most destructive armaments, and his mental-emotional development, which has left him still in a state of marked narcissism with all its pathological symptoms.'[53] The philosopher Günther Anders (1902 to 1992) spoke of a 'Promethean gap' to describe the 'final rupture', in this technical age, of the link between knowledge, ability and action on the one side and comprehension, feeling and conscience on the other. Human beings, he thought, were not up to the challenge posed by 'their inner Prometheus'. The consequences of this gulf could destroy

50   Gebser, loc. cit., p. xxvii.
51   Ibid., p. 297.
52   Ibid., p. 294.
53   Fromm, Erich. 2010. The Heart of Man. Riverdale NY: American Mental Health Foundation, p. 86.

humanity.[54] Fromm, too, stresses that the contradiction between human intellectual and emotional development could 'easily' lead to a catastrophe.

According to Fromm, it can be assumed that the narcissistic drive, just like the sex drive and the instinct for self-preservation, has an important biological function, since in the interests of their own survival all human beings are bound to treat themselves as more important than anyone else. However, it is only an *optimal* narcissism, not a *maximal* one, that serves the goal of survival. The biologically necessary quantum can only be so great as to remain compatible with social cooperation. Fromm describes the process whereby individual narcissism transmutes into group narcissism. In place of the self, the family, the clan, the people or the nation becomes the object of the narcissistic drive. 'Thus, narcissistic energy is maintained but used in the interests of the survival of the group rather than for the survival of the individual', Fromm observed.[55]

Ideally, the solution would lie in a gradual reduction and eventual overcoming of narcissism in every individual human being in the course of *an expansion of consciousness*. For now, however, according to Fromm, the simpler option lay in *at least changing the object* towards which narcissistic energy was directed. Fromm was thinking of an orientation towards the planet and the human race. 'If the individual could experience himself primarily as a citizen of the world and if he could feel pride in mankind and in its achievements, his narcissism would turn toward the human race as an object, rather than to its conflicting components.' And, he added, '[t]he image of the human race and of its achievements as the object of benign narcissism could be represented by supranational organizations such as the United Nations'. However, Fromm noted, 'it is clear that such a development can occur only inasmuch as many and eventually all nations concur and are willing to reduce their national sovereignty in favor of the sovereignty of mankind; not only in terms of political, but also in terms of emotional, realities. A strengthened United Nations and the reasonable and peaceful solution of group conflicts are the obvious conditions for the possibility that humanity and its common achievements shall become the object of group narcissism'. Among the main preconditions that had to be achieved first before destructive group narcissism could be overcome and Man could 'experience in himself all of humanity' Fromm included the 'subordination of national sovereignties *to the sovereignty of the human race and its chosen organs*' (emphasis added).[56]

---

54 Anders, Günther. 1956. Die Antiquiertheit des Menschen 1: Über die Seele im Zeitalter der zweiten industriellen Revolution. München: Verlag C.H. Beck, pp. 267ff.
55 Fromm, loc., cit., p. 70.
56 Ibid., pp. 87-90.

The problem of cultural lag

It is notable that the revolutionary developments in technology have had strangely little impact on international political structures. The author and critic of technology Lewis Mumford pointed out this phenomenon in the middle of the 1970s. 'By turns the steamboat, the railroad, the postal system, the electric telegraph, the airplane, have been described as instruments that would transcend local weaknesses, redress inequalities of natural and cultural resources, and lead to a worldwide political unity – "the parliament of man, the federation of the world." Once technical unification was established, human solidarity, "progressive" minds believed, would follow. In the course of two centuries, these hopes have been discredited.'[57] Clearly, what we are dealing with here is the phenomenon of 'cultural lag', as described in 1922 already by the sociologist William Ogburn (1886 to 1959). According to this theory, every society requires a little time to adjust to dealing with new technologies and their applications. Thus the problem is not only the great and ever-increasing speed of change in modernity, but also the differing rates at which cultures manage, to a greater or lesser degree, to come to terms with those changes.[58] The Westphalian international system of states, which dates back to 1648, is in this respect the most extreme anachronism in our time. Ogburn wrote in 1957 that 'the lag in adjusting to the atomic bomb' was 'a lag of great danger'.[59] In fact, *to this day* there has been no adjustment at all to this destructive technology. As we have shown, to be successful and sustainable, such an adjustment would have to consist in the establishment of a demilitarised, federal world peace order.

Interestingly, the inter-state rivalry for power inherent in the Westphalian system is an important driver of the dynamic of acceleration. The states system is the calm at the eye of the raging hurricane tearing through the world. The philosopher Paul Virilio, who has examined the development of the modern world under the aspect of speed, has spoken of 'dromocratic politics', that is, the politics of the race. In an outstanding study of 'time structures in modernity', the sociologist Hartmut Rosa writes that the unfolding of the modern process of acceleration 'can only be adequately grasped in light of the military and state-centered competition for the conquest, control, and defense of national territories'. Modernization, he continues, 'is an accelerative project of national states that was driven by nothing more than the political striving to preserve and accumulate power within a system of competing national states that took

---

57 Mumford, Lewis. 1970. The Myth of the Machine: The Pentagon of Power. Harcourt, Brace & World, p. 296.
58 Ogburn, William Fielding. 1922. Social Change with Respect to Culture and Original Nature. New York: The Viking Press, pp. 200ff.
59 Id. 1957. 'Cultural Lag as Theory'. Sociology and Social Research XLI: 167–74.

shape after the Treaty of Westphalia.' In his view, the nation states have now mutated in some respects into obstacles to acceleration. He writes: 'in a complete inversion of the circumstances of classical modernity, acceleration in late modernity is not achieved by state regulation of social, cultural, and economic processes and relations, but by their *deregulation*'. However, he concedes that overall they remain 'decisive agents of acceleration'. What has changed is merely the mode. The forces of acceleration have globalised, and compel the states, in a self-reinforcing dynamic, to push forward their own erosion. 'The political project of modernity has perhaps come to its end as a result of the desynchronization of socioeconomic development and political action', Rosa observes.[60] But that would only be the case if the 'cultural lag' were to persist, i.e. if the Westphalian system were to continue and there was therefore no adjustment in the global political structures. The elites are still managing to block the obvious solution, namely *the globalization of state power itself*. Within the world population, meanwhile, the outlines of the necessary change of consciousness are already clearly beginning to emerge.

For William E. Scheuerman, the question arises whether meaningful democracy is still possible 'amidst a state system whose fundamental temporal dynamics seem fundamentally inconsistent with careful, slow-going democratic deliberation and debate'. He then goes on to suggest where a possible solution might lie. 'If social acceleration represents a dangerous yet indispensable facet of the modern state system, how might we reconfigure that system so as to at least minimize the obvious dangers at hand, not the least of which remains the terrible specter of (high-speed) nuclear war? Might an alternative model of inter-state relations - some form of transnational democracy I perhaps - at least provide a better starting point than the Westphalian system for doing so?'[61] Democratic decision-making takes time. Paradoxically, a global democratic legislative system based on qualified majority voting might even lead to faster and more effective outcomes than international law, which is extremely slow. And a world parliament is also a political instrument that could be used to delay developments, to speed them up or even to block them entirely. It could serve to contain the self-propelling forces of acceleration.

60 Rosa, Hartmut. 2015. Social Acceleration. A New Theory of Modernity. Transl. by Jonathan Trejo-Mathys. New York: Columbia University Press, pp. 311, 204ff., 313.
61 Scheuerman, William E. 2003. 'Speed, States, and Social Theory: A Response to Hartmut Rosa'. Constellations (10) 1: 42–48, p. 47.

Global identity and the Other

In view of the developmental dynamic of human evolution to date, it has been argued that the emergence of a global government is simply impossible, since the Earth does not face any external opponent or any kind of external entity which would make possible the development of a global identity or political integration on a planetary scale. The anthropologist Richard Newbold Adams sums up the identity issue thus: '[i]dentity is fundamentally the binary differentiation of some set of "we" from some set of "other"'.[62] And Volker Rittberger wrote, 'without strong externally generated adaptation pressures there seems little likelihood of a world state' – without, however, wanting to entirely exclude the possibility.[63] US President Ronald Reagan addressed the issue in 1987. 'In our obsession with antagonisms of the moment, we often forget how much unites all the members of humanity', he said in a speech before the UN General Assembly. 'Perhaps we need some outside, universal threat to make us recognize this common bond. I occasionally think how quickly our differences worldwide would vanish if we were facing an alien threat from outside this world.'[64] As the Canadian political scientist Arash Abizadeh writes in an article on this topic, Georg Friedrich Hegel argued already in his 'The Phenomenology of Spirit' that the emergence of a consciousness of the self, and thus of identity, presupposes the recognition of that self by another. Following on from that, more recently the philosopher Charles Taylor emphasized that identity was always formed in dialogue or in dispute with others.

In Abizadeh's view, however, it is a mistake to simply assume that what is true for *individual* identity formation applies equally to *collective* identity formation. Unlike an individual, so the core of the argument runs, a collective can also constitute itself through recognition by its individual members. Recognition by another external collective is also a possibility, but not an absolute precondition.[65] The political scientist Alexander Wendt gets to the heart of the matter. 'The world state' he writes, 'would be recognized by the individuals and groups that constitute its parts, and it in turn would constitute and recognize them. This is possible because even though parts and whole are mutually constitutive, they are not identical; there is a boundary or difference between them.

---

62 Adams, Richard Newbold. 1975. Energy and Structure. A Theory of Social Power. Austin, London: University of Texas Press, pp. 210, 304.

63 Rittberger, Volker. 1973. Evolution and International Organization. Toward a New Level of Sociopolitical Integration. Den Haag: Nijhoff, p. 48.

64 Reagan, Ronald. 21 September 1987. 'Address to the 42nd Session of the United Nations General Assembly in New York, New York'.

65 Abizadeh, Arash. 2005. 'Does Collective Identity Presuppose an Other? On the Alleged Incoherence of Global Solidarity'. American Political Science Review (99) 1: 45–60, pp. 47ff.

The members of a world state have their own subjectivities that constrain its behavior, and the world state has a subjectivity that constrains their behavior.' Wendt also points out that global identity formation in a world state could also be engendered by means of *self-differentiation from a past that has been left behind*, and from its obsolete values. 'In Hegelian terms we could say that 'history' becomes the Other in terms of which the global Self is defined', he explains. Identity is based on stories, which can distinguish between *a past and a present self*, he continues. Germany, for example, draws part of its identity today from the demarcation separating it from the Nazi regime and its crimes '[H]umanity's own past provides a rich and terrifying repository in contrast to which cosmopolitan identity could constitute its "difference"', Abizadeh observes.[66]

The vision of a humanity transformed by history, the promise 'Never again!', is thus a part of the formation of a global identity. In a passionate plea for a planetary perspective, the French philosopher Edgar Morin dates the beginning of the planetary era to around 1500, when the small western European nations began to circumnavigate the world. Morin believes that this ushered in a 'planetary Iron Age', which he also calls the 'prehistory of the human spirit'.[67] In this age, in light of the threat posed by war, nuclear weapons, environmental destruction and overshoot, the dangerous 'Other' lies *in humanity itself*. An awareness that human history is actually just beginning, and a determination to finally overcome war, genocide, exploitation and environmental destruction, are important constituent parts of a global identity.

Humanity must address the issue of its collective shadow. This includes the structural violence perpetrated by the international system. A *global truth commission*, following the example of national commissions like that in South Africa, could be helpful in this and could accompany the transition to a democratic world order. One of the tasks of such a commission might be to investigate from a global perspective and to make public, in a manner as objective and free from ideology as possible, the circumstances surrounding the most serious crimes against humanity, wars and internal conflicts of recent and present times, to identify the culprits, to recognize and honour the victims, and to create a basis for reconciliation. As Heikki Patomäki and Teivo Teivainen emphasize, the moral and political legitimacy of such a commission is of the utmost importance.[68] It could be set up by a UNPA and continued within the framework of a world parliament. In the opinion of Michael Hardt and Antonio Negri, the

---

66 Ibid., p. 58.
67 Morin, Edgar, and Anne Brigitte Kern. 1999. Homeland Earth. Cresskill, NJ: Hampton Press, pp. 8, 58.
68 Patomäki, Heikki, and Teivo Teivainen. 2004. A possible World: democratic transformation of global institutions. London, New York: Zed Books, p. 136.

work of such commissions is 'an exemplary Enlightenment project of modernist politics, and the critique of it in these contexts could serve only to aid the mystificatory and repressive powers of the regime under attack'.[69]

The 'Overview Effect' and a planetary worldview

Even though there is no extra-terrestrial 'Other', the experience of seeing the planet as an integral entity, from the outside, is one of epochal significance for the self-knowledge and awakening consciousness of humanity. The first two full-face pictures of the Earth are among the most influential and important photographs ever taken. The photos in question are 'Earthrise', taken during the Apollo 8 mission on 24 December 1968, and the famous 'Blue Marble', taken on 7 December 1972 during the Apollo 17 mission. The television coverage of the moon landing in 1969 was followed by hundreds of millions of people, who were confronted with an outside perspective on the planet. The picture of the Earth in its totality is without question *the* symbol of our age. The author Frank White called the impact of the planetary perspective the 'Overview Effect'. It is not necessary to travel into space to experience this effect. 'Anyone who flies in an airplane and looks out the window has the opportunity to experience a mild version of it', said White.[70] Top-quality satellite and aerial images are now part of our everyday media experience. Programmes like Google Earth enable us to explore the entire globe from above, virtually.

The best descriptions of the 'Overview Effect' come from those who have experienced it themselves - the astronauts. Since the beginning of space travel, they have reported how deeply they were changed by the view of the planet from space. They describe being gripped by a feeling of unity, of home, and of vulnerability. The German astronaut Ulf Merbold, for example, was in space for 40 days all told in the course of three missions. 'The first sight of the Earth horizon', he reported, 'took my breath away. Not because I was surprised by the curve of the line of the horizon; it was more the royal blue colour of the atmosphere that enchanted me. But how thin this life-preserving layer was! This was the moment that all astronauts had talked of ... The Earth lay spread out below us. Its beauty was captivating – no language can describe it – yet how vulnerable it looked! ... We looked for the dividing border lines that are so clearly present between the countries on all the maps. But they don't exist.'[71] 'When you go

69   Hardt, Michael, and Antonio Negri. 2000. Empire. Cambridge: Harvard University Press, p. 156.
70   White, Frank. 2014. The Overview Effect. 3rd ed. Reston, VA: American Institute of Aeronautics and Astronautics, p. 1.
71   This and the subsequent quotation from Merbold are translated from the preface of the German edition of 'The Overview Effect': White, Frank. 1993. Der Overview-Effekt. München: Goldmann.

around the Earth in an hour and a half,' said the pilot of the Apollo 9 moon landing, Russell Schweickart, 'you begin to recognize that your identity is *with that whole thing.*' (emphasis added) '[I]t comes through to you so powerfully that you're the sensing element for man. You look down and see the surface of that global that you've lived on all this time, and you know all those people down there and they are like you, they are you – and somehow you represent them.' So for Merbold, the greatest significance of space travel may lie in the development of *'a global consciousness'*.

The German-American political scientist John H. Herz, well-known for his theory of the 'security dilemma', argued in a 1980 essay that 'for the first time, a truly planetary worldview seems plausible'. 'It arises out of the view the astronauts had of the small, blueish sphere that is the Earth, the realization of its uniqueness, its limitedness and its vulnerability.' Although this may be only one of many possible worldviews, 'the others are provincial, antagonistic, and under the new conditions of worldwide interdependence they carry within them the risk of the devastation or even the extinction of humanity. And for that reason, the global worldview presents itself even to a moral relativist as more fundamental than all the others, because it gives moral precedence to the survival of humanity, without which all other measures of worth are meaningless'.[72]

The planetary worldview has already had important and direct effects on world politics. Mikhail Gorbachev made a major contribution to the ending of the Cold War through glasnost and perestroika as well as his committed efforts towards détente with the USA and NATO. The inferno of an atomic self-destruction of the human race was averted, for the time being at least. According to Gorbachev, the planetary perspective was of considerable significance for his politics. 'Ultimately, human beings, with the gift of reason, must understand that they are global human beings, individuals who must take responsibility not only for themselves and their own fate, their own community, but also for planet Earth, for the whole of humanity.' This is how Gorbachev sketched out the so-called 'New Thinking' that he claimed served as his political guideline. 'The whole history of thought is a story about pushing back its own limits, expanding its own horizon. The time has now come for this horizon to encompass the entire globe. Already today we can see how mankind is embracing a broader, a global worldview', the former General Secretary of the Communist Party of the Soviet Union and his advisers wrote in a book published in 1997.[73]

---

72   Herz, John H. 1980. 'Weltbild and Bewußtwerdung - vernachlässigte Faktoren beim Studium der Internationalen Beziehungen'. Aus Politik and Zeitgeschichte 11: 3–17, p. 15.
73   Gorbatschow, Michail, Vadim Sagladin, and Anatoli Tschernjajew. 1997. Das Neue Denken. Politik im Zeitalter der Globalisierung. München: Goldmann, pp. 205f.

Although the 'New Thinking' may have had a considerable influence on world politics and contributed to 'a consolidation of the civilising process' (as Gorbachev put it)[74], so long as the switch to a planetary consciousness is not also reflected in changed institutional global structures the world will remain trapped in a dangerously unstable condition of cultural lag. 'A system which can only maintain the peace of the world so long as it is in the hands of first-rate men', wrote Lionel Curtis, 'is a standing danger to peace. It is self-condemned, for no system has a right to count on an unbroken succession of first-rate leaders to see that it works. The only systems to be trusted are those which continue to maintain peace when run by leaders of average ability.'[75] The only lasting solution lies in overcoming the anarchic basic structure of the international system.

Identity, demos, and state formation

The emergence of a global identity and the development of global state structures are inextricably intertwined. On the one hand, a planetary perspective is the foundation on which a world parliament will arise. Conversely, a world parliament is perhaps the most important vehicle for the promotion of a planetary perspective. The development of institutions and the growth of solidarity and identity are reciprocal processes – neither can originate or establish itself without the other. This is well illustrated by the emergence of the nation states. In his influential book on nation states as 'Imagined Communities', the political scientist Benedict Anderson describes nationality and nationalism as 'cultural artefacts'. In Anderson's view, the nation should be understood in an anthropological sense as 'an imagined political community'. 'It is *imagined*', he elucidates, 'because the members of even the smallest nation will never know most of their fellow-members, meet them, or even hear of them, yet in the minds of each lives the image of their communion.'[76] The idea of such a national community is not innate, or natural, but *historically constructed*. According to Jürgen Osterhammel, there is a growing tendency within recent work on the theory of nationalism to see the nation state 'not as the almost inevitable result of a mass construction of consciousness and identity from below', but rather as 'the product of a concentrated and deliberate exercise of power from above'. It was

74 Ibid., p. 209.
75 Curtis, Lionel. 1949. World Revolution in the Cause of Peace. Macmillan Co., p. 42.
76 Anderson, Benedict. 1991. Imagined Communities: Reflections on the Origin and Spread of Nationalism. Verso, pp. 5ff.

a project of powerful elites, or – as Osterhammel stresses – of anticolonial or rev-olutionary counter-elites.[77] State formation was often not the outcome, but only the beginning – and the most important instrument – of the process of becoming a nation. The Italian politician of the 1860s Massimo d'Azeglio is famously sup-posed to have said: 'We have made Italy. Now we must make Italians.'[78]

The academic study of history, as it developed in the 19th century, per-formed an important service as midwife at the birth of the new nation states. It set about constructing ancient national histories. 'Rather than neutral instru-ments of scholarship, the modern methods of researching and writing history were developed specifically to further nationalist aims', wrote the historian Pat-rick Geary. Programmes of education were put together to spread the national ideology and the 'national language', usually used initially only by a minority, among the population. Geary rightly cautions against dismissing national ide-ologies as trivial only because they were largely products of the imagination.[79] They had a very real impact. Nationalism was able to mobilize the people in their masses and to lead them into war. It is an example of the construction of an in-group morality that shows how significant the division into a 'We' and an 'Other' can be. William E. Scheuerman points out that '[t]he construction of na-tional identities permitted elites, for example, to call on common people to fight against social peers – sometimes living just across the border – chiefly because they saw themselves as French, for example, rather than Dutch or German'.

But what defines a nation and a constitutive people – a demos? Eric Hobsbawm points out that, historically, ethnic, linguistic or religious criteria were not para-mount. 'Indeed, if "the nation" had anything in common from the popular-rev-olutionary point of view, it was not, in any fundamental sense, ethnicity, lan-guage and the like, though these could be indications of collective belonging also. As Pierre Vilar has pointed out, what characterized the nation-people as seen from below was precisely that it represented the common interest against particular interests, the common good against privilege ... Ethnic group differ-ences were from this revolutionary-democratic point of view as secondary as they later seemed to socialists.'[80] It was only later that theorists, and nationalist programmes, tried to narrow down the concepts of the people and the nation

---

77   Osterhammel, Jürgen. 2003. Geschichtswissenschaft jenseits des Nationalstaats. 2nd ed. Göttingen: Vanden-hoeck & Ruprecht, p. 325.
78   Hom, Stephanie Malia. 2013. 'On the Origins of Making Italy: Massimo D'Azeglio and 'Fatta l'Italia, bisogna fare gli Italiani''. Italian Culture (XXXI) 1: 1–16.
79   Geary, Patrick J. 2003. The Myth of Nations: The Medieval Origins of Europe. Princeton University Press, pp. 16f.
80   Hobsbawm, Eric. 1992. Nations and Nationalism Since 1780: Programme, Myth, Reality. Cambridge Uni-versity Press, p. 20.

on the basis of such criteria. In fact, most of the world's states are unquestionably multicultural and have large minorities. The homogenous 'nation state' is largely a fiction. The multi-faith and multi-ethnic state of India, with its 1.24 billion inhabitants and countless language communities, is a good illustration of the fact that a homogenous culture, a common religion or a minimum threshold of prosperity do not represent prerequisites for a demos or a functioning democracy. The French scholar Ernest Rénan recognised in 1882 that ethnic categorizations were fundamentally problematic, and that membership of a nation cannot be purely dependent on linguistic, religious and geographical criteria either. In Rénan's view, a nation is 'a great solidarity constituted by the feeling of sacrifices made and those that one is still disposed to make. It presupposes a past but is reiterated in the present by a tangible fact: consent, the clearly expressed desire to continue a common life'. 'A nation's existence', he summed up forcefully, 'is a daily plebiscite.'[81] It is based on the mutually acknowledged self-identification of its members.

The demos does not exist in isolation, detached from institutions. The demos only comes into being through state formation. The political scientists Michael Zürn and Gregor Walter-Drop point out that 'a demos is never externally given, but always the result of political institutions and intensified transactions'. They cite the examples of France and Great Britain to illustrate that it was primarily the state which, at an early point in its history, created a symbolic framework supporting the development of an imagined community and a strong national identity.[82] The demos is a legal entity that arises out of a political act, namely the founding of the state; its membership is defined by citizenship of that state. This applies just as much to the world state as to territorial states: the formation of a world demos is similarly not a precondition for, but a consequence of, global state formation. The difference, however, lies in the fact that the community of humanity as a collective of all human beings is natural and innate. From a cosmopolitan perspective, there are no problems of segregation here, as there are with national citizenship. Everybody is included, and a part of the potential world demos. Homogeneity, in any respect, is not a requirement. The world society is and will remain multi-cultural, multi-ethnic, multi-faith and multi-lingual. 'If the Indian Union and the European Union can organize

81 Rénan, Ernest. 1992. 'What Is a Nation? Text of a Lecture Delivered at the Sorbonne on March 11th, 1882', published in: the same, Qu'est-Ce Qu'une Nation?, Paris, Presses-Pocket. Transl. by Ethan Rundell.
82 Zürn, Michael, and Gregor Walter-Drop. 2011. 'Democracy and representation beyond the nation state'. In: The Future of Representative Democracy, ed. by Sonia Alonso, John Keane, and Wolfgang Merkel, 258–81. Cambridge University Press, p. 265.

a parliament, then the world can do it, too', Johan Galtung argued. The establishment of a world parliament will call into being a planetary demos. And the demos embodied in the world parliament will represent *the common interests of humanity* and will defend them against the particularistic interests of the states and the privileges of the transnational elite. Even though antidemocratic governing elites and antimodern extremists may deny it, the Universal Declaration of Human Rights and the other established treaties on human rights, above all the two Covenants, on Civil and Political Rights and on Economic, Social and Cultural Rights, have already served to bring about a common global set of shared basic values. Surveys document a 'dramatic international consensus' on fundamental human rights among the world population.[83] This provides a broad foundation of shared values on which a world parliament, and with it a world demos, can be built.

The philosopher Peter Singer believes the moral significance of national borders needs to be reconsidered in the context of globalization. 'We need to ask', he writes, 'whether it will, in the long run, be better if we continue to live in the imagined communities we know as nation-states, or if we begin to consider ourselves *as members of an imagined community of the world* (emphasis added).'[84] National and global identity are not mutually exclusive here. The sociologist Georg Simmel (1858 to 1918) described identity as the product of *individually combined affiliations* to social circles and groups.[85] Each group affiliation is accompanied by feelings of solidarity and identity, of varying strength, which if necessary have to be reconciled and balanced off. Ultimately, national citizenship is merely one affiliation among many. The economist and philosopher Amartya Sen emphasizes in his book 'Identity and Violence' that people must not be reduced to one identity. Identities are 'robustly plural' and overlap, and 'the importance of one identity need not obliterate the importance of others'. For that reason, he writes, it is not necessary 'that our national allegiances and local loyalties be altogether *replaced* by a global sense of belonging, to be reflected in the working of a colossal "world state." In fact, global identity can begin to receive its due without eliminating our other loyalties.'[86]

83 Patrick, Stewart M. 8 December 2011. 'Surprising International Human Rights Consensus'. Council on Foreign Relations - The Internationalist (blogs.cfr.org).
84 Singer, Peter. 2004. One World: The Ethics of Globalization. New Haven: Yale University Press, p. 171.
85 Simmel, Georg. 2013. Soziologie. Untersuchungen über die Formen der Vergesellschaftung. Gesamtausgabe Band 11. 7th ed. Frankfurt: Suhrkamp. Ch. 6, Die Kreuzung sozialer Kreise, pp. 456-511.
86 Sen, Amartya. 2007. Identity and Violence: The Illusion of Destiny. London: Penguin Books, pp. 19, 185.

The progressive attitude of the world population

As the spread of postmaterial values and of a planetary perspective might lead us to expect, more and more people already consider themselves to be citizens of the world too, and as such they feel solidarity with one another. The online network Avaaz, for example, can very quickly mobilize millions of people across the world for global issues. 'Why should women and men from one part of the world worry about the fact that people in other parts of the world are getting a raw deal if there is no sense of global belonging and no concern about global fairness?' asks Amartya Sen, writing about the anti-globalization protest movement. 'Global discontent, to which the protests give voice, can be seen as evidence of the existence of a sense of global identity and some concerns about global ethics.'[87] This finding is confirmed by representative international surveys carried out over the last ten years. In the fifth wave of the WVS survey, for example, a global average of 72 per cent of respondents in the 46 countries surveyed reported that *they regarded themselves as citizens of the world.*[88] This group includes the so-called 'cultural creatives', as described by the sociologist Paul Ray and the psychologist Ruth Anderson in 2000. The authors believe this group represents a new subculture, alongside traditionalists and modernists, one that makes up a third of the population of the industrialised societies. The cultural creatives focus on the things that all people have in common. They think holistically, and do not believe in business as usual. They take account of the welfare of future generations in their deliberations. '[T]hey are the people most concerned about the condition of our global ecology and the well-being of the people of the planet', according to Ray and Anderson.[89]

Whether it is measures to lessen the effects of climate change, observance of international law, implementation of human rights, participatory democracy, the abolition of nuclear weapons or the strengthening and democratization of the United Nations: majorities can be found across the world *in support of all these aims.* Their thinking in these areas is much more advanced than that of the government officials who act in their name in international negotiations and who only pursue their own national interests. '[I]t does appear that in many cases publics tend to be at least one step ahead of their governments', sums up the director of the research programme WorldPublicOpinion.org, Steven Kull.

---

87 Ibid., p. 123.
88 Council on Foreign Relations. 2011. 'Chapter 1: World Opinion on General Principles of World Order'. In: Public Opinion on Global Issues. New York: Council on Foreign Relations, p. 11.
89 Ray, Paul H., and Sherry Ruth Anderson. 2001. The Cultural Creatives: How 50 Million People Are Changing the World. New York: Broadway Books, p. 11.

'This dynamic is especially true', he writes, 'when it comes to dealing with problems of a global nature that require international cooperation. Nation states as institutions have proven reluctant to cooperate in ways that compromise their sovereignty or their freedom to pursue their maximal national interest. ... But it appears that individuals as a whole are more ready to cooperate in a global framework and are not as constrained by competitive national narratives.'[90]

In a survey carried out in 16 countries, 87 per cent of people overall thought that their country had a responsibility to take measures against climate change. A majority in 13 countries – an average across all countries of 63 per cent – was of the opinion that their government was not doing enough in this area. In another survey, a majority in 15 of 19 countries surveyed thought their government should give a higher priority to combating climate change - an international average of 60 per cent. When asked if changes to individual lifestyles were necessary to reduce climate emissions, an international average of 83 per cent across 21 countries agreed.[91] There is strong support for the idea of an 'international agreement for eliminating all nuclear weapons', to explicitly include oversight measures to ensure compliance in all countries. 76 per cent of those surveyed across 21 countries agreed with this idea, including large majorities in the five atomic powers in the UN Security Council.[92] Another survey asked in 20 countries if the UN Security Council had a responsibility to use military means to protect civilian populations against serious violations of human rights or genocide. An overall average of 61 per cent said yes, and only 21 per cent disagreed. In addition, an international average of 66 per cent of respondents in 22 countries called for the establishment of a permanent UN peace corps, to be selected and trained by the UN and under its command.[93] Other surveys also show support for democratising the UN. In 2005, for example, people were asked if their country's official representative at the UN General Assembly should be elected by the people. In all 19 countries surveyed a majority was in favour, the average majority being 74 per cent. The pollsters also tested public attitudes on 'creating a new UN Parliament, made up of representatives directly elected by citizens, having powers equal to the current UN General Assembly'. This idea received majority support in all 18 countries surveyed. On average the support stood at 63 per cent, with an average of 20 per cent against.[94] In a more

90   Kull, Steven. 2010. 'Listening to the Voice of Humanity'. Kosmos Journal, Spring-Summer: 26–29, p. 27.
91   Council on Foreign Relations. 2011. 'Chapter 5a: World Opinion on the Environment'. In: Public Opinion on Global Issues. New York: Council on Foreign Relations, pp. 6f.
92   Global Zero. 9 December 2008. 'Launch Press Release' (www.globalzero.org).
93   Council on Foreign Relations. 2012. 'Chapter 3: World Opinion on Violent Conflict'. In: Public Opinion on Global Issues. New York: Council on Foreign Relations, p. 2.
94   Id. 'Chapter 2: World Opinion on International Institutions'. In: ibid., pp. 6f.

recent survey across eight countries, on average 85 per cent said that they believed that the UN needs to be reformed and 71 per cent thought that a new
supranational organisation should be created 'to make enforceable global decisions' to address global risks.[95]

Global history and education for world citizenship

The planetary perspective has had an impact on the writing of history, too. Historians speak of a veritable global history boom in the academic literature, in
research and in teaching. Sebastian Conrad, an academic historian who teaches
in Berlin, writes in an introduction to this new approach that 'cross-border processes and exchange relationships, but also comparative studies within the
framework of global connections' are at its centre. 'The starting point is always
the interconnectedness of the world, and the circulation and exchange of things,
people, ideas and institutions are among the most important topics for this approach', he explains. Global history can mean universal history in the tradition
of Arnold Toynbee or H.G. Wells, but 'the most interesting questions often
arise at the intersection between global processes and their local manifesta-
tions'. According to Conrad, three 'ideal-typical forms' of global history can be
distinguished: world or universal history with a global horizon, the history of
global interdependence, and the history of global integration.[96] Global history
represents a decisive turn away from the discipline's previous fixation on the
nation state framework, and at the same time an attempt to abandon all Euro-
centrism completely. 'Following the end of European domination of the world,
in an epoch of rapidly advancing intercontinental connections, and in light of
growing doubts about the universal normative validity and practical benefits of
conceptions of modernity originating from Europe, the discipline of history,
too, finds itself confronted with the irrefutable need for all the problems to be
seen in a global context', writes Jürgen Osterhammel, a professor of history in
Konstanz regarded as a pioneer and leading figure of global history. It is quite
clear that global history is also being seen here as a political project. 'It is time
for *a history with a cosmopolitan agenda* to step up alongside history with the
self-appointed role of building national historical identity and teaching national
values, and that which sees its role as the strengthening of a European historical
identity', writes Osterhammel, who since 2012 has been working together with
former Harvard professor Akira Iriye on a new six-volume 'History of the

---

95 Global Challenges Foundation. 2017. Attitudes to global risks and governance. Carried out by ComRes in
    Australia, Brazil, China, Germany, India, South Africa, the United Kingdom and the United States.
96 Conrad, Sebastian. 2013. Globalgeschichte. Eine Einführung. München: C.H. Beck, pp. 9f.

World'.[97] Global history, Sebastian Conrad observes, is 'usually written in a cosmopolitan spirit'. It is 'a political project with emancipatory potential', and 'a step
on the path to a global consciousness which opens possibilities for cross-border
communication and interaction. Just as the study of history as practised in the
19th century was intended to produce national subjects, so a global perspective is
a prerequisite for an understanding of oneself as a citizen of today's world'.[98]

The arrival of global history as an acknowledged school within the discipline
serves to create an important foundation for the formation of a global identity
and to complement the process of global state formation. Unlike national history writing in the 19th century, which first had to construct a national subject,
the history of humanity finds its subject – the human species – ready and waiting.
What is more, in the Anthropocene it is clear that the human species is a genuine
'Schicksalsgemeinschaft', that is, it shares a common destiny, since the wellbeing of
all people, including coming generations – indeed, perhaps the very survival of
human civilization – is essentially dependent on the management of the world
system, of the global common public goods, and of the global existential risks.

In schools, especially, there is considerable potential for a greater use of work
based on a global history approach or perspective. The United Nations is now
actively promoting the incorporation of the idea of global citizenship in the
school curriculum. In the 'Global Education First' initiative set up by UN General Secretary Ban Ki-moon in 2012, fostering global citizenship in schools is
one of three global priorities, along with improving the general quality of learning and enabling every child on the planet to have a school education. In the
UNESCO education programme, one of the strategic aims is to help states to
integrate global citizenship education in their education systems. 'Global Citizenship Education', UNESCO claims, 'equips learners of all ages with those values, knowledge and skills that are based on and instil respect for human rights,
social justice, diversity, gender equality and environmental sustainability and
that empower learners to be responsible global citizens.'[99]

'Big History' as a modern creation story

Seeing the human species in its cosmological context is a part of what it means
to have a planetary perspective on human history. One's gaze is directed not
just backwards from space onto the Earth, but also outwards into the universe.

---

97 Osterhammel, Jürgen. 2003. Geschichtswissenschaft jenseits des Nationalstaats. 2nd ed. Göttingen: Vanden-
    hoeck & Ruprecht, pp. 47, 9.
98 Conrad, loc. cit., p. 26.
99 UNESCO. 28 May 2015. 'Global Citizenship Education' (www.unesco.org).

Spectacular images such as those from the Hubble Space Telescope encourage us to think about life on Earth and existence as a whole. Thus, in the tradition of popular authors such as Carl Sagan, Isaac Asimov and Stephen Hawking, global history becomes a part of what the historian David Christian and the biochemist Fred Spier call 'Big History'. The time horizon of this new interdisciplinary field stretches from the Big Bang, about 13.8 billion years ago, up to today. The home of the human race, 'Spaceship Earth', is a small planet orbiting one of up to 400 billion stars that form the galaxy we call the Milky Way. The Milky Way in turn is only one of perhaps 200 billion galaxies, grouped in clusters and superclusters, that make up the known universe. The nearest solar system to ours, Alpha Centauri in the Andromeda galaxy, is 4.3 light years or over 40 trillion kilometres away. In between is empty space, traversed by cosmic radiation. In view of these cosmic distances, as things stand it is very unlikely that even the tiniest proportion of the human race will ever live anywhere but on the Earth. The common denominator in the history of the universe, according to Spier, is 'the emergence and decline of complexity' within the self-regulating systems of the world of inorganic matter, of life and of human culture under conditions of increasing entropy.[100]

The perspective of 'Big History', writes Spier, 'may stimulate another type of identity, namely the idea that all of us belong to one single, rather exceptional, animal species, which emerged on a rather exceptional planet somewhere in the universe; that our closest cousins are the primates; that we are, in fact, related to all life forms and that, seen from a cosmic perspective, our far cousins are the rocks, the water, and even the stars. For if the current big history account provides a reasonably accurate overview of the past, everything would have descended from the "fire mist" of tiny particles that emerged immediately after the big bang'.[101] 'Big History' provides an account of the origin of all existence and of life on Earth on a strictly scientific basis. The cosmological worldview thus helps us on the path to an integral consciousness and creates an important frame of reference for planetary identity.

One of the leading thinkers in the field of 'Big History' is the US American historian David Christian. At the beginning of his work 'Maps of Time' from 2004, he observes that every human community tries in one way or another to answer the question of the origins of existence. Creation stories have helped people to see their existence in an overall context, to give it meaning and to develop a sense of belonging within the whole. In the modern world, however, Christian laments, while there may be more information and knowledge than

---

100 Spier, Fred. 2011. Big History and the Future of Humanity. Malden, MA: Wiley-Blackwell, pp. 24ff.
101 Ibid., p. 139.

ever before, it is present only in unrelated fragments and not in the context of a universal story. 'Big History' represents the attempt to bring these fragments together into a 'modern Creation myth'.[102] If it were to address the great questions such as our place in the universe, then history could play just as important a role in modern industrial societies as traditional creation myths did in non-industrial communities, Christian believes.[103]

The continuation of the project of modernity

For advocates of postmodernism such as Jean-François Lyotard, the fact that people are no longer able to believe in overarching guiding ideas like progress, enlightenment or socialism is a characteristic feature of our time. By 2007, with the beginning of the global financial crisis, market fundamentalist neo-liberalism – one of the potential 'Grand Narratives' still remaining following the collapse of 'actually existing socialism' - was delegitimised. As the German philosopher and expert on Lyotard Wolfgang Welsch emphasizes, postmodernist thinking is suffused by the conviction that no narrative able to claim *universal* validity and legitimacy is possible any longer anyway. This version of postmodernism has abandoned all concepts of universality and focuses on the particular. 'This, if you like, is now our meta-narrative', writes Welsch.[104]

Postmodernist thinking is itself a proposal for a new meta-narrative – against its own will, as it were. Its master idea is that there can and should no longer be any universal master ideas. Its attempt to provide a post-modernist narrative has itself failed, ironically, and should be regarded as finished. Without a shared sense of self and a common orientation, world civilization will not be able to survive for long. Even with a post-modernist mindset, it should not be possible to avoid giving serious thought to the need and the necessary conditions for a global form of government as a prerequisite for the survival of humanity in the Anthropocene, if one is not prepared to simply give up on humanity altogether. Welsch emphasizes that both the defenders of modernity and the advocates of post-modernism want to 'diagnose and treat the pathologies of modernity'.[105] But post-modernist thinking in the manner of Lyotard cannot offer solutions to the global problems. In effect, it inherently excludes global approaches, as the social scientist David Harvey sums up the situation in

---

102 Christian, David. 2011. Maps of Time: An Introduction to Big History. Berkeley: Univ. of California Press, p. 2.
103 Id. 1991. 'The Case for ‚Big History'.' Journal of World History (2) 2: 223–38, p. 227.
104 Welsch, Wolfgang. 2008. Unsere postmoderne Moderne. Berlin: Akademie Verl., pp. 172f.
105 Ibid., p. 165.

his book 'The Condition of Postmodernity'.[106] From a post-modernist perspective, the problem, as Welsch puts it, lies in the fact that 'totality can only arise from making one particularity into an absolute, which is inevitably linked to the suppression of other particularities'.[107] The totalization of the particular, within nationalism for example, and the resulting fragmentation of international law and of global governance, is a typical feature of modernity. Since it excludes the possibility of a shared cosmopolitan perspective, Lyotard's postmodernist thinking does not overcome this state of affairs but further cements it. But why should a holistic perspective – in the sense of an integral consciousness – not be able to allow room for the particular at the same time?

As Karl-Otto Apel noted, in Lyotard's view not only the 'universal narrative of emancipation' but also the idea of 'humanity as the singular subject of history, to be realised in the future' have foundered. For Lyotard, the reason lay 'in the failure of cosmopolitan solidarity in the modern period, from the nationalism of the French Revolution and Stalinism to the power struggles within the capitalist economic system'.[108] With respect to core concerns of the Enlightenment such as democracy and human rights, the empirical basis for the postmodernist theory of the end of meta-narratives is highly questionable. The spread of democracy and the increasing establishment of human rights throughout the world demonstrate that the lust for liberty remains unbroken. Growing global empathy and the trend towards a planetary perspective are laying the foundations for a cosmopolitan solidarity. Apel pointed out over twenty years ago that, although the deterministic assumption of a 'fixed path of history' is obsolete, by contrast the belief in 'progress, in the sense of the cosmopolitan unity of human history, which must remain a goal to be pursued and invoked at all times, and resilient against all frustrations, remains more topical and urgent than ever'.[109]

The characteristic feature of our time is not the failure but on the contrary the *continuation* of the modern project of emancipation, albeit focused on the planetary level. Following the argument made by Jürgen Habermas, who has set himself decidedly against the idea of postmodernity, modernity should be seen as an 'unfinished project', one which must now be continued in a 'post-national constellation' under the banner of a 'radicalised enlightenment' in order to 'develop new forms of democratic self-control of society'.[110] Habermas has written frequently in more detail about his ideas for the necessary 'constitution of a

---

106 Harvey, David. 1990. The Condition of Postmodernity. Malden, MA: Blackwell, p. 52.
107 Welsch, loc. cit., p. 181.
108 Apel, loc. cit., pp. 396f. with reference to 'Discussion entre Jean-Francois Lyotard et Richard Rorty'. Critique 456: 559–85 (May 1985).
109 Apel, loc., cit., pp. 410f.
110 Habermas, Jürgen. 1998. Die postnationale Konstellation. Frankfurt: Suhrkamp, p. 134.

community of citizens of the world', which include a world parliament made up of representatives of the states and of the world citizenry.[111] If it is considered necessary to speak of an epochal change, then Ulrich Beck's concept of a transition to a *second modernity* offers the most convincing approach. The focus here is on the erosion of the institutions and systems associated with the nation state and on the risks and side-effects engendered by modern industrial societies. Nevertheless, so Beck asserts, the question of what is disintegrating 'is immediately countered by the question of what is coming into being – the meaning of the emergent outlines, principles and opportunities of a second, non-linear, global modernity with a cosmopolitan agenda'.[112] One could also speak of a transition to a *planetary modernity*.

The philosopher Peter Sloterdijk has expressed the thought that '[t]he wretchedness of the conventional forms of grand narrative by no means lies in the fact that they were too great, but that they were *not great enough*' (emphasis added). If the grand narratives known so far 'have been seen through as unsuitable attempts to seize power over the world's complexity', he added, 'this critical realization neither delegitimizes the narration of things past nor exempts thought from striving to cast an intense light on the comprehensible details of the elusive whole.' Accordingly, 'the talk of the end of the grand narratives overshoots the mark as soon as it is no longer content to reject their intolerable simplifications.'[113] 'Not great enough' for us means not self-reflexive enough and not comprehensive enough. This brings to mind the development of utopian thinking. Reflections on the ideal form of the state and an ideal society constitute a distinct literary genre, beginning with Plato's 'Republic' around 370 BCE. It is named after the novel 'Utopia', written by Thomas More in 1516, which laid the foundations for utopian thinking in the modern era. If utopian literature was at first characterised by static, descriptive models of the state such as More's, it has now produced more reflexive stories. In Ursula K. LeGuin's 1974 utopian novel 'The Dispossessed', for example, the conditions for and the problems with the concept itself are debated and critically analysed.

What is needed is not a closed narrative but rather an inclusive, integral and vibrant approach. The knowledge of one's own limitations and a self-critical stance, with the aim of steady and constant further development, are important features of a new grand narrative seeking to claim universal validity. It is clear

---

111 In recent times see for example: Habermas, Jürgen. 2011. Zur Verfassung Europas. Berlin: Suhrkamp, pp. 85ff.

112 Beck, Ulrich, Anthony Giddens, and Scott Lash. 1996. Reflexive Modernisierung. Eine Kontroverse. Frankfurt am Main: Suhrkamp, p. 19.

113 Sloterdijk, Peter. 2013. In the World Interior of Capital: Towards a Philosophical Theory of Globalization. Transl. by Wieland Hoban. 1st ed. John Wiley & Sons, pp. 5, 4.

that it cannot represent any kind of static and final wisdom. In a now-famous 1958 lecture on liberty, the Russian-British philosopher Isaiah Berlin (1909 to 1997) identified the problems with closed worldviews. 'One belief, more than any other', Berlin said, 'is responsible for the slaughter of individuals on the altars of the great historical ideals - justice or progress or the happiness of future generations, or the sacred mission or emancipation of a nation or race or class, or even liberty itself, which demands the sacrifice of individuals for the freedom of society. This is the belief that somewhere, in the past or in the future, in divine revelation or in the mind of an individual thinker, in the pronouncements of history or science, or in the simple heart of an uncorrupted good man, there is a final solution.'[114]

The new 'Grand Narrative' is the story of human history itself, global history embedded in the 'Big History', from the formation of the Earth to its end, when in a billion years the increase in solar radiation will mean the end of life on our planet. It is a story in which the human species becomes gradually ever more aware of itself and its actions. It is the story of the development of a planetary democracy that ensures the wellbeing and peaceful coexistence of all people in harmony with all other life on Earth. It is a meta-narrative in that it draws from the failure of previous narratives claiming exclusivity and truth the conclusion, in the spirit of Isaiah Berlin, that it is not closed but ever changing and developing in the light of self-criticism and self-reflection. 'We need to try to understand our universe even if we can be certain that our attempts can never fully succeed', is how the historian David Christian encapsulates the fundamental approach of 'Big History'. He has pointed out how people unfailingly search for stories that give them a sense of purpose and direction. We should therefore not be afraid to offer an enlightened, universal picture of the world. 'Only when a modern creation myth has been teased out into a coherent story will it really be possible to take the next step: of criticizing it, deconstructing it, and perhaps improving it. In history as in building, construction must precede deconstruction.'[115]

The new global Enlightenment

With regard to social organization, the new 'Grand Narrative' revolves around the development of democracy and emancipation over the course of human socio-political intellectual and spiritual evolution. There will always be differing opinions on politics and on the associated distribution conflicts. Democracy as

---

114 Berlin, Isaiah. 1969. Four Essays on Liberty. Oxford University Press, p. 167.
115 Christian, loc. cit., pp. 10f.

a means of making decisions must always remain subject to constant improvement. Under planetary modernity, a world parliament is the principal institution for the preservation and improvement of democracy as a form of government. At the same time, it is the focal point of the new global Enlightenment which, following a period of uncertainty and disorientation, goes together with the third democratic transformation. The new global Enlightenment does not have to be proclaimed. With advancing human cognitive and moral development and with the spread of a planetary consciousness, it is taking place already. A large proportion of the world's population has understood that humanity has to take responsibility for the actions of the human race in order for life on Earth and humanity itself to have any future. As Edward O. Wilson argues, this knowledge is an important component of 'a new Enlightenment'.[116] The crisis of the early phase of planetary modernity is caused by humanity's inability to live up to this responsibility as a collective. The inspiration and motivation behind the new global Enlightenment is to change this and to liberate humanity from its disenfranchisement, through the construction of a planetary democracy.

---

116 Wilson, loc. cit., p. 294.

PART III

Shaping the future: the design and realization of world democracy

The establishment of a democratic world parliament has been regarded since the beginning as a practical political project. It was not philosophers but revolutionaries like Anacharsis Cloots and social reformers like Constantin Pecqueur who were its most important early proponents at the end of the 18th and the middle of the 19th centuries. It was they who first spelt out the principles of universal equality and the sovereignty of peoples in a rigorous and cosmopolitan approach. They regarded a world parliament as both goal and product of a process of global unification and of the democratic self-realization of humanity. This perspective is inseparably bound up with the idea of a world parliament.

The transition from intergovernmental inter-national law to a cosmopolitan world law has become an urgent necessity. The creation of a directly elected world parliament with legislative powers must be accomplished as soon as possible. Worldwide cooperation must become a project of political integration. Global governance must be recognised for what it is, namely a part of rapidly proceeding global process of state formation. The practical realization of world democracy, however, and the fundamental reconstruction of the UN – or its replacement by a new world organization – are not suitable for over-hasty and risky experiments. While a sudden and radical improvement in the political and social conditions for the establishment of a world parliament cannot be entirely excluded, it would be better, for the time being, to expect the process to be gradual and evolutionary. Under the currently prevailing conditions, then, a world parliament may be a distant goal, but the first pragmatic step to set the process in train has long been possible, and indeed overdue. A *parliamentary assembly* should accompany the process of reaching global agreement, providing a vehicle for the ongoing formation of a democratic supranational community: no integration without representation. In the spirit of the project of a new global enlightenment, it will support the development of a global civil society and a democratic world public sphere.

The same fundamental issues are always raised for discussion. How should the deputies for such a parliamentary assembly be selected? How to deal with the fact that democratic elections are still not possible in some countries? How should the seats be allocated? What powers should a world parliament have? In addition to dealing with these and other questions, it will be important to have a picture of the practical step by step process over time of bringing the world parliament into being. In the historical development of the European Parliament in the course of European integration, an instructive example exists that can serve as a foundation.

26.
Building a world parliament

The example of the European Parliament

The European Parliament emerged out of the Common Assembly of the European Coal and Steel Community (ECSC), which came into being in 1952. From the beginning, the Common Assembly was more than just an advisory body. In line with the ECSC Treaty, it exercised supervisory powers over the executive body of the Community, the High Authority. Again in line with the Treaty, it was left to the individual states to decide whether its deputies were to be representatives selected by and from the national parliament or to be directly elected. However, the latter option was not taken up. Thus the Assembly was initially comprised of 78 delegates sent by the national parliaments of the six founding states of the ECSC. The delegates organised themselves not by national origin but in transnational political groupings. They formed committees corresponding to the areas of responsibility of the High Authority. The Assembly debated the annual financial report submitted by the High Authority, and had the power, with a two-thirds majority vote, to compel the Authority to resign.

With the Treaty of Rome in 1957, the European Economic Community (EEC) and the European Atomic Energy Community (Euratom) were established alongside the ECSC as independent organizations. A parliamentary assembly was foreseen as a part of all three communities. In order to avoid a three-part structure, in the course of the negotiations on the Treaties the Common Assembly was transformed into an organ for all three communities. The clause allowing the option of direct election of the deputies was dropped. However, the EEC Treaty included a provision for the Assembly to submit proposals for direct elections following a common procedure in all member states. The Assembly was now made up of 142 deputies and called itself a European Parliament. Its first meeting in this new configuration took place in 1958. The Merger Treaty which came into force in 1967 completed the joining together of all the remaining community organs. From 1975 onwards the parliament acquired the right of co-decision on the community budgets. As the practical powers of the European Communities grew, so too did the need for greater democratic legitimacy at the European level. Agreement on the introduction of direct elections was finally reached in 1976, albeit without a common procedural basis, and this was formally ratified by the member states. Since 1979 the members of the European Parliament have been directly elected. Politically strengthened in this way, the EP rejected the Commission's proposed budget for the first time in 1980.

In the early 1980s, the European institutions became bogged down in a complex of problems on account of the requirement for unanimity. The fact that each of the now twelve governments could block any decision often meant that no decisions were taken at all. In response to this situation, in 1984 the European Parliament under the leadership of Altiero Spinelli drew up a draft constitution for a federal European Union with a genuine legislature based on the principle of majority rule. This initiative helped gain the support of the governments to drive forward institutional reform of the Communities. It is not necessary here to go over the further development of the European Treaties from the Single European Act (1985) via Maastricht (1992), Amsterdam (1997) and Nice (2000) to the establishment of the European Union as an independent legal personality with the Treaty of Lisbon in 2007. The decisive point is that the European Parliament evolved from the Assembly of the ECSC, made up of national parliamentarians, to a directly elected legislative and supervisory organ of the European Union. Together with the Council of Ministers it decides on the Union's budget, and in most areas of policy it legislates on an equal basis with the Council, albeit *as yet* still without a right of initiative. In the course of European integration, the European Parliament has developed into a centre of power which in the European landscape wields more influence than national parliaments.

The European experience offers several lessons for the development of a global parliamentary body in terms of its structural framework and possible developmental stages. These include, with regard to the framework: 1. its remit (with which intergovernmental organizations and organs is it linked institutionally, and with respect to which policy areas); 2. how its powers are exercised; 3. how its members are elected (by the parliaments, directly, or optionally by either method). One objective is for all forms of public authority and public policy decision-making at the global level to be democratically accountable and also subject, where appropriate, to co-decision-making by the Parliament.

The proposal for a UNPA

At the time the idea of a UNPA was first put forward, there was a general willingness to accept that it could start off with only a bare minimum in terms of the three aspects identified above. It could be established as a subsidiary organ under Article 22 of the UN Charter by a resolution of the UN General Assembly. This would circumvent the need for a revision of the Charter, which would require the approval of two-thirds of all member states and all five of the veto powers in the Security Council – a difficult hurdle. The assembly was conceived as providing support for the work of the committees of the General Assembly as an advisory parliamentary body, made up of deputies from the national parliaments of the member states and possibly also from international parliamentary institutions (IPIs) such as the European Parliament. The model for this kind of assembly is not the Common Assembly of the ECSC, which of course also had supervisory rights from the outset, but above all the Parliamentary Assembly of the Organization for Security and Co-operation in Europe (OSCE PA), which was established in 1990 and met for its first formal session in 1992. A potential objection to taking the Common Assembly of the ECSC, or indeed the European Parliament (or the Parliamentary Assembly of the Council of Europe) as a model is the fact that they are only regional, or specifically European, in character and therefore not easily applicable to worldwide or UN organizations. However, the OSCE has 55 member states and 12 partner states, spanning the whole of the northern hemisphere, including four of the five permanent members of the UN Security Council (the exception being China). The 320 members of the OSCE PA include parliamentary deputies from all the OSCE member states. The task of the Assembly is to contribute to security and the development of democracy in the OSCE region. It passes resolutions, makes recommendations and is known especially for its electoral observation work.

As in the European Parliament, deputies in the UNPA should not be organised by national origin but in *transnational groups* organised around common political orientations. So in all probability there would be a conservative group, and socialist, liberal, green, left and other groups. Existing international party associations - such as the conservative Centrist Democrat International, the Socialist International, the new social democratic Progressive Alliance, the Liberal International and the Global Greens - could cooperate with the relevant groups in a UNPA. To date, their political influence is extremely small; but that could change through cooperation with affiliated political groups in a global parliamentary body. The path to a world parliament would thus help to encourage the formation of *global parties*.

The extension of powers and responsibilities

The supporters of the international campaign for a UNPA are in favour of the idea of the assembly being developed gradually once it has been set up. In the appeal for a UNPA, signed by parliamentarians from across the world, it is stated that the assembly 'could initially be composed of national parliamentarians. Step by step, it should be provided with genuine rights of information, participation and control vis-à-vis the UN and the organizations of the UN system. In a later stage, the assembly could be directly elected'. The call for a UNPA is relatively cautious, and for many people it does not go far enough. The European Parliament, for example, believes that the assembly should be equipped from the outset with the right to information, monitoring and participation. A purely advisory function is regarded as inadequate. In addition, it has now been suggested that participating states should have the option of directly electing their delegates from the beginning. Some more progressive countries would introduce direct elections for the selection of their delegates, others would only follow later, and some would prefer to maintain indirect selection through the national parliament for the longer term. On the model of the ECSC Assembly, the first step could also consist in the establishment of a parliamentary assembly within an organization with a narrower specialised remit, for example the WTO or the UN Climate Change Conference.

The next steps would involve broadening the remit and powers of the assembly. Extending its remit seems sensible not least because it is impossible on practical grounds alone to equip each of the dozens of different intergovernmental organizations and UN programmes with its own parliamentary body. Instead, mirroring the structure of the UN system, the work of the UNPA would be thematically focused through committees, which in contrast to plenary sessions would be able to meet more flexibly. The parliament would develop gradually into a 'common assembly' for the organizations and programmes of the UN system and in this way counteract the fragmentation of the system. Alongside the national parliamentarians, representatives of the so-called 'major groups' as defined by the UN in the course of Agenda 21 should also take part in the committee meetings. These groups are: indigenous people, women, children and youth, workers and trade unions, farmers, local authorities, the scientific community, business and industry, and NGOs. The deliberations of the committees would thus take on the character of cosmopolitan conferences.

The UN General Assembly cannot confer more powers on the assembly than it has itself. This sets limits on the possible extension of supervisory and co-decision-making powers under Article 22. But the powers of the General Assembly should also not be underestimated. It can exert direct influence on the programmes and funds it has set up, such as the children's fund UNICEF, the development programme UNDP, the refugees' commission UNHCR and the environment programme UNEP and their governing regulations. It would certainly be feasible to confer questioning, citation and interpellation rights, as well as the right to involvement in the approval of the budget or the selection of directors. In principle a UNPA could be given the same prerogatives by the General Assembly as are enjoyed by the General Assembly itself. This includes, for example, drawing the attention of the Security Council to crises, or submitting legal questions to the International Court of Justice. In political terms, the assembly could in principle involve itself in all areas relevant to the UN, including for example exercising parliamentary oversight over peace missions or offering advice on moving to a sustainable economy and society. The international Campaign for a UNPA advocates that the assembly's overriding objective should be 'a reform of the present system of international institutions and global governance'.[1] The Campaign's appeal calls for the assembly to become 'a political catalyst for further development of the international system and of international law'. The ECSC Assembly was tasked already in 1952, its founding year, with drafting a treaty for the establishment of a political Union.

In order to differentiate more clearly, as soon as its remit was extended to cover the International Monetary Fund, the World Bank Group or the World Trade Organization, the assembly could be referred to as a Global Parliamentary Assembly or GPA. Its establishment under international law could perhaps similarly be achieved without the necessity for treaty amendments by means of cooperation agreements. However, following the model of the Rome Convention on certain institutions common to the European Communities, we could ultimately picture an intergovernmental treaty which would amend all the relevant existing agreements and establish the GPA as a common body with extensive rights with respect to all the relevant institutions of global governance. This would for example be a way of embedding the right to be involved in the selection of the Directors of the IMF, the World Bank Group and the WTO. The assembly should additionally have the right to send its own delegations to the relevant intergovernmental negotiations, for example with regard to the WTO, the Climate Change Convention and the Conference on Disarmament. It should also be able to take part in the global setting of norms and standards and to have democratic oversight over this process. If it were politically feasible, it is not impossible to imagine leapfrogging the Article 22 process and establishing the assembly instead directly as a GPA by means of an intergovernmental treaty of this kind.

The most important step, ultimately, would be the change to a world parliament. The use of that term would demonstrate that the assembly had now become a part of a *global legislative system* which, under certain conditions and

---

1   Campaign for a UN Parliamentary Assembly, November 2007. 'Conclusions regarding policies of the Campaign for a UN Parliamentary Assembly' (en.unpacampaign.org).

within certain parameters, could pass binding world law. By this point, if not earlier, subject to the detail, numerous changes to international law - and in some countries also to national constitutions - would become necessary. The act of creating a system of world law would be undertaken in the name of humanity, but in itself it would be an act under international law. The world parliament would be founded as a main organ of a world organization of the third generation. As a main pillar of a world peace order it would be involved in decision-making on any coercive measures or peace missions, and would be part of the global inspection system working towards total nuclear disarmament. New supranational institutions which are already being discussed and will sooner or later come on to the political agenda, such as a world central bank, a world tax authority, a global antitrust office, police force and intervention force, as well as the introduction of global taxes or of a global basic income, require democratic legitimation and parliamentary oversight exercised by a world parliament. A world parliament is an indispensable basis for legitimate, democratic and binding majority decisions for the regulation of global issues, and especially the management of global common goods such as the atmosphere and global public goods such as the financial system.

Growing democratic challenges

Many supporters of a UNPA would agree that important preconditions for the step to a world parliament are not yet in place. With respect to its democratic legitimacy, this applies above all to the level of democratization in the community of states. One important difference from the European example is that not all the countries have unquestionably democratic constitutions, or even constitutions that can be called democratic at all. The European integration process has only involved democracies. However, the Campaign for a UNPA advocates that the assembly should be open to delegates from all the member states of the UN. How else would it be able to claim global validity as a platform for world domestic policy, and be integrated into the existing system of global governance? Unlike in Europe, global integration without regard to the form of government of the participating countries is quite far advanced already, for example within the framework of the World Trade Organization. We believe that the objective of democratic world government and of a world parliament can be reached faster and more easily via a universal approach than via an exclusive gathering of the slowly growing cohort of democracies, which as yet have no direct points of contact with the global decision-making centres. However, democracies and democratic delegates must in any event play a deciding role in the establishment and further development of the global parliamentary assembly. To this end, the democratic delegates to the assembly should organize themselves into a cross-party network. The Community of Democracies and their parliamentary forum could make it their task to support the process in this way.

Nevertheless, countries in which free democratic elections are not yet possible, or only possible with restrictions, should in principle be included, and especially China, with its massive population. The establishment of a UNPA must also be seen in this context as *a measure for the promotion of democracy*. It can be expected that the many transition countries will thereby gain in terms of a strengthening of their parliamentary opposition. Lessons can be learned in this regard from existing international parliamentary institutions. As international networks of deputies, they are regarded as 'schools for democracy' where learning and persuasion take place. The political scientist Beat Habegger also speaks of a socialization function.[2] The world's first multinational parliament, the Imperial Council of the Austro-Hungarian Empire, which lasted until 1918 and which comprised deputies from eight nationalities, was optimistically seen as the 're-cruiting school for the Central and Southeast European democracies' by Karl Renner, one of the founders of the first Austrian republic.[3] Renner, incidentally, advocated a world state composed of autonomous national components following the example of Switzerland and Austria-Hungary.[4] In any event, the socialization effect is one of the arguments for making a UNPA open to all UN member states. Deputies would at least have to be elected by their national parliaments, however. Anyone holding a government office should not be permitted to be a member of the assembly. Possible 'pseudo-parliamentarians' would come under the positive influence of the democratic deputies and the parliamentary culture of interaction and debate. It is questionable whether some autocratic governments want their country to take part in a UNPA at all. Step by step, the requirements for compliance with democratic norms will grow. The international Campaign therefore clearly states, with an eye to the future development of the assembly, that 'direct elections of the UNPA's delegates are regarded as a precondition for vesting the body with legislative rights'.[5] Such elections must be free, fair,

---

2   Habegger, Beat. 2005. Parlamentarismus in der internationalen Politik: Europarat, OSZE and Interparlamentarische Union. 1st ed. Baden-Baden: Nomos, pp. 34, 228.

3   Cit. from Österreichisches Parlament, Parlamentskorrespondenz Nr. 98, 18 Feb. 2002 (www.parlament.gv.at).

4   Renner, Karl. 1915. ‚Der Krieg und die Wandlungen des nationalen Gedankens'. Der Kampf 8:8–23. See also Riehle, Bert. 2009. Eine neue Ordnung der Welt: föderative Friedenstheorien im deutschsprachigen Raum zwischen 1892 und 1932. V&R unipress, pp. 89ff.

5   Campaign for a UN Parliamentary Assembly, loc. cit.

equal, universal and secret. In some states, this will not be possible in the foresee-able future. But to wait until the community of states has been fully and success-fully democratised before the first step is taken is not a realistic alternative.

The allocation of seats

Using the four models we have considered so far as methods for the allocation of seats in a UNPA, and on the basis of the data from Freedom House for the year 2015, we have concluded that between about 60 and 70 per cent of the roughly 800 deputies would come from countries classified as electoral democ-racies. Moreover, between 68 and 76 per cent would come from free or partially free countries.[6] Given the ongoing progress of the third wave of democratiza-tion, the tendency will be for these proportions to rise steadily. In any event, the number of democratically legitimate deputies would be larger than might be expected purely on the basis of these classifications. This is because in those countries classified as 'unfree' there can nevertheless be a genuine parliamen-tary opposition. The widespread belief that a majority of deputies in a world-wide parliamentary body would of necessity be under the control of autocratic governments is erroneous.

In order to ensure that different opinions within a country would be repre-sented at a UNPA, our models assumed that regardless of population size each country would send at least two delegates. In the absence of direct elections, the allocation of seats to each country should reflect the political spectrum in the national parliament as accurately as possible. Thus, even in the case of very small countries, at least one delegate could represent the governing majority and one the opposition. The remaining seats can then be allocated to countries ac-cording to varying formulae, for example proportionally to population size. This would help prevent the complete marginalization of small countries, because un-der a directly proportional allocation system and 800 seats in total, 71 countries would fail to reach the threshold of four million inhabitants which would entitle them to one deputy. Yet together these countries amount to 90 million inhabit-ants. Conversely, the ten countries with the biggest populations would send about 60 per cent of all the deputies. Even if all 800 seats were allocated in direct pro-portion to population share, by our calculations 58 per cent of seats would be taken by deputies from electoral democracies. In the view of the US American geographer and world federalist Joseph Schwartzberg, who drew up detailed models for the allocation of seats at three different progressive developmental

---

6   See Bummel, Andreas. 2010. The composition of a Parliamentary Assembly at the United Nations. 3rd edi-tion. Berlin: Committee for a Democratic UN.

stages of an assembly, given their very small populations it would be sufficient if in the first stage the microstates were each to be allocated only one seat.

Existing IPIs do not use a directly proportional allocation, nor is it to be recommended for a UNPA. Indeed, at the Pan-African Parliament and the Latin-American Parliament, national delegations are all equal in size. Other IPIs use population size as an allocation criterion, but with a gradation to prevent the marginalization of small countries and the disproportionate predominance of large ones. The example of the European Parliament is again especially instructive here. The method of allocation of seats is stipulated in the EU Treaty, which reads: '[t]he European Parliament shall be composed of representatives of the Union's citizens. They shall not exceed seven hundred and fifty in number, plus the President. Representation of citizens shall be degressively proportional, with a minimum threshold of six members per Member State. No Member State shall be allocated more than ninety-six seats.'[7] The key here is the principle of 'degressive proportionality'. The larger the population of a state, the greater the number of people represented by each deputy. The EU Treaty does not include a mathematical formula. The precise allocation is decided by the European Council and European Parliament in keeping with the stated principles. In the eighth legislative period, Malta, the smallest EU member state, had six seats, meaning one deputy for each 70,000 inhabitants, while Germany, the most populous country, had 96 seats, meaning one deputy for each 833,000 inhabitants.

This unequal representation has been the subject of constitutional complaints in Germany. Two judgements have been made on the subject by the Federal Constitutional Court, and they contain interesting observations. In its judgement pertaining to the Maastricht Treaty of 1993, the Federal Constitutional Court noted that in a community of states 'democratic legitimation cannot be established in the same form as it can within a state system uniformly and conclusively regulated by a single state constitution'.[8] In its judgement pertaining to the Lisbon treaty of 2009, the Court again considered the question of the democratic legitimacy of the EU and stated that '[a]s a representative body of the peoples in a supranational community, characterised as such by a limited willingness to unite, it cannot, and need not, as regards its composition, comply with the requirements that arise at state level from the equal political right to vote of all citizens'[9]; and further, that '[t]he democratic basic rule of equal opportunities of success ("one man, one vote") only applies within a people, not within a supranational representative body, which remains a representation of

---

7   Article 14 para. 2.
8   BVerfG, 2 BvR 2134, 2159/92, 12 October 1993 - Maastricht, no. 93.
9   BVerfG, 2 BvE 2/08, 30 June 2009 - Lisbon, no. 271.

A WORLD PARLIAMENT

the peoples linked to each other by the treaties albeit now with special emphasis on citizenship of the Union'.[10]

A graduated allocation of seats in a UNPA is certainly defensible, and it is politically imperative. As the models cited above demonstrate, it is also feasible, even though a balance has to be struck between a plethora of mini-states on the one hand and the population giant China on the other. As the Federal Constitutional Court pointed out, the inequality within the European Parliament is only acceptable 'if the German Bundestag retains own responsibilities and competences of substantial political importance'.[11] The degree of democratic legitimacy required corresponds to the depth of supranational integration. Seen from this perspective, a graduated allocation of seats within a UNPA would not represent a problem, since its legal competences would initially be limited so as to be roughly comparable with those of the European Parliament. As these competences were extended over the course of a progressive evolution into a world parliament, the issue of the democratic representation of the citizens would certainly later play an increasing role. Over the longer term, the allocation of seats would have to approach ever closer to the world law principle of 'one person, one vote'. Once at the level of a world parliament, consideration would have to be given to creating constituencies of roughly equal size throughout the world for the direct election of deputies, which would mean shared parliamentary representation for many small countries. This is an idea taken up by Schwartzberg in his developmental scenarios. In any event, these states could continue to have equal representation in the General Assembly or in any body that might replace it. The principal purpose of the parliament, on the other hand, would be the democratic representation of the world's population.

10 Ibid., no. 279.
11 Ibid., no. 246. Cf. also no. 263.

27.
Creating world law

International law and world law compared

One of the most important tasks for a global parliamentary assembly will be to grapple with the questions of how a constitutional system of world law might look in detail and how it might be brought about. In addressing this task, it will be able to draw on numerous preparatory studies that have already been mentioned in this book. Here, we would like only to briefly outline some important features of world law and of the process of global legislation. In an important study from 2007, the academic law expert Angelika Emmerich-Fritsche set out, over 1200 pages, the history of the development of world law. As she explains, the purpose of world law 'is not that of reconciling the diverging interests of states, which is what international law exists to do, but rather that of meeting the elemental needs and interests of the whole of humanity'.[1] The nature and character of world law can be best seen by examining the most significant respects in which it differs from international law:

- In international law, the *state* is the most important entity, while in world law it is the individual as *a citizen of the world*. World law has its roots in the idea of world citizenship. Individuals are innately and directly endowed with rights and duties.
- Whereas international law as a rule applies only to states and must be implemented via national law, world law can in principle apply *directly* to everyone, everywhere.
- International law is based on intergovernmental treaties, which states can *voluntarily* choose to ratify or not, whereas world law has *universal application*, not only to states but also in principle to individuals and companies.
- The central paradigms of international law are *national independence* and the sovereign equality of states, whereas the corresponding principles in world law are *global interdependence* and *the equality of all people*.
- The dominant perspective in the intergovernmental system is that of the *national interest*, or Raison d' État, while in world law it is that of the *planetary*

1   Emmerich-Fritsche, Angelika. 2007. Vom Völkerrecht zum Weltrecht. Berlin: Duncker & Humblot, p. 340.

interest of humanity. Yehezkel Dror has coined the apt term 'Raison d'Humanité' for this.[2]

– The creation of new rules in international law by means of intergovernmental treaties is based on the *consensus principle*, whereas world law is based on democratic decision-making by *qualified majorities*.

– In intergovernmental negotiations and councils, representation is generally through officials *nominated by the executive branch of national government*, while representatives in the decision-making bodies of world law are *democratically elected by the world population*. As a rule, the guiding principle for representation in international law is *'one state, one vote'*, whereas in world law it is *'one person, one vote'*.

– In contrast to international law, where the question of precedence is *at the discretion of the states*, world law *always takes precedence* over national and international law.

– Under international law principles, a state is able to decide whether or not, and under what conditions, to accept external jurisdiction, on a *voluntary* basis. Under world law, submission to external jurisdiction is *obligatory*.

World law is concerned not only with the welfare of individuals but simultaneously with the wellbeing and the survival of the entire species and of its habitat, the Earth. As Emmerich-Fritsche noted, fundamental elements of world law can in principle be realised within the framework of international law. Agreements under international law are an appropriate vehicle for this purpose if and when they are approved by almost all states, so that they have practically universal applicability. The creation of a world legislature is in such cases 'not absolutely imperative'.[3] Traces of world law are indeed already present in the international law system. This applies for example to the binding status of UN Security Council decisions under Chapter VII of the UN Charter, to the concept of the common heritage of humanity in the Convention on the Law of the Sea, the obligatory dispute settlement procedure of the WTO, the powers of the International Criminal Court to prosecute individuals and the emergent principle of the state's responsibility to protect, which sets limits on state sovereignty.

It is open to question, however, whether officials of national governments are able to legitimately define the interests of humanity and willing to do so. As has been outlined already in the tragedy of international law, in negotiations in

---

2   Dror, Yehezkel. 1995. Ist die Erde noch regierbar? Ein Bericht an den Club of Rome. Transl. by Hans-Jürgen Baron von Koskull. 1st ed. C. Bertelsmann, pp. 116ff.

3   Emmrich-Fritsche, loc. cit., p. 458.

international law there is a tendency towards the lowest common denominator among particularistic individual state interests. The international law system has given plenty of evidence over decades of its dysfunctional nature in such key areas as nuclear disarmament and climate change. Moreover, the development of international customary law is painfully slow and ineffective. A parliament democratically elected by the world population is the appropriate mechanism for continuously defining the common interests of humanity. Free and fair planetary elections to a world parliament equipped with legislative powers is the most powerful symbolic expression of a fully developed system of world law and of a *democratic* system of world government.

A bicameral world legislature

Notwithstanding this, the states will remain the most important organs of governance in the world, and for many people a key point of reference for their identity. In a federal world legal system, they represent an indispensable level of government and decision-making. Just as the German federal states carry out administrative responsibilities on behalf of the Federation, so the nation states, if they have functioning state structures, can take over the implementation of some elements of a world law system. As Otfried Höffe, Jürgen Habermas and Václav Havel have all argued, the legitimation of a third-generation world organization requires institutional representation of both the states and the world population. A global legislative system should be based on two chambers, an assembly of the states and a democratically elected world parliament. It should be a fundamental principle that the approval of both chambers is required for world laws to be passed. Depending on the matter being legislated, different levels of qualified majority could be required. Votes in the chamber of states could also be linked to specific majority requirements subject to the matter under consideration; for example, a majority might require a specified minimum proportion of global GDP or of worldwide CO_2 emissions. For binding global legislation, it will remain unlikely for a considerable time to come that a simple majority in both chambers would represent adequate legitimation.

Weighted voting has also been proposed for the chamber of states, to reduce the imbalance there between small and large countries. Joseph Schwartzberg has worked out a model for the UN General Assembly, since '[u]ntil such time as the United Nations adopts a system of weighted voting that realistically reflects the actual global distribution of power, it seems doubtful that any major state will willingly grant the GA, the most representative organ within the UN system, the authority to make binding decisions'.[4] However, if an acceptable balance is achieved in the world parliament, then it could be that the introduction of strong weighted voting in the chamber of states would no longer be necessary. The chamber of states would instead be the place to ensure that due weight was also given to the interests of small countries.

As an additional means of enabling feedback between global law-making and the electorate, the national parliaments should also be involved in the process. In order to ensure the efficacy of a global system of legislation, there must not be a requirement for global laws always to be ratified by a specific majority of national parliaments. However, the decisions of the chamber of states and the world parliament should only come into force if objections are not raised by a specified number of national parliaments within a specified time period. This accords with a proposal formulated already in 1905 by US American lawmakers.[5] As in the law-making process in the EU, at least two types of global legislation should be envisaged: firstly, framework laws, which have to be fleshed out in detail and transposed into national law by the national parliaments within a specified time limit; and secondly, laws with direct and immediate applicability.

A world constitutional court

World law is based on primary constitutional law and secondary legislation. Universal basic and human rights are to be enshrined in a world constitution. Whether the decisions of the world legislature and the actions of global governmental institutions are in accordance with human rights and with the legal division of competences must be subject in principle to judicial review. To this end, a world constitutional court should be established. The European Court of Justice has stated, with respect to sanctions imposed by the UN Security Council, that already under the current framework of international law 'a judicial review is indispensable to ensure a fair balance between the maintenance of international peace and security and the protection of the fundamental rights and freedoms of the person concerned..., those being shared values of the UN and

---

4   Schwartzberg, Joseph. 2013. Transforming the United Nations System. Designs for a Workable World. Tokyo, New York, Paris: United Nations University Press, p. 17.

5   Lange, Christian (ed.). 1911. 'Un Congrès International, Conférence de Bruxelles, 1905'. In: Union interparlementaire: Résolutions des Conférences et Décisions principales du Conseil, 2nd ed., 93–94. Brussels: Misch & Thron, see point 8.

the European Union'.[6] Following the 2011 revolution, Tunisia proposed the establishment of an 'international constitutional court' to enable the supervision of national elections and changes of government by an independent international court. The responsibilities of such a court could later be extended as appropriate in the course of the transition to a world legal order.

Conversely, a world parliament has considerable significance for the legitimation of a world constitutional court, and indeed of *any form of global jurisdiction*. Armin von Bogdandy and Ingo Venzke have pointed out that international courts, too, are 'actors of global governance' and 'somehow require democratic legitimation conveyed by representative institutions'. 'Their establishment and legal basis [i.e. of international courts] are mostly enshrined in international treaties that draw their democratic legitimation from the domestic procedure of parliamentary ratification. While we do not question the democratic significance of this parliamentary consent, we see limits to its legitimatory power: limits that render it advisable – given the development of many international courts – to open up additional sources of legitimation.' At the centre of their democratic legitimation must be 'the individuals whose freedom is shaped by judicial decisions, however indirectly'.[7] Angelika Emmerich-Fritsche makes it clear in her study that 'world courts that make legal decisions with binding effect on the citizens of the world' require, as a matter of fundamental principle, 'deeper democratic legitimation'. What this means in practice is that the judges must be elected by either the citizenry under their jurisdiction, or their parliament, or a democratically appointed selection committee. In Emmerich-Fritsche's view, it would be a 'pragmatic and sensible' step for a world court to set up a selection committee for judges 'composed of members drawn from the national parliaments and/or the world parliament and from among the highest judges in the states, sitting jointly'.[8] The involvement of the world parliament, representing the world population, should be regarded as indispensable.

6   European Court of Justice. 18 July 2013. 'Judgement of the Court, Kadi v. Council, Joined Cases C-584/10 P, C-593/10 P and C-595/10 P', para 131.
7   Bogdandy, Armin von, and Ingo Venzke. 2014. In Whose Name? A Public Law Theory of International Adjudication. Oxford University Press, pp. 207, 148, 149, 212.
8   Emmerich-Fritsche, loc. cit., pp. 651f.

28.
The necessary conditions
for the transformation

The structural conditions for institutional change

A world legal system with a world parliament will not come about simply because it is ethically and morally superior to the present system of international
law and because in any rational debate it has the more persuasive arguments.
That may be a good starting position, but in and of itself it is of course not sufficient. The international law expert Richard Falk has pointed out that '[i]n
world order studies it is traditional to propose a better system of world order
and then argue for its adoption. Such an approach tends to be "utopian" or "ro-
mantic" in the sense that it overlooks the transition from "here" to "there."'. It
was assumed that the better arguments would prevail. However, this dispute
will be settled not in the debating clubs but in the political arena. 'Those who
benefit from existing arrangements of power and interest', writes Falk, 'are unlikely to be swayed, except in marginal or cosmetic respects, by appeals based
on argument or values.' He argued that power can be transformed only by
countervailing power. 'No world order solution which presupposes the substantial modification of the state system can be achieved unless the advocates of
the new system are aligned with important social and political forces within the
existing world structure.'[1] It is in the nature of the third democratic transformation and the new global enlightenment that their goals, values and perspectives will spread gradually through world society and thereby gain ever more
potential. This process will be driven forward by the long-term economic, social
and cultural changes associated with global industrialization and post-industri-
alization. We have already looked, for example, at the significance of sustained
prosperity and rising levels of education for an emancipatory shift in values and
ultimately for the evolution of a post-conventional morality. The ever more
widespread experience of global interconnectedness and the global growth of
empathy are other factors we have looked at. The ambitious middle classes in
the developing countries on the one side and the squeezed middle classes in the

1   Falk, Richard. 1975. A Study of Future Worlds. Amsterdam: North-Holland Publishing Company, p. 277.

industrialised countries on the other represent – together with the global pre-cariat – the social forces which, as part of a 'transformative subject', will be the principal social agents of the third transformation.

However, this does not mean that this trend will inevitably continue and end in the realization of a world democracy. The powers of persistence within the status quo, and the resistance from its beneficiaries to a new global social con-tract and a new global class compromise as part of an eco-social and pacifist world legal order, must not be underestimated. In the area of climate policy, for example, representatives of the oil and coal industries work ceaselessly to thwart the international negotiations, to discredit the findings of climate research and to influence public opinion in their favour. US President Donald Trump is one of their most powerful allies today. Moreover, there is a real danger of a serious setback to civilization, or even of collapse on a global scale. The new precariat and the squeezed middle classes also have an anti-modern, nationalistic-reac-tionary potential that demagogues may mobilize for their purposes. Based on the latest data of the seventh wave of the World Values Survey, researchers rec-ognize signs of a 'democratic deconsolidation' that may also be looming in the established Western democracies, and they caution against the idea that a breakdown of democracy in these countries is impossible.[2] Democracy support-ers fear that this is exactly what could happen in the United States under Trump. As Norbert Elias pointed out, the civilizing process 'is never finished and always under threat.'[3]

Ronald Inglehart and Christian Welzel have described how long-term value shifts in society create the foundation for institutional changes. As an illustra-tion of this, they point to the slow but steady trend to greater emphasis on self-determination and self-realization in the populations of the Eastern European countries in the decades preceding 1989. This shift in values built up a pressure for change in society that finally, under specific historical circumstances, quite suddenly and unexpectedly resulted in the fall of the Wall and the collapse of the communist regimes in Eastern Europe. According to Inglehart and Welzel, the exact point in time when a long-term value shift of this kind leads to an institutional breakthrough is usually determined by the removal or overcoming of blocking factors *at the level of the elites*. In their view, the turning point in the revolutions in Eastern Europe was when Mikhail Gorbachev made clear in 1988 that, unlike in 1956 in Hungary or 1968 in Czechoslovakia, the Soviet Union

---

2   Foa, Roberto, and Yascha Mounk. 2016. 'The Democratic Disconnect'. Journal of Democracy (27) 3: 5–17.
3   Elias, Norbert. 1992 [1989]. Studien über die Deutschen, Frankfurt: Suhrkamp, p. 225.

would not support collapsing governments of allied states with military force.[4] An interesting aspect of the example they choose is that, at least according to Gorbachev's own account, a decisive factor for him personally was a shift to a planetary perspective.

In the face of sustained blocking at the elite level, social tensions can sometimes increase to the point when they find release in a violent explosion. In 2013, the World Academy of Art and Science (WAAS), together with the Club of Rome and other institutions, started a project on a new 'integrated perspective' for the solution of global problems. The aim is to establish a global consortium to implement 'a new paradigm of human development'. In an essay outlining the project, Ivo Šlaus and Garry Jacobs from the World Academy wrote that radical change in history usually comes in the form of violent revolutions. These are directed against elites who doggedly refuse to relinquish any power. Occasionally, however, far-sighted leaders had recognised the urgent need for rapid social evolution to stave off such revolutions. For example, the English elites had consciously sought to prevent a repeat there of the bloodshed of the French Revolution, which had wiped out the French aristocracy, through an opening up towards the middle classes.[5]

A cosmopolitan movement

The situation with regard to the world system is different in that there is no political power centre for any revolution – even only in theory – to attack. In contrast to the development of the nation states in the 19th century, which was driven forward by the adoption of ideas of nationhood and state formation at the elite level, there is also as yet virtually no sign that any parts of the transnational elite want to establish any such power centre. The more difficult it is for counter-movements to get any kind of hold on the machinery of the transnational state, the better it is for the interests of the transnational elite. It means that such counter-movements cannot then direct their efforts effectively at a global level. For Jean Rossiaud, the co-Director of the new World Democratic Forum, this is precisely the reason why the efforts of social movements to bring about global change largely come to nothing. The lack of a world state limits social movements to resistance, a repertoire of defensive or reactive actions, at the local or national level. However, the crucial steps need to happen at a global

---

4   Inglehart, Ronald, and Christian Welzel. 2005. Modernization, cultural change, and democracy: the human development sequence. Cambridge University Press, pp. 41ff.

5   Šlaus, Ivo, and Garry Jacobs. 2013. 'In Search of a New Paradigm for Global Development.' Cadmus (6) 1 (www.cadmusjournal.org).

level, Rossiaud believes. In the 'first' or 'early modernity' period, national movements pushed for the establishment of nation states. For the new social movements, the time has now come, according to Rossiaud, for a 'democratic cosmopolitarian movement' whose most important demand is for the establishment of a world state. This would then provide the institutional foundation for the realization of the movement's real aims.[6] What is important here is not that the movement reaches a unified position on each of these aims in detail. Unity is important only with regard to the objective of establishing a democratic global institutional framework which would enable a consciously global politics to be effectively pursued *at all*. It seems reasonable to assume that the social movements of the *second* democratic transformation, which in many countries continue to fight for democratization at the nation state level, will also see themselves as part of the cosmopolitan movement. After all, they share a common goal in the establishment and strengthening of democracy - just at different levels.

The idea of such a cosmopolitan movement is attracting increasing attention. 'The global transformation will require the awakening of a new social actor: a vast movement of global citizens expressing a supranational identity and building new institutions for a planetary age', says Paul Raskin of the Tellus Institute.[7] The Institute is working together with others as part of a 'Great Transition Initiative' to bring such a 'global citizens' movement' into being. An Institute paper states that the establishment of a world parliament should be one of the projects of the movement.[8] In a more recent essay titled 'Journey to Earthland', Raskin imagines a scenario in which after phases of crisis and emergency an 'Earthland Parliamentary Assembly' adopts a world constitution in 2048 that brings a 'Commonwealth of Earthland' into being. At the pinnacle of the formal structure sits a world assembly with regional and at-large members selected by popular vote in world-wide elections.[9] Three international conferences were also held between 2013 and 2015 on the creation of a world citizens' movement. They were organised under the umbrella of a civil society project with the name DEEEP, which also regards itself as part of the movement for a 'Great Transformation'.

6   Rossiaud, Jean. 2012. 'For a Democratic Cosmopolitan Movement.' Forum for a New World Governance, pp. 11f.
7   Raskin, Paul. 2010. 'Imagine All the People: Advancing a global citizens movement.' Tellus Institute, pp. 1, 3.
8   Raskin, Paul, Orion Kriegman, and Josep Xercavins. 2010. 'We the People of Earth: Toward Global Democracy.' Tellus Institute.
9   Raskin, Paul. 2016. Journey to Earthland. The Great Transition to Planetary Civilization. Boston: Tellus Institute, pp. 75, 87.

The role of the NGOs

The political pressure created by civil society and the new social movements does not consist only of resistance. But it is directed primarily towards achieving *intrasystemic* change, that is, at achieving specific goals within the continuing framework of the existing system; and this fails to address the problems arising from the anarchic system of international law, let alone solve them. The growing pressure for change in society must be steered towards a radical transformation of the *institutional and legal basis* of the system itself. Although the big international NGOs could play an important role in this by exerting pressure on the elites, the pioneers of the cosmopolitan movement prefer not to rely on them. Up until now they have not appeared as significant actors in the 'Great Transformation' pressing for a change in the institutional structures of the world system. Over the past thirty years, for example, attempts to persuade the biggest NGOs to join together in major shared campaigns for a reform of the United Nations have repeatedly come to nothing. Like companies who want to focus on their core business, their horizons rarely extend beyond their own immediate concerns. Their activities are largely determined by the shifting concerns of day-to-day politics, and focus on the achievement of short-term goals that are easy to measure and present. Even though a systemic change towards a world legal order might often be the best means of achieving their goals on a lasting basis, this approach strikes them as too distant. Beyond symbolic actions, they have little inclination to address questions of the world order, which requires an overarching, long-term perspective. Just like the worlds of politics and business, and indeed our society as a whole, they are trapped in what the business consultant Pero Mićić recently described as 'the short-term trap'.[10]

However, the root causes of their lack of success in this respect lie even deeper. In their 2014 book 'Protest Inc.', the political scientists Peter Dauvergne and Genevieve Lebaron describe how the big NGOs now increasingly look, think and act like businesses, and are thus turning into supporting pillars of the system. 'One consequence for world politics', they write, 'is that activism is now less "radical" than it was forty or fifty years ago, at least in terms of demanding systemic and far-reaching change.' Only rarely do 'career activists' today call for a world government or a new international economic order. They are woven into the existing system, and therefore incline towards a conservative 'realist' position. Dauvergne and Lebaron believe that the de-radicalization of the professional NGO world, and its increasing pragmatic closeness to government, business and sources of finance, explains why so many people are now seeing

10 Mićić, Pero. 2014. Wie wir uns täglich die Zukunft versauen Raus aus der Kurzfristfalle. Berlin: Econ.

signs of a global uprising while at the same time the world order 'remains so immune to demands from below for systemic reforms'.[11] Pressure from the streets is not taken up and channelled in the way it should be.

The growing gulf between the professional NGO world and ordinary people was acknowledged as a problem by representatives of the NGO world themselves in a self-critical open letter published in 2014. Signatories including the then head of Greenpeace, Kumi Naidoo, and the director of Oxfam, Winnie Byanyima, wrote '[w]e offer this critique because we have watched with increasing anxiety as civil society has been co-opted by processes in which we are outwitted and out manoeuvred ... Our actions are clearly not sufficient to address the mounting anger and demand for systemic political and economic transformation that we see in cities and communities around the world every day'.[12] More and more civil society activists are no longer prepared to accept this, and are discussing how to contribute to effective systemic changes as part of a 'Great Transformation'. The Smart CSOs Lab founded in 2011 enables them to get together with researchers and funders to discuss new approaches. On the website of the Lab can be read: 'We believe civil society organizations (CSOs) have a crucial role to play in catalysing transformative social and economic change, yet new ideas and strategies are needed to address the challenges we face. Our current focus on single issues and short-term goals means that while we may win many battles, we are losing the war'.[13]

A UNPA as a catalyst for change

The more the societal value shift and the new global enlightenment take hold, the greater will be the pressure – and the desire – felt by the big professional international NGOs to see their work in the broader context of the 'Great Transformation' and to actively support aims such as that of a world parliament. And the more likely it is that progress can be made on the gradual path described towards a world parliament. The key milestone is to get the process going by setting up a UNPA. The social basis for the establishment of a directly elected UNPA with powers similar to those of the General Assembly is already in place, as is confirmed by the 2005 survey referred to above. A more radical worldwide mobilization in pursuit of this goal is possible, and in the right constellation could be successful, even though direct elections are not yet possible

11 Dauvergne, Peter, and Genevieve LeBaron. 2014. Protest Inc. The Corporatization of Activism. Polity Press, pp. 4, 1, 136.
12 'An open letter to our fellow activists across the globe: Building from below and beyond borders.' CIVICUS' Blog, 6 August 2014 (blogs.civicus.org).
13 'The Smart CSOs Lab'. SmartCSOs. Accessed 21 September 2016 (smart-csos.org).

or even desired in all countries. The crucial hurdle here are *the blocks at the elite level*. Instead of dissipating their energy over too broad an area, the tender green shoots of the 'Great Transformation' should be concentrated mainly at one point so as to break through these very blocks. As was recognised by world federalists such as Dieter Heinrich in the early 1990s, '[s]uch an assembly of parliamentarian actors, if we could just get it established, would provide the onward momentum necessary to its further evolution as a house of the people at the UN'.[14] In a mutually reinforcing process, the assembly would contribute to the formation and growth of a cosmopolitan movement, which in turn would mobilize public support for the extension and development of the assembly. Progressive deputies in the assembly would be perhaps the most important motor of a cosmopolitan movement. A UNPA is the crucial vehicle for giving global expression to the social forces for systemic change and for concentrating the political pressure for change on governments and the elite. At the same time, it is the decisive political and institutional fulcrum for the creation of a world state structure on the way to a world parliament.

The global social shift in values and consciousness does not seem at this point in time to be far enough advanced for the goal of a world parliament on a 'one person, one vote' basis to be achievable yet. A survey carried out for the BBC in 2007 in 15 countries asked respondents how likely they would be 'to support a Global Parliament, where votes are based on country population sizes and the global parliament is able to make binding policies?' In only two of the countries surveyed, namely India and Dubai, did a relative majority of respondents unconditionally support this proposal. In six further countries, support was positive on balance, though with reservations; in the remaining seven countries, the attitude was predominantly negative.[15] In order for a world parliament to be established, both educational work and a firm desire for change on the part of the elite are required so that *social blocks* can be removed. The assembly, set up initially in the form of a UNPA, would itself be one of the most important actors in this process. Given a tiered allocation of seats, clear limits to its powers, and the involvement of the General Assembly and the national parliaments in the decision-making process, we would in any event expect greater support.

---

14 Heinrich, Dieter. 2010. The Case for a United Nations Parliamentary Assembly. Extended reprint, originally published 1992. Berlin: Committee for a Democratic UN, p. 42.
15 Bummel, Andreas. 2010. The composition of a Parliamentary Assembly at the United Nations. 3rd edition. Berlin: Committee for a Democratic UN

Four factors

When, under what circumstances and in what form the global values shift might help the efforts for a word parliament to achieve an institutional break-through cannot be foreseen. This cannot be considered a surprise. Historic events often arrive suddenly and unexpectedly, even for professional observers. In spite of all the advance signs, almost nobody saw the Fall of the Berlin Wall coming when and how it did on 9 November 1989, or more recently the Arab Revolutions of 2011. Few people would have believed it possible that the com-munity of states would be able, only nine years after the Fall of the Wall, to approve the founding constitution of a permanent International Criminal Court, and that this document would be ratified within four years by 60 states, despite the opposition of the USA, and would enter into force. In any scenarios for the possible realization of a world parliament, four factors are likely to play important roles in one way or another, and in one combination or another.

The stealthy revolution

As was the case with the ICC, in the initial phase progress will be made in the political background, largely unremarked in the public sphere. It will proceed slowly, step by step. Support will grow in civil society, in academic and intellec-tual circles, among experts, politicians and governments. This process has al-ready begun. We have set out its long prehistory in this book. Just as interna-tional support for the ICC was coordinated and propelled by a coalition of NGOs, so there has been since 2007 an international Campaign for a UNPA. The starting position has been fundamentally transformed for the better by the progress of the second democratic transformation, the global values shift and globalization. While it is true that following the Second World War there was widespread public support in many countries for a world parliament and world citizenship, support that one could certainly characterize in historical terms as a cosmopolitan movement, the *second* transformation was not yet sufficiently far advanced. The Soviet Union, for example, the main victorious power along-side the USA, was ruled by the mass murderer and dictator Joseph Stalin, and decolonization was only just beginning. This factor could be called 'the stealthy revolution'. It creates the basis required, but by itself it is unlikely to be enough to achieve the necessary breakthroughs.

The revolution from below

When the decisive milestones are reached on the path to the establishment and further development of a UNPA, then at that point the blocks in place at the elite level will probably only be overcome if the social pressure for change becomes visible as mass support for a world parliament. This factor could be called 'the revolution from below'. The international surveys conducted so far on the issue of a global parliament suggest that the potential for this is indeed present in the world population. Sooner or later, the calls could be prominently taken up not only by leading international NGOs but also by the new social movements. In addition, cities and local authorities could play an important role. According to David Wylie, who was a member of the Cambridge city council, initiatives at the municipal level could be decisive in circumventing the resistance of nation-states.[16] All this could mark the birth of a new cosmopolitan movement. Through resolutions by cities and municipalities as well as mass protests and demonstrations, with the call for a world parliament at their centre, it could take its place on the world stage and on the agenda of day-to-day political debate. This might happen in the course of a new global wave of protest such as was last released by the Arab Revolutions. The Tunisian Revolution of 2011 not only spilled over into Egypt, Libya and Yemen, where the governments were also overthrown, but sparked protests around the world. The anti-austerity movement of 15 May arose in Spain, and its call for 'real democracy now' was taken up by demonstrators in other countries. The occupation of Zucotti Park in New York by the 'Occupy Wall Street' movement in September 2011 was inspired by the occupation of Tahrir Square in Cairo. The Occupy protests spread through the USA, Great Britain, Germany and other countries. The commonalities and links between the different movements need to be considered in detail, but the World Economic Forum noted with regard to protests in eleven countries in 2013, including Egypt, Brazil, China, Thailand, Turkey and Ukraine, that 'popular discontent with the status quo is already apparent among rising middle classes'.[17] The idea that the establishment of a world parliament could become the central rallying-call for mass protests is not entirely far-fetched. The international network of Occupy groups adopted a statement for the globally coordinated day of protest on 15 May 2012 calling for a 'systemic transformation' of the global economic and political system and the democratization of international institutions. In the text published by the *Guardian* it is stated that '[a]ll decisions affecting all mankind should be taken in democratic

16 Wylie, David A. 2009. City, Save Thyself! Boston: Trueblood Publishing.
17 World Economic Forum. 2014. Global Risks 2014. Geneva, p. 28.

forums like a participatory and direct UN parliamentary assembly or a UN people's assembly, not rich clubs such as G20 or G8'.[18] This is the 'new cycle of struggles' of which Michael Hardt and Antonio Negri spoke.

The revolution from above

Another important factor for the realization of a world parliament will be support from enlightened elites. This is the 'revolution from above'. Elements of the transnational elite, small at first but then growing larger, will recognize that it lies in their own interests to actively drive forward global democratic reforms. Only in this way will it be possible to ensure the necessary social backing for the continuation of economic integration and global modernization and the stability – even the survival – of world society. World law, on account of its universal validity, can be made to work for all economic actors without distortion of competition. Business spokespersons may see advantages in regulation through world law compared with the current international law system. But support from elite business and regulatory circles will not be motivated by calculated self-interest and social pressure alone. The advance of post-conventional morality, of empathy and of a planetary perspective does not stop when it reaches their doors. This could not have been better illustrated than by Mikhail Gorbachev's 'new thinking'. This example suggests that it could be the determined initiative of one influential head of government that achieves the institutional breakthrough for a 'global perestroika'. 'The path to a world order leads via the voluntary renunciation of advantage by the powerful, whether because they heed the call of their own humanity or because in their wisdom they foresee the collapse of their own power if they fail to join forces with the others', wrote Karl Jaspers.[19] Moreover, significant support – not least financial – for a cosmopolitan movement and for the push for a world parliament could even come from the circle of the super-rich. Microsoft founder Bill Gates, for example, with a personal fortune of about 80 billion US dollars, heads the *Forbes* magazine list of the world's richest people. In an interview with the *Süddeutsche Zeitung* in early 2015 he briefly touched on the issue of a world government. There he bemoaned the lack of 'a form of global governance' for climate change. 'We need a world government?' the interviewers pressed him. 'We have global problems, so it is badly needed', he replied.[20] According to billionaire Mark Zuckerberg,

18 'The GlobalMay manifesto of the Occupy movement'. The Guardian, 11 May 2012 (www.guardian.co.uk).
19 Jaspers, Karl. Rechenschaft and Ausblick. München: Piper, 1958, p. 301.
20 Gates, Bill. 28 January 2015. Du darfst keine Zweifel haben. Interview by Michael Bauchmüller and Stefan Braun. Süddeutsche Zeitung.

who founded Facebook in 2004, 'our greatest challenges also need global responses - like ending terrorism, fighting climate change, and preventing pan-
demics. Progress now requires humanity coming together not just as cities or
nations, but also as a global community'.[21]

The trigger

Studying the history of the international system tells us that the most important
institutional breakthroughs and paradigm shifts often occur only after dramatic
and decisive events. The paradigm of sovereignty was an outcome of the Thirty
Years' War. The League of Nations, the first intergovernmental organization
for collective security, and the international law prohibition against war in the
Kellogg–Briand Pact were a consequence of the First World War. The replacement of the League of Nations as a universal world organization by the United
Nations and the European integration process, with its conceptual basis in
shared sovereignty, were consequences of the Second World War. The establishment of the International Criminal Court was a delayed consequence of the
Holocaust and the Nuremberg Trials. Concrete political trigger events of this
kind in the first half of the 1990s were the crimes and genocide on the territory
of the former Yugoslavia, and the genocide in Rwanda, for each of which the
UN Security Council set up its own tribunal.

One often encounters the idea that the next evolutionary step towards a
third-generation federal world organization will not be possible without a similar experience of suffering and shock. 'To create, by anything in the nature of
a fresh start, a new world system to avert a third world war', wrote Wilfred Jenks
in 1969, 'would be a task requiring political imagination and determination of
an order which neither history nor current experience gives us any right to expect.'[22] Randall Schweller recently wrote that the only solution 'is an enormous
shock to the system, a calamity of huge proportions that cracks through the
closed system's outer crust and injects the world with new, useful energy to do
work again'. He was thinking of 'an appalling natural disaster, global pandemic,
or series of coordinated worldwide terrorist attacks against major cities', or a
world war. Only such destruction, thought Schweller, could prepare the ground
for global renewal.[23] For the physicist Leó Szilárd (1898 to 1964), as for many
other scientists involved in the development of the atom bomb, there was no

21 Zuckerberg, Mark. 16 February 2017. 'Building Global Community' (www.facebook.com).
22 Jenks, C. Wilfred. 1969. The World Beyond the Charter. London: George Allen & Unwin Ltd., p. 11.
23 Schweller, Randall L. 2014. Maxwell's Demon and the Golden Apple: Global Discord in the New Millennium.
    Baltimore, Maryland: Johns Hopkins University Press, p. 140.

doubting that a world government had to be created, whether in order to control nuclear technology or for the maintenance of peace. As he wrote in 1946, the issue that we have to face is 'whether we can have such a world government without going through a third World War'.[24]

The scenario of a Third World War is one we have no desire to describe. 'This atomic blast', wrote Carl Friedrich von Weizsäcker, 'will never be forgotten while people still tell their children stories. It will be the ultimate symbol of the abyss into which the corruption of the human heart once led us.'[25] If the remnants of human civilization following an atomic war were sufficient to enable the construction of any kind of world government, it would probably not be democratic. Such a scenario as a trigger event for the establishment of a democratic world legal order is not only emphatically not to be wished for, but almost certainly impossible anyway. 'The primary purpose in the formation of a democratic cosmopolitarian movement should be to prevent a third World War', according to Jean Rossiaud. The historic task of the movement is to try to ensure a 'gentle transition'. 'The trade union movement and Socialist International failed in this task in 1914', he writes, drawing a historical parallel.[26]

Anticipating and averting the horror

The biggest challenge lies once again at the level of consciousness. As Ulrich Bartosch notes, 'the hope that the painful path of experience can be supplanted by the sensible path of rational understanding' was expressed already by Carl Friedrich von Weizsäcker. For if 'the actual experience of a horrific final world war would bring about the change in human consciousness, which means that that change in consciousness is indeed possible, then the anticipatory experience of the horror must be a sufficient condition for the possibility of a change of consciousness without war', Bartosch concludes. Such a change of consciousness 'could empower people to pre-emptively construct a politically underpinned world peace order. All the significant elements of a postwar period can be recognised in the present and can be comprehended, which means they can be reflected upon. The only thing we don't have is the actual experience of pain,

24 Szilard, Leo. 1946. 'Can we Avert an Arms Race by an Inspection System?' In: One World Or None, ed. by Dexter Masters and Katharine Way, 167–79. New York: The New Press, p. 178.
25 Weizsäcker, Carl Friedrich von. 1979. Der ungesicherte Friede. 2nd ed. Göttingen: Vandenhoeck & Ruprecht, p. 103.
26 Rossiaud, loc. cit., p. 19.

of fear and devastation'.[27] To put it in a nutshell, being able to imagine the hor-
rors of a third world war should mobilize the necessary strength to prevent such
a future from occurring, and to make it permanently impossible through the
creation of a world peace order. But that alone is probably not enough. As Joseph Baratta sums up, '[a]tomic fear has proven too shallow a motivation for
the great work of establishing world government. Humanity will not be fright-
ened into delegating its sovereign powers to a common or federal government.
Something like love of country - love of the earth - is needed. People must want
a higher level of government to guarantee their liberties, their property, and
their security. A positive vision is needed'.[28]

The establishment of a world legal order can be achieved without a shock
event on the scale of a third world war, a global pandemic or an unprecedented
natural disaster. Nevertheless, the revolution from below and the revolution
from above will probably need trigger events to enable them to develop the
force needed for a breakthrough. An important spark for the ignition of the
'Occupy' protests was not only the occupation of Tahrir Square but also the
global financial crisis of 2007 and the bank bailouts. It is possible to imagine
scenarios in which unforeseen but powerful events bring about sudden historic
reconfigurations that enable a huge leap forward. A collapse of the international
financial and banking system with an accompanying global economic crisis is
not inconceivable. The US Joint Chiefs of Staff wrote in their US Military Strategy paper for 2015 that 'the probability of U.S. involvement in interstate war
with a major power is assessed to be low but growing'.[29]

Climate-induced events

What seems certain is the increased incidence and strength of extreme climate-
induced events such as storms, floods, heat waves, cold spells and droughts. Climate change will force many millions of people, perhaps hundreds of millions,
to become refugees. How exactly it will unfold, and with what consequences,
cannot be foreseen. But there is good reason to be worried. For example, with
regard to long-term effects, recent research results – unlike the IPCC scenarios
– assume that even if the two degrees target is achieved a sea level rise of several
metres must be anticipated. Moreover, this could happen far faster than has

27   Bartosch, Ulrich. 1995. Weltinnenpolitik. Zur Theorie des Friedens bei Carl Friedrich von Weizsäcker. Ber-
     lin: Duncker & Humblot, p. 311.
28   Baratta, Joseph Preston. 2004. The Politics of World Federation. From World Federation to Global Govern-
     ance. Vol. 2. Westport, Connecticut; London: Praeger Publishers, p. 528.
29   Joint Chiefs of Staff (ed.). 2015. 'The National Military Strategy of the United States of America 2015', p. 4.

been assumed to date. The ecological and social consequences could be 'devastating' according to a study published in 2015. 'It is not difficult to imagine that conflicts arising from forced migrations and economic collapse might make the planet ungovernable, threatening the fabric of civilization', it goes on.[30] Low-lying coastal regions, which include areas like New York and large parts of Bangladesh, would become uninhabitable. In addition, the changes that have already been set into motion will leave at least a quarter of the world's land more arid.[31] An overwhelming number of studies warn against such upheavals. However, in a report to the Club of Rome on forecasts for the year 2052, Jørgen Randers assumes that there is 'no chance' that CO_2 emissions will be reduced far and fast enough to keep global warming below two degrees.[32] Another study notes that the combustion of all remaining reserves of coal, gas and oil over the coming centuries would mean a rise in sea levels of over 50 metres.[33] In the negotiations over a third generation world organization, the decades-long failure of the world community to halt anthropogenic climate change will be the chief witness. A federal world order may be inevitable as a way of dealing with the consequences.

A democratic China

It is not impossible to imagine that under certain conditions a serious initiative could be instigated by an enlightened US President with a cosmopolitan inclination and enjoying the support of both the House of Representatives and the Senate. But a 'global perestroika' could also originate from a quarter which today seems unlikely. A decisive development in world politics that would make the third democratic transformation almost impossible to stop would be the democratization of China. The democratization of China would mean that the proportion of the world's population living in democracies would jump in one stroke from 60 per cent today to 80 per cent.[34] The remaining autocratic regimes would come under increasing pressure, and the goal of a total democratization of the community of states would be very close. In addition, the democratic legitimation of the great majority of deputies to a world parliament could hardly be questioned. A democratic China would decisively alter the global political landscape,

30 Hansen, J., et al. 23 July 2015. 'Ice melt, sea level rise and superstorms: evidence from paleoclimate data, climate modeling, and modern observations that 2 °C global warming is highly dangerous.' Atmos. Chem. Phys. Discuss. (15) 14: 20059–179, pp. 20121, 20119.
31 Park, Chang-Eui, et al. 2018. 'Keeping Global Warming within 1.5 °C Constrains Emergence of Aridification'. Nature Climate Change 8 (1): 70.
32 Randers, Jorgen. 2012. 2052. White River Junction, Vt: Chelsea Green Publishing Co, p. 118.
33 Winkelmann, Ricarda, et al. 4 September 2015. 'Combustion of Available Fossil Fuel Resources Sufficient to Eliminate the Antarctic Ice Sheet.' Science Advances (1) 8.
34 'China's Charter 08'. Transl. by Perry Link. The New York Review of Books, 15 Jan. 2009 (www.nybooks.com).

and could throw its economic and demographic weight into the scales so as to finally bring about a democratization and strengthening of global governance.

A successful democratization in the near future seems unlikely, not least in view of the total surveillance of Chinese society by the state security services and the suppression of any organised opposition. But history has always been able to surprise us. One aspect of the question that has been much discussed is socio-economic development. At over 7,000 US dollars, average per capita incomes in China have already passed the threshold at which many social scientists believe a process of democratization is almost inevitable. The political scientist Minxin Pei notes with regard to China that, with the exception of oil-producing countries, hardly any autocratic regimes have been able to survive once per capita income has reached 6,000 US dollars.[35] According to surveys conducted in 2003, at that time already 72.3 per cent of Chinese respondents said that democracy was desirable for China.[36] 60 years after the adoption of the Universal Declaration of Human Rights, a 'Charter 08' calling for a new democratic constitution for China was published, and was signed by thousands of courageous Chinese citizens. This document, supported by many prominent Chinese figures, states that authoritarianism is in decline all around the world, and that this process will not halt at the Chinese border.[37]

The theoretical and ideological foundation on which a cosmopolitan initiative for a new democratic leadership in China could be based is already being laid down. It consists in a new interpretation, from the perspective of global modernity, of the concept of 'Tianxia' from the time of the Zhou dynasty. The philosopher Zhao Tingyang, apparently a star in China's intellectual circles, believes that through the adoption and implementation of this concept China could become a world power and take on responsibility to the benefit of all – not as an oppressive or aggressive empire, but as a progressive force contributing to the realization of a Tianxia system in the world. According to Feng Zhang from Tsinghua University in Beijing, the central idea is that of 'transforming the world into a home for all peoples'. The concept goes beyond the nation state as the highest political unit and requires the establishment of a world institution able to deal with all global issues. 'This, in effect, amounts to saying a world government is necessary in the tianxia system', Zhang sums up.[38]

35 Pei, Minxin. 13 February 2013. '5 Ways China Could Become a Democracy.' The Diplomat (thediplomat.com).
36 Chu, Yun-Han, Larry Diamond, Andrew J. Nathan, and Doh Chull Shin (ed.). 2010. How East Asians View Democracy. New York: Columbia University Press, p. 22.
37 'China's Charter 08'. loc. cit.
38 Feng, Zhang. 2009. 'The Tianxia System: World Order in a Chinese Utopia.' GlobalAsia (4) 4: 108–12, pp. 108ff.

It would be based explicitly on an inclusive world constitution.[39] With this initiative, in the judgement of Allen Carlson from Cornell University in New York, for the first time in the country's history China's foreign policy elite has begun to question the normative structures of the international system, based as they are on Western thinking; and with that, 'a potentially far-reaching ... reconsideration of international order is underway in China'.[40]

In the beginning

At the core of the third democratic transformation is a change in values and consciousness. As Michael Koenig-Archibugi from the London School of Economics has observed in a valuable essay, the possibility of a global democracy is dependent to some extent on people's belief in the possibility of a global democracy.[41] In this book we have tried to show that global democracy is not only necessary but possible. But it will not come about by itself, but only as a result of our efforts. And we will need staying power. The process of structural transformation into a world democracy will take a long time. Meanwhile there are countless acute problems that require immediate attention. Nevertheless, it would be a fatal error not to put our energies into the necessary long-term transformation for that reason. Short-term thinking will not bring about an evolutionary leap forward, and will lead us further down a blind alley. A fantastic and fulfilling future for humankind in harmony with nature is possible. As the Anthropocene advances and we continue to master the challenges of our age, so people will increasingly grasp the fact that the last 10,000 years of human history were only the beginning.

As H.G. Wells wrote nearly 100 years ago in 'The Outline of History', '[h]istory is and must always be no more than an account of beginnings. We can venture to prophesy that the next chapters to be written will tell, though perhaps with long interludes of setback and disaster, of the final achievement of world-wide political and social unity. But when that is attained, it will mean no resting stage, nor even a breathing stage, before the development of a new struggle and of new and vaster efforts. Men will unify only to intensify the

---

39 Tingyang, Zhao. 2012. 'All-Under-Heaven and Methodological Relationism.' In: Contemporary Chinese Political Thought, Ed. by Fred Dallmayr and Zhao Tingyang, 46–66. Lexington: Univ. Press of Kentucky, p. 64.

40 Carlson, Allen. 2011. 'Moving Beyond Sovereignty? A brief consideration of recent changes in China's approach to international order and the emergence of the tianxia concept.' Journal of Contemporary China (20) 68: 89–102.

41 Koenig-Archibugi, Mathias. 2011. 'Is global democracy possible?' Europ. Journal of Int. Rel. (17) 3:519–42, p. 523.

search for knowledge and power, and live as ever for new occasions'.[42] Human-kind will finally be able to develop and deploy to the full its creativity and energy, and in a productive way, for the optimal benefit of all people and of all life on earth. This dream *can* become reality. It *must* become reality, if humankind is to have a future.

42   Wells, Herbert George. 1920. The Outline of History. Being a Plain History of Life and Mankind. Vol. II. New York: The MacMillan Company, p. 594.

Index

ABOUT THE PUBLISHER

DEMOCRACY WITHOUT BORDERS is a non-governmental organization that supports a holistic approach to democracy promotion that spans from the local to the global level and at the same time embraces the dimensions of representation, participation, deliberation and co-decision. As it is no longer the nation-states where key decisions are being taken, Democracy Without Borders advocates a democratic world order in which citizens participate beyond national boundaries. While advocating ongoing democratization at all levels, we focus on promoting democracy in transnational regional and global institutions. The establishment of a democratic world parliament is one of our key goals.

Visit our website at
www.democracywithoutborders.org

Lightning Source UK Ltd.
Milton Keynes UK
UKHW02f1603290418
321697UK00006B/94/P

9 783942 282130